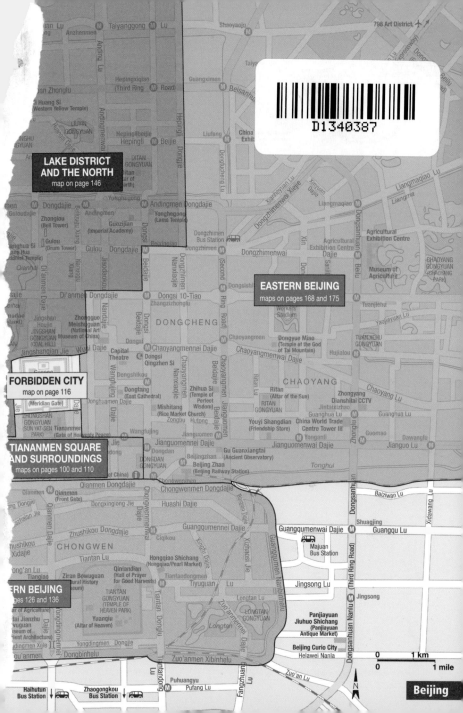

CUNARD

THE MOST FAMOUS OCEAN LINERS IN THE WORLD™

½

24 Hour Loan Only

Library Services by Ocean Books

APA PUBLICATIONS

Part of the Langenscheidt Publishing Group

How to Use This Book

This book is carefully structured both to convey an understanding of the city and its culture and to guide readers through its attractions and activities:

◆ The Best Of section at the front of the book helps you to prioritise. The first spread contains all the Top Sights, while the Editor's Choice details unique experiences, the best buys or other recommendations.

◆ To understand Beijing, you need to know something of its past. The city's history and culture are described in authoritative essays written by

specialists in their fields who have lived in and documented the city for many years.

◆ The Places section details all the attractions worth seeing. The main places of interest are coordinated by number with the maps.

◆ Each chapter includes lists of recommended shops, restaurants, bars and cafés.

◆ Photographs throughout the book are chosen not only to illustrate geography and buildings, but also to convey the moods of the city and the life of its people.

◆ The Travel Tips section includes all the practical information you will need, divided into five key sections: transport, accommodation, activities (including nightlife, events, tours and sports), an A–Z of practical tips and a language guide. Information may be located quickly by using the index on the back cover flap of the book.

◆ A detailed street atlas is included at the back of the book, with all restaurants, bars, cafés and hotels plotted for your convenience.

PLACES AND SIGHTS

Chapters are **colour-coded** for ease of use. Each neighbourhood has a designated colour corresponding to the orientation map on the inside front cover.

A locator map pinpoints the specific area covered in each chapter.

Margin tips provide extra snippets of information, whether it's a practical tip, a whimsical quote, an historical fact, or advice on shopping and eating.

A four-colour map shows the area covered in the chapter, with the main sights and attractions coordinated by number with the text.

PHOTO FEATURES

Photo features offer visual coverage of various aspects of the city, from its ancient *hutong* lanes to the burgeoning modern art scene.

SHOPPING AND RESTAURANT LISTINGS

Shopping listings provide details of the best shops in each area. **Restaurant listings** give the establishment's contact details, opening times and price category, followed by a useful review. Bars and cafés are also covered here. The coloured dot and grid reference refers to the atlas section at the back of the book.

6525-1071. Open: 11am–11pm. **$$** 60 p287, C4
A fun pub atmosphere at this boisterous Xinjiang restaurant with belly dancers and other shows. The roast mutton, kebabs and naans are good. Book ahead if possible.

TRAVEL TIPS

Travel Tips provide all the practical knowledge you'll need before and during your trip: how to get there, getting around, where to stay and what to do. The A–Z section is a handy summary of practical information, arranged alphabetically.

Contents

Places Names Usage:

For all places listed in this guide, rather than following a rigid system of English followed by the standard pinyin transliteration in brackets, or the other way round, we have simply used the best-known and most appropriate name for tourist purposes. On the whole, this means English with pinyin in brackets, but there are many exceptions, particularly for those temple names where the English is unwieldy. Thus Tiananmen Square (Tiananmen Guangchang), the Great Wall (Wanli Changcheng) and the Lama Temple (Yongheggong), but also Baiyunguan (Temple of the White Cloud) and Fayuansi (Temple of the Source of Buddhist Teaching).

Maps

LEFT: Mao-era relics for sale at Panjiayuan Market.

Travel Tips

THE BEST OF BEIJING: TOP SIGHTS

From the Forbidden City to the Great Wall, Tiananmen Square and the Temple of Heaven, Beijing has no lack of magnificent sights. Here are ten of the best

▷ **The Back Lakes area**
For all the neon-lit bar action, the few remaining *hutong* and locals' outdoor activity makes the area around Houhai perhaps the most picturesque part of the city, particularly on summer evenings. *See page 152.*

△ **Imperial Palace Museum (Forbidden City)**
One of the few remaining parts of the ancient capital and centre of the city. *See page 113.*

▽ **National Stadium (Bird's Nest Stadium)**
Built for the 2008 Olympics, the latticework structure is an iconic design, and a superb – albeit costly – legacy of the sporting spectacular. *See page 59.*

▽ **Great Wall**
Though Badaling is most popular with domestic tourists, the crowds make it less appealing to foreign visitors. Simatai is better. *See page 225.*

△ **Tiananmen Square**
This gigantic open space at the heart of the city is simply like nowhere else on earth. *See page 99.*

◁ **New Summer Palace**
Conceived on a grand scale, this is one of the most beautiful gardens in the world. *See page 202.*

▽ **798 Art District**
The creative centre of the capital, and of China. *See page 176.*

△ **Beihai Park**
Part of 2,000 years of landscape design in Beijing, Beihai is a wonderfully relaxing place to unwind. *See page 145.*

▽ **Temple of Heaven**
Dramatic ancient buildings set amid what is arguably the nicest park in the city. *See page 135.*

▽ **Lama Temple**
This venerable Tibetan place of worship is the most interesting temple in the city. *See page 155.*

The Best of Beijing: Editor's Choice

Setting priorities, saving money, unique attractions...
here, at a glance, are our recommendations, plus some
tips and tricks even the locals won't always know

Ancient Buildings

- **Tiananmen Gate**
  The iconic landmark from which Mao proclaimed the founding of the PRC, and which still features his portrait. *See page 105.*
- **White Dagoba**
  This large white Buddhist stupa in the midst of verdant Beihai Park has long been a city landmark. *See page 148.*
- **Hall of Prayer for Good Harvests**
  The iconic circular building at the centre of the Temple of Heaven complex. *See page 139.*
- **Hall of Mental Cultivation (Forbidden City)**
  The living quarters of Emperor Qianlong, the Empress Dowager and Pu Yi. *See page 122.*
- **Marco Polo Bridge (western fringes)**
  This magnifcent old bridge survived being the site of the first battle in the build-up to World War II. *See page 215.*
- **Tomb of Yongle (Ming Tombs)**
  The best Ming tomb. Yongle was largely responsible for building the ancient capital. *See page 219.*
- **Little Potala Temple, Chengde** An extraordinary copy of Lhasa's Potala Palace in the Qing emperors' relaxing summer resort. *See page 241.*

Above: the unique East is Red dining experience.

Only in Beijing

- **Natural History Museum** Attractions include preserved human cadavers. *See page 140.*
- **Beijing City Planning Museum** A huge scale model of the city. *See page 111.*
- **Ancient Observatory** A unique sight, astronomical equipment dating back to the 13th century. *See page 172.*
- **The East is Red** Beijing does retro-kitsch like nowhere else – and nowhere more vibrantly than at this unusual restaurant. *See page 177.*
- **798 Space** Beijing's unique art district in the northeast of the city features numerous venues in converted factories. *See page 176.*
- **Chocolate Wonderland** An extraordinary addition to Beijing's list of sights. *See page 160.*

Left: Tiananmen Gate, iconic sight.

A FLAVOUR OF OLD BEIJING

ABOVE: the essence of the old city at the Bird and Fish Market.

• *Hutong* Wandering around the streets that thread their way through the fast-disappearing old neighbourhoods is the best way to connect with the city's past. Prime areas are around the back lakes. *See page 164.*

• **Laoshe teahouse** The city's most famous traditional teahouse hosts daily performances of Beijing Opera. *See page 126.*

• **Huguang Guild Hall** Another old-style venue in which to witness Beijing Opera. *See page 127.*

• **Courtyard hotels** Staying at the Lusongyuan and other similar hotels is a great way of experiencing the old character of Beijing. *See page 263.*

• **Bird and Fish Market** Caged songbirds, crickets and koi carp for sale. *See page 189.*

MODERN BEIJING

• **National Centre for the Performing Arts** Known locally as "the Egg", this was the city's first avant garde modern building. *See page 104.*

• **CCTV headquarters**. This spectacular modern structure lies close to the Third Ring Road. *See page 170.*

• **National Aquatics**

Centre The water cube. *See page 59.*

• **Sanlitun Village** This bar and restaurant district is probably the best place in the city to get a feel for the new generation of youthful, moneyed, aspirational Beijingers. *See page 175.*

ABOVE: the Great Wall at Jinshanling.

THE GREAT OUTDOORS

• **Simatai Great Wall** The best views of the unreconstructed Great Wall. *See page 231.*

• **New Summer Palace** The most beautiful imperial garden in China. *See page 202.*

• **Fragrant Hills Park** Stunning in autumn. *See page 209.*

• **Imperial Flower Garden** Relief from the oppressive surroundings of the Forbidden City. *See page 123.*

• **Olympic Forest Park** Expansive open area in the north of the city. *See page 59.*

• **Old Summer Palace** Pleasant lake-studded parkland northwest of the city. *See page 199.*

• **Jingshan Park** Amazing views of the Forbidden City from this artificial hill to its immediate north. *See page 150.*

• **Cave of Precious Pearls** Great views of Beijing from the Western Hills – if you're lucky and it's a clear day. *See page 213.*

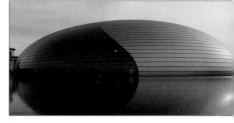

ABOVE LEFT: traditional bronze lion at the Forbidden City.
ABOVE: the National Centre for Performing Arts (aka "The Egg").

BEST EATS

- **Roast duck** Though Quanjude is the most famous place for Peking Duck, some say Da Dong is the best for the city's signature dish. *See pages 73, 141, 178.*
- **Gui Jie** Pick any restaurant on this lively street to the south of the Lama Temple. *See page 160.*
- **The Courtyard** Ultra-glamorous dining just a stone's throw away from the Forbidden City. *See page 177.*

- **Beijing Noodle King** Noodles are a staple of the Beijing diet, and this is probably the best place in town to sample some. *See page 161.*
- **Red Capital Club** Recaptures the essence (albeit somewhat sanitised) of 1950s China. *See page 177.*
- **Donghuamen Night Market** An abundance of outlandish street food just around the corner from Wangfujing. *See page 171.*

LEFT AND BELOW LEFT: memorabilia is the name of the game at the Red Capital Club. **ABOVE:** a well-stocked bar in the Houhai area. **BELOW:** modern cool at the Green T. House. **BOTTOM:** Yanjing Beer and Beijing Beer are the two local brews.

BEST BARS

- **Capital M** Afternoon tea with views of Qianmen Gate and Tiananmen Square. *See page 141.*
- **Green T. House** The apogee of contemporary Chinese interior design. *See page 177.*
- **Drum and Bell Café** Rooftop overlooking a quiet square where local people gather. *See page 163.*
- **Nanluoguxiang** Experience Beijing's nascent café culture in this picturesque "back lakes" *hutong*. *See pages 161, 163.*
- **Face Bar** One of Beijing's top bars. *See page 179.*

BEST SHOPPING

- **Wangfujing** Oriental Plaza is just one of several large malls on Beijing's most famous shopping street. *See page 169.*
- **Jianguomen: Silk Street Market, Friendship Store** These two totally different shopping experiences each has a lot to offer. *See page 174.*
- **Hongqiao Market** Specialises in pearls but also a great place to buy clothes, shoes and watches. *See page 138.*
- **Panjiayuan Antique Market** The best place to look for souvenirs of all kinds. *See page 138.*
- **Antiques Market, Tianjin** An interesting shopping alternative outside Beijing. *See page 249.*

ABOVE: merchandise at Silk Street Market – a good place to look for cut-price designer clothing.

ANCIENT TEMPLES

- **Baiyunguan** The city's most atmospheric Daoist temple. *See page 132.*
- **Biyunsi** A beautiful location out in the Fragrant Hills. *See page 211.*
- **Guangjisi** A well-used Buddhist temple in the west of the city. *See page 185.*
- **Dongyue Miao** A thriving Daoist centre. *See page 173.*

LEFT: Baiyunguan, the Temple of the White Clouds, is Beijing's leading Daoist temple. **ABOVE:** Biyunsi Temple in the Fragrant Hills west of the city.

MONEY-SAVING TIPS

Taxi Hire Taxis are cheap in Beijing, and metres are always installed. Consider hiring a taxi for a day's sight-seeing outside the city. Bargain hard and agree the fare before you set off – it shouldn't be too expensive, and will give you control and flexibility to do what you want *(see page 258)*.

Hotels You should not have to pay the standard "rack rate" for a hotel room in Beijing. Discounts are available at various times of the year, or at week-ends, or simply by asking at the desk. Booking your room online can also lower the price *(see page 260)*.

Tipping is not generally expected in China *(see page 276)*.

International telephone calls are quite expensive; invest in an IP card, and pay less than half the rate *(see pages 276–7)*. Calls from land lines within the city are usually free.

Mobile / cellphones are cheap to use if you purchase your own SIM card (Rmb 50) in one of the many mobile phone shops dotted around the city *(see page 277)*.

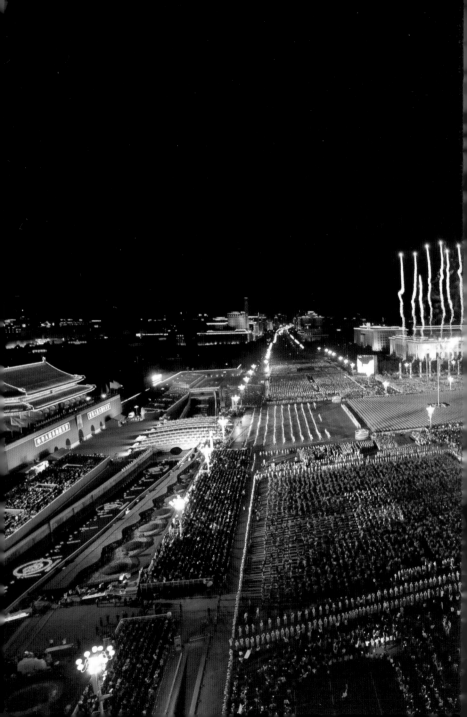

CHINA'S ANCIENT CAPITAL

Laid out according to ancient geomantic principles, modern Beijing is a dynamic and increasingly sophisticated city

Beijing is a city of opposites and extremes – it captivates and confuses, excites and exasperates, all in equal measure. As the capital of the People's Republic, it is both the seat of the world's largest communist bureaucracy and the source of the policy changes that have turned China into an economic powerhouse. Its walled compounds and towering ministries are full of bureaucrats who technically legislate in the name of Marx and Mao, while the streets outside are a riot of speeding cars, flashing neon and cellphone-wielding citizens whose aspirations and lifestyles are increasingly akin to those of London or New York. Beijing may lack the futuristic glow of Shanghai – it remains altogether a grittier place than its southern rival – but nonetheless the changes in the past few years are remarkable.

Repression and freedom exist side by side in this vast city. Open political dissent is not tolerated. But politics is a favourite subject of Beijingers, who like nothing better than a witty joke at the expense of their leaders or the Communist system. Barely veiled political critiques abound on the capital's stages and in its growing number of art galleries.

The Olympic Games in 2008 prompted a rapid and exhaustive makeover. Ancient buildings were ruthlessly torn down before plans for their replacements had even been drawn up, new subway lines snaked and bifurcated into the city's furthest suburbs, and the skyline became a playground for the whim of foreign architects. But for the thousands of migrants from home and abroad who pour into the capital each week, and the emerging urban middle class struggling to carve out a life and identity, this is only the beginning. The dusty old city of bicycles, Mao suits and political slogans seems a distant memory. The new Beijing has well and truly arrived. ❑

PRECEDING PAGES: the bright lights of Wanfujing; celebrating the 60th anniversary of the PRC in Tiananmen Square. **LEFT:** the Hall of Prayer for Good Harvests at the Temple of Heaven. **ABOVE RIGHT:** Tiananmen Gate. **ABOVE LEFT:** Beijing Opera.

THE BEIJINGERS

Beijingers, with their distinctive burr, love to talk. And the economic and social changes of recent years have certainly given them plenty to talk about...

Stereotyping Chinese from other parts of the country is a favourite pastime in China. As residents of the nation's capital, Beijingers are a favourite target and, indeed, are not above playing the game themselves. It is perhaps unsurprising that the traits Beijing residents like to ascribe to themselves are somewhat different from those that non-Beijingers tend to ascribe to them.

Indeed, if you ask a Beijing resident to describe his fellow citizens, he is likely to tell you that they are generous, affable, loyal, hardworking and patriotic people, who love to talk, especially about politics. But if you ask someone from outside Beijing, he is more likely to describe a typical Beijinger as someone who is arrogant, eager to get rich but unwilling to do hard or menial work, and full of talk but short on action. If the person you ask happens to be Shanghainese, he is likely simply to sniff and say that Beijingers are *tu*, which roughly translates as "country bumpkins".

Boom town

Stereotypes aside, the reality is that it gets harder to define a typical Beijinger with each passing year, as the economy booms and the city evolves at breakneck speed. Like most big capital cities, Beijing attracts leading entrepreneurs, actors, singers, models, bureaucrats, politicians, generals, scientists and sports stars. It also attracts poor rural residents from around the nation, who come to the capital to take on the menial tasks

that many Beijing residents no longer care to do. These days there are so many poor migrants working as construction workers, household servants, nannies, waitresses, janitors and refuse collectors, that public and private life in Beijing would virtually cease to function if they all went home. About 50 percent of the 16-plus million living in Beijing, either those now carrying the coveted *hukou* residence permit, or temporary residents, were not born in the capital. These one-time *waidiren*, literally "outside place people", often strive to assimilate by dropping their native accents and adopting local manners. And although red propaganda banners can be seen exhorting the populace to "build a new capital",

---

LEFT: living standards have improved beyond all recognition. **RIGHT:** Beijingers face a bright future.

most people simply dream of building a decent life for themselves with a home, car and family.

Long gone are the days Beijing was considered a hardship post by expats, and an increasing number of foreigners choose to set up home in the city by purchasing a house and raising children who often attend local schools, thus soaking up the Chinese language and culture. Chinese "Green Cards" are still something of a rarity, however. By 2009, barely 300 foreigners had been granted permanent residence in Beijing.

Work and leisure

Contrary to stereotype, most people work hard. The cellphones carried by all but the city's poorest, oldest and youngest residents are generally used for business communications rather than chit-chat. Because so much of their time is devoted to work, most white-collar workers – and even some labourers – hire others to care for their children and do their cleaning and cooking. Some couples even board their toddlers at live-in nursery schools during the working week.

Too Many People, Too Few Surnames

When Genghis Khan was asked how he would conquer northern China, it is said that he replied, "I will kill everybody called Wang, Li, Zhang, and Liu. The rest will be no problem." With well over a billion people, it is natural to assume that China would have a surplus of surnames to go around. Yet of the 12,000 surnames that once existed in China, today there remain just 3,000. Nearly a third of the population shares just five family names, and 90 million share the name Li, by default the world's most common surname. In the US, by comparison, there are only 2.4 million people with the name Smith, the most common family name in the English-speaking world.

Much of the problem began centuries ago, when non-Han Chinese, seeking to blend into the dominant culture, abandoned their own surnames and adopted common names of the Han. In modern China, with its vast population, literally thousands of people can share the same full name, leading to numerous frustrating cases of mistaken identity.

A recent trend is for parents to choose archaic or uncommon characters for their children's given names. This can cause major problems when they have to register with police or other institutions, as computer systems cannot always cope with these characters. There have been cases of banks refusing customers with unusual names.

The material rewards of all this hard work are everywhere to be seen. Over 4 million Beijing residents now own a car, more than in either Shanghai or Guangzhou, and about half own their own homes. Goods that were once seen as luxuries – telephones, air-conditioning, refrigerators, stereos – are taken for granted. Consumers are now dazzled by window displays of all the latest mobile phones, laptop computers and digital camera equipment. If the prices of these international brands are too high, Chinese versions – often copyright-infringing – are an ever-present budget option. Holidaying in other parts of China or even overseas is increasingly popular, and some of the city's wealthiest residents even own second homes.

Though people may have less free time than they once did, they have more money to spend on it, so leisure-time activities are booming. Watching television and pirated DVDs, eating out and shopping are the main leisure pursuits for most Beijingers. Wangfujing is the capital's premier promenading street, but diners and window-shoppers can be found in any corner of the city at almost any time of day.

Countless bars, cafés and nightclubs form the backbone of Beijing's nightlife. Though the capital's bar culture is certainly based on

> *China's post-80s generation are often branded materialistic and bereft of values. But many are intensely patriotic, and sensitive to perceived Western media bias against their country.*

the Western model, many Beijingers feel at something of a loss merely sitting in a bar and drinking, so added entertainment such as dice-games, karaoke and floor shows are not uncommon. Ostentation and one-upmanship come with Chinese characteristics: thus well-heeled partiers sip Chivas Regal mixed with green tea or order bottles of champagne that arrive at their table topped by a lit sparkler.

Far Left: roasting chestnuts in an old *hutong* neighbourhood. **Left Top:** promoting family planning. **Left:** communal dining. **Above Top:** at the World of Suzie Wong's bar. **Above:** policeman on a bike. **Above Right:** market vendor on Dazhalan shopping street.

NOT-SO-LITTLE EMPERORS

Since the one-child policy was introduced in 1979, a single child often has a monopoly over two parents and four doting grandparents. Boys, seen as inheritors of the family line, are spoilt more. Memories of hard times, and the desire to get the most out of one offspring, mean many parents believe bigger is better. Obesity has become common among urban children puffed up by Western fast food and countless brands of snacks and sweets.

In return for all the attention, the "little emperors" face increasing pressure to succeed in their exams. Yet sympathy is in short supply: "Many of them are selfish, lazy, arrogant and uncaring," wrote *China Daily*.

> *A 2007 survey showed that 91 percent of Chinese supported equal rights in employment for homosexuals but 70 percent opposed the legalisation of same-sex marriages. In early 2010, China hosted its first ever gay parade.*

Exercise is increasingly trendy, with health clubs, yoga centres and a few rock-climbing walls springing up around the city. Education is also a prime leisure-time activity, especially learning English. "Crazy English", in which students are told to shout out the words, has caught on after promotion at evangelist-style rallies, so don't be alarmed to hear students bellowing out simple phrases of English in the city's parks.

Because old habits die hard – and because many Beijingers live in cramped, sub-standard accommodation – much leisure activity still takes place on the city's busy streets and in its narrow *hutong*. Walk around a major intersection and you will see families flying kites over the road, boys kicking a football around on the grass verges and elderly people chatting on bridges. On summer evenings, along the pavements and under the bridges sit barbers, bicycle repairers, fruit and vegetable vendors, neighbourhood committee wardens and fortune-tellers. *Qi gong* practitioners and *Yang Ge* dancers use whatever space remains. And there, keeping order among the motley procession of pedestrians, cyclists, drivers and passengers, are the ever-watchful eyes of authority; the police, flag-waving traffic wardens, and bicycle and car park attendants.

Alienation and the generation gap

Unsurprisingly, there is also a downside to the fast-changing lifestyle that prosperity has brought to Beijing. High-rise apartments with private baths and kitchens are more comfortable than crumbling low-rises with shared facilities, but they are also isolating. Older people, in particular, find it hard to adjust. While some gather to chat in the front entrances of their shiny new buildings or do t'ai chi together in the early morning, others succumb to loneliness and despair. The young and seemingly successful are not immune to such feelings either – China's suicide rate is several times the world average, and it is the leading cause of death among people aged 15–34.

If families have more money and freedom, they also seem to feel more pressure. The one-child policy to which most city dwellers are subject causes parents to place inordinate hopes on their single children, or "little emperors". Many kids are expected not only to excel at school,

but also at extra-curricular study courses, languages and music lessons. Children who used to run around in the street are now confined to high-rises where they watch TV, play video games or do homework while their parents work. This increasingly sedentary lifestyle – supplemented with junk food – has led to an obesity rate topping 10 percent among Beijing

> A preference for male offspring combined with the one-child policy has led to widespread sex-specific abortions. By 2020, more than 24 million Chinese men could find themselves without a spouse.

children (*see panel, opposite*). Those with no siblings sometimes find it hard to play with others and are often considered to be somewhat spoilt, and are often stressed by the time they become teenagers. Indeed, between 16 and 25 percent of college students are believed to be suffering from some sort of mental disorder.

Left: a billboard promotes the one-child policy.
Above Top & Above: playground at Ditan Park.
Above Right: the Long Corridor at the Temple of Heaven park is a favourite hangout for Beijingers.

The media write of the "psychological plague" on college campuses, though individual suicides are not always reported for fear of encouraging copycats.

The older generation benefited from job security working for state-run companies. Their job, housing and furniture were assigned by their work unit, and even marriages had to be approved by a supervisor. The advice given by parents – those who grew up in that very different China – to their children can seem absurdly outdated, and young people turn to social groups, often based around online computer games and forums, for guidance and information.

The institution of marriage has also come under considerable pressure. A negative side-effect of China's increasing freedom is the huge rise in prostitution. Prostitutes generally work in massage parlours, hairdressers' salons, bars, clubs and hotels, and can be a regular part of a business trip or an evening with work colleagues. Extra-marital affairs are commonplace and are a major contributor to the city's escalating divorce rate. Extra-marital sex also contributes to the increasing rate of STD infection and even HIV.

In 2009, state media reported that HIV/Aids had become the nation's deadliest infectious disease. The most at-risk group was found to be migrant workers who were having unprotected sex with prostitutes with alarming frequency. This spurred a more open approach to public discussion of the problem and educational campaigns. Condom makers such as Durex benefited greatly from this openness and their slick adverts can be seen in primetime television slots.

With Beijing's rising divorce rates, second and third marriages are common. Couples marry later and have children later – or not at all – and young people often live together before marriage. More people are opting to remain single, and the number of women who choose to become single mothers is slowly starting to grow. Women in particular are more ambitious and demanding in their search for the perfect partner, and a regular wage is no longer seen as a sufficient draw.

Migrants and minorities

Beijing's 4 million-strong migrant workforce plays a crucial role in the city's economy. Most are men who transport waste on heavy tricycle carts, unblock drains and canals or construct roads, housing and shopping centres. Some sell fruit and vegetables, often sleeping under makeshift stalls in summer. Many women find live-in jobs as waitresses, cleaners, beauty-shop workers, nannies or servants.

But migrant workers do not receive much of a welcome. Much of Beijing's "disorder" – from unplanned births to crime and pollution – is

> China's migrant workers were named runners-up in Time magazine's "Person of the Year" award 2009, for their outstanding contribution to propping up the Chinese economy during the global financial crisis.

blamed on them, and they have few rights or privileges. Until the outbreak of SARS, those employed by construction firms were often crammed into dorms that slept 100 people; now the regulation is that there must be no more than 14 to a room. Although they are paid much less than a Beijing resident would be for the same job, they frequently have trouble col-

lecting any money at all. Few have insurance or access to health care, and most must rely on the good will of their employers if they are injured on the job. When swine flu swept the capital in 2009, it was permanent residents who received the first inoculations.

While many migrants are young and single, some have children, and for them life is particularly difficult. Hefty surcharges are levied on migrant children who attend public school, and parents who cannot afford these fees must send their children to illegal, makeshift schools run by other migrant parents. Faced with such a choice, many choose to leave their children back home to be raised by grandparents or other relatives,

Beijing's minority population consists of both migrants and permanent residents. The most visible are the Tibetan merchants, with their long hair and flowing sheepskin robes, who sell jewellery and religious items. Otherwise, the Hui Muslims are the capital's most obvious minority (see pages 66, 129).

Beijing's increasing worldliness is bolstered by its ever-growing number of foreign residents, both Western and Asian, who are particularly in evidence in the Chaoyang District in the east of the city. ❑

FAR LEFT: a school outing to Jingshan Park. **LEFT:** sitting in the winter sunshine. **ABOVE:** construction is a major employer in the city. **RIGHT:** there are fewer bicycles (and tricycles) these days, but many are still used for transporting materials.

DECISIVE DATES

Early History

c.3000 BC
Neolithic villages are established in the area around present-day Beijing.

c.700 BC
Trading between the Chinese, Koreans, Mongols and northern tribes starts to take place around the site of the modern city.

475–221 BC
Warring States period. Rise of the city of Ji, the forerunner of Beijing.

221 BC
Qin Shi Huangdi unifies China to found the first imperial dynasty, and creates the Great Wall. Beijing (still known as Ji) becomes the administrative centre of Guangyang prefecture.

206 BC
Han dynasty founded; capital in Chang'an.

165 BC
Civil service examinations instituted.

2nd century AD
Trade between China and Asia/Europe thrives. The first Buddhist temples are founded in China. Beijing (Ji) develops into a strategic garrison town between the warring kingdoms of northern China and the lands of the Mongols and other nomads.

220
Abdication of the last Han emperor. Wei, Jin, and northern and southern dynasties divide China.

581
After nearly four centuries of division, the Sui dynasty reunifies China.

589–610
Repairs of early parts of the Great Wall. Construction of a system of Grand Canals linking northern and southern China.

618
Tang dynasty proclaimed. Government increasingly bureaucratised.

Mongol Dynasties (916–1368)

907–960
Fall of Tang dynasty. Five Dynasties and Ten Kingdoms partition China. Beijing, (called Yanjing or Nanjing), becomes the southern capital of the new Khitan (Mongol) empire under the Liao dynasty.

1040
Development of neo-Confucianism, which continues through the 11th and 12th centuries.

1125
The Nüzhen, another Mongol tribe, overthrow the Liao to begin the Jin dynasty.

1153
Beijing (Zhongdu) is the Nüzhen capital.

1215
Genghis Khan destroys the city.

1267
Kublai Khan starts construction of Khanbaliq, known in Chinese as Dadu (Great Capital), using Confucian ideals. An imperial palace is built in today's Beihai Park.

1279
Mongol armies rout the Song court to establish the Yuan dynasty, reinstating Beijing (Khanbaliq/Dadu) as capital. Trade along the Silk Road flourishes.

1293
City rebuilding completed. Tonghua Canal links the city with the Grand Canal.

Ming Dynasty (1368–1644)

1368
Han Chinese overthrow the Mongols. Ming dynasty is founded. Dadu is renamed Beiping ("Northern Peace") and the capital is moved south to Nanjing.

1403
Beiping reinstated as capital of the empire by the emperor Yongle.

1406–20
During Yongle's reign the city is rebuilt around the new Imperial Palace and its basic layout is established.

1553
Macau becomes a Portuguese trading port and the first European settlement in China. Completion of Beijing's city wall.

15th–17th centuries
Rebuilding of the Great Wall to make the "10,000 Li" Wall.

FAR LEFT: watercolour of old China.
LEFT: Genghis Khan, destroyer of the city.
ABOVE: Emperor Kangxi. **RIGHT:** Boxer rebels guarded by foreign troops, 1900.

Qing Dynasty (1644–1911)

1644
The Manchu, a non-Han Chinese people from Manchuria, seize Beijing, to initiate the Qing dynasty.

1661–1722
Reign of Emperor Kangxi.

1736–95
Reign of Emperor Qianlong.

1800
First edict prohibiting the

importation and local production of opium.

1838
All trade in opium banned. The following year, the Qing court terminates all trade between England and China.

1840–2
First Opium War.

1842
Treaty of Nanjing signed. More Chinese ports are forced to open to foreign trade, and Hong Kong island is surrendered to Great Britain "in perpetuity".

1851–64
The Taiping Rebellion.

1858–60
Second Opium War. Treaty of Tianjin signed, opening more ports to foreigners.

1894–5
China is defeated by Japan in the Sino-Japanese War.

1900
The Boxer Rebellion.

1911
Republican Revolution: Sun Yat-sen is chosen president, but soon steps down. Abdication of the last emperor, Pu Yi.

Post-Imperial China

1912–16
Yuan Shikai takes over as president. Several provinces proclaim independence. After Yuan dies, the warlord period ensues.

1919
On 4 May in Beijing, a large demonstration demands the restoration of China's sovereignty, thus beginning a Nationalist movement.

1921
Founding of the Communist Party in Shanghai.

1925
Sun Yat-sen dies.

1934–6
The Long March: Commu-
nists forced to abandon their stronghold in southern China. Only 30,000 of the original 100,000 who began the march arrive at the northern base in Yan'an (Shaanxi province).

1937
The Marco Polo Bridge Incident prompts Communists and Nationalists to unite to fight the Japanese.

1945
Japan defeated in World War II; full-scale civil war ensues in China.

People's Republic of China

1949
Mao Zedong declares People's Republic in Beijing on 1 October; Nationalist army flees to Taiwan.

1950–3
Chinese troops support North Korea.

1958–61
Mass famine kills more than 30 million.

1960
Split between China and the Soviet Union.

1965–6
Beginning of the Cultural Revolution.

1972
President Richard Nixon visits China.

1976
Zhou Enlai (Jan) and Mao Zedong (Sept) die. Tangshan earthquake kills 242,000 east of Beijing.

1978
Deng Xiaoping becomes leader, instituting a policy of economic reform and openness to the West.

ABOVE: Mao Zedong addresses a crowd of supporters, 1944. **RIGHT:** the spectacular opening ceremony at the 2008 Olympics.

1979
The US formally recognises China. Democracy Wall movement crushed.

1989
Pro-democracy demonstrations in Tiananmen Square brought to an end by a brutal military crackdown on 4 June. China is heavily criticised in the West.

1992
Deng restarts economic reforms.

1997
Deng Xiaoping dies. Hong Kong reverts to Chinese sovereignty on 1 July.

1999
Vehement anti-US protests in Beijing following the accidental bombing of the Chinese embassy in Belgrade.

2001
Beijing is named host city of the 2008 Olympic Games. China joins the World Trade Organization after a 15-year quest.

2002
The Party's 16th congress ends with significant changes to the constitution. Jiang Zemin replaced as president by Hu Jintao.

2003
An outbreak of the SARS virus brings panic to Beijing, with schools closed.

2006
The high-altitude China–Tibet railway line begins operation.

2007
China carries out missile test in space, shooting down an old weather satellite. Military build-up causes concern abroad. Hu Jintao tours African nations to boost trade and investment.

2008
Anti-China protests in Tibet escalate into violence and fatalities. Beijing hosts Olympic Games, and China wins 51 gold medals.

2009
Mass celebrations mark 60 years of Communist power.

2010
Google pulls out of China after suspecting the government of sabotaging its operations.

FROM ANCIENT TIMES TO 1949

Once a frontier town at the edge of fertile lowlands,
Beijing served as the capital of imperial dynasties
for more than 1,000 years

The geographical position of Beijing has been one of the leading factors in its eventful history. Lying at the northern edge of empire – where the very different cultures of the settled Chinese farmers and the nomads of the steppes collided – the city became the prey of each victorious faction in turn, a fact reflected by the many changes to its name throughout the centuries.

Evidence of human settlement in the area goes back half a million years or so with the discovery of Peking Man *(Sinanthropus pekinensis; see page 216)*. This find, in Zhoukoudian, 50km (30 miles) southwest of Beijing, revealed that Peking Man belonged to a people who walked upright, were already using stone tools and who knew how to light fires.

Around 3000 BC, neolithic villages were established in the area of modern Beijing, inhabited by people familiar with agriculture and the domestication of animals. There is to this day dispute as to the existence of the first dynasty recorded in Chinese historical writings, the Xia dynasty (21st to 16th centuries BC). The dynasty's legendary Yellow Emperor, Huangdi, is thought to have ruled between 2490 and 2413 BC and to have fought battles against the tribal leader Chiyo here, in the "Wilderness of the Prefecture of Zhou". It is presumed that Zhuluo, to the west of Beijing, was the earliest settlement in this area. It was here that Huangdi's successor, Yao, is said to have founded a capital named Youdou, the "City of Calm".

LEFT: Emperor Kangxi practising calligraphy.
RIGHT: a sculptor's impression of Peking Man.

Throughout Beijing's prehistory, the hills to the north, northeast and northwest served as a natural frontier for the people who settled here and who traded with the nomadic tribes living beyond the passes of Gubeikou and Naku. These northern hill tribes also had close ties with the people who occupied the Central Plain, which stretched along the Yellow River to the south and southwest of Beijing. Its important role as a trading post promoted the settlement's rise to become the ancient city of Ji.

During the Warring States period (475–221 BC), the count of the state of Yan annexed this area and made Ji his central city. In the 3rd century BC, the first emperor of the Qin dynasty

and of China, Qin Shi Huangdi, made the city an administrative centre of the Guangyang Command, one of 36 prefectures of the unified, centrally organised feudal empire. With the construction of the Great Wall during his reign (221–210 BC), Ji became a strategically important trade and military centre, a position it retained for approximately 1,000 years, until the end of the Tang dynasty. During this time, it was often the subject of wars and conflict.

Beijing, the imperial city

At the beginning of the Tang dynasty, Ji was not that different from the other great cities of feudal China. But by the end of the dynasty, the Great Wall had lost much of its protective function, leaving it more vulnerable to attack from the north.

The city became an imperial seat when the Khitan conquered northern China and founded the Liao dynasty in AD 936. The Khitan renamed Ji "Yanjing", meaning "Southern Capital" (it was also known as Nanjing – not to be confused with the city of the same name in east-central China, to which the Ming later decamped). As the southern centre of the nomad empire, this area became a point of support and departure for many expedi-

tions of non-Chinese peoples – Khitan, Nüzhen and Mongols – on their way to the south.

In relation to today's Beijing, Yanjing lay roughly in the western part of the city. The temple of Fayuansi was in the southeastern corner of the old walls, the Forbidden City lay to the

> The official view of Qin Shi Huangdi has been constantly re-evaluated throughout China's history. Often portrayed as a tyrant, the first emperor can also be seen as a reformer who made important changes to politics and law.

southwest and the markets were in the northeast corner. Each of the city's four quarters was surrounded by massive walls.

In the early part of the 12th century, the Nüzhen, another nomadic tribe from the northeast, vanquished the reigning Liao dynasty and replaced it with the Jin dynasty. In 1153, they moved their capital from Huiningfu (in the

modern province of Liaoning) to Yanjing, and renamed it Zhongdu, "Central Capital". New buildings were constructed, and the Jin moved the centre of their capital into the area to the south of today's Guanganmen Gate. But it only lasted a few decades: in 1215, Mongol cavalry occupied Zhongdu and the city was completely destroyed by fire.

The Great Khan's capital

It was not until 1279 that Kublai Khan made Zhongdu the capital of the new Yuan dynasty. He completely rebuilt the city and gave it the Chinese name of Dadu, meaning "Great Capital". In the West, it was mostly known by its Mongol name, Khanbaliq or Khambaluk.

The building of Dadu continued until 1293, while Kublai Khan ruled the empire. The centre of the city at that time was moved to the vicinity of the northeast lakes. In the south, Dadu reached the line of today's Chang'an Avenue, with the observatory marking the southeast corner. In the north, it reached as far as the present Lama Temple, which was at that time the site of

Left: Kublai Khan and the Ming emperors Hongwu and Wanli. **Above:** an early view of the Forbidden City.

the trade quarters by the Bell and Drum Towers. The population was about 500,000.

Emperor Yongle's city

Beijing's role as capital city continued during the Ming and Qing dynasties. With the conquest of Mongol Dadu by Ming troops in 1368, Beijing became Chinese once more and was renamed Beiping ("Northern Peace"). Zhu Yuanzhang, founder of the Ming dynasty, at first made the more modern Nanjing, hundreds of

---

MARCO POLO AND KHANBALIQ

In 1266, Marco Polo was welcomed into Kublai Khan's court at Khanbaliq before being sent back to the Pope with the Khan's written request for missionaries. In his journals Marco Polo wrote:

"There are in Khanbaliq unbelievable numbers of people and houses, it is impossible to count them. The houses and villas outside the walls are at least as beautiful as those within, except, of course, for the imperial buildings … Nowhere in the world are such rare and precious goods traded as in Khanbaliq … just imagine, every day more than 1,000 wagons arrive fully laden with silk and precious jewels."

miles to the south, his capital and gave Beiping to one of his sons as a fief. When the latter succeeded to the throne in 1403, taking the ruling name of Yongle, he moved the country's capital back up to Beijing.

At first the city was made smaller. The outer city wall was demolished and rebuilt more towards the south, between today's Deshengmen Gate and Andingmen Gate. One can still see remains of the demolished northern wall of Dadu outside the Deshengmen. Local people call it the Earth Wall, since only a broken row of hillocks remains. From 1406 to 1420, the new Beijing was built, with the Imperial Palace that still exists today at its centre.

Most ancient buildings in today's inner city date back to this time. Like Kublai Khan, the Ming emperors followed the square pattern dictated by the old rules. The main axis ran southwards and the city was completely enclosed by walls with three gates on each side. Civil engineers dug moats and canals, planned Beijing's extensive road network and, in 1553, completed a massive city wall to protect their

thriving capital. The ground plan resembled a chessboard, with a network of north–south and east–west streets, at the heart of which nestled the Forbidden City, surrounded by high red walls. To the south, starting from today's Qianmen, an Inner City was built.

Yongle's decision to make Beijing his capital may seem surprising, as the city's northerly position brought with it the permanent danger of attack by the Mongols or other nomadic tribes (which did indeed follow in the 16th and 17th centuries). In all probability, it was an expression of his drive for expansion. Under his rule, the imperial boundaries were pushed north as far as the River Amur (the present-day border with Russia). Moving the capital to the edge of the steppe zone could also be viewed as a sign that the Ming dynasty planned to restore the pre-eminence of the Chinese empire in Asia, the foundations of which had been laid by the Mongols. This ambition later became the hallmark of the entire Qing dynasty. The Ming also undertook China's greatest ever public-works project: the "10,000 Li" Great Wall, which linked or reinforced several older walls. Yet this costly project ultimately failed to save their empire. In 1644, Li Zicheng led a peasants' revolt, conquered the city of Beijing and toppled the Ming dynasty. A mere 43 days later, Manchu troops defeated Li's army and marched into Beijing, making it their capital.

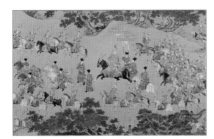

The Manchu rulers

The Manchu did not change the orientation of the city. They declared the northern part of the city, also known as the Tartar City, their domain, in which only Manchu could live, while the Ming Inner City to the south was renamed the Chinese City. The new Qing dynasty left its mark on the architecture of the Forbidden City, but did not change the basic structure.

Though the Qing emperors continued to observe the Confucian rites of their predecessors, they also brought their own language and customs with them. Chinese and Mongolian were both used in official documents. Tibetan Buddhism, which had flourished among the northern tribes since the Mongols promoted it in the 12th and 13th centuries, was the main Manchu religion. The Qing brought the fifth Dalai Lama from Lhasa to Beijing in 1651 to oversee the introduction of Tibetan Buddhism (Lamaism) to the capital. The White Dagoba (stupa) in Beihai Park commemorates the Dalai Lama's visit; the Lama Temple (Yonghegong) and the temples at the imperial 'resort' of Chengde are other legacies of the Qing emperors' religious faith.

Foreign influence

At around this time, the outside world began to make inroads into China. In 1601, the Italian Jesuit Matteo Ricci arrived in Beijing, followed in 1622 by Johann Adam Schall von Bell (1592–1666), who later received permission to build the city's first Catholic church (Nantang, or South Cathedral, *see page 128*). Jesuit missionaries

quickly won influence at court because of their astronomical and other scientific knowledge.

By the beginning of the 19th century, at the time when the Qing empire was at its peak, Beijing had a population of 700,000, including a small foreign community. But signs of decay were beginning to surface – due to cor-

> In 1293, the Tonghua Canal was completed, linking the capital with the Grand Canal and making it possible to bring grain from the south into the city by boat.

ruption within the imperial household, and the gradual wresting of power away from the centre by warlords and princes. Revolts increased and secret societies sprang up everywhere, rapidly gaining influence. Xenophobia grew with the rise in Han nationalism. The first persecutions of Jesuits and the destruction of churches took place. Emperor Qianlong, still self-confident, supposedly told the ambassador of the British queen that the Middle Kingdom had no need of

FAR LEFT: massive rebuilding of the Great Wall failed to save the Ming dynasty. **LEFT:** Emperor Yongle created much of the ancient city of Beijing. **ABOVE:** detail from a 15th-century scroll painting of the imperial procession to the Ming Tombs. **ABOVE RIGHT:** Chinese and German troops do battle during the Boxer Rebellion,1900.

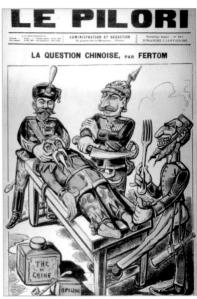

"barbarian" products, for the Middle Kingdom produced all that it required. And yet the time of humiliation for Beijing and for all of China was just around the corner, with the advance of foreign colonial powers from the time of the First Opium War (1840–2) onwards.

At the end of the Second Opium War (1858–60), the emperor was forced to flee from the Western armies, who went on to destroy part of the city, including Yuanmingyuan, the Old Summer Palace (the ruins can still be seen today, *see page 199*), and plundered Beijing's treasuries. The emperor was obliged to grant concessions to the foreign powers. Extra territorial areas were granted and the diplomatic quarter in the southeast part of the imperial city was put at the disposal of the foreigners, which became the Legation Quarter *(see page 109)*. Many Chinese, however, were unwilling to accept this humiliation, and hostility gradually increased. During the 1880s and 1890s a programme of Chinese "self-reliance", supported by the powerless Emperor

PU YI, THE LAST EMPEROR

Pu Yi was one of the tragic figures of 20th-century China. Born into the imperial family in 1906, he acceded to the throne aged two, but was forced to abdicate just four years later, although he continued living in the Forbidden City for another 12 years until a military coup forced him to move to Tianjin. During China's uncertain 1920s, he wavered between different ideas and considered emigration, but later hoped to persuade warlords to unite in restoring the throne. The growth of anti-Qing sentiments in Tianjin forced Pu Yi to take refuge in the Japanese legation, which led, in 1932, to his appointment as "chief executive" of Japanese-occupied Manchuria, and "emperor" status two years later.

After liberation by Soviet troops he was captured and imprisoned in Siberia, where he was allowed to live in relative comfort. Pu Yi was then sent back to China in 1950, and spent 10 years in Fushun War Criminals Prison, where he was "re-educated" in revolutionary ideology. After his release, he lived as an ordinary citizen of Beijing until his death in 1967. China's last emperor ended his days an apparently zealous Communist: in a strong echo of George Orwell's *Nineteen Eighty-Four*, Pu Yi's response to being awarded a special pardon by the Party was: "Before I had heard this to the end I burst into tears. My motherland had made me into a man."

Guangxu, was instituted. It centred on the construction of railways, docks and other infrastructural projects that had hitherto been built and controlled by foreigners. The programme met with opposition from the imperial court, and after China's defeat in the Sino-Japanese War of 1894–5 it effectively collapsed. All this added momentum to the demands of extremist groups, and slogans such as "Drive the barbarians from our country!" were to be heard everywhere.

Two years later, in 1900, followers of a secret society named the Society for Peace and Justice – known in the West as the Boxers – rebelled. For two months, partly supported by imperial troops, they besieged the foreign embassies. Western countries quickly sent forces to Beijing. The empress dowager Cixi fled to Xi'an, and the Boxer Rebellion was crushed. A foreign newspaper based in Beijing reported: "The capital of the emperors was partly destroyed, partly burned down. All that was left was a dead city. The streets were choked with the bodies of Chinese, many charred or eaten by stray dogs."

Once again, the increasingly weak Manchu regime had to pay great sums in reparations, while the foreigners received further privileges. As Beijing continued to decay, the imperial court carried on in the same old way, cut off from reality, bound up as it was in luxury, corruption and intrigue.

End of empire

In October 1910, an advisory council met for the first time in Beijing. By then the middle-class Xinhai revolution, led by Dr Sun Yat-sen, had become a real threat to the Manchu imperial house. The prince regent recalled the Imperial Marshal, Yuan Shikai, the strongman of Cixi, dismissed earlier in 1909. He was appointed supreme commander and head of the government. However, Yuan Shikai wanted to prepare a change of dynasty in the traditional style. He avoided confrontation with the republican forces in the south, elected himself president of the National Assembly in November 1911, and the next month forced the child emperor Pu Yi to abdicate, effectively sealing the fate of the Qing dynasty.

The long rule of the Sons of Heaven was over. Chinese men could finally cut off their hated pigtails – the external symbol of servitude imposed by the Manchu. But the city continued to decay and social problems became more acute. Yuan Shikai failed in his attempt to defeat the republicans – who had organised

FAR LEFT: Pu Yi as a young child. LEFT: an 1898 caricature of the carve-up of China by Western imperialists. ABOVE: Sun Yat-sen. RIGHT: a depiction of the Long March.

The May Fourth Movement was not just a surge of nationalism, it also represented a cultural and literary revolution in which many intellectuals sought to abandon the values of ancient China and build a new nation based around Western ideals.

themselves as the Guomindang (Kuomintang), the National People's Party, led by Sun Yat-sen. Yuan died in 1916 and the dynasty was overthrown, but the social and political problems remained unsolved. Beijing stagnated in a half-feudal state.

Warlords struggled for control, dashing any hopes of unity and peace. The north and Beijing, which remained the nominal capital of the republic after 1911, were badly affected by these battles. Social and political problems became more acute, and the misery of the poor was indescribable.

Expansionist foreign powers remained greedy for profit and influence in China. In the Treaty of Versailles of 1919, the former German concessions – Qingdao and the adjacent Jiaozhou Bay – were not returned to China but given to Japan. This deeply wounded national pride. More than 300,000 young Chinese, mostly students and intellectuals, demonstrated in Beijing on 4 May 1919 to demand national independence and territorial integrity. A manifesto passed at the demonstration ended with the words: "China's territory may be conquered, but it cannot be given to foreign powers. The Chinese people may be slaughtered, but they

will not surrender. Our country is in the process of being destroyed. Brothers, defend yourselves against this!"

As a result of this May Fourth Movement – considered a turning point in modern Chinese history – the Chinese workers' movement grew. Trade unions and the Communist Party came into existence, the latter soon becoming active in Beijing. At that time, the party's future leader, Mao Zedong, was a librarian at Beijing University. In the 1920s, Guomindang and Communist Party forces still fought side by side against the warlords in the north. But after the right wing of the Guomindang gained the upper hand in 1928, the Communist Party was banned. Chiang Kai-shek, the Guomindang leader, moved his capital to Nanjing.

Beijing in the 1920s was a vibrant yet poor and chaotic city, with a street life of fortune-tellers, opera troupes, nightclub singers, foreign businessmen and adventurers. Modernity was slowly creeping in; the network of streets was extended, water pipes were laid, hospitals were established and banks opened branches.

Yet the outside world influenced Beijing far less than it did Shanghai, an open treaty port with foreign concessions ruled by foreigners

and in which foreign law applied, almost like a colony: the official languages here were French or English and the people making the laws were foreign. Beijing was still China, far less hospitable in terms of living or business conditions for foreigners.

The Japanese and World War II

The years leading up to World War II were overshadowed by the threat of the Japanese. Already, in 1931, Japan had occupied northeast China, which they named Manchuria. In 1935, huge anti-Japanese demonstrations marched through the streets of Beijing. Following the 1934–6 Long March from the south, surviving Communist troops regrouped in Shaanxi province, to the southwest of Beijing. The Guomindang, responding to popular pressure, made a new alliance with the Communists, this time to fight against Japan.

A confrontation choreographed by the Japanese in 1937 on the Marco Polo Bridge, on the western outskirts of Beijing, served the Japanese as a pretext for occupying Beijing and then all of China.

Life became worse for the people of Beijing during World War II, a time when the foreigners remained "neutral" and the Japanese secret police controlled everything. By 1939, Japan had seized all of eastern China and the Guomindang had retreated to Chongqing in Sichuan province, far to the southwest. The US began supplying the Guomindang troops, hoping that they would oust the Japanese and, later, the Communists – still at that time fighting alongside their rivals against the common enemy. In 1941, an attack on Communist troops by a rogue Guomindang unit split the alliance, although both sides continued separate action against the Japanese.

Towards the end of the war, Communist guerrillas were operating in the hills around Beijing, but after the Japanese surrender the Guomindang took control of the city, supported by the Americans. However, by 1948 their position was weakening daily, as the Communists gained support across the Chinese countryside, and eventually in 1949 the People's Liberation Army marched victorious into the city. ❏

Far Left: beggars in Beihai Park, 1917.
Above Left: Chinese troops defend themselves against Japanese attack, 1937. **Above:** Nanjing falls to the Japanese, 1938.

COMMUNISM AND MODERN TIMES

After decades of turmoil which reached its nadir during the brutal Cultural Revolution, the Deng era brought bold economic reforms. The ensuing economic growth continues to accelerate, with implications for China's world role

On 31 January 1949, Beijing was taken without a struggle. On 1 October, Mao Zedong proclaimed the foundation of the People's Republic of China from Tiananmen, the Gate of Heavenly Peace. Just like the emperors before them, the Communists moved their centre of power into part of the Forbidden City, to Zhongnanhai, west of the Imperial Palace.

All government bodies were based in Beijing. Important schools and colleges moved here, and new factories were built. The city, which had just 1.2 million inhabitants in 1949, grew through the incorporation of eight rural districts of Hebei province in 1958. Urban reshaping began in the 1950s. The slum areas were cleared, new buildings erected and the streets widened. Despite pleas by planning experts, Mao insisted on demolishing Beijing's ancient city walls. Grey and dusty Beijing was to become a green city within the decade.

As the centre of political power, the capital led several fierce ideological campaigns in the 1950s. During the Korean War (1950–3), it rallied support for its North Korean allies against "US imperialists". In 1956, Mao issued his infamous edict, "Let a hundred flowers bloom, let a hundred schools of thought contend." It sounded too good to be true, and sure enough – whatever the original intent – the Hundred Flowers movement soon became a vehicle for flushing out dissenting voices. Many of those who heeded Mao's call found themselves purged or arrested. At least 300,000 intellectuals, most of them committed Communists, were labelled "rightists" or "capitalist roaders" and sent to remote labour camps for "re-education". Many were from Beijing; some would never return.

Khrushchev's 1956 condemnation of Stalin shocked the Chinese leadership. When the Soviet premier later criticised Mao, shock turned to anger, and a full-scale diplomatic rift. In July 1960, all remaining Soviet experts left China. Beijing residents were largely unaffected by the focus of Khrushchev's concern, the Great Leap Forward. Party secrecy also ensured ignorance of the mass famine in the countryside. From 1958 to 1961 over 30 million people starved to death, mainly due to misguided Great Leap policies. In the middle of this rural catastrophe, in 1959 the capital

celebrated the 10th anniversary of Communist rule with a huge rally and 10 major construction projects, including the Great Hall of the People and the huge museums which flank Tiananmen Square.

Redder than red

As if the traumas of the Hundred Flowers and the Great Leap movements were not enough, in 1965 the first rumblings of the Cultural Revolution began with the launch of a campaign, exhorting the people, in typically lyrical fashion, to "Hand over the Khrushchevs sleeping next to Mao". Defence minister Lin Biao henceforth orchestrated the rise of Mao to godlike status. Images of the Great Helmsman decorated Beijing's public buildings and homes, and everyone wore Mao badges. Red Guard groups mushroomed across the capital. Encouraged by Mao, students abandoned their lessons and persecuted their teachers and other authority figures. They took over factories and

offices to pursue "class struggle". Some even fought pitched battles with other groups to prove ideological supremacy. The Red Guards also ransacked many of Beijing's ancient cultural sites, and searched homes for "bourgeois" or "feudal" items. Mao's wife, Jiang Qing, and supporters of her Gang of Four, used Beihai Park throughout the Cultural Revolution as a private domain.

At the end of the 1960s a new fear gripped Beijing, as soldiers and civilians hurriedly

---

LEFT: the PLA marches into Beijing in 1949.
ABOVE TOP & ABOVE: the cult of Mao; the Great Helmsman and Red Guards, 1965.
ABOVE RIGHT: propaganda image from the 1940s.

MELTDOWN MANIA

Beijingers did not starve to death during the Great Leap Forward, but they were expected to participate by doing "more, cheaper, better, faster". To meet ludicrous steel-production goals, families melted down pots and pans in backyard furnaces. The city's Central Philharmonic Orchestra, eager to demonstrate its patriotism by "producing" more, doubled its annual number of performances from 40 to 80. In the near-hysterical atmosphere, it was soon decided that this was not ambitious enough, and the number was doubled again, to 160; and then again, to 320; and again, to 640; they finally settled on the nice round number of 1,200 concerts a year.

Maomorabilia

Mao's personality cult lives on in the vast quantities of kitsch 1960s and '70s merchandise for sale in the city

Away from Tiananmen Gate, the most likely place you will see the image of Mao Zedong is in one of the city's curio markets. In a recycling of an icon that has endured for over 40 years, the vast sea of kitsch created during the 1960s and early 1970s in his honour has in recent years become fashionable again. Mao attained Messianic status during the mayhem of the Cultural Revolution which began

in 1966, a time when his likeness appeared on some 2 billion pictures and 3 billion badges, when Red Guards waved his "Little Red Book" of quotations during huge rallies; more than 350 million were printed between 1964 and 1966, and translations into all major languages followed. The arms of waving Red Guards became the hands of Cultural Revolution alarm clocks, while double-image Mao medallions, rubber stamps, resin busts and ceramic ornaments all fuelled the personality cult.

Despite the huge volume produced, some items have become valuable collec-

tors' pieces, especially original postage stamps, paintings and posters. A few Cultural Revolution paintings have sold for more than $1 million. Many badges were thrown away or used as scrap metal but an estimated 300 million have survived, with some passing hands for up to Rmb 10,000.

In the run-up to the 60th anniversary of the founding of the People's Republic in 2009, prices for Chairman Mao porcelain statues and mint-condition quotation books doubled. The demand appears to have been sparked partly by a State Council issued "Ten-Year Plan to Develop Red Tourism" in 2004, and partly by rose-tinted nostalgia among a patriotic new generation too young to have experienced the horrors of the Cultural Revolution.

Panjiayuan Market and Beijing Curio City (see page 138) are good places to look for items, with striking Mao propaganda posters on sale for under Rmb 30. Look out, too, for ornaments and pictures of Lei Feng – a young soldier in a fur-lined hat with earflaps, regarded as a model of selfless devotion – and gun-toting young women dressed in pale blue short suits. *The Red Detachment of Women* was one of seven model stage works allowed by Mao's wife Jiang Qing, a former film actress and self-appointed cultural arbiter.

The cult of Deng Xiaoping has shadowed the Mao trend to some extent. Souvenir stalls sell Deng watches, musical lighters, T-shirts, and pendants for car windscreens. But for some people, Deng will always be second best. For them, Mao remains the greatest hero of the 20th century, if not China's entire history. ❑

LEFT: Mao kitsch is easy to find in city markets.
ABOVE: millions of Mao badges were made.

built a vast network of tunnels and air-raid shelters, preparing for possible war with the Soviet Union. The two powers had skirmished along China's northeast border, and Mao was convinced the Soviets planned an invasion.

War was avoided, but the internal struggles continued. In 1971 the heir apparent, Lin Biao, died in a plane crash, allegedly while fleeing China after a failed coup attempt. But Lin's death merely left the way clear for a second faction to manipulate the Mao personality cult. The Gang of Four hijacked Mao's "Criticise Lin Biao and Confucius" campaign, launched in 1973. Zhou Enlai, probably China's most popular premier, became "Confucius" and was criticised, but remained in office.

US president Richard Nixon made a historic visit to Beijing in 1972, marking the beginning of the end of China's international isolation. But it did not signal the end of the Cultural Revolution, which would last another four years, until the momentous events of 1976.

ABOVE TOP: Zhou Enlai (second left) and Mao (far right) in the 1930s. **ABOVE LEFT & ABOVE CENTRE:** more images of Mao. **ABOVE RIGHT:** typical Social Realist revolutionary imagery dating from the Cultural Revolution period.

Signs of change

In early April 1976, during the week of the Qingming Festival when the Chinese remember their dead, the silent rage of the people found expression in a massive demonstration. Dissatisfaction had increased because of food rationing and the poor quality of goods available. Support and trust in the leadership, even in Mao, had evaporated.

The people of Beijing gathered by the thousands for several days in Tiananmen Square, to pay homage to the recently dead President Zhou Enlai, and to protest against Mao and the radical leaders of the Cultural Revolution. The first demands for modernisation and democracy were heard, signalling the end of the Cultural Revolution. In response to the unrest, a new face was presented to the Chinese people: Hua Guofeng, who was named First Vice-Chairman, second only to Mao.

When Mao died on 9 September machines everywhere stood still, shops closed and people gathered on the streets. The television showed pictures of mourners weeping. But an astute observer would have concluded that the Chinese were shocked less by the death itself than by the uncertainty of what the future, after Mao Zedong, would bring.

First came the toppling of the Gang of Four, in October 1976. Hua had the four radical leaders, one of whom was Mao's widow Jiang Qing, arrested during a Party meeting. They were convicted of creating and directing the Cultural Revolution. Jiang Qing died in prison.

By spring 1977, the new Chairman Hua's portrait was prominently displayed in the capital. A large poster showed him at the deathbed of the Great Helmsman. Attributed to Mao, the caption read: "With you in charge, my heart is

A FATEFUL YEAR

The Chinese, great believers in omens and portents, have always viewed natural disasters as signs from heaven of great changes to come. In July 1976, a massive earthquake destroyed the city of Tangshan, to the east of Beijing, and claimed hundreds of thousands of victims. In imperial times this would have been interpreted as a sign that a change of dynasty was imminent. The shockwaves reached as far as Beijing, toppling buildings, and within a few weeks a comparable jolt struck the political landscape. Mao Zedong, the Great Helmsman who had led China out of feudal servitude, died on 9 September 1976.

at ease." Hua, however, remained in power only a short time. A veteran of the revolution was waiting in the wings, one who had twice disappeared into obscurity during the intra-party struggles: former vice-premier Deng Xiaoping, who emerged as China's leader in late 1978.

From 1978 to 1980, Beijing was the scene of countless demonstrations by dissatisfied Chinese from all over the country. Most were young students who courageously joined the Democracy Wall movement in spring 1979. On the wall by Xidan Market, *dazibao* (big character posters) reappeared. These were familiar from the Cultural Revolution years but were significantly different in their content. Officials were accused of corruption, and individuals demanded justice for past wrongs. One concise wall poster asked: "Who knows the representative of my district, who is supposed to represent me in the People's Congress?" Space for name, address and telephone number were left pointedly blank, a plain reference to the fact that National People's Congress (NPC) members in China were selected by the higher echelons of the Communist party and in practice no elections took place.

Students at the Xidan Wall sold journals that they had produced themselves. It was through these journals that many city dwellers learned for the first time of the mass poverty in the countryside. Petitions were handed in daily, putting considerable pressure on the Party, and while many of the leaders of these demonstra-

ABOVE LEFT: city buildings are damaged by the Tangshan earthquake of 1976. **ABOVE:** Deng Xiaoping assumed leadership in 1978. **RIGHT:** street scene from the late 1970s.

tions were arrested, some of their ideas became official government policy.

Opening the doors

In 1982, a new Constitution came into being. An open-door policy to foreign countries was one important step in the modernisation programme designed to quadruple China's economic power by the year 2000. Soon, the first free markets arrived, seen at many major crossroads. In contrast to the state-run shops, they were able to offer

China's first special economic zone was established in 1980, at the then unknown town of Shenzhen on the border with Hong Kong. Since then, its population has swelled from 30,000 to more than 14 million.

fresh fruit and vegetables. For years, independent work and private trade had been condemned. Now cooks, cobblers, hairdressers, tailors and carpenters simply started to work for themselves.

The city seemed to have awoken from a long sleep, and the pace was hectic. People enjoyed

the new beginning. The time of forced participation in political events and campaigns was over and interest in politics faded away. New horizons opened for the young, and never before had they been known to study so eagerly. Careers as scientists, engineers and technicians, study trips abroad, and freedom and prosperity beckoned.

Television showed pictures from abroad and spread, intentionally or subliminally, the message of the blessings of consumerism. Suddenly the three "luxury goods" – a bicycle, clock and radio – were no longer enough. The department stores filled up with refrigerators, washing machines, television sets and expensive imported goods. Fashion shows and magazines, as well as pop singers and film stars, awoke the desire of women and men to look attractive and different. In contemporary literature, young lovers no longer vowed to fight to the death for the revolution and their homeland. Instead, they would study hard and help with the modernisation of their country.

All of this reform, however, was not without controversy. After Deng Xiaoping's protégé Hu Yaobang became general secretary of the Party and Zhao Ziyang became premier, opposition

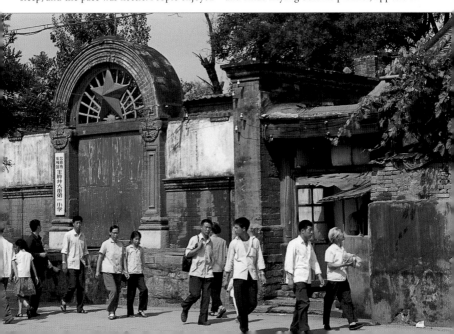

grew in Conservative circles, especially in the army. At the end of 1983, a campaign began against "spiritual pollution". Many serious criminals were publicly executed as a deterrent, but the fight was mainly against intellectuals and artists, and against fashions such as long hair and Western music, which were being steadily imported from Hong Kong.

Coca-Cola became the first wholly foreign-owned firm in China on 13 December 1978. Kentucky Fried Chicken arrived in 1987, followed three years later by McDonald's.

For some, economic freedom was not enough. At the end of 1986, student protests that began in Hefei reached their peak in Shanghai, where they ended peacefully. This led to Conservatives pressuring party secretary Hu Yaobang to retire, as he had sympathised with the students' calls for greater democracy and curbs on corruption. Zhao Ziyang, who was regarded as a relative liberal, succeeded Hu, and in 1988 Li Peng took over from Zhao as premier.

Pro-democracy demonstrations

The discontent that had been mounting as the 1980s wore on found an outlet in April 1989 with the death of former Party secretary Hu Yaobang. Since Hu had previously shown sympathy for students and their needs, his death was both a cause of sorrow and a perfect pretext for protests veiled as demonstrations of mourning. Students initially proceeded with caution, coming out to demonstrate only in the small hours of the night and returning to their campuses by morning. But by the time of Hu's funeral a week later, they had become far more daring, making demands on the government and occupying Tiananmen Square.

The protests soon spread across the rest of China. Beijing remained the epicentre, however, and many adventurous students jumped aboard trains – generally allowed to ride for free by sympathetic workers – and travelled to the capital to join the demonstrators. The government's willingness to allow the protests to continue astonished many and gave them hope, but was in actuality a sign of a leadership deeply divided over how to handle the situation. Finally, in mid-May, the moderates led by Zhao Ziyang lost the battle and martial law was declared in Beijing on 19 May. Zhao visited the Tiananmen protesters at 4am and sobbed as he said, "We have come too late." His political career was over, and it was only a matter of time until the protests would be forcibly ended.

The end duly arrived on 4 June, when Deng Xiaoping sent in the People's Liberation Army "to end the counter-revolutionary rebellion". The soldiers turned their tanks and guns on the students and on the many citizens of Beijing who supported them. Estimates of the number of people killed range from the hundreds to the thousands. The Chinese government has never given a full account of what happened.

In the weeks and months that followed, Beijing and much of the nation remained in a state of shock. Foreigners left China en masse and the economy spluttered as foreign investment dwindled. Jiang Zemin, who as Party secretary of Shanghai had handled the protests there with relative aplomb while also demonstrating his loyalty to Beijing, was named to replace Zhao Ziyang as general secretary.

Deng Xiaoping had severely damaged his reputation as an open-minded reformer, but, if he had proven himself willing to resist political change at all costs, he was still determined to continue with his pragmatic policies of economic reform and opening to the outside world. To make this clear, he travelled to several special economic zones in the south and to Shanghai in 1992, using every opportunity to reaffirm explicitly the Party's commitment to continued economic reform. This helped to provide the spark for a burst of economic development and reassured foreign investors, who began increasing the number and size of their investments in China.

With economic development back on track, Deng retired from all his official positions (except that as head of the Chinese Bridge Players' Association) in 1993, although he remained important behind the scenes. When he died in 1997, the unofficial position of "core" of the Communist Party leadership passed to Jiang Zemin. Later that year, the Hong Kong handover and a visit to the United States gave Jiang two opportunities to show his new stature to people in China and abroad. He continued to push for greater economic development and worked to strengthen China's international standing, aided by Premier Zhu Rongji.

The PRC celebrated its 50th anniversary in 1999 and that same year enshrined "Deng

FAR LEFT: the Chinese population exceeded the 1 billion mark in the early 1980s. LEFT TOP: modern architecture in eastern Beijing. LEFT: new economic freedom: a street vendor in 1983. ABOVE: Tiananmen demonstrators, 1989. RIGHT: famous image from 4 June 1989.

Xiaoping Thought" in the Constitution, thereby giving Deng's theories a status equal to Mao's. Collections of his writings and speeches were published and his sayings were promoted, including the catchy "To get rich is glorious", and "It doesn't matter if the cat is black or white, as long as it catches the mice." Despite 1989, Deng's position as the pragmatic, courageous and far-seeing architect of China's economic reform remains intact.

Jiang Zemin

Jiang Zemin did not share the war-hero status of Deng Xiaoping, and his oversized glasses and tendency to show off awkwardly by speaking poor English, reciting poetry or singing songs made him an easy butt of jokes. In the early years of his tenure, many expected him to be a flash in the pan and even compared him to Hua Guofeng, Mao's ill-fated successor. But Jiang proved smarter than his critics. His determination to join the World Trade Organization paid off, and in 2001 China was finally admitted. This was a highly significant development not only because of the trading privileges it brought, but also because it cemented China's status in the global community.

Jiang's desire to improve China's diplomatic status in general, and its relations with the US in particular, encountered several serious obstacles. In the spring of 1999, thousands of practitioners of a martial art known as Falun Gong surrounded the Zhongnanhai leadership compound in a silent protest against the treatment their members had received in Tianjin. Jiang was smart enough not to call in the army, but he did unleash a crackdown in which the movement was banned and many of its followers arrested, drawing international criticism.

During the Kosovo War of 1999, the accidental bombing of the Chinese embassy in Belgrade by a US NATO plane sent US–China relations into a tailspin and brought student protesters onto the streets. This time, however, the protests were an eerie mirror-image of those of 1989, with students demonising America and its values instead of glorifying them – and the Chinese government permitting, even encouraging, their activities. In April 2001, another diplomatic incident occurred when a US spy plane collided with a Chinese fighter jet over the South China Sea. The Chinese pilot died, but the Americans survived after landing on Hainan Island, where they were immediately detained by the Chinese and released only after 11 days of intense public propaganda and private negotiations.

ABOVE LEFT: Jiang Zemin and George W. Bush at an economic summit in 2001, the year China was admitted to the World Trade Organization. **ABOVE & RIGHT:** the Tibetan protest movement exploded into violence in 2008.

These and other less public disagreements made the road ahead look rocky for US–China relations. However, the shocking tragedy of the September 2001 terrorist attacks in New York proved a turning point for relations, and indeed, for China's international diplomatic position. As the US and other Western nations focused their attention on fighting terrorists, China suddenly became a needed ally rather than a convenient target for governments and politicians who wanted to show their support for human rights. The Chinese government – ever mindful of its own simmering separatist problems in Xinjiang and Tibet – remained largely silent as the US went to war first in Afghanistan and then in Iraq. Tensions over North Korea's suspected nuclear weapon programme also benefited China, which found itself sought after as a vital intermediary in negotiations with its hermetic neighbour. In 2004 the US–China relationship was on its best footing since before the events of 1989.

In the last few years of his tenure, Jiang Zemin began to put forward a new theory called the "Three Represents" with the intention of making the ruling Communist party more responsive to the needs of its population and inclusive of the new wave of entrepreneurs and businessmen *(see panel, page 50)*. Despite opposition from hard-line Communists, the Three Represents was added to both the Party and State constitutions and may prove to be Jiang's most important legacy.

Hu Jintao's leadership

Jiang Zemin relinquished his position as Communist Party secretary in 2002, as state president in 2003, and as head of the Central Military Commission in 2004. He was replaced in all three positions by Hu Jintao, a native of Anhui province who studied engineering at Beijing's prestigious Tsinghua University. Hu had risen quickly through the ranks of the Communist Party based on his own merit and hard work, and is believed to have been hand-picked as future leader of China by Deng Xiaoping as early as 1992. Deng liked him for being reform-orientated yet tough: in March 1989, Hu had overseen a bloody suppression of Tibetan rebels that some say became a model for the Tiananmen crackdown in June.

Hu had something of a baptism by fire when the SARS epidemic broke out almost as soon as he assumed office. Institutionalised obfuscation

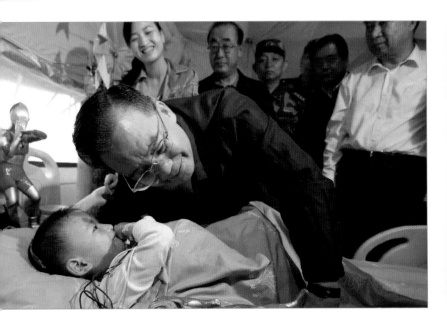

significantly worsened the problem, but once Hu recognised that the cover-up was nearly as dangerous as the disease, he fired those who had lied and opened China up to international disease experts. His background gave him a deep understanding of the problems in rural areas, and he adopted a somewhat more populist governing approach than his predecessor. His premier, Wen Jiabao, also has a strong interest in rural affairs and is a well-liked populist; he is still remembered by many for having accompa-

nied Zhao Ziyang on his visit to the students in Tiananmen Square in May 1989. Wen is often used to display the caring side of the Communist leadership. When China's worst snow storms for half a century buffeted central and southern areas of the country in January 2008, it was Wen who visited stranded passengers at two major train stations to show sympathy and call for order. He was also hailed for rapidly responding to the magnitude-8 Sichuan earthquake just four months later, with a personal visit and hands-on approach to rescue work and the recovery effort.

Though a pragmatic leader, Hu Jintao still seeks to guide the hearts and minds of the people. In March 2006 he released his "Eight Honours and Eight Shames", a set of moral codes for Party cadres to follow as an example to all Chinese. The list was topped by a call for patriotism: the ideology behind education, the standpoint of state media and the justification for China's rising global influence. The call to follow science and disregard superstition can also be seen as characteristic of Hu's ideals, which were written into China's Constitution under the banner of the "Scientific Development Concept" in October 2007.

THE "THREE REPRESENTS"

The basic idea of the Three Represents is that the Communist Party must strive to represent the requirements of China's "advanced productive forces", "advanced culture" and the interests of the overwhelming majority of the Chinese people. Even to someone versed in the opaque language of the Communist bureaucracy, the theory is virtually unintelligible, and it was at first the subject of much muttered ridicule. However, the underlying purpose was, and is, of great importance: to allow capitalists to join the Communist Party and to guarantee their basic rights and protection. It also enshrined Jiang Zemin's principles in the Constitution alongside those of Mao and Deng Xiaoping.

Olympics, unrest and the future

Both Hu and Wen were reappointed in March 2008 in the run-up to August's Olympic Games. Their pledge was to oversee China's continued economic development and the construction of a harmonious society. The concept of har-

> The Sichuan earthquake of May 2008 led to so-called "disaster diplomacy", with Beijing accepting aid from foreign countries including Japan and even the breakaway island of Taiwan.

mony is seen as necessary to ensure that the huge disparity in distribution of wealth that remains across China's territories does not spill over into riots and social disorder. The peaceful coexistence of the 56 officially recognised ethnic minorities is also a major issue. Deadly riots erupted in the restive regions of Tibet in March 2008 and Xinjiang in July 2009. Though much of the public support the notion of a harmonious society, the concept is also derided as the force behind harsh crackdowns on dissenting voices, freedom of expression in the print media and online, political petitioners and anyone whose views might be seen as "unharmonious". Foreign information providers such as Microsoft, Yahoo! and Google have to omit sensitive web pages from their Chinese-language results, though the last gave a rare show of defiance in early 2010 when it temporarily stopped censoring results of its search engine.

China's image abroad is also of more importance than ever as, hungry for raw materials, it seeks to expand its influence into Africa while giant state-owned companies acquire assets from Western companies bankrupted by the global economic crisis. Though many political observers see it as triumphantly confident after a successful Olympics and having stubbornly refused to cede to outside influences that would have the nation fall more into line with their values, others recognise ongoing development problems and urge its leaders to continue to follow the advice of both Deng Xiaoping and ancient strategists: "Hide one's capabilities and bide one's time." ❑

LEFT: Wen Jiabao visiting children injured in the 2008 Sichuan earthquake. **ABOVE:** celebrating Chinese National Day (1 October).

LIFE IN THE NEW CHINA

The Chinese economic miracle has transformed the lives of the citizens of Beijing as much as anywhere in the country. The sheer rapidity of change has, however, resulted in a plethora of social, political and environmental problems

Boom times: winners and losers

The Communist Party stakes its unchallenged authority on economic results. More than 250 million people have been lifted out of poverty since economic modernisation was initiated at the end of the 1970s. Within a population of 1.3 billion, a Chinese "middle class" has emerged numbering more than 100 million. Though definitions of this group vary, they are generally the owners of cars and homes, the people

> In 2009, China's most talked about TV programme was Woju, an accurate portrayal of the difficulties of purchasing property, and the importance of salary in determining who to marry.

Modern China defies category. The unprecedented model of a planned economy coupled with a capitalist marketplace has led to growth nearing double digits every year since 1979, the year when foreign investment was first allowed in. While Western economists and politicians struggle to understand the shift in the global balance – the unfamiliar often leading to fear – Chinese scholars tend to see the new global order as the inevitable rise of a great nation. They refer to the current era as the new Tang dynasty: an economic and cultural renaissance. Provided the financial juggernaut keeps steaming forward, the captains of industry and government have no fear of widespread mutiny.

with sufficient disposable income to eat out at restaurants, travel and take an active approach to their children's education. Social problems still exist within this group, however. A flurry of speculation in the housing market has caused Beijing property prices to rise beyond the grasp of even highly educated urban workers.

On the other side of the tracks, migrant workers and farmers are less fortunate, seeing only a fraction of the enormous wealth that circulates – some 70 percent of GDP is controlled by just one percent of the population. Average income for urban residents rose to Rmb 18,858 (US$2,765) in 2009, while in the countryside it was just Rmb 5,153 (US$755) – just over a quarter of the urban wage.

A comprehensive labour law introduced in 2008 guaranteed factory workers' basic rights and security, though employers can find ways around the rules to remain competitive. Land-grabs are now rampant on the overpopulated mainland. Farmers often have to cede their land to commercial developments with little or no compensation provided – with the threat of violence or false imprisonment if they resist. Any disquiet among these disadvantaged groups is treated as a bigger threat to social stability than the abuses themselves, and is given short shrift by the authorities.

Unprecedented freedoms

Communist China has always frowned on dissent, be it political, religious or the orientation of its estimated 30 million homosexuals. But within a liberalised, international marketplace and with more than a quarter of the population gaining regular access to the outside world online *(see following page)*, the government has been relaxing control of any group not seen as a direct threat to its absolute authority.

The mainland's first government-sanctioned gay bar opened in the bohemian tourist town of Dali, Yunnan province, in 2009 – a venture that would have been unthinkable even a few years before. Though some hailed the move as an acceptance of alternative lifestyles, the focus of the bar is the prevention of the spread of HIV/Aids rather than any explicit promotion

PRECEDING PAGES: standing guard in the snow at Tiananmen. LEFT: Hu Jintao. ABOVE TOP: vision of the future at the City Planning Museum. ABOVE: the spirit of the age. ABOVE RIGHT: shopping is a favourite pastime; huge shopping malls have sprouted all over the city.

RAGE AGAINST THE RICH

With its conspicuous and growing wealth disparity, it is no surprise that anti-rich sentiment is on the rise in China. Property developers are public enemy number one for their perceived market manipulation that keeps home ownership out of the means of many, but anyone who has made a fortune for themselves is likely to be suspected of having done so through cronyism rather than their own hard work. Graduates from poor families can find their high grades are nullified by a lack of personal connections or *guanxi*, seen as essential for almost any business dealing. Some predict a return to a time of less ostentatious flaunting of wealth and status symbols.

THE GREENING OF CHINA

China is currently the world's largest exporter, and the number one producer of greenhouse gases. Every day it sucks in huge quantities of raw materials for its core manufacturing industry and to supply its frenzy of construction. As the population gravitates towards the prosperous cities, the greatest urbanisation the planet has ever seen is creating a surge in energy demand.

Efforts are being made to bring the country into line with global environmental targets, however. Huge wind and solar power projects may help China reach an

ambitious goal of 20 percent renewable energy by 2020, although many would dispute that this is likely. Pollution is still a huge problem. Factories routinely ignore regulations and use their influence to avoid censure and muzzle public opposition. Waste products from industry have led to toxic heavy metals percolating into the nation's rivers, and subsequently poisoning the water supply and the food chain. This has led to a rash of "cancer villages", where incidences of the disease are sky-high and claim the lives of otherwise healthy adults and children alike.

of tolerance. The opening night was delayed to avoid publicity as many potential customers shied away from having their preferences made public. China's first gay beauty pageant was set to be held in Beijing in 2010, but was shut down by police on the pretext that event organisers did not have the correct permits. It is estimated that 80 percent of homosexuals on the Chinese mainland marry a person of the opposite sex to create the public impression of a conventional lifestyle.

Religious practice has seen a remarkable revival in recent years. Traditional faiths such as Taoism and Buddhism are even regarded as rather fashionable, but it is Christianity that has captured the hearts and minds of the masses. Surveys estimate the number of mainland Christians worshipping outside of state churches at 100 million. Technically illegal, house churches provide a sense of faith and security in a nation that has seen often devastating clashes of ideologies in recent years. Many predict the authorities will only become more accepting of the religion if they believe it can assist in the building of a harmonious society.

China goes online

China now has more than 380 million internet users, a number greater than the population of the United States. These so-called "netizens" use the net for similar reasons to Western users: for news, information, social interaction, games and pornography. The freedoms provided by

the internet and its rapid introduction have led to some startling phenomena. Young men devote hours each day to playing online games, and internet addiction has become classified as a clinical disorder thought to affect more than 10 million.

On a more positive note, the internet's power in allowing netizens to act as public watchdog and wage campaigns against misconduct and injustice has been significant. When photographs of a government official in Nanjing wearing a luxury watch and smoking expensive cigarettes were posted online, public outcry led to an investigation and his eventual sacking for corruption.

But the Chinese mainland's internet is far from free. Many sites are blocked arbitrarily and without explanation, and internet search results are carefully controlled to prevent controversial topics from appearing. Foreign companies such as Yahoo! and Microsoft have been criticised for self-censoring their search results in China and even providing personal information on political dissidents to authorities. In 2010, internet information provider Google became the first company to stop censoring its Chinese-language search engine. The unprecedented free flow of information lasted only for a few days.

Building the creative industries

As the workshop of the 21st-century world, China is an export-driven producer of low-value-added goods. The world's tools, toys, shoes and a million other goods are manufactured here at low cost thanks to near-limitless, cheap labour and low standards of workers' rights and environmental protection.

However, this economic model is no longer desired by an ambitious nation looking to develop innovative Chinese brands for the domestic market. Yet this laudable aim is compromised by an ingrained lack of respect for intellectual property rights. Almost every product imaginable is counterfeited in China, from software to clothes, cigarettes and medicine. This trend has led to the emergence of a *shanzhai*, or "knockoff" culture, originating with cheap mobile phones that imitate the design and features of more expensive models. Many consider that *shanzhai* simply shows how China lacks true innovation. While the government throws money at the problem, building industrial parks for the creative industries and dangling financial rewards in front of potential talent, it has so far failed to stem the production of counterfeit goods. ❑

FAR LEFT TOP: China is the world's largest producer of greenhouse gases. FAR LEFT: the gay community has gained a degree of liberation in the past few years. LEFT: Christianity is on the rise. ABOVE: Western brands – sometimes fake – are everywhere. RIGHT: internet cafés are very popular.

The Legacy of the Olympics

Beijing's superhuman efforts to host the most spectacular Olympics ever have left a rather mixed legacy

At 8.08pm on the eighth day of the eighth month of 2008, the Games of the XXIX Olympiad opened in Beijing. Such an auspicious time and date illustrated the optimism that this momentous event would place Beijing firmly on the map of the world's great cities and

demonstrate beyond all doubt that China was not only taking a stand on the rostrum of global power but had ambitions to take the gold.

Following Beijing's successful bid to host the Games in 2001, the city witnessed a dizzying – and, for many, painful – transformation. Dozens of sporting venues were upgraded to Olympic standard or built from scratch, the airport and subway system were expanded and tens of thousands of residents relocated.

The lust for change didn't stop there. The promise of a green Olympics was set to transform Beijing into a model of environmental protection. As the city geared up for the big event, nothing seemed beyond the reach of the drive towards Olympic glory: public civility was "upgraded", national fitness improved, pollution dispersed. Even the weather was manipulated.

And then, after the final climax of nationalism, hope and triumph, some disappointments emerged. The high cost of operating the lavish Olympic venues saw many closed, or left empty, and the city's air remained choked. Temporary freedoms granted to the international press and the free flow of information were quickly repealed.

But for most residents of Beijing – particularly those fortunate enough to own homes that skyrocketed in value – the changes were largely positive. Though the term "cosmopolitan" still sits uneasily on the shoulders of the ancient capital, it must be said that its infrastructure and facilities are now truly world-class.

Getting around

Perhaps the Olympics' greatest physical legacy is the public transit upgrades. Three subway lines were opened in 2008 alone, and by 2015, some 8 million passengers a day will have access to 20 lines, comprising one of the world's largest metro systems. Beijing Airport's vast Terminal 3 has increased its capacity to 76 million passengers a year, while the rail network's new South Station boasts the world's fastest conventional trains, rushing towards Tianjin at a top speed of 350kmh (220mph).

The Green Olympics

When Ethiopian runner Haile Gebrselassie pulled out of the Olympic marathon event over fears of health problems, Beijing's air-quality problems received international attention. But the skies over the city had already been on the receiving end of a massive clean-up operation. Coal-burning was banned within the Fourth Ring Road in the run-up to the Games, many high-polluting factories were relocated outside the city limits, and private vehicle use was restricted on certain days according to licence-plate numbers. But the number of cars on Beijing's

roads had hit 4 million by the end of 2009, doubling in just six years and making a mockery of the notion of "blue-sky days".

National fitness

China topped the Olympic gold-medal tally in 2008 with 51, leaving the United States a distant second at 36. August 8 was established as an annual day to promote sports participation among those outside the athletic elite, but the nation's youngsters still trail behind others in the amount of regular exercise they get. The pressure of study keeps many indoors, and Beijing's internet cafés remain full of youngsters avidly playing computer games for hours on end.

Cultural heritage

While countless ancient streets and sites of historic interest were cleared for Beijing's Olympic developments, it seemed only foreign observers and a few hidebound Chinese heritage experts were speaking out in protest. With such a long history, little of central Beijing could have been touched without permanently damaging or destroying irreplaceable cultural relics, and the wrecking ball invariably won any argument. Of course, some historically significant buildings have state protection as tourist sites, but large areas of historic *hutong* have gone for ever.

The venues
The National Stadium
To build a truly iconic stadium for the Olympics, Beijing spent an eye-watering US$423

LEFT: the Bird's Nest Stadium under construction in 2007. **ABOVE:** Olympic lift-off. **ABOVE RIGHT:** Beijing's subway system has expanded enormously.

---

million on a radical design of criss-crossing steel trusses by Swiss architects Herzog and de Meuron. Resembling a bird's nest or piece of cracked Chinese porcelain, the thatched exoskeleton leaves the building porous to its surroundings and wandering between the soaring columns is akin to a walk through a giant steel forest. Although the future of the stadium is in doubt – operating costs may prove too high for it to remain a sporting venue – the "Bird's Nest" is now one of Beijing's top attractions.
Tel: 8437-3008. www.n-s.cn
Transport: Olympic Green or Olympic Sports Center subway stations (line 8)

The National Aquatics Centre
The futuristic appearance of the Olympic swimming venue known as the "water cube" is owed to its surface layer of plastic bubbles which provides strength, light and reduces the cost of heating and illuminating the building. Key to the promise of a "green" Olympics, the venue includes water collection and recycling technology. The centre houses a water park and fitness facilities.
Tel: 8437-1588. www.water-cube.com
Transport: Olympic Green or Olympic Sports Center subway stations (line 8)

Olympic Forest Park
Built to accommodate tennis, archery and hockey events during the Games, the park is now split into two by a bird reserve in the northern section and a garden to the south. Electric vehicles are available to rent.
Transport: Forest Park subway station (line 8)   ❏

RELIGION

Daoism, Buddhism and Confucianism are slowly regaining popularity, after the Cultural Revolution abruptly halted one of the world's richest spiritual traditions

Although only one major religion, Daoism, actually originated in China, the nation has absorbed all the world's major faiths over the centuries and is now home to millions of Buddhists, Muslims and Christians. The practices and doctrines of all these religions have been sinified in varying degrees, with Buddhism having been so significantly assimilated that it is now common to speak of "Chinese Buddhism" as one form of the religion. Indeed, the Chinese approach to all religion has historically been so syncretic that it is somewhat difficult to isolate religious practices – a Daoist temple might have a statue of Confucius or Buddha, while a portrait of the Virgin Mary might be hard to distinguish from a rendering of Guanyin, the Buddhist goddess of mercy.

New gods are readily adopted into local religious practice; peasants in some parts of the country now pray for good harvests before statues of Mao Zedong. Religion in China is now growing among newly affluent urbanites as well as rural peasants.

Ancestor worship

The ancestor worship of the Chinese is based on the belief that a person has two souls. One is created at the time of conception. After death, its strength dwindles, although it remains in the grave with the corpse and lives on the sacrificial offerings, until it eventually leads a shadow existence by the Yellow Springs in the underworld. However, if no more sacrifices are

Left: the Jade Emperor, a Daoist deity appropriated by popular religion. **Right:** ancestor worship.

offered, it will return to earth as an ill-willed spirit and cause damage.

The second soul emerges at birth. During its heavenly voyage after death, it is threatened by evil forces, and is dependent upon the sacrifices and prayers of living descendants. If the sacrifices cease, then this soul, too, turns into an evil spirit. But if the descendants continue to make sacrificial offerings and maintain the grave, the deceased may offer help and protection.

Originally, formal ceremonies of ancestor worship were exclusive to the king, but around 500 BC peasants began to honour their ancestors. At first, people believed the soul of the ancestor would search for a human substitute, usually the

grandson of the honoured ancestor. About 2,000 years ago, genealogical tables were introduced as homes for the soul during sacrificial acts. Until then, the king and noblemen had used human sacrifices for ancestral worship. Today they offer their ancestors sacrifices of food and gifts, for example, during the Qingming Festival.

Popular beliefs

The original popular Chinese religion focused on the worship of natural forces. Later on, people began to worship the Jade Emperor, a figure from Daoism; from the 14th century onwards the Jade Emperor became the most important god in popular religion. Guanyin, the goddess of mercy, originated in Mahayana (Great Wheel) Buddhism. There were also earth deities, and every town, large or small, worshipped its own town god. Demons of illness, spirits of the house and even the god of latrines had to be remembered. The deities of streams and rivers were considered particularly dangerous and unpredictable.

ANCESTRAL RITES

The Qingming Festival, often known as Tomb Sweeping Day, has been taking place at the beginning of April since the 8th century as a date to make offerings to one's ancestors and maintain their graves. According to ancient Chinese belief, the dead can influence the fate and fortune of the living, a belief that has led to the observation of elaborate rituals.

The Tang emperor Xuanzong is said to have established the Qingming Festival to limit extravagant ceremonies honouring ancestors to just one day. Today, the Chinese usually take Qingming – literally "clear and bright" – as an opportunity to pay respects to more recently deceased relatives such as parents or grandparents with offerings including incense, flowers and spirit money – paper notes resembling real currency that are burned with the intention of sending them to the afterlife where ancestors might make use of them. Shops near Beijing's Babaoshan Cemetery provide a modern take on what the deceased might need for a happy and comfortable afterlife by selling cardboard televisions, DVD players and washing machines.

A national holiday since 2008 – there are far more public holidays now than was the case just a few years ago – the Qingming Festival is a means by which families can enjoy outdoor activities such as kite-flying and picnicking.

Until the founding of the Qin empire in 221 BC, China was divided into many small states, with a variety of contending schools of philosophical thought. From these myriad doctrines, only Confucianism and Daoism had gained wide acceptance. Buddhism, China's other major religion, arrived from India in the 1st century AD, though it remained small-scale for several more centuries.

Daoism

Two of the central concepts of Daoism are *dao* and *wuwei*. *Dao* means the way or path, but also means method or principle. *Wuwei* is sometimes simply defined as passivity, or "swimming with the stream". The concept of *de* (virtue) is closely linked to this, not in the sense of moral honesty, but as a virtue that manifests itself in daily life when *dao* is put into practice. The forces of *yin* and *yang* determine the course of events in the world. The masculine, brightness, activity and heaven are considered *yang* forces; the feminine, weak, dark and passive elements of life are *yin*.

In popular religion, Laozi *(see panel, page 64)* is seen as the founder of Daosim, and its classic work is the *Daodejing*. It now seems certain

LAOZI

Laozi is usually seen as the founder of Daoism, although people today still argue about his historical existence. He was born, it is said, in a village in Henan province in 604 BC into a distinguished family. Among the colourful myths is one that relates how his mother was pregnant with him for 72 years and that he was delivered into the world through her left armpit. For a time, he held the office of archivist in the then capital, Luoyang. He later retreated into solitude and died in his village in 517 BC.

that more than one author wrote this tome. The earliest, and most significant, followers of Laozi were Liezi and Zhuangzi. Liezi (5th century BC) was concerned with the relativity of experiences, and he strived to comprehend the *dao* with the help of meditation. Zhuangzi (4th century BC) is especially famous for his poetic allegories. The abstract concepts of Daoism did not attract ordinary people, but by the Han period (206 BC–AD 220) there were signs of a popular and religious Daoism. As Buddhism also became more popular, it borrowed ideas

ABOVE LEFT & ABOVE: during the Qingming Festival, paper "spirit money" is burned to ensure the wealth of deceased ancestors. **RIGHT:** statue of Laozi, founder of Daoism.

from Daoism, and vice versa, to the point where one might speak of a fusion between the two.

Religious Daoism developed in various directions and schools. The ascetics either lived in monasteries or retreated to the mountains and devoted all their time to meditation. Daoist priests assumed important social functions as medicine men and interpreters of oracles. They carried out exorcism and funeral rites, and read mass for the dead or for sacrificial offerings. Many of these practices drew on ancient shamanism.

Baiyunguan Temple (The Temple of the White Cloud) in southwestern Beijing is an important, and thriving, Daoist centre *(see page 132)*.

Confucian influence

For Confucius, too, *dao* and *de* are central concepts. For more than 2,000 years, the ideas of Confucius (551–479 BC) have been an important part of Chinese culture, and have in turn influenced neighbouring lands such as Korea and Japan.

Confucius – or Kong Fuzi (Master Kong) – came from an impoverished family of the nobility who lived in the state of Lu (near Qufu in western Shandong province). Having failed to gain office with one of the feudal lords, he became an itinerant scholar, preaching his ideas and gaining a modest following – although it wasn't until centuries after his death that his ideas really caught on. Confucius significantly reinterpreted the idea of the *junzi*, a nobleman, to that of a noble man, whose life is morally sound and who is, therefore, legitimately entitled to reign. Humanity *(ren)* was a central concept, based on fraternity and love of children. A ruler would only be successful if he could govern according to these principles.

Confucius defined the social positions and hierarchies very precisely. Only if and when every member of society takes full responsibility for his or her position will society as a whole function smoothly. Family and social ties – and hierarchy – were considered fundamental: between father and son (filial piety), man and woman (female subservience), older brother and younger brother, friend and friend, and ruler and subordinate.

Confucianism has had many incarnations. After the Han-dynasty emperors adopted it, it became a religion of law and order, which ensured popularity with subsequent dynasties. It

It is debatable whether Confucianism is a religion in the strictest sense, including as it does strong elements of social theory and philosophy. Confucius himself has long been worshipped as a deity.

became the official state religion and the basis of all state examinations, a determining factor for Chinese officialdom until the 20th century. Mao tried to annihilate Confucianism – and all religion – in the Cultural Revolution, but non-religious Confucianism is slowly finding favour with a new breed of pragmatists who value the ancient religion's emphasis on order and social hierarchy. The Confucius Temple (Kong Miao) in northeastern Beijing is a centre for religious Confucianism *(see page 158)*.

FAR LEFT: a statue of Confucius. TOP LEFT & ABOVE LEFT: prayers written on pieces of paper are tied to trees next to Confucian temples. ABOVE TOP: Buddha at Biyunsi Temple in the Fragrant Hills. ABOVE LEFT, ABOVE & ABOVE RIGHT: worshippers and monks at the Lama Temple.

Buddhism

The Chinese initially encountered Buddhism at the beginning of the 1st century AD, when merchants and monks came to China over the Silk Road. The type of Buddhism that is prevalent in China today is the Mahayana (Great Wheel) school, which – as opposed to Hinayana (Small Wheel) – promises all creatures redemption through the Bodhisattva (redemption deities).

Two aspects were particularly attractive to the Chinese: the teachings of karma provided a better explanation for individual misfortune, and there was a hopeful promise for existence after death. Nevertheless, there was considerable opposition to Buddhism, which contrasted sharply with Confucian ethics and ancestor worship.

Buddhism was most influential during the Tang dynasty (618–907). Several emperors officially supported the religion; the Tang empress Wu Zetian, in particular, surrounded herself with Buddhist advisers. However, following Wu Zetian's abdication in 705, anti-Buddhist sentiment again began to grow. Some critics faulted it on nationalist grounds, noting that Buddha was "of barbarian origin" and could not even speak Chinese. Others saw it as an economic drain, pointing out the huge number of monasteries that were exempt from taxes, the hundreds of thousands of monks and nuns who did not plant or weave, and the large amounts of precious metal that were used to make statues. The emperor Wuzong further came under the influence of Daoists who viewed Buddhism as a competitive threat, and in 845 launched a massive suppression of the "insignificant Western religion", in which more than 40,000 temples and 4,600 monasteries were destroyed and more than 250,000 monks and nuns returned to the laity.

Wuzong died the following year and the suppression was quickly ended, but the blow it had

> *The masters of Chan Buddhism considered meditation to be the only path to knowledge, achievable through total absorption in one's normal activity. The most important method was a dialogue with the master, who asked subtle and paradoxical questions.*

struck was one from which the religion would never fully recover.

Even so, 10 Chinese schools of Buddhism emerged, eight of which were essentially philosophical in nature and did not influence popular religion. Only two schools have remained influential: Chan (School of Meditation or Zen Buddhism) and Pure Land (Amitabha), a form of Mahayana Buddhism that has dominated in China since the 14th century.

In Mahayana Buddhism, worship focused on the Bodhisattva Avalokiteshvara. Since the 7th century AD, the ascetic Bodhisattva has been a popular female figure in China. She is called Guanyin, a motherly goddess of mercy who represents a central deity for the ordinary people.

In the 7th century AD, Buddhism was introduced from Tibet from India. With the influence of the monk Padmasambhava, Tibetan Buddhism (Lamaism) incorporated shamanist beliefs and rituals from the indigenous Bön religion. One of Beijing's most popular sights, the Lama Temple (Yonghegong; *see page 155)* is a reminder of the historic links between Beijing, Mongolia and Tibet.

The arrival of Islam

Islam probably reached China in the 7th century via the Silk Road, as well as by sea to the southeast coast. During the Yuan dynasty (1279–1368), it finally became permanently established, while territorial expansion of the empire into central Asia brought more Muslims into the empire.

Muslims have perhaps suffered more persecution than other religious groups in China, partly because their faith is still considered "foreign", unlike Daoism and Buddhism. In the 18th century, slaughtering animals according to Islamic rites was forbidden, and the building of new mosques and pilgrimages to Mecca was not allowed, while marriages between Chinese and Muslims were illegal.

After another round of persecution during the Cultural Revolution, Chinese Islam has been allowed to revive. Beijing has several mosques and Islamic cultural centres, as well as Muslim districts like Niu Jie, with its ancient mosque *(see page 129).*

More than half of Chinese Muslims are ethnic Han Chinese, known as Hui, and have the distinction of being the only minority group

recognised solely on the basis of religion, and the only one whose members do not share a common language. Hui women wear head-scarves, and men usually wear white skullcaps similar to those worn in Muslim countries. The men often grow beards, but otherwise resemble China's Han majority *(see panel, page 129)*.

The capital's other main Muslim group, Uighurs from Xinjiang in the far west of China, look more Turkish than Chinese. Thanks to

Although religious freedom is supposedly guaranteed under China's constitution, many overseas groups say that religious persecution is widespread.

more enlightened policies and, some say, the Chinese government's need for oil from Muslim countries, Chinese Muslims are allowed to worship freely, to celebrate traditional festivals, and even to make pilgrimages to Mecca. There is little sign in Beijing of the Han–Uighur tensions that exploded into violence in the cities of Urümqi and Kashi in 2009.

Christianity

Christianity was first brought to China by the Nestorians in AD 635, who, in spite of persecutions, managed to spread the word to all regions

of the empire. Around the mid-14th century, initial contacts were made between China and the Roman Catholic Church, and during the Ming period, Catholic missionaries began to be very active in China. The Italian Matteo Ricci was one of the leading Jesuit missionaries to China. When he died, there were about 2,000–3,000 Chinese Christians.

The Jesuits used their knowledge of Western sciences to forge links with Chinese scholars, but other Catholic Orders were more dogmatic and caused tensions. At the onset of the 19th century, the Protestants began their missionary activities. By 1948, there were some 3 million Catholics and 1 million Protestants in China.

The Vatican's vigorous anti-Communist stance after World War II resulted in the Chinese government proclaiming that the Catholic Church in China should no longer consider itself accountable to Rome. To this day, the Pope recognises only the Taiwanese government. Yet relations are slowly improving. China now has an officially recognised 10 million Protestants and 4 million Catholics worshipping in state-sanctioned churches, and many more Christians who attend independent house churches within a legal grey area. ❑

Left: Buddha statue at Beihai Park. **Above:** Hui Muslims at Niu Jie Mosque. **Right:** the East Cathedral (St Joseph's) off Wangfujing.

TRADITIONAL CHINESE MEDICINE

Healthcare in China is split between modern Western practice and the traditional local variety, usually reserved for minor ailments

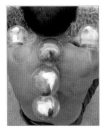

The mention of traditional Chinese medicine often conjures up images of the near-mystical application of needles, aromatic herbs and strange animal parts. Yet, despite its exotic stereotype, traditional Chinese medicine has gained respect from both scientists and the general public in the West.

In China, scepticism and debate arose as to the value of traditional medicine during the first half of the 20th century. After 1949, competition between Western and Chinese medicine was eradicated for practical as well as ideological reasons, with an attempt to integrate the two systems.

This approach has persisted, and today medical care in China often consists of a mixture of both Western and traditional Chinese medicine, although Western-style medicine *(xiyi)* tends to dominate. Large public hospitals *(renmin yiyuan)* in cities across the country offer both traditional Chinese and Western treatment. Hospitals dealing exclusively with traditional Chinese medicine *(zhongyi)* tend to be smaller and less well equipped *(see page 275)*.

Beijingers will usually visit a doctor trained in Western medicine if they are seriously ill and need to be treated quickly. If the problem is less urgent, the patient will most likely seek out a traditional doctor, who can better restore harmony to the body.

ABOVE: the massage of pressure points around the body, including those in the feet, is an important part of Chinese medicine. **TOP LEFT:** cupping, a form of acupuncture. **ABOVE LEFT & RIGHT:** a traditional apothecary is full of dried seeds, herbs and plants.

ABOVE: preparing herbal ingredients at Tongrentang pharmacy.

RIGHT: a Chinese medical poster showing the body and its organs.

ABOVE: during an initial consultation, practitioners seek to gain an overall appraisal of the state of the subject's health.

TONGRENTANG PHARMACY

A traditional Chinese apothecary has a unique smell made up of thousands of scents emanating from jars and cabinets stocked full of dried plants, seeds, animal parts and minerals.

Among them are the well-known ginseng roots, dried or immersed in alcohol. You will also recognise the acupuncture needles and the cupping glasses made of glass or bamboo.

One of the most famous Chinese apothecaries is the legendary Tongrentang pharmacy, located in Beijing's Dazhalan *(see page 126)*, which has been in business for over 300 years. It was once a royal dispensary during the Qing dynasty and still produces all the pills and secret concoctions once used by royalty. The name Tongren is derived from the *I Ching* and means "harmonious and selfless" and "treating others equally", philosophies the founder, a senior court physician, prescribed to.

The size of this pharmacy is overwhelming, as is the selection of remedies: small and large eggs, snakes coiled in spirals, dried monkeys, toads, tortoises, grass-hoppers, fish, octopuses, stag antlers, rhinoceros horns and the genitalia of various unfortunate – and sometimes endangered – animals. And then there are the myriad varieties of dried and preserved herbs, blossoms, roots, berries, mushrooms and fruits.

RIGHT & BELOW: all kinds of ingredients are used, from plants and fungi to (often illegal) animal parts from endangered species.

FOOD AND DRINK

Eating out is one of the main pleasures in a city that not only offers its own specialities but also acts as a melting pot for cuisine from all over China. A fast-growing number of other Asian and Western restaurants have added variety, and everything is pleasingly affordable

Beijing cuisine has traditionally existed in two largely separate forms; the imperial food of the royal court and the home-style cooking enjoyed by the ordinary citizen.

Over the centuries, the finest chefs were attracted to the imperial court, and the best among them could count on being given the rank of minister. In the palace kitchens, cooks created dishes that belonged at the pinnacle of world cuisine, dishes made from rare ingredients and prepared with great culinary skill. This is where dishes that belong to every sophisticated Chinese kitchen originated: Peking Duck, Phoenix in the Nest, Mandarin Fish, Lotus Prawns, Mu Shu Pork and Thousand Layer Cake, among others.

In contrast, the traditional cuisine of the capital's workers, peasants and soldiers was simple, with plenty of onions and garlic. The

The great importance of eating in China is expressed by the common greeting "Chiguole?" or "Chifanlema?" (Have you eaten?) – roughly equivalent to the Western custom of enquiring about one's health.

variety of vegetables available further south in China was lacking – in winter, it was common to see nothing but cabbages filling the markets. Improved transportation and the widespread

use of greenhouses means that today's residents can get pretty much anything they need, albeit at a higher price.

Beijing's modern cuisine is a mixture of these two traditions, allied to influences from across the country. The main meal of a family of four usually consists of rice, noodles or steamed bread, soup and three or four freshly prepared hot dishes. Many families will eat three cooked meals a day, which makes for a lot of domestic work; many working people – especially those on lower incomes – eat in workplace canteens.

"Food first, then morals", wrote the dramatist Bertolt Brecht, a maxim particularly appropriate to China. During its long history, it has

LEFT: preparing Peking Duck at Quanjude restaurant.
ABOVE RIGHT: street stalls at Donghuamen Night Market.

suffered repeated famines. Even today, the problem of an adequate food supply is by no means solved, despite the generous supply of goods in Beijing's stores and markets.

The government constantly reminds its critics that China feeds 22 percent of the world's population on just 7 percent of its arable land. Much of China's land is unsuitable for agriculture, which explains why in fertile areas every square metre is used for growing something edible, even in spaces barely large enough for a single head of cabbage. Pasture or fallow land is rarely seen.

Local favourites

Western palates generally have little difficulty adjusting to and thoroughly enjoying Chinese cooking – and there are few better places than Beijing for sampling it. The most famous local dish is unquestionably Peking Duck *(see below)*, but many other culinary styles and specialities have found fame here. Traditional Beijing haute

---

WHERE TO EAT IN BEIJING

Wherever you are in Beijing you will never be far from one of the city's countless restaurants, cafés, kebab stands and snack shops.

While five-star hotels boast excellent restaurants, they often focus on Western food for those with generous expense accounts. The embassy and nightlife area Sanlitun showcases an invasion of global cuisines at competitive prices. Gui Jie, to the south of the Lama Temple, is a neon-lit, all-night dining boulevard of

spicy hotpots, de luxe private rooms and rowdy street life. The university district Haidian offers minority restaurants catering to students from around China and throngs of inquisitive diners. Traditional Beijing food is not ubiquitous, but a collection of time-honoured local food stalls can be enjoyed at Jiumen Xiaochi (Lake District and the North chapter).

For full listings of recommended restaurants, refer to the end of each Places chapter.

明珠鲍鱼

纸火锅涮鲍鱼

阳光冰鲍

鱼翅泡饭

cuisine is said to reflect two styles of cooking: imperial, which is based on Qing-dynasty palace dishes; and Tan, named after the Tan family, a synthesis of salty northern cuisine with sweeter southern cuisine.

For northern China's *laobaixing* (ordinary people; literally, "old hundred names"), the most common specialities are *jiaozi* (meat- and vegetable-filled pasta parcels), *baozi* (steamed buns stuffed with minced meat and vegetables), noodles, cornbread and pancakes – rice is not grown in the harsh climate of the north. Stir-fried and boiled dishes often feature cabbage and potatoes.

Hotpot, sometimes called Mongolian hot-pot – although Mongolians claim it originated in Korea – is another speciality. This combines fondue-style cooking – usually in a communal hot-pot – with unlimited meat and vegetables. A newer challenger has also caught on: Sichuan "yin-yang" hot-pot, divided into two compartments. Beware the fiery *yang* half.

Above Left: the art of making noodles. **Above Top:** ingredients are cut up into small pieces before stir-frying at high heat. **Above:** sweet and sour pork. **Above Right:** Beijing has plenty of fast-food joints – Chinese and Western.

"Thousand-year-old" eggs *(pidan)* remain one of Beijing's most popular appetisers. These are duck eggs that have been packed raw into a mass of mud, chalk and ammonia and left for two weeks or so – not 1,000 years. When fully preserved, the egg white turns a transparent, dark-greenish black and the yolk turns milky

> The Chinese believe strongly in the nutritional benefit of most of the foods they eat following the proverb "He who takes medicine and neglects diet wastes the skill of his doctors."

yellow-green. The eggs are then cut into wedges, sprinkled with soy sauce and sesame oil, and served with pickled ginger. To many Westerners the taste is an acquired one, but nonetheless worth trying at least once.

The city's signature dish

A prerequisite for true Peking Duck is a special kind of duck bred in and around Beijing, which is force-fed for about six months before it is

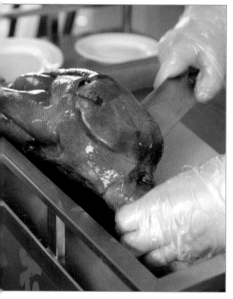

slaughtered. Preparing the duck so that it has the perfect, world-renowned melt-in-the-mouth crispness requires great skill. After slaughter, plucking and cleaning, air is carefully blown through a hole in the neck, so that the skin is loosened from the flesh. This process helps to make the skin as crisp as possible after roasting. The duck is then painted with a mixture of honey, water and vinegar and hung up to dry for three days. Afterwards, still hanging, it is slowly grilled in a special oven.

CHOPSTICKS

Chopsticks, or *kuaizi*, date back thousands of years. Although bone, ivory, gold, jade and steel have all been used, most chopsticks are now made of wood, and thrown away after each meal. Once a luxury, disposable chopsticks are found in most restaurants (except, ironically, the more expensive places). This is primarily for reasons of hygiene; greasy chopsticks have in the past helped spread epidemics of hepatitis and other diseases. Some diners now bring their own chopsticks to restaurants, however, following a widespread media campaign on the environmental damage of intensive logging to produce the throwaway items.

Equally important to the Peking Duck experience are the dishes served alongside it: very thin pancakes, little sesame-seed rolls, spring onions and *haixian* (or *hoisin*) sauce, a sweetish bean sauce flavoured with garlic and spices.

An authentic meal of Peking Duck begins with a selection of appetisers, most of which derive from various parts of the duck: fried liver, deep-fried heart with coriander, intestines, boiled tongues and the webbed skin of the feet cut very finely – in Chinese cooking, little is wasted. Next, the cook brings the roast duck to the table and cuts it into bite-sized pieces of skin and meat. Take one of the pancakes, use the chopped spring onion to spread *haixian* sauce on it and put a piece of duck over the spring onion. Then roll the whole thing up and eat it using your fingers.

It is this combination that provides the highest gastronomic pleasure and makes the often rather fatty meat digestible. For the final course,

ABOVE LEFT: the city's signature dish. **ABOVE TOP:** Peking Duck is served with thin pancakes, *hoisin* sauce and spring onions. **ABOVE:** roasting in a coal-fired oven. **RIGHT:** Beijing is known for its street food, from large savoury pancakes (*jian bing*) to skewered seafood.

Monosodium glutamate (weijing; MSG) is very common in Chinese cooking. You can ask for it not to be included in your food, but it is present in most pre-prepared sauces, such as soy sauce.

you will be served a soup made of the remains of the duck – mostly bones.

Full duck banquets don't come cheap; in fact, they are too expensive for most Chinese families, and reserved for special occasions. There are a number of cheaper duck restaurants in Beijing, but sadly many have become pure mass-production centres.

Gastronomic melting pot

Beijing has assimilated food from many Chinese regions into its *jia chang cai* (home-style dishes). These are the standard dishes you will find in restaurants and homes. Sichuan, Guangdong (Canton), Dongbei (the northeast),

Shanghai, Shandong and Hunan are some of the regions that continue to influence typical Beijing menus. Milder Sichuan dishes, such as *Mala Doufu* (spicy tofu) and Gongbao Chicken (with chilli and peanuts), can be found in most large restaurants. Sizzling rice-crust, called *guoba*, also originated in Sichuan.

Apart from the dishes that have already joined the ranks of the city's *jia chang cai*, Beijing has many restaurants specialising in cuisine from different regions of China, especially the spicy cuisine of Sichuan and Hunan, and the stir-fries and rice dishes from Guangdong in the deep south, universally known as "Chinese" to the rest the world. You can eat lean, grilled mutton and beef at restaurants run by China's Korean and Uighur minorities. The Uighurs, from Xinjiang in China's far northwest, make flatbreads and kebabs similar to those found in the Middle East. Hand-cut, stir-fried pasta pieces served in spicy tomato sauce, called *chaopian'r*, are another Xinjiang speciality. Restaurants run by Dai (from Yunnan), Mongolian and Tibetan people offer further tastes of China's remote frontiers.

and going. Diners order a range of dishes, which are whisked through the restaurant and clattered down. Noodles, usually eaten with a thick sesame- and soy-based sauce, are standard fare.

Countless snack restaurants, some open 24 hours, offer a relaxed atmosphere in which you can try much more than noodles. You will also find an endless choice of snacks like red-bean porridge, sesame cakes, *jiaozi*, *baozi*, *hundun* (wonton, like *jiaozi* soup), and *guotie* (fried *jiaozi* "pot stickers"). Many department stores and shopping malls, such as Oriental Plaza, Parkson and Sun Dongan Plaza, feature food courts serving snacks from around China.

For a quick breakfast try *jidan guan bing* (egg pancakes), sold at roadside stalls. Or sample *you- tiao*, deep-fried bread sticks (like doughnuts) usu- ally eaten with hot *dou jiang* (soy milk). They are a delicious traditional start to the day and the ideal fuel for a hard morning exploring all that the city has to offer. They go well with a glass of *dou jiang*, a soybean drink served hot or cold.

Street food is also worth seeking out at other times of day. Look out for *jian bing* savoury pancakes or *xianer bing* – a meat-filled variety, as well as wonton soup, *jiaozi* and *baozi*. The Donghuamen Night Market *(see page 171)* just

Thanks to the number of Chinese travelling abroad and the number of Westerners coming to China, there are now also a large number of Western restaurants in Beijing. Some of these are fast-food joints familiar the world over, such as McDonald's, KFC (there are over 100

> China's ganbei *culture has come under fire in recent years after a number of officials died from alcohol poisoning after downing excessive glasses of strong liquor at banquets.*

branches of each in the city, as well as Chinese imitations) and Pizza Hut, which are favoured by young Chinese. Others are more sophisti- cated – it is possible to find quite good French, Italian, Middle Eastern and many other types of international cuisine around the city.

To balance this culinary invasion, "Old Bei- jing" fast food and the lively dining style com- mon before 1949 have made something of a comeback. Traditionally dressed waiters shout across the restaurant, announcing those coming

Above Left: a local fast-food joint offers a variety of Chinese and foreign food. **Above:** hot street food on a cold winter's day. **Above Right:** a trendy Sanlitun bar; together with the area around Houhai Lake, this is the city's main nightlife district. **Far Right:** Maotai liquor.

off Wangfujing is a good place to try regional specialities, such as skewers of spiced meat (*kaorou chuaner*), but there are street-food vendors on many street corners all over town (less so around Tiananmen Square).

A liking for liquor

Alcohol is often an integral part of a Chinese meal. A warning to take care is not unwarranted here, as Chinese men often drink very strong grain liquor. The expensive Maotai, named after its place of origin, is famous, as is Wuliangye from Sichuan. Erguotou, the most popular Beijing brand, gives you 56 percent alcohol by volume for just a few *kuai*. Spirits are usually found in every restaurant and home, and are in special abundance at any type of official gathering. Many wealthy Beijing businesspeople now prefer Rémy Martin XO or similar luxury brandies. In property, construction and many other industries, bottles of brandy are used as small gifts to oil networks of *guanxi* (connections), especially among officials.

Sweet liqueurs, more popular in the south of China, are also drunk, as is beer (*pijiu*), which is a standard mealtime drink – Chinese beer (Tsingtao is the leading brand) is generally good. Several Sino-French joint ventures produce passable, inexpensive wines. Dragon Seal, Dynasty and Great Wall are among the better brands. Mineral water (*kuangquan shui*) and soft drinks are universally available. ❑

TIPS ON ETIQUETTE

If you are invited into someone's home to eat, it is usual to bring a gift – alcohol, cigarettes or small presents typical of your home country. The Chinese are not judgemental when it comes to how you eat. No one will think less of you if you cannot use chopsticks or if you don't know where to put your bones – just do as others are doing, or what comes naturally to you.

On the other hand, you may be pressured to eat considerably more than you want to, or to sample foods that you may not really desire. It is perfectly acceptable to say no, as long as you do so politely. If the thought of eating something doesn't appeal, then don't eat it – profess an allergy, explain that you prefer something else, or just tell the truth. If you are full, say so. If your hosts continue to pressure you, just take a tiny bite.

Take care of your neighbours at the table, serving them some of the food, especially from dishes that they cannot reach easily. Remember also not to pick out the best pieces on each dish, but to take food from the side of the dish closest to you.

At the meal, the host will drink toasts to the guests. *"Ganbei!"* (empty cup) means you should empty your glass in one shot, and turning your glass upside down shows that you have followed this instruction.

ARTS AND CRAFTS

Silk, jade and cloisonné epitomise China's rich artistic heritage, yet the Chinese consider painting and calligraphy as their highest art forms. Performance arts include classical music and spectacular acrobatics, as well as Beijing Opera

The arts have long played a crucial role in Chinese society, culture and government. In Confucian China, for instance, music was believed to reflect the state of society, and a proper gentleman was someone who could write beautiful calligraphy, play an instrument and craft a poem. The Communists regarded art as an important propaganda tool and devoted many resources to creating a new, proletarian art that would help win people over to their viewpoint.

To this day, the government is the nation's biggest arts patron, supporting hundreds of opera companies, orchestras, drama troupes and art schools, as well as untold numbers of writers, poets, composers and musicians. Chinese leaders still believe that they must demonstrate proficiency at music, poetry and calligraphy; Jiang Zemin, for instance, played the piano and published his poetry and calligraphy on the front page of the *People's Daily*.

Beijing is the most important arts centre in China and – somewhat surprisingly – is also artistically freer than many other cities. Artists find it easy to hide between the cracks of its many bureaucracies, or to play one ministry off against another in order to get approval for an avant-garde exhibition or performance. Thanks to officially recognised cultural zones such as the 798 Art District and the buzz being created by a new wave of contemporary Chinese artists, Beijing is now marked boldly on any international art tourist's map.

LEFT: an acrobatics show in the capital.
ABOVE RIGHT: brush painting.

VISUAL ARTS AND CRAFTS
Brush painting

Writing and painting have always enjoyed an intimate association due to the original pictographic nature of the Chinese script. This is evident from the customary incorporation of written words, such as a poem or the name of the artist, into most Chinese paintings.

In China, painting comprises various different disciplines: calligraphy; monochromatic and coloured work in ink on fabric or paper; mural reproductions such as woodblock prints; other related techniques, such as embroideries and woven pictures; and purely decorative paintings.

THE FOUR TREASURES OF THE STUDY

Writing and painting materials are referred to in China as the Four Treasures of the Study, consisting of the brush, ink stick, rubbing stone and paper. Such tools have long been held in high esteem by Chinese poets, scholars and painters; there are reliable records which show that brush and ink were being used as early as the 1st century BC, during the Han period. Chinese ink was only taken up in Europe as a distinct kind of paint in the 17th century. The attractive shops along Liulichang *(see page 127)* are the best places in Beijing to buy traditional brushes, paper, ink sticks, rubbing stones and other artists' materials.

Because of their close connection, painting skills are learned in much the same way as writing: through copying old masters or textbooks. A painter is considered a master of his art only when the necessary brushstrokes for a bird, a chrysanthemum or a waterfall can flow effortlessly from his hand. The strong emphasis placed on perfection quickly leads to specialisation by painters on specific subjects. In this way, for instance, Xu Beihong (1895–1953) became known as the painter of horses, just as Qi Bai-Shi (1862–1957) was famous for his shrimps. Many of Xu's best works are displayed at the Xu Beihong Memorial Hall *(see page 189)*.

One of the most favoured painting forms in China is landscape painting. Notable characteristics of this form are perspectives that draw the viewer into the picture, plain surfaces (unpainted empty spaces) that add a feeling of depth and the harmonious relationship between man and nature, with man depicted as a small, almost vanishing, figure in nature.

Oil painting was introduced by Jesuit missionaries, along with such Western painting techniques as the use of perspective. It never caught on, except as an export product, until the Communist era, when it became a popular medium for producing Socialist-Realist art. Many of China's best-known contemporary painters also work in oil paints.

Contemporary art is big in Beijing, visible at private galleries and at performance-art exhibitions. The city suburbs are home to several colonies of artists from around the country, although their lifecycle tends to follow the familiar pattern of growth, gentrification and abandonment when public taste changes. The

contemporary art scene has moved rapidly through styles, including pop art and a horrific mid-1990s focus on "body art", which involved the use of corpses and body pieces as art materials. In recent years, the trend has been towards installations, film and video. China is now in

> Genuine antiques are hard to come by in China because, in order to protect the country's valuable heritage, the government prohibits the sale of articles pre-dating the First Opium War.

the midst of a renaissance with architecture, design and fashion spurring the public imagination, often from studios and workshops located in the cultural capital of Beijing.

Silk

The cultivation of the silkworm is said to go back to the 3rd millennium BC. Legend has it that the wife of the mythical Xia dynasty Yellow Emperor Huangdi began the tradition of plant-

ing mulberry trees and keeping silkworms. For centuries, silk held the place of currency: civil servants and officers as well as foreign envoys were frequently paid or presented with bales of silk. The precious material was transported to the Middle East and the Roman empire via the famous Silk Road.

The Chinese maintained a monopoly on silk until about 200 BC, when the secret of its manufacture became known in Korea and Japan. In the West – in this case the Byzantine empire – such knowledge was acquired only in the 6th century AD. The Chinese had prohibited the export of silkworm eggs and the dissemination of knowledge of their cultivation, but a monk is said to have succeeded in smuggling some silkworm eggs to the West.

Today's centres of silk production are areas in the east of China around Hangzhou, Suzhou and Wuxi. Hangzhou has the largest silk industry, while Suzhou has the finest embroidery.

Porcelain

The Chinese invented porcelain in the 7th century AD, 1,000 years before Europeans. The most widespread original form was celadon, a product of a blending of iron oxide with the

FAR LEFT: modern brushes. **LEFT TOP & LEFT:** calligraphy for sale in a Liulichang shop. **ABOVE:** scroll paintings. **RIGHT:** close-up of the classical Chinese landscape style of painting.

glaze that resulted, during firing, in a characteristic green tone. *Sancai* ceramics, ceramics with three-colour glazes from the Tang dynasty, became world-famous, while the Song period celadons – ranging in colour from pale or moss green, pale blue or pale grey to brown tones – were also technically excellent.

As early as the Yuan period, a technique from Persia was used for underglaze painting in cobalt blue to distinctive effect. These days, wares decorated in such a way are generically known as Ming porcelain. Common themes seen throughout the subsequent Ming period were figures, landscapes and theatrical scenes. At the beginning of the Qing dynasty, blue-and-white porcelain *(hua qing)* attained its highest level of quality.

From the 14th century, Jingdezhen in Jiangxi province has been the centre of porcelain manufacture, although today relatively inexpensive porcelain can be bought throughout China.

Jade, China's cherished stone

With its soft sheen and rich nuances of colour, jade has been valued by the Chinese since antiquity, but it became widely popular only in the 18th century. Colours vary from white to

As a dense stone, real jade feels heavy in your palm. Held up to the light, the genuine article should reveal irregularities, always feels cool and cannot be scratched with a knife.

green – in China, a clear emerald-green stone is valued most highly – but there are also red, yellow and lavender jades.

In jade-carving workshops there are as many as 30 kinds of jade in use. The most famous are those in Qingtian (Zhejiang province), Shoushan (Fujian province) and Luoyang (Hunan province). Masters of jade work include Zhou Shouhai, from the jade-carving establishment in Shanghai, and Wang Shusen in Beijing, the latter specialising in Buddhist figurines. In government shops, jade can be trusted to be genuine. On the open market and in private

ABOVE LEFT: carving in nephrite jade. **ABOVE:** classical-style porcelain vase. **RIGHT TOP:** jade Buddha. **RIGHT:** a bonsai tree is expensively adorned with jade and coloured glass. **FAR RIGHT:** creating a cloisonné jar.

shops, however, caution is advised. Quality depends on the feel of the stone, its colour, transparency, pattern and other factors. If in doubt, consult a reputable expert.

The Chinese traditionally used a distinctive style in the making of shadow puppets. Translucent cow hide would be used for the characters, whose shadows would be cast onto a white cloth by lamplight.

Lacquerware

The glossy sheen of lacquerware is not only attractive to the eye but also appealing to the touch. It is made by coating an object, such as a bowl or vase, with extremely fine layers of a lacquer that comes from the milky sap of the lacquer tree *(rhus verniciflua)*, which grows in central and southern China. If soot or vinegar-soaked iron filings are added to the lacquer, it will dry into a black colour; cinnabar turns it red. The colour combination of red and black, first thought to have been applied in the 2nd century BC, is still considered a classic.

CHINESE SCROLLS

Chinese brush painting and calligraphy are generally mounted on a hanging scroll. In days gone by, the scroll was rolled up, stored away and brought out on special occasions to be slowly unfurled, revealing only parts of a scene, subtly drawing the observer into the picture. Thus the picture was handled while being scrutinised. With horizontal scrolls, always unrolled little by little, the hands were in constant movement. The same applies to the two other formats for classical painting – the fan that needed unfolding and the album leaf that needed pages turned. The idea was to create a bond between picture and observer; painting on panel or canvas imposes a rational distance.

The carved lacquer technique, which began in the Tang dynasty, when large lacquerware Buddhist sculptures were produced, reached its highest peak during the Ming and Qing periods. The core, often of wood or tin, is coated with mostly red layers of lacquer. When the outermost coat has dried, decorative carving is applied, with the knife penetrating generally to the lowest layer so that the design stands out from the background in relief. Today, lacquer-

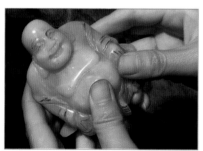

ware is mainly produced in Beijing, Fuzhou and Yangzhou; best-known is the Beijing work, which goes back to the imperial courts of the Ming and Qing dynasties.

Cloisonné

The cloisonné technique, a way of decorating metal objects with enamel, reached China from Persia in the 8th century AD, was lost and then rediscovered in the 13th century. In cloisonné, metal rods are soldered to the body of the metal object. These form the outlines of the ornamentation, while the spaces between the rods are filled with enamel paste and fired in the kiln, usually four or five times. Finally, metal surfaces not already covered with enamel are gilded. Cloisonné jewellery and ornaments are available all over Beijing.

THE PERFORMING ARTS

For Beijing Opera, see pages 88–9.

Classical music

Western classical music came to China by way of Western missionaries, and was eventually adopted by Chinese reformers who believed it would help to improve the morals and

behaviour of their fellow citizens. Even the Communists saw its usefulness as a diplomatic tool and founded a symphony orchestra at their revolutionary base at Yan'an. During the Cultural Revolution, Western music was banned, but Western instruments were introduced into all the "model operas", several of which were created and performed around the nation. The upshot of all this is that classical music is now deeply rooted in China's cities. Beijing has two major orchestras – the China National Symphony Orchestra and the China Philharmonic – and more than half a dozen others that perform less regularly. It is also home to the Central Conservatory of Music, which was founded in the early 1950s at Zhou Enlai's behest, and is arguably the best conservatory in the country. The Beijing International Music Festival held every October has grown into a major international event with scores of top-notch performers from around the world.

Above Left & Top: hard at work on cloisonné painting at the Beijing Mosaic Factory. **Above:** a performance at the National Centre for the Performing Arts. **Right:** acrobatics shows tend to include all kinds of balancing acts.

Western opera was first introduced to China through foreigners resident in Shanghai in the 1920s and 1930s, but its more formal introduction came via Soviet advisers during the 1950s. Beijing has a major opera company and many

> Spoken drama enjoys an especially large and faithful audience in Beijing, whose people are known for their love of conversation. The capital's taxi drivers often listen to storytelling on their car radios: the histrionic performance is fascinating even if you can't understand the words.

conservatory students study opera, but the cost of staging productions is so prohibitive that there is no formal opera season.

The influence of Western-style symphonic music has been so strong in China that during the 1950s orchestras of traditional Chinese instruments were created. Because these were not intended to be played in huge ensembles,

many technical changes had to be made and new instruments invented. Purists still scoff at the whole idea, but Beijing's China National Traditional Orchestra is here to stay. For a list of classical music venues *see page 267*.

Theatre

Spoken drama was first introduced to China by Chinese students studying in Japan around the turn of the 20th century. It was seen as modern and progressive because it differed from traditional Chinese drama – which was always sung and accompanied by music – and because it frequently dealt with social issues. It soon caught on among young people in the main cities, who flocked to see productions of plays like Ibsen's *A Doll's House* (Mao Zedong's wife, Jiang Qing, even performed the role of Nora in her younger years). Chinese writers soon became involved, and the works of such playwrights as Guo Morou, Cao Yu and Lao She have become classics.

The Beijing People's Art Theatre is the nation's most illustrious drama company, performing to full houses in the Capital Theatre on Wangfujing. It has a tight-knit group of actors who perform both Chinese and foreign plays

and whose acting style is instantly recognisable. The National Theatre Company of China is considered of comparable standard and can be seen performing at the National Centre for the Performing Arts, a venue that drama aficionados hope will help promote the art. For a list of theatres, *see page 267.*

> *Today you can still see Tang-dynasty dances performed at theatres. One eye-catching example uses extremely long, flowing sleeves made of ramie that female dancers twirl through the air.*

Dance

Dance has been a part of ordinary people's entertainment in China since antiquity. It played a key role at the imperial court during the cosmopolitan Tang dynasty – some scholars believe that foot-binding first developed because fashionable women began to imitate the way Tang court dancers wrapped their feet (a practice that did little to help the develop-

ment of dance for the next millennium and more). Most of China's 56 official minority groups have strong folk-dance traditions, and dance has also traditionally formed a regular part of rural entertainment for Han Chinese, especially at the Spring Festival (Chinese New Year). However, institutionalised, formal performances are a relatively modern phenomenon, and Beijing has played a key role in their development.

China's first ballet company, the Central Ballet of China, was founded in Beijing in 1959 with the help of Soviet experts. It performs both Western and Chinese repertoires, including a "model opera" from the Cultural Revolution, *The Red Detachment of Women.* The Central Song and Dance Ensemble performs dance of all kinds from around the world, while the Central Nationalities Song and Dance Ensemble focuses on the dances of China's ethnic minorities. The People's Liberation Army Song and Dance Ensemble is also a top-notch dance group. It was the ex-PLA dancer and foreign-trained Jin Xing who founded Beijing's first modern dance company in 1995. The troupe has performed at the

Venice Biennale, the Berlin Arts Festival and other prestigious events. For a list of venues *see page 267.*

Acrobatics

Acrobatics has a history in China of close to 3,000 years. The art form spread along the Silk Road and was for many centuries highly popular entertainment. Its star began to fade as early as the 13th century, when early forms of Chinese opera started to develop, but it remained popular in rural areas. The Cultural Revolution era saw something of a comeback for acrobatics, since leftist revolutionaries considered it to be a respectable "proletarian" art form, and today there are about 80 professional acrobatics troupes in China. Beijing's troupe is one of the best, and the city is also home to an acrobatics school that trains young acrobats from around the world.

Nonetheless, the art is very lacking in crea-

tivity and is still rather staid; the acrobatics performances generally staged in Beijing are intended to impress foreign tourists (and of course collect their money), and they serve this purpose – once. After that, it is sad to say, these performances staged day after day are hard to view as anything more than highly skilled acrobats performing kitsch. Beijing residents themselves rarely go to see acrobatics, unless out of duty to a guest from afar. For details on where to see performances *see page 266.* ❑

FAR LEFT: a ballet performance of *Raise the Red Lantern.*
LEFT ABOVE & LEFT: *The Red Detachment of Women,* a ballet at the National Centre for the Performing Arts.
ABOVE, ABOVE RIGHT & RIGHT: acrobatics are mainly performed for tourists these days, but the shows are still spectacular, if sometimes lacking in inspiration.

BEIJING OPERA

The emphasis in Beijing Opera is on Confucian ethics and morality: goodness is upheld and evil is punished

Although Chinese theatre in the form of skits, vaudeville, puppet shows and shadow plays has existed for over 1,000 years, formal music-drama has its origins in the 13th-century Yuan dynasty. This evolved into more than 300 different styles of Chinese Opera, but today the highly stylised Beijing (*jingxi*) variety – dating from the 1800s – is by far the most popular.

Beijing Opera is a composite of different expressive art forms: literature, song, dialogue, mime and acrobatics. Plots are based on historical stories or folklore with which audiences are already familiar. The main division is between *wenxi* (civilian plays), and *wuxi* (military dramas), but there are also comedies. *Wenxi* pieces are more like Western drama, and describe daily life. The *wuxi*, on the other hand, consist mainly of fights, and tell of historical wars and battles, making great use of acrobatics. Many operas draw upon popular legends, folk or fairy tales, or classical literature; tales such as *The Three Kingdoms*, *The Dream of the Red Mansions* or *Journey to the West* are much better-known in China than their equivalent literary classics in the West.

In the old days, permanent theatres were a rarity, even in Beijing. As a result, opera was performed on the streets and in the market places – a sign of its popularity with ordinary people. It was a useful way for them to learn about life outside the narrow circle of their own day-to-day existence.

ABOVE: whether in soliloquies, spoken verse, songs or dialogue, the words used in any Beijing Opera performance are almost always colloquial. The opera was meant from the start to be watched by the common people. Audiences are usually noisy, but appreciative.

ABOVE: today, Beijing Opera is alive and kicking in the capital. Performances can be seen at the spacious, high-tech Mei Lanfang Theatre or smaller and more traditional Zhengyici (pictured). *See page 267 for details.*
LEFT: performers are resplendent in silk costumes.

THE ART FORM OF OPERA TRAINING

Beijing Opera is considered one of the most conventionalised forms of theatre to be found anywhere in the world, requiring years of training to master.

Actors often undergo seven years of training as children, after which they are selected for specific roles, with numerous subdivisions, though before the 1930s all were required to be played by men.

A female role is referred to as *dan*, and many troupes include a young and older performer to take these parts. The *sheng* is usually the main male role, often involving acrobatics and martial arts. The distinctive painted face that has come to represent the art abroad is the *jing*, the secondary male role who may be expected to equal the female characters in singing and mime. The clown role, or *chou*, is regarded as of lesser importance, though it can be demanding as it involves both acrobatics and humour.

An actor's training includes learning how to apply the elaborate make-up that serves to identify each character.

LEFT: a performance in a city shopping mall. **BELOW:** Beijing Opera was one of the main forms of entertainment in the past.

RIGHT: the ancient art was dealt a blow during the Cultural Revolution when only a handful of operas were approved by Mao Zedong's wife and its appeal faded. During the 1990s, the lengthy performances were shortened and changes permitted to costumes and make-up to help reverse the decline.

ABOVE: colours are highly symbolic. Red, in this instance, signifies loyalty, while yellow stands for aggression and blue cruelty. Audiences can tell the personality of characters on the stage by their painted faces.

PLACES

A detailed guide to the city, with the principal sites clearly cross-referenced by number to the maps

In traditional Chinese thought, the world was not imagined as the flat, circular disk of the Ptolemaic system familiar in the West, but as a square. A city was also supposed to be square, a reflection of the cosmic order, and in no other city in China was this basic idea realised as completely as in Beijing. Screened from the north by a semicircle of hills, the city lies on a plain which opens out to the south. All important buildings are built to face south, thus protecting them from the harmful *yin* influences of the north – be they the vicious Siberian winter winds or enemies from the steppes. A line from north to south divides Beijing into eastern and western halves, with a series of buildings laid out as mirror images to their equivalents on the opposite side of the city. These northern and southern approaches converge at the Forbidden City, which the meridian line bisects.

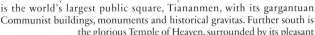

Immediately south of the Forbidden City is the world's largest public square, Tiananmen, with its gargantuan Communist buildings, monuments and historical gravitas. Further south is

the glorious Temple of Heaven, surrounded by its pleasant park. To the east are the shiny modern shopping centres around Wangfujing, and further east the business and expat district of Chaoyang, full of gleaming skyscrapers and hotels, as well as a wide variety of restaurants and bars. To the west and north is beautiful Beihai Park and the attractive back lakes area, full of atmospheric old *hutong*, and plenty of bars and cafés.

No visit to Beijing is complete without a trip out to the Great Wall, and several sections are within easy reach. Further afield are the magnificent Imperial Resort at Chengde and the old treaty port of Tianjin, where many handsome 19th-century houses built by foreign merchants still stand.   ❏

PRECEDING PAGES: smiling statue in the 798 Art District; crowds and red lanterns at the Ditan Park temple fair. **LEFT:** Kunming Lake, Yiheyuan. **ABOVE RIGHT:** street market off Wangfujing. **ABOVE LEFT:** a benevolent dragon, symbol of imperial power, at the Forbidden City.

Beijing

Renmin Daxue (The People's University of China) Renmindaxue

Yiheyuan (New Summer Palace), Beijing Daxue (Beijing University), Zhongguancun

Dazhongsi (Temple of the Great Bell)

Xueyuan Lu

Wudaokou

Suzhou Dajie

Beisanhuan Xilu

Beisanhuan Zhonglu

Dazhongsi

SHUANGXIU GONGYUAN

Xizhimen Beidajie (Second Ring Road)

Beisanhuan Beilu

Beisanhuan Xilu

Weigongcun Lu

Xueyuan Nanlu

Xueyuan Nanlu

Xinjiekouwai Dajie

Deshengmenwai Dajie

Weigongcun

Gaoliangqiao Lu

Suojafen Lu

Deshengmen Bus Station

Xiangshan (Fragrant Hills)

Banjing Lu

Wanshousi (Longevity Temple)

Baishiqiao Lu

Zhongguo Guojia Tushuguan (National Library of China)

National Library

Wutasi (Temple of Five Pagodas)

Beijing Haiyang Guan (Beijing Aquarium)

Sidaokou Lu

Xizhimen Railway Station

Deshengmen Xidajie

Jishuitan

Xu Beihong Jinian Guan (Xu Beihong Memorial Hall)

Xinjiekou

Song Qingling Guju (former Home of Song Qingling)

Desheng

Xianshan Zhonglu (Third Ring Road)

ZIZHU YUAN GONGYUAN (PURPLE BAMBOO PARK)

Zizhuyuan Lu

Beijing Dongwuyuan (Beijing Zoo)

Beijing Zhanlanguan (Beijing Exhibition Centre Theatre)

Xitang (West Cathedral)

Jishui

Hou

Baiyun Lu

Xizhimenwai Dajie

Beijing Zoo

Xizhimennei Dajie

Xizhimen

Xinjiekou Beidajie

Xinjiekou

Mei Lanfang Jinian Guan (Mei Lanfang Memorial)

Guo

Chegongzhuang Xidajie

Chegongzhuang Dajie

Ping'an Ring Rd)

Ping'anli Xidajie

Gangwashitang (Earthenware & Brick Market Church)

Ping'anli

Resid Guo

Di'an

Fushi Lu

Sanlihe Lu

Baiwanzhuang Jie

XICHENG

Lu Xun Bowuguan (Lu Xun Museum)

Chengongzhuang (Second Ring Rd)

Baitasi (Temple of the White Pagoda)

Guangjisi (Temple of Universal Rescue)

Xisi Beidajie

Beitang (North Cathedral)

Xishiku Dajie

GON

Fucheng Lu

Fuchengmenwai Dajie

Fuchengmen

Nanlishi Lu

Fuchengmennei Dajie

Baitasi

Xisi

Xihuangchenggen Nanjie

Wenjin

YUYUANTAN GONGYUAN

Yuyuan

(SONG QINGLING CHILDREN'S SCIENCE PARK)

Sanlihe Lu

Yuetan Beijie

Nanlishi Lu

Lidai Diwang Miao (Temple of Emperors of Successive Dynasties)

Lingjinghutong

Xidanbei Dajie

Taipingqiao Dajie

Zhongna

Zhonghua Shiji Tan (China Millennium Monument)/ Beijing World Art Museum

Cuiwei Lu

Renmin Geming Junshi Bowuguan (Military Museum of the Chinese People's Revolution)

Yuetan Nanjie

Yuetan Donglu

YUETAN GONGYUAN (ALTAR OF THE MOON PARK)

Picai Hutong

Minzu Wenhuagong

Xidan Beidajie

Xinhua (Xinhua

Fuvou Jie

Fuxing Lu

Gongzhufen

Yangfangdianxi Lu

Yangfangdian Lu

Muxidi

Nanlishilu

Fuxingmen

Fuxingmennei Dajie

Xidan

Xichang

Jungshibowuguan

Shoudu Bowuguan (Capital Museum)

Baiyun Lu

Baiyunguan (Temple of the White Cloud)

Changchunjie

Xuanwumen Xidajie

Nantang (South Cathedral)

Xuanwumennei Dajie

Guojia Daju (National Cen the Performing

Hepingmen

Xuanwumen

Lianhuachi Donglu

Huaibaishu Jie

XUANWU ART GARDEN

Caishikou

Xisanhuannan Lu

Lianhuach Xilu

Lianhua (Lotus Pond)

Beijing Xi Zhan (West Railway Station)

Tianning Si (Temple of Heavenly Tranquility)

Guang'anmen Nanbinhelu

Xiaanmennei Dajie

Baoguo Si (Baoguo Temple)

Guang'anmennei Dajie

Luomashi Da

Guang'an Lu

Guang'anmenwai Lu

Guang'anmenwai Lu

Niu Jie Qingzhensi (Ox Street Mosque)

Huguang Huiguan

Liu Li Qiao Bus Station

Maliandao Lu

Nanxiang Jie

Fayuansi (Temple of the Source of Buddhist Teaching)

Guang'an Lu

Guang'ammen Railway Station

XUANWUMEN

Zaolinqian Jie

Niu Jie

WANSHOU GONGYUAN

Taoranting

Baizhifang Xijie

Baizhifang Dongjie

TAORANTIN GONGYUAN (HAPPY PAVILI PARK)

Sanluju Lu

Liucun Lu

DAGUANYUAN (GRAND VIEW GARDEN)

Caiyuan Jie

You'anmen

Lize Qiao Bus Station

Fengtai Beilu

Fengtai Beilu

You'anmen Xibinhelu

Beijing South Railway Station

Yongdingn Bus Statio

Beijing South Railway Station

Liangshui

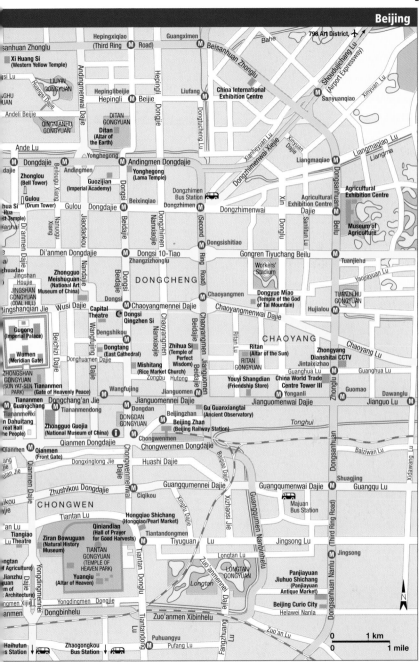

798 Art District,

Xi Huang Si
(Western Yellow Temple)

LIUYIN GONGYUAN

QINGNIANHU GONGYUAN

Hepingxiqiao
(Third Ring Road)

Guangximen

Beisanhuan Zhonglu

Bahe

Shoudujichang Lu
(Airport Expressway)

Hepinglibeijie

Hepingli

Beijie

Liufang

China International
Exhibition Centre

Sanyuanqiao

Andeli Beijie

Ande Lu

DITAN GONGYUAN

Ditan
(Altar of
the Earth)

Yonghegong

Andingmenwai Dajie

Dongzhimenwai Xiejie

Liangmaqiao Lu

Liangma

Zhonglou
(Bell Tower)

Andingmen

Guozijian
(Imperial Academy)

Yonghegong
(Lama Temple)

Dongzhimen
Bus Station

Agricultural
Exhibition Centre

Agricultural
Exhibition Centre Beilu

Gulou
(Drum Tower)

Gulou Dongdajie

Beixinqiao

Dongzhimen

Dongzhimenwai

Museum of
Agriculture

Nanluogu Xiang

Di'anmen Dongdajie

Dongsi 10-Tiao

Dongsishitiao

Gongren Tiyuchang Beilu

Tuanjiehu

Tuanjiehu Lu

Yaojiayuan Lu

Zhongguo
Meishuguan
(National Art
Museum of China)

DONGCHENG

Workers'
Stadium

TUANJIEHU
GONGYUAN

JINGSHAN
GONGYUAN
(COAL HILL)

Wusi Dajie

Capital
Theatre

Dongsi

Chaoyangmennei Dajie

Chaoyangmen

Dongyue Miao
(Temple of the God
of Tai Mountain)

Hujialou

Gugong
(Imperial Palace)

Dongsi
Qingzhen Si

Chaoyangmenwai Dajie

CHAOYANG

Chaoyang Lu

Wumen
(Meridian Gate)

Dengshikou

Zhihua Si
(Temple of
Perfect
Wisdom)

Ritan
(Altar of the Sun)

Zhongyang
Dianshitai CCTV

Dongtang
(East Cathedral)

RITAN
GONGYUAN

Jintaixizhao

Guanghua Lu

ZHONGSHAN
GONGYUAN
(SUN YAT-SEN
PARK)

Mishitang
(Rice Market Church)

Zongbu   Hutong

Youyi Shangdian
(Friendship Store)

China World Trade
Centre Tower III

Guomao

Tiananmen
(Gate of Heavenly Peace)

Wangfujing

Jianguomen

Yonganli

Dawanglu

Tiananmen
Guangchang

Dongchang'an Jie

Jianguomennei Dajie

Jianguomenwai Dajie

Jianguo Lu

Tiananmenxi

Tiananmendong

Dongdan

Gu Guanxiangtai
(Ancient Observatory)

Dahuitang
reat Hall
he People)

Zhongguo Guojia
(National Museum of China)

DONGDAN
GONGYUAN

Beijingzhan

Beijing Zhan
(Beijing Railway Station)

Tonghui

Balziwan Lu

Qianmen
(Front Gate)

Qianmen Dongdajie

Chongwenmen

Chongwenmen Dongdajie

Dongxinglong Jie

Huashi Dajie

Shuagjing

Zhushikou Dongdajie

CHONGWEN

Guangqumennei Dajie

Guangqumenwai Dajie

Guangqu Lu

Tiantan Lu

Ciqikou

Hongqiao Shichang
(Hongqiao/Pearl Market)

Majuan
Bus Station

Tiangiao
Lu Theatre

Ziran Bowuguan
(Natural History
Museum)

Qiniandian
(Hall of Prayer
for Good Harvests)

Tiantandongmen

Tiyuguan   Lu

Jingsong Lu

Jingsong

TIANTAN
GONGYUAN
(TEMPLE OF
HEAVEN PARK)

Longtan Lu

LONGTAN
GONGYUAN

Panjiayuan
Jiuhuo Shichang
(Panjiayuan
Antique Market)

Yuanqiu
(Altar of Heaven)

Longtan

Beijing Curio City

Helawei Nanla

Dongbinhelu

Zuo'anmen Dongjie

Zuo'an Lu

Yongdingmennei

Zuo'anmen Xibinhelu

Puhuangyu

Zhaogongkou
Bus Station

Pufang Lu

0   1 km

0   1 mile

TIANANMEN SQUARE AND SURROUNDINGS

The giant open space at the heart of Beijing, where imperial and Communist monuments meet as nowhere else, reflects China's tumultuous history

Main Attractions

TIANANMEN SQUARE
NATIONAL CENTRE FOR THE PERFORMING ARTS
TIANANMEN GATE
FOREIGN LEGATION QUARTER
BEIJING CITY PLANNING MUSEUM

Maps and Listings

MAP OF BEIJING, PAGES 96–7
MAP OF TIANANMEN SQUARE, PAGE 100
MAP OF FOREIGN LEGATION QUARTER, PAGE 110
RESTAURANTS, PAGE 111
ACCOMMODATION, PAGE 261

Tiananmen Square ❶ (Tiananmen Guangchang; 天安门广场) is the symbolic centre and political heart of Beijing, and it is to this immense plaza – said to be the world's largest public square – that most first-time visitors to the Chinese capital are initially drawn. This is the place where classical heritage and revolutionary symbolism meet head on. Imperial gateways, representing the feudal centuries of the Middle Kingdom, face the monuments and museums erected by the Communist regime that flank the square. Overlooking all is the iconic Tiananmen Gate, with its Mao portrait, entrance to the Forbidden City.

At the centre of things

For many Westerners, the words "Tiananmen Square" have become synonymous with the democracy demonstrations of 1989 and their brutal suppression. For most Chinese the square is a place that conjures up a broader range of images, both joyous and dark. Since the end of imperial times it has been at the heart of Chinese politics, both for dissent and (stage-managed) celebration. It was

here, on land once occupied by imperial office buildings, that May Fourth protesters gathered in the spring of 1919 to demand that their government reform itself and the nation. Thirty years later, on 1 October 1949, hundreds of thousands of cheering soldiers and citizens gathered in the square to hear Mao Zedong proclaim the founding of the People's Republic from atop Tiananmen Gate. In the 1950s the square was quadrupled in size and paved with concrete so it could accommodate up to a million

LEFT: carved *huabiao* pillars outside Tiananmen Gate symbolise dialogue between emperors and their subjects.
RIGHT: kite-flying in Tiananmen Square.

ABOVE: the Mao Mausoleum in the middle of the square continues to pack in the crowds.

people for public gatherings. Based on Moscow's Red Square, and under Soviet supervision, the work included the demolition of two major gates and the widening of Chang'an Avenue to 10 lanes. The first military parade was held in 1953, showcasing advanced Soviet weaponry. The Great Hall of the People and the National Museum of China were completed on either side of Tiananmen Gate by 1959 in time for the 10th anniversary of the People's Republic. This enlarged space then became the site of near-hysterical gatherings of Red Guards during the Cultural Revolution in the late 1960s.

In April 1976 the square again took centre stage – this time in the form of popular protest – as thousands of locals gathered to leave paper flowers and poems in memory of Zhou Enlai, whose death in January they felt had been too lightly acknowledged by their leaders. Five months later Mao was dead, and China set out on a new path – one that was to lead to Deng Xiaoping's reforms and, eventually, to the bloodshed of 1989.

In the late 1990s, the square was again renovated, this time in readiness for the October 1999 celebrations of the PRC's 50th anniversary.

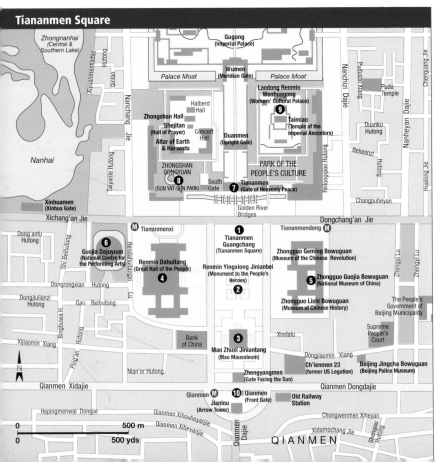

Tiananmen Square

This involved it being closed to the public for almost a year – a time which conveniently encompassed the 10th anniversary of 4 June 1989. The cement blocks were replaced with granite slabs – which could bear the weight of armoured vehicles without a scratch. On 1 October 2009, the 60th anniversary of the founding of the People's Republic, a huge military parade rolled through the square. Some 10,000 troops, several hundred tanks and missile-laden vehicles were proudly displayed before the country's top leaders and international media.

Every Chinese visitor to Beijing makes a visit here a top priority, along with the obligatory photograph. Early birds arrive before dawn to witness the national **flag-raising ceremony** at the north end of the square. The Chinese flag is unfurled at dawn and taken down at dusk each day in a ceremony that, on national holidays, can attract thousands of spectators. Two columns of immaculately dressed soldiers march out of Tiananmen Gate and across Chang'an Jie to approach the flagpole and perform the ceremony in an atmosphere of hushed reverence.

On a day-to-day basis, the square functions as a kind of concrete park, albeit one with an unusually high security presence. Kite-flying is a favourite hobby, and local kite-flying veterans are eager to share advice with novices.

In the middle of Tiananmen Square is the **Monument to People's Heroes ❷** (Renmin Yingxiong Jinianbei; 民英雄纪念碑), an obelisk dedicated in 1958 to the soldiers who fell in the Revolution. It stands on a double pedestal, and at a height of 37 metres (123ft) is 4 metres (14ft) taller than the Tiananmen Gate. The lower part of the base is ornamented with bas-reliefs portraying the stages of Chinese revolutionary history, from the first Opium War (1840–2) to the founding of the People's Republic.

Mao Mausoleum ❸

Address: central Tiananmen Square
Tel: 6513-2277
Opening Hrs: Tue–Sun 8–11.30am, Aug–May also Tue, Thur 2–4pm
Entrance Fee: free, but with small charge for compulsory bag deposit across the street

A complex network of tunnels is rumoured to lie beneath the austere surface of Tiananmen Square. Built in the 1970s during a period of frosty relations between China and the USSR, the compound was intended to accommodate all of Beijing's inhabitants in the event of nuclear war. A section accessible from the Qianmen area was opened as a tourist attraction in 2000 but closed for renovation in 2008.

BELOW: the Revolutionary Heroes Statue next to the Mao Mausoleum is a fine example of Socialist Realist art.

TIP

Be sure to store bags and cameras in the facility provided before queuing to enter the Mao Mausoleum or you'll be turned away. Once inside, it is advisable to maintain a respectful demeanour, speak quietly and look fast – visitors are herded past Mao's corpse by brusque soldiers who brook no lingering.

BELOW: the Mao Mausoleum.

Transport: Qianmen (line 2) or Tiananmen East (line 1) subway stations

To the south, in front of Zhengyangmen Gate, is the **Mao Mausoleum** (Mao Zhuxi Jiniantang; 毛主席纪念堂). After the death of Mao Zedong in 1976, political circumstances dictated the building of an everlasting memorial to the leader of the Revolution, founder of the state and Party chairman. In contrast, President Zhou Enlai, who died in the same year, had his ashes scattered to the winds. Mao's body was embalmed – by Vietnamese experts, it is said – and placed on display here. The mausoleum was built in only nine months in 1978 and also contains rooms commemorating other state and Party leaders. It was renovated in 1999 for the 50th anniversary of the PRC. Nowadays, however, some Chinese regard the monument as an unfortunate reminder of the personality cult of Mao.

There are massive group sculptures by the front and rear entrances to the mausoleum, depicting the people's common struggle for socialism – typical examples of the style of Socialist

Greening the Grey

Stage to the proclamation of the founding of the People's Republic, Tiananmen Square is akin to holy ground for the ruling Communist Party. Eyebrows were raised, therefore, in 2007 when leading architect Ma Yansong proposed paving the vast, empty space with trees and grass in a Chinese interpretation of New York's Central Park. Ma claimed his concept would heighten environmental awareness and spur debate on the use of public space. Domestic media reports on the proposition were muted, though such a daring suggestion could be seen as a indication of freer debate on sensitive political topics. It is now considered extremely unlikely to happen, and today the square remains grey.

Realism. The body of Mao lies in state in a crystal coffin in the Central Hall of Rest. He is dressed in the typical blue suit and covered with the flag of the Communist Party. In the southern hall beyond, calligraphy by Mao himself can be seen, bearing the

title "Reply to Comrade Guo Moruo", a poem Mao wrote in response to verse sent to him by the influential revolutionary writer *(see page 188)*.

The mausoleum was visited by countless Chinese in the months after it was opened, with people queuing patiently across Tiananmen Square. These days it is rather less frequented, although it can still be busy. Mao's status in 21st-century China is odd – he is at once the father of the nation and the man who, in the official words of the Party, got it "30 percent wrong"; still revered as something like a god by many, yet largely removed from public display throughout the land – the famous portrait at Tiananmen *(see page 104)* being one exception. The rapid rise of the Mao memorabilia phenomenon *(see page 42)* further muddies the waters.

Great Hall of the People ❹

Address: west side of Tiananmen Square
Tel: 6309-6156
Opening Hrs: daily 9am–5pm
Entrance Fee: charge
Transport: Tiananmen West subway station (line 1)

Tiananmen Square is flanked by vast Soviet-style edifices dating from the days of close relations between the two countries in the 1950s. The **Great Hall of the People** (Renmin Dahuitang; 人民大会堂), on the west side of the square, is the largest of these behemoths and the venue for meetings of the National People's Assembly (the Chinese parliament). Various official departments are also housed here, as is a banquet hall that seats 5,000. In addition, the hall is used to receive political delegations from abroad and to hold concerts by major visiting orchestras, though the acoustics are abysmal. There isn't much specific to see, but walking around the dimly lit, cavernous halls with their red carpets and polished

wooden floors certainly gives a feel of the Party spirit.

National Museum of China ❺

Address: 16 Dong Chang'an Jie; www.nationalmuseum.cn
Tel: 6513-2801
Opening Hrs: currently N/A
Entrance Fee: charge
Transport: Tiananmen East subway station (line 1)

Over on the eastern side of Tiananmen Square, directly opposite the Great Hall of the People, is the **National Museum of China** (Zhongguo Guojia Bowuguan; 中国国家博物馆). The two-winged four-storey hulk, constructed at great speed for the celebrations of the PRC's 10th anniversary in 1959, has been undergoing major renovation work for several years. When completed in late 2010, it will have tripled in size.

The museum is divided into two sections. The **Museum of the Chinese Revolution** (Zhongguo Geming Bowuguan), at the northern end, chronicles the history of the

ABOVE: the large auditorium in the middle of the Great Hall of the People.
BELOW: a wintry scene on the square.

Communist Party in China, the revolutionary civil wars and the campaign of resistance against the Japanese. During the Cultural Revolution, the displays had to be constantly readjusted to fit in with whatever was the current campaign (rather like the Ministry of Truth in George Orwell's *Nineteen Eighty-Four*), but the aim is now to provide a more objective record – even if that means a governmentally approved objective record.

The southern section of the museum houses the **Museum of Chinese History** (Zhongguo Lishi Bowuguan), opened in 1926. Many of the pieces on display were donated from private collections in China and elsewhere in the world, offering a chance for visitors to see many rare and precious Chinese artefacts. Among them is a valuable blue-glazed lamp from the Southern Dynasties period (AD 420–589), Tang figures and an embroidered silk portrait of the Celestial Kings. Ancient bronzes, jade pieces and bones, and ceramics from the Tang and Song dynasties are also on show. In addition, the museum features Chinese discoveries such as

printing, gunpowder, the compass and paper manufacture.

National Centre for the Performing Arts (National Grand Theatre) ❻

Address: 2 Xi Chang'an Jie; www.chncpa.org
Tel: 6655-000
Opening Hrs: Tue–Sun 9am–5pm
Entrance Fee: charge
Transport: Tiananmen West subway station (line 1)

Behind (to the west of) the Great Hall of the People is the **National Centre for the Performing Arts** (Guojia Dajuyuan; 国家大剧院), a striking titanium-and-glass dome surrounded by water that opened to the public in September 2007. Land for the structure was set aside by Premier Zhou in the late 1950s, but the vagaries of politics and the inability to agree on a design caused the project to be delayed for four decades. The decision finally to proceed in the late 1990s only led to more controversy – there were objections to the budget (which ballooned to an estimated Rmb 2.7 billion), to the idea of putting mul-

Mao's Portrait

As Mao's body lies in its mausoleum, his seemingly ageless likeness looks down from the Tiananmen Gate. The gigantic portrait of the leader measures 6 metres by 4.5 metres (20ft by 15ft) and weighs nearly 1.5 tonnes. It is cleaned every year before Labour Day (1 May) and replaced before National Day (1 October), when Mao is joined by the founder of the Republic, Sun Yat-sen. The portrait first appeared at the founding of the New China in 1949 and was originally hung only for these two occasions, but it became a permanent fixture during the Cultural Revolution – though a black-and-white picture briefly replaced it after Mao's death in 1976.

Ge Xiaoguang, the latest of four artists who have maintained the image, has painted 19 giant portraits of the Great Helmsman. The paintings are reinforced with plastic and fibreglass and have to be lifted into place by crane. Used portraits are apparently kept in case of demonstrations like those in 1989, when paint bombs added a touch of Jackson Pollock to Ge's work. Ge, incidentally, became a minor celebrity after he appeared on TV in 1994. As an employee of the Beijing Art Company, he receives no extra payment for his special assignment.

tiple theatres under one roof, and to the exclusion of foreign architects from the bidding process. When no Chinese design was deemed suitable, a second round of bidding was held that included designs by foreigners. The choice of French architect Paul Andreu's design – which supporters likened to a water pearl and detractors to a duck egg – caused an uproar, with critics complaining that it was "un-Chinese" and utterly incompatible with its surroundings. This is true in a way, as it was the city centre's first unconventional modern building. The distancing "moat" and high cost of tickets also gives the project a sense of elitism – a politically incorrect, if inevitably common, phenomenon in a rapidly developing but nominally Communist capital. The "Egg", as the building has been dubbed, is certainly impressive, though, with a total of four magnificent and unique theatres, including an opera hall seating 2,416, and a similarly capacious music hall. An entrance ticket permits access to public spaces – including the underwater corridor, roof terrace and resource centre – and exhibition halls, certainly worth considering even if the performances on offer don't grab you.

Tiananmen Gate ➐

Address: north end of Tiananmen Square
Tel: 6511-8600
Opening Hrs: gate, daily 8.30am – 5pm; viewing platform, daily 8.30am–4.30pm
Entrance Fee: gate, free to pass through; viewing platform, charge
Transport: Tiananmen East or Tiananmen West subway stations (line 1)

Separated from the northern end of Tiananmen Square by the 38-metre (125ft) wide Chang'an Jie, the iconic **Tiananmen Gate** (Gate of Heavenly Peace; 天安门), marking the southernmost extent of the Forbidden City, is reached via seven marble bridges across a small moat. This famous building was once the meeting place of the divided city, where the various levels of the

ABOVE: the unmistakable dome of the National Centre for the Performing Arts.
BELOW: lush grass and flower beds flank Tiananmen Gate.

traditional pyramid of authority – the city to the south of Qianmen, the Imperial City and the Forbidden City – came into contact with each other.

When the emperors left the Forbidden City to celebrate the New Year rites at the Temple of Heaven, they made their first offerings at Tiananmen Gate. On important occasions, imperial decrees were lowered from the gate in a gilded box. The civil servants, kneeling, were to receive them, copy them and then distribute them all over the country. Thus it was in a decidedly imperial manner that Mao Zedong proclaimed the People's Republic of China from this spot on 1 October 1949, and received the adulation of millions of Red Guards during the Cultural Revolution.

Tiananmen Gate has become the symbol of Beijing and, indeed, the People's Republic. It is the only public building in the city still to display the portrait of Mao on the outside. To the left of this portrait is a sign in Chinese characters: "Long live the People's Republic of China." The sign on the right says, "Long live the great unity of all the peoples of the world."

The earliest structure here, the Guomen (Gate of the Empire), was built out of wood in 1417, then rebuilt in stone after fire damage. In 1651, the gate was again rebuilt after destruction by Manchu troops and renamed Tiananmen. Finally, the side gates were demolished in 1912 to open up the square. Today there are five passages through the massive gate walls. The central one follows the imperial route and was reserved for the emperor; today it is open to all. Subjects are said to have put up petitions to the emperor, along with suggestions for improvements, on the carved marble pillars (*huabiao*) in front of the gate.

On the other side of the passageway is a large courtyard full of souvenir and drinks vendors and parading soldiers. The ticket office for the **viewing platform** above the Mao portrait on Tiananmen Gate is on the left (ie west; daily 8am–4.30pm; entrance fee; bag deposit compulsory).

Continue north through the Upright Gate (Duanmen) to reach the ticket office for the Imperial Palace (*see page 113*). The complex itself is entered through the Meridian Gate (Wumen).

ABOVE: an army of workers keep Tiananmen Square spotlessly clean at all times.
BELOW: traditional lions keep guard outside Tiananmen. **BELOW RIGHT:** a tour group leader; Tiananmen Square is top of the itinerary for Chinese tourists.

Zhongshan Park ⓮

Address: 1 Zhonghua Lu, west of Tiananmen Gate
Tel: 6605-5431
Opening Hrs: daily winter 6.30am–8pm, summer 6am–9pm
Entrance Fee: charge
Transport: Tiananmen West subway station (line 1)

To the left of the promenade leading from Tiananmen Gate to the Meridian Gate, and separated from the Imperial Palace by a wall and a moat, **Zhongshan Park** (Sun Yat-sen Park; 中山公园) is a fine example of the fusion of imperial architecture and garden design. Over 1,000 years ago this was the site of the Temple of the Wealth of the Land, but the ancient cypresses are all that remain from that time. The park was named after Sun Yat-sen following his death.

From the main entrance to the park in the south, the path first goes through a white **marble arch**. In 1900, the German ambassador Baron von Ketteler was shot dead on Hatamen Street (modern-day Chongwenmen), on his way to the Chinese Foreign Ministry, by one of the rebellious Boxers. In reparation, the imperial family were required to build a triumphal arch on the spot, with the inscription: "In memory of the virtuous von Ketteler." However, after 1919, Germany no longer existed as an imperialist power, and the arch was moved to its present position and inscribed: "Justice will prevail." In 1953, it was reinscribed again, this

time by poet Guo Moruo *(see page 188)*, and reads: "Defend peace."

Further north, in the centre of the park, is a great square area, where the **Altar of Earth and Harvests** (Shejitan; 社稷坛) once stood. The altar's shape is a reminder of the old Chinese concept of the earth as a square. Twice a year, in the grey light of dawn, the Ming and Qing emperors brought their offerings here in the hope of obtaining divine support for a good harvest. During the sacrifice, the altar was covered with five different types of coloured earth, and these colours can still be seen today, repeated in the tiles that cover the low surrounding walls.

The five colours are thought to represent the points of the compass (north, south, east, west and centre). To the north of the altar is the **Zhongshan Hall** (中山堂), built of wood, a typical example of Beijing's classical architecture. Also inside the park is a modern concert hall, which puts on concerts by Western and Chinese orchestras.

To the east, on the other side of the promenade between Tiananmen

Zhongshan Hall was used to store the coffin of Sun Yat-sen after he died in 1925. In 1929 his body was moved to Nanjing, where it was buried in a huge mausoleum at the foot of the Purple Mountains.

BELOW LEFT: the courtyard at the centre of Zhongshan Park.
BELOW: a traditional gateway in the park.

and Meridian gates, is the **Workers' Cultural Palace** ❾ (Laodong Renmin Wenhuagong; 劳动人民文化宫; daily, summer 6am–8pm, winter 6.30am–5pm; entrance fee) – the grounds of which are used for temporary exhibitions and cultural events. In the centre of the complex is a venerable temple dating from the 15th and 16th centuries – the **Temple of the Imperial Ancestors** (Taimiao; 太庙). Five times a year the wooden ancestor tablets, upon which the names of the dead forefathers of the imperial family were recorded, were taken from the central hall to the southern hall, where the emperor paid his respects to his forefathers.

The veneration of ancestors is one of the oldest practices in the Chinese spiritual tradition, hingeing on the belief that the well-being of the dead is dependent on the offerings and veneration of the living. The dead, in turn, are thought to be able to influence the fate of the living *(see page 61)*. The imperial ancestors received extraordinary honours and respect, as they were believed to be responsible for the well-being of the whole country. The

Taimiao thus functioned as one of the country's most important ritual sites.

After 1949, the temple complex was restored and equipped for its new life as a workers' college and pleasure garden. Now, the "sacred halls" are used for leisure activities, further education courses and occasional high-profile performances billed by promoters as "Forbidden City" concerts.

Qianmen

At the southern end of Tiananmen Square, **Qianmen** ❿ (Front Gate; 前门) was once the outer, southern entrance into the old Inner (Chinese) City from the Outer (Tartar) City, and dates from 1421 during the reign of Yongle. The gate in fact comprises two separate structures: the stone **Jianlou** (Arrow Tower; 箭楼), which burned down in 1900 and was reconstructed in 1903; and the main gate, the wooden **Zhengyangmen** (Gate Facing the Sun; 正阳门), just to the north, also damaged in 1900 and reconstructed, to which the city wall was connected. The gates are free to walk through, but a ticket is required if you want to

ABOVE: Zhengyangmen Gate. **BELOW:** Jianlou formed the southern part of Qianmen Gate.

ascend (both daily 8.30am–4pm; separate entrance fees). Zhengyangmen, the tallest gate in Beijing at 40 metres (130ft), has a collection of old photographs and models upstairs showing how it looked in the past when it was joined with Jianlou. Unusually, all are captioned in English.

Foreign Legation Quarter

In contrast to Shanghai and neighbouring Tianjin (see page 246), European traders never established much of a presence in Beijing. Yet after the Second Opium War, the British and the French, followed by various others, were grudgingly permitted to establish a concession in the heart of the city. At first they made use of existing palace buildings, and the quarter where they lived was integrated into the rest of the city. But during the 1900 Boxer Rebellion, which culminated in a 55-day siege on the quarter, almost the entire area was destroyed. In the subsequent rebuilding, high walls were added for protection, and colonial-style edifices replaced the older Chinese buildings. Eventually evicted from the premises in 1950, the foreigners left behind these anomalies of colonial-style architecture.

The city government considers the area an unwanted relic of an ignominious period in China's history, and many old buildings have disappeared to be replaced by offices and apartments. A lavish complex comprising restaurants, bars and even a nightclub called Ch'ienmen 23 (see panel, below) on the site of the former US legation sets the tone for the future of the area. Several of the old colonial buildings remain almost unchanged, however, and are used by various government departments. They are off limits to the public and hidden behind high walls and guarded gates, but, even so, the area is well worth strolling through; the villas and mansions remain ensconced in quiet, tree-lined streets, a world away from the crowded, jostling arteries of downtown Beijing.

A stroll around the quarter

Towards the northern end of Taijichang Dajie (formerly Rue Marco Polo), the grand red-brick towers of the former **Italian Legation Ⓐ** are now the headquarters of the Chinese People's Friendship Association. The building was also used to accommodate "foreign friends" who supported the Chinese Revolution. Down the *hutong* to the east is the grey-and-white Greek-temple facade entrance to the **Austro-Hungarian Legation Ⓑ**,

These legations under the wall are greatly out of conceit with the encircling city. They do not even harmonise with one another. It is as though each first Plenipotentiary of the Powers concerned brought with him a shipload of building material from the homeland and tried to assemble it when he came to his journey's end.

Gilbert Collins, 1925

ABOVE LEFT:
the entrance to
the old French
Legation building.

Ch'ienmen 23

The area surrounding Tiananmen Square has been kept relatively free of large commercial ventures in order to preserve the sanctity of such a politically charged setting. Breaking the mould, albeit in restrained and sensitive fashion, is Chi'enmen 23 (www.chienmen23.com), a modern and luxurious development in the former American Legation compound. The project was supervised by China's "king of high culture", American-born Handel Lee, the man behind the Courtyard, Beijing's first international-standard restaurant and art gallery, which opened near the Forbidden City in 1996. His subsequent Shanghai project, Three on the Bund, was credited with reviving the once-dilapidated riverfront into a centre of culture and self-indulgence.

Keen to replicate that success, Lee set to work on Chi'enmen. The project took more than three years to come to fruition, with countless bureaucratic hurdles to overcome before it finally opened in 2008. The tastefully retro interior accommodates upmarket restaurants, exclusive clubs and a well-appointed theatre. There is also a multi-level exhibition space, the **Beijing Center for the Arts** (Tue–Sun 10am–10pm), an impressive platform for contemporary Chinese artists.

ABOVE: a typical tree-lined street in the Legation Quarter.

now housing the Institute of International Studies. Back on Taijichang is the grey-blue-walled **Peking Club** ❸. Built in 1902, complete with tennis courts and a swimming pool, this is the exclusive haunt of high-ranking Chinese Communist Party officials.

Further south, on the corner of Dongjiaomin Xiang and partly hidden by a newer building, is **St Michael's Catholic Church** ❹, built by the French Vincentian fathers in 1902. It was nearly destroyed during the Cultural Revolution, then renovated in 1989. The rear entrance to the expansive grounds of the former **Belgian Legation** ❺ is across the street. The buildings, originally modelled after a villa belonging to King Leopold II (1835–1909), now function as a state guesthouse. Nearby is the old **French Legation** ❻, the Beijing residence of Cambodia's King Sihanouk, distinguished by an imposing grey gate with red doors and two large stone lions standing guard.

On the corner of Dongjiaomin Xiang and Zhengyi Lu is the large red-and-white-brick building of the **Yokohama Specie Bank** ❼, where the Empress Dowager Cixi supposedly took out a loan. Looking south is the site of the **Grand Hôtel des Wagon-Lits**, which was *the* fashionable place to stay, and was close to the old railway station outside the wall. The station still stands, just southeast of Tiananmen Square, but is now used as a shopping mall.

Head north on Zhengyi Lu, an attractive street with shady parkland running up the middle, and you will come to an impressive red-towered gate. This is the **Japanese Legation** ❽, and it was here that the Chinese were forced to accept the infamous "Twenty-One Demands" on 7 May 1915, whereby the Japanese obtained special rights over Manchuria. Almost opposite is the old **British Legation** ❾. Previously a prince's palace, this building was the city's largest foreign

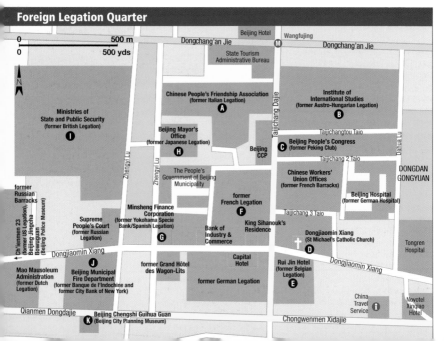

Foreign Legation Quarter

legation. Many sought refuge here during the siege of 1900. It is now occupied by the Ministries of State and Public Security. South on Qianmen Dongdajie are the buildings of the **Banque de l'Indochine** and the **City Bank of New York 〇**.

Other sights

The **Beijing City Planning Museum 〇** (Beijing Chengshi Guihua Guan; 北京城市规划馆; Tue–Sun 9am–4pm; entrance fee), at 20 Qianmen Dongdajie, has displays that illustrate 3,000 years of the city's history. For an unforgettable confirmation of the sheer sprawl of modern Beijing, a huge model of the city takes up an entire floor. One of the museum's prize possessions is a 90-sq-metre (35-sq-ft) bronze relief that depicts Beijing

on the eve of liberation. The relief includes an astonishing 5,000 people, 60,000 trees and 118,000 structures. Two on-site theatres screen films on the city's urban development, including a glimpse into a future metropolis entirely free of old *hutong*.

Also worthy of a visit is the **Beijing Police Museum** (Beijing Jingcha Bowuguan; 北京警察博物馆; Tue–Sun 9am–4pm; charge) located just 500 metres/yds east of Mao's mausoleum, showcasing the history of China's police force, forensic methods and an impressively comprehensive collection of old-fashioned torture devices. The fourth floor contains an assortment of modern and improvised weapons used by the police and their adversaries and a video shooting range. ❏

ABOVE: part of the giant model of Beijing in the City Planning Museum.

RESTAURANTS

Cantonese

ZEN 1903
蝶1903
Ch'ienmen 23, 23 Qianmen Dongdajie. Tel: 6559-9608. Open: 11am–10pm. **$$$**
❶ p288, B2
Cantonese classics such as dim sum and seafood soups are delicate and fresh at this reasonably priced but decidedly upmarket restaurant.

French

Maison Boulud
布鲁宫法餐厅
Ch'ienmen 23, 23 Qianmen Dongdajie. Tel: 6559-9200. Open: Mon–Fri 11.30am–2pm, 6–10.30pm; Sat–Sun 11am–4pm, 6–10.30pm.
$$$$ ❷ p288, B2
Celebrity chef Daniel Boulud's innovative creations make this Beijing's finest French

restaurant. The brunch menu (11am–4pm) represents good value for money.

Imperial

Laijinyuxuan
来今雨轩饭庄
West side of Zhongshan Park. Tel: 6605-6676. Open: 10.30am–10pm. **$$ ($$$ for Red Mansions Banquet)**
❸ p288, A1
Resembling a traditional garden house, this renowned restaurant in Zhongshan Park serves up food featured in the famous Qing-dynasty novel *Dream of the Red Mansions*. A Red Mansions banquet must be booked in advance.

Tiananmen Fangshan
仿膳饭庄
37 Dongjiao Minxiang. Tel: 6523-3105. Open: 11am–

2pm, 5–8pm. **$$$$** ❹ p288, B2
Sumptuous imperial cuisine in a luxurious setting. Boxed desserts are available to buy as gifts for friends and family.

Italian

Ristorante Sadler
Ch'ienmen 23, 23 Qianmen Dongdajie. Tel: 6559-1399. Open: 11.30am–2pm, 6–10.30pm. **$$$$** ❺ p288, B2
Fine Italian dining from the kitchen of Michelin-starred chef Claudio Sadler, with dishes paired to wines from an extensive list.

Muslim

Tiananmen Donglaishun
东来顺天安门店
44 Dong Jiaominxiang, near SE corner of Tiananmen Square. Tel: 6524-1042. Open: 11am–2pm, 5–8pm.

$$$ ❻ p288, B2
A branch of the well-known Muslim restaurant, with mutton hotpot cooked over charcoal fires.

Peking Duck

Tiananmen Quanjude
全聚德天安门店
44 Dong Jiaominxiang, near SE corner of Tiananmen Square.
Tel. 6512-2265. Open: 11am–2pm, 5–8pm; fast food available all day.
$$$$ ❼ p288, B2
A branch of the famous Peking Duck restaurant specialising in Shandong cuisine.

• • • • • • • •
Prices are for a typical dinner for one (three dishes with beer in Chinese restaurants, or a three-course meal with a half-bottle of house wine in Western-style restaurants). $ = under Rmb 50, $$ = Rmb 50–100, $$$ = Rmb 100–200, $$$$ = over Rmb 200.

THE FORBIDDEN CITY

The great palace complex at the heart of Beijing functioned as the fulcrum of the ordered cosmos that was imperial China

At the heart of modern Beijing lies the most complete historical site in all of China. This remarkable complex, a full square kilometre (¹/₃ sq. mile), is simply a must-see for any visitor to the city: to avoid the crowds try to get here early in the day, and note that some of the halls have exhibitions which require you to buy additional tickets.

The Forbidden City, also known as the **Imperial Palace** (Gugong; 故宫), was the hallowed nucleus of the Chinese empire for nearly five centuries. Within its thick red ramparts a succession of emperors lived and ruled, aided and served by tens of thousands of officials, eunuchs, maids and concubines. The emperor was considered to be the Son of Heaven, the divinely appointed intermediary between heaven (*yang*) and earth (*yin*), who was responsible for peace, prosperity and the orderly life of the world.

As the theoretical centre of the terrestrial world, the Forbidden City was a sacred ground in which ceremony and ritual dominated every aspect of life for all inhabitants, from the emperor himself to the lowliest serving girl. Its expansive courtyards were regularly filled with processions of officials robed in embroidered silk gowns of many colours. Through its labyrinthine side corridors coursed a stream of young maid-servants – 9,000 of them in the Ming dynasty – and eunuchs. While the maids usually served only during their teenage years, the eunuchs were employees for life, and their mincing footsteps, high voices and – some said – scent of urine were a fixture of palace life. So, too, were the concubines, highly educated young women for ever cut off from their families and the world outside, fated to spend their days

LEFT: the enormous doors at Duanmen Gate.
RIGHT: keeping tradition alive.

ABOVE: the Imperial Throne in the Palace of Heavenly Purity. **BELOW:** huge urns were filled with water as a precaution against fire, a constant threat to the palace's wooden buildings.

sewing – and, perhaps, conniving – as they awaited the emperor's pleasure.

The Forbidden City today in some ways resembles a well-touristed ghost town. Indeed, in recognition of this fact, the Chinese no longer refer to it as a "city" at all, but as a "museum", and its official appellation is now the **National Palace Museum** (Gugong Bowuguan; 故宫博物馆). But, with a little reading and imagination, it is still possible to conjure an image of life as it was once lived at the heart of imperial China.

History of the palace

The Mongols (Yuan dynasty, 1279–1368) built their palace to the west of today's Forbidden City, before moving the capital to Nanjing in central China. In 1403, the third Ming emperor, Yongle, decided to move the capital back to Beijing. He ordered a new palace to be built, of which the basic structure has remained to the present day. According to legend, Yongle received the plans from the hands of a Daoist priest who had descended from heaven especially for that purpose. Between 1406 and 1420 some

200,000 people were occupied in the construction, and the palace was finally occupied in 1421. The stones had to be brought on wagons from quarries in the countryside around Beijing. In winter, they were drawn on ropes over the icy ground.

The buildings were mostly wooden and were constantly being altered; the wood came from the provinces of Yunnan and Sichuan in the southwest of China. Their main enemy was fire, and often entire great halls burned down. For this reason, there were a number of large water containers in the palace, many made of gilded copper and still present today, albeit supplemented by modern fire-fighting equipment, although even as recently as 1987 one of the smaller buildings fell victim to fire. Most of the present buildings date from the 18th century. Many of them have names based on Confucian philosophy – endless combinations of "harmony", "peace" and "quiet" – which were considered to have fortunate connotations.

In 1900 there were still some 10,000 people living within the Forbidden

City, and until the overthrow of the last emperor, the general public were barred from entry. Although the older parts were made into a museum as early as 1914, the last emperor and his court lived in the rear parts of the palace until 1924. The first tourists were admitted in the 1920s, but after 1937 there was not much left to look at, as items were removed to Nanjing and Shanghai for safekeeping from the advancing Japanese. From there, palace treasures were in turn "removed for safekeeping" to Taiwan, during Chiang Kai-shek's retreat in 1949, and remain there to this day.

Following the founding of the People's Republic, extensive restoration work was undertaken. Zhou Enlai is credited with protecting the renovated palace from zealous Red Guards during the Cultural Revolution. Today, the complex is protected by law.

Orientation

The Forbidden City is entered from the south through Tiananmen Gate, although the Imperial Palace Museum itself – the area which you have to pay to enter – lies beyond the Meridian Gate (Wumen) – *see below.*

The complex covers an area of 720,000 sq metres (861,000 sq yards), running a distance of 961 metres (1,050yds) from north to south and 753 metres (823yds) from east to west. It is surrounded by a broad moat and protected by a rectangular wall 10 metres (35ft) high, with mighty watchtowers standing at the four corners. The buildings are aligned on north–south lines, the most important of them orientated to face south, towards the sun. The precise geometric pattern reflects the strongly hierarchical structure of imperial Chinese society, with its fixed and ordered harmony as an expression of cosmic order.

There are two main areas within the walls – the southern (front) section or **Outer Courtyard**, comprising three large halls, in which the Ming and Qing emperors held state ceremonies, and the residential northern (rear) section or **Inner Courtyard**, consisting of three large palaces and a few smaller ones, as well as the Imperial Gardens.

ABOVE: the largest courtyard in the Forbidden City is the Court of the Imperial Palace (or Outer Court).

Follow Xi Chang'an Jie for a few hundred metres/yds west from Tiananmen Gate. On the right-hand side, framed by red walls, is Xinhuamen, the gate leading into Zhongnanhai, the seat of the Communist Party of China and a modern-day Forbidden City. It was here that Mao Zedong used to reside as the Great Leader; today this area is still the inner sanctum of the Party leaders.

Forbidden City

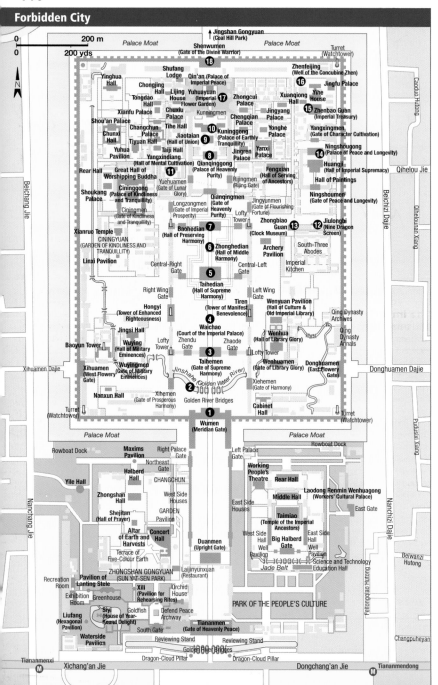

Palace Moat

Shenwumen (Gate of the Divine Warrior)

Palace Moat

Turret (Watchtower)

18

0 200 m
0 200 yds

N

Zhenfeijing (Well of the Concubine Zhen)

16

Jingfu Palace

Yinghua Hall

Shufang Lodge

Qin'an (Palace of Imperial Peace)

Chongjing Hall

Lijing House

Yuhuayuan (Imperial Flower Garden)

17

Zhongcui Palace

Xuanqiong Hall

Yihe House

Tongdao Hall

Chuxiu Hall

Kunningmen

Jingyang Palace

15 Zhenbao Guan (Imperial Treasury)

Xianfu Palace

Tihe Hall

Chengqian Palace

Shou'an Palace

Changchun Palace

Jiaotaian (Hall of Union)

10 Kunninggong (Palace of Earthly Tranquillity)

Yonghe Palace

Yangxingmen (Gate of Character Cultivation)

Chunxi Hall

Tiyuan Hall

9

Jingren Palace

Yanxi Palace

Yuhua Pavilion

Taiji Hall

Yangxindiang (Hall of Mental Cultivation)

8 Qianqinggong (Palace of Heavenly Purity)

14 Ningshougong (Palace of Peace and Longevity)

Rear Hall

Great Hall of Worshipping Buddha

11

Yuehuamen (Gate of Lunar Glory)

Rujingmen (Rijing Gate)

Fengxian (Hall of Serving of Ancestors)

Huangji (Hall of Imperial Supremacy)

Qihelou Jie

Ciningong (Palace of Kindliness and Tranquility)

Qianqingmen (Gate of Heavenly Fortune)

Hall of Paintings

Shoukang Palace (Palace of Kindliness and Tranquility)

Ciningmen (Gate of Kindliness and Tranquillity)

Longzongmen (Gate of Imperial Prosperity)

Jingyunmen (Gate of Flourishing Fortune)

Ningshoumen (Gate of Peace and Longevity)

Xianruo Temple

CININGYUAN (GARDEN OF KINDLINESS AND TRANQUILITY)

7 Baohedian (Hall of Preserving Harmony)

Lofty Tower

Zhongbiao Guan (Clock Museum)

13

12 Jiulongbi (Nine Dragon Screen)

Linxi Pavilion

6 Zhonghedian (Hall of Middle Harmony)

Archery Pavilion

South-Three Abodes

Central-Right Gate

5

Central-Left Gate

Imperial Kitchen

Taihedian (Hall of Supreme Harmony)

Right Wing Gate

Left Wing Gate

Tiren (Tower of Manifest Benevolence)

Wenyuan Pavilion (Hall of Culture & Old Imperial Library)

Qing Dynasty Archives

Hongyi (Tower of Enhanced Righteousness)

4 Waichao (Court of the Imperial Palace)

Qing Dynasty Annals

Jingsi Hall

Zhendu Gate

Zhaode Gate

Wenhua (Hall of Library Glory)

Baoyun Tower

Wuying (Hall of Military Eminence)

Lofty Tower

3 Taihemen (Gate of Supreme Harmony)

Lofty Tower

Donghuamen (East-Flowery Gate)

Xihuamen (West Flowery Gate)

Wuyingmen (Gate of Military Eminence)

Wenhuamen (Gate of Library Glory)

Donghuamen Dajie

Nanxun Hall

Xihemen (Gate of Prosperous Harmony)

Jinshahe (Golden Water River)

2 Golden River Bridges

Xiehemen (Gate of Harmony)

Cabinet Hall

Xihuamen Dajie

Turret (Watchtower)

Turret (Watchtower)

1 Wumen (Meridian Gate)

Palace Moat

Palace Moat

Beichang Jie

Beichizi Dajie

Qihelounan Xiang

Puduskou Xiang

Caodou Hutong

Rowboat Dock

Maxims Pavilion

Right Palace Gate

Left Palace Gate

Rowboat Dock

Yile Hall

Halberd Hall

Northeast Gate

CHANGCHUN

Working People's Theatre

Rear Hall

Laodong Renmin Wenhuagong (Workers' Cultural Palace)

Zhongshan Hall

West Side Houses

East Side Houses

Middle Hall

East Gate

Nanchang Jie

Shejitan (Hall of Prayer)

GARDEN PAVILION

Taimiao (Temple of the Imperial Ancestors)

Altar of Earth and Harvests

Concert Hall

West Side Hall

Big Halberd Gate

East Side Hall

Beiwanzi Hutong

Terrace of Five-Colour Earth

Well Pavilion

Well Pavilion

Recreation Room

Pavilion of Lanting Stele

ZHONGSHAN GONGYUAN (SUN YAT-SEN PARK)

Duanmen (Upright Gate)

Jade Belt

Science and Technology Education Hall

Beiwanzi Hutong

Exhibition Room

Greenhouse

Xili (Pavilion for Rehearsing Rites)

Orchid House

Laijinyunxuan (Restaurant)

PARK OF THE PEOPLE'S CULTURE

Feitonglong Hutong

Liufang (Hexagonal Pavilion)

Siyi (House of Year-Round Delight)

Goldfish

Defend Peace Archway

Changpuheyan

Waterside Pavilion

South Gate

Tiananmen (Gate of Heavenly Peace)

Reviewing Stand

Reviewing Stand

Golden Water Bridges

Dragon-Cloud Pillar

Dragon-Cloud Pillar

Tiananmenxi

Xichang'an Jie

Jichang'an Jie

Dongchang'an Jie

Tiananmendong

The Imperial Palace Museum

Address: 4 Jingshan Qianjie;
www.dpm.org.cn
Tel: 8500-7421
Opening Hrs: daily Apr–Oct 8.30am–5pm, Nov–Mar 8.30am–4.30pm
Entrance Fee: charge; extra fee payable for the Clock Museum and Imperial Treasury
Transport: Tiananmen East or Tiananmen West subway stations (line 1)

To the north of Tiananmen Gate *(see page 105)*, past the Duanmen Gate, is the massive bulk of the **Meridian Gate ❶** (Wumen; 午门), the main entrance to the Forbidden City (you can also buy tickets and enter at Shenwumen at the northern end). At 38 metres (125ft) it is the tallest gate of the palace. Because of the five pavilions on its U-shaped base, this gate was also known as the Gate of the Five Phoenixes. The number five is of great symbolic importance as it represents the five Confucian cardinal virtues – humanity, justice, refinement, education and trust. The emperor could only represent the *dao* of heaven, the order that pervades the world, and bring harmony on earth if he remained faithful to these virtues.

From a throne in the middle pavilion of the gate the emperor reviewed military parades, announced new calendars and ordered rebellious officials to be punished. The only other people allowed to use this gate were the empress on her wedding day, and scholars who had passed the palace examinations.

Once inside the Meridian Gate you enter a large courtyard, bisected by the **Golden Water River ❷** (Jinshahe; 金水河), crossed by five marble bridges. Across this first courtyard to the north is the **Gate of Supreme Harmony ❸** (Taihemen; 太和门), rebuilt in 1890. Inside it there is a large map of the palace. Beyond this gate is the largest courtyard in the complex, the **Court of the Imperial Palace ❹** (also known as the Outer Court; Waichao; 外朝), where the imperial shops selling silk and porcelain were situated.

Halls in harmony

There are three large audience and throne halls at the end of the Court

ABOVE: the palace's huge wooden doors feature lions and heavyweight golden knobs – the number of which signifies the door's importance.
LEFT: seven bridges cross the Golden Water River.
BELOW: looking north from Tiananmen Gate to Duanmen Gate.

A Forbidden City branch of Starbucks opened in 2000 to a public outcry that was rekindled in 2007 by TV personality Rui Chenggang. He claimed the American-run coffee shop marred the solemnity of the Forbidden City and undermined Chinese culture. His campaign was successful and the café was replaced by an alternative outlet selling similar drinks though managed by the Palace Museum.

BELOW: the Court of the Imperial Palace (Outer Court).

of the Imperial Palace: the Hall of Supreme Harmony, the Hall of Middle Harmony and the Hall of Preserving Harmony. They stand on a marble platform some 8 metres (26ft) high, which is divided into three levels. The balustrades on each level are decorated with dragon heads that spout water when it rains.

The **Hall of Supreme Harmony ❺** (Taihedian; 太和殿) is the largest of the three, and in the time of the Ming and Qing dynasties, its 35 metres (115ft) made it the tallest building in Beijing – its pre-eminence ensured by an imperial decree that forbade any other city buildings from exceeding its height. Within the hall stood the **Dragon Throne**, from where the emperor ruled. Only he could enter the hall by walking up the ramp adorned with dragon motifs. On the platform in front of the hall are two symbols – a grain measure on the left and a sundial to the right – representing imperial justice and agriculture. Also present are bronze figures of cranes and tortoises – symbols of good luck and longevity.

On state occasions, such as a coronation, the first day of the New Year or the empress's birthday, a formal court ceremony was conducted in the hall. Outside the hall, officials and the more important dignitaries lined up according to their rank, waiting to be summoned before the emperor. Incense and bells strengthened the impression of the other-worldly nature of the emperor.

The roof of the hall is supported by 72 pillars, with the inner six adorned by dragons. The hierarchy of Chinese feudal society was even reflected in roofs, which were designed to indicate the social position of the householder. The roofs of the Imperial Palace symbolised the highest degree of power through their colour, construction and material. Their breath-taking beauty makes it worth taking the time to see them again and again from different perspectives. The U-shaped corbels typical of Chinese wooden buildings – all built without the use of nails – were reserved for great palaces and temples.

The Hall of Supreme Harmony has the most imposing roof in the

Prolonging the Dynasty

At night, the Forbidden City emptied of mandarins and other royal relatives, leaving the emperor the sole mature male. During the Qing dynasty, he might have had over 120 empresses and concubines at his disposal. They were not all chosen for their beauty, but for their political ties; this perhaps explains why some emperors found their way outside the walls, in disguise, to the brothels at Qianmen.

To prolong the dynasty, there were rules for ensuring that the primary empress was impregnated. It was thought that the male life force *yang* (ie semen) was limited, while the female life force, *yin* (her bodily fluids), was inexhaustible. To build up sufficient potency to father a Son of Heaven, the emperor required a great deal of *yin*. The best way for the female life force to transfer to the emperor was for him to engage in lots of sex with his concubines without achieving an orgasm. In this way he could store up lots of *yang* for his one monthly tryst with his empress. In practice, the emperors did not always restrain themselves. Most of them found one concubine that they liked, and ended up impregnating her. Cixi, for instance, got her start this way, providing the emperor Xianfeng with his only male heir.

palace, with a horizontal ridge, four rooftrees and double eaves. The varnished ornaments are also a sign of the building's status. Its dragons, for instance, at a weight of 4.5 tonnes and a height of 3 metres (11ft), are the largest in the palace. These dragons are supposed to attract clouds and water and so protect the building from fire. Altogether, there are the figures of 10 animals on the roof, and one immortal, to serve as protection against evil spirits.

In the smallest of the three halls, the **Hall of Middle Harmony** ❻ (Zhonghedian; 中和殿), the emperor prepared for ceremonies before entering the main hall. There is an imperial palanquin on display here. The last of the three great halls, the **Hall of Preserving Harmony** ❼ (Baohedian; 保和殿), was used in the lavish New Year's banquets, as well as for examinations.

Once beyond the Hall of Preserving Harmony stairs lead down from the platform. In the middle of the stairs, along the former Imperial Way, lies a ramp hewn from a single block

of marble weighing 250 tonnes and decorated with dragon motifs.

The rear courtyards

The northern section of the Imperial Palace is entered through the **Gate of Heavenly Purity** (Qianqingmen; 乾清门), which leads to three large palaces: the Palace of Heavenly Purity, the Hall of Union and the Palace of Earthly Tranquillity. These palaces were the living and working quarters of the Ming and Qing emperors, and the scene of plots and intrigues between eunuchs and concubines in their manoeuvrings for power and influence within the court.

The **Palace of Heavenly Purity** ❽ (Qianqinggong; 乾清宫) was the bedroom of the Ming emperors, but the Qing used it for audiences with officials and foreign envoys, and also for state banquets. The inscription above the throne reads "just and honourable". The successor to the imperial throne was announced from here.

Immediately to the north is the **Hall of Union** ❾ (Jiaotaian;

ABOVE LEFT: as a court concubine, Cixi provided Xianfeng with his sole male heir. **BELOW:** the dragon and phoenix figures perched on the palace rooftops bring protection against lightning and fire. The phoenix-riding figure at the outermost tip is the son of the Dragon King – ruler of the sea, with powers over the waters.

The Golden Prison

Within the palace walls, the emperors lived a strictly controlled life with little personal freedom

It may not be obvious from a visit to the Imperial Palace that although the emperor and his court moved daily around buildings of stunning beauty, contemplated extraordinary collections of art and played in gardens beyond compare, their privileged life of luxury came at a price.

Reginald Johnston, tutor to Pu Yi, wrote: "If ever there was a palace that deserved the name of a prison, it is that palace in the Forbidden City of Peking, in which emperor Shunzhi pined for freedom, and in which the last but one of his successors, the emperor Guangxu, ended his dismal days nearly twelve years ago."

From the first, a Chinese emperor was a slave to a system built around the cult of his divine personality. His life, and the lives of his empress and concubines, were effectively not their own. From the moment they rose to the moment they went to sleep – and even while they slept – they were kept under scrutiny by attendant eunuchs, so that they never experienced any real privacy.

The emperor could not leave the confines of the palace grounds without official escort and usually not unless it was to attend an official function or to travel to another palace. Empresses and concubines led even more sheltered lives, because their sex made it impossible for them to be seen by any males outside the immediate family circle.

Days in the palace were governed by routine. Rising as early as three or four in the morning to ready themselves for official audiences, they would be bathed by eunuchs and servants who carried water from the Golden Water River. When necessary, a chamber pot was brought, placed in the corner of the room, and emptied immediately.

The young sons of the emperor, and perhaps a privileged cousin or two, spent their days in lessons with the most learned of Confucian scholars, learning Chinese language, calligraphy and the Confucian classics, the philosophy on which the civil service was based and which governed official life. This prepared them for the day when one of them would be emperor and the others his officials, who would have to accept and write imperial memorials at court. Memorials, written on scrolls, were the way in which officials from all over China communicated with the emperor.

Even when the emperor moved from one part of the palace to another, it was a major expedition involving a considerable amount of organisation. Pu Yi described a walk in the garden in his autobiography: "At the head marched a eunuch, a herald whose function was like that of a car horn. He walked twenty or thirty yards in front of the others, constantly hissing 'chi, chi' to shoo away any other people in the vicinity. He was followed by two of the higher eunuchs walking like crabs on both sides of the path... If I was carried in my palanquin, two of the younger eunuchs walked at my side, ready to attend to my wishes at any time. If I was walking, they held me under the arms to support me. Behind me followed a eunuch with a great silken canopy. He was accompanied by a great crowd of eunuchs carrying all kinds of paraphernalia..." ❑

LEFT: an audience with the emperor.

交泰殿), where imperial concubines were officially approved. Within the hall are the imperial jade seals as well as a water clock dating back to 1745. The third palace, to the rear, is the **Palace of Earthly Tranquillity ❿** (Kuninggong; 坤宁宫), the residence of the Ming empresses. The Qing rulers, following their religious traditions, also used the rear part of this hall for ritual sacrifices that entailed slaughtering pigs and cooking votive offerings. In the eastern wing is the bridal chamber of those Qing emperors who married after their accession, namely Kangxi, Tongzhi and Guangxu.

The last time the room was used for this purpose was in the winter of 1922, by the deposed last emperor Pu Yi. He later wrote: "After we had drunk the marriage cup at our wedding and eaten cakes to ensure children and children's children, we entered this dark, red chamber. I felt very uncomfortable. The bride sat on the *kang*, her head lowered. Sitting beside her, I looked about for a while and saw nothing but red: red bed curtains, red bedclothes, a red jacket, a red skirt, red flowers in her hair, a red face… everything seemed to be made of red wax. I felt most dissatisfied. I did not want to sit, but to stand was even less desirable. Yangxindiang [the Hall of Mental Cultivation] was, after all, more comfortable. I opened the door and went back to my accustomed apartments."

To the sides of the Palace of Heavenly Purity lie the **East and West Palaces**, grouped like the constellations around the pole star. Here, the emperor was the only mature adult male, surrounded by concubines, eunuchs, the empress, serving women and slaves.

The male palace servants were without exception eunuchs, therefore ensuring that after dark the emperor would be the only male capable of begetting a new generation. For many Chinese, especially for the poor, it was lucrative to enter the imperial service as a eunuch. Surgeons, called "knifers", stationed themselves at the gates to the Forbidden City. Here, they would perform castrations at "reasonable rates", but then sell the sexual organs back to the victims at

TIP

The Forbidden City's website, www.dpm.org. cn, was expanded in 2009 as part of efforts to use digital technology to bring the wonders of the Imperial Palace to the masses. The academic resources are all in Chinese, though the site is worth a visit for its interactive maps and lush photography.

ABOVE: detail on the Hall of Preserving Harmony. **BELOW:** the Hall of Middle Harmony.

ABOVE: on display in the Clock Museum, an ornate Qing-dynasty celestial globe maps the heavens. **BELOW:** the Nine Dragon Screen, made of 1,773 glazed bricks.

a high price, for the organs had to be presented in a bottle for inspection at the palace.

As eunuchs were the only people who lived permanently in the Forbidden City – and were allowed to leave and return – they became not only well informed, but also skilled at intrigue. Some of them became powerful people in their own right – and a few virtually ruled the country. Corruption was a problem amongst eunuchs; the Jesuit Matteo Ricci called them "monsters of vice".

One of the most important buildings in the palace, the **Hall of Mental Cultivation ⓫** (Yangxindiang; 养心殿) functioned as the living quarters of Emperor Qianlong (1736–96) and, a century later, the empress dowager Cixi. Pu Yi also had his private apartments here. The working, living and sleeping rooms can be seen, as can the room where Cixi received audiences while hidden behind a screen. Strict Confucian protocol required that as a

woman, and as an empress, she could not be seen by any Chinese of low birth or foreigners.

Dragons and longevity

To the southeast is the **Nine Dragon Screen ⓬** (Jiulongbi; 九龙壁), built of brightly coloured glazed bricks. The dragon is a symbol of heaven and, therefore, of the emperor, as is the number nine, the highest unit. It is no surprise that the dragon had, according to Chinese mythology, nine sons. Each of these nine dragons had different skills. Chao Feng, for instance, loves danger and is set on roofs to protect against fire – as seen in the Hall of Supreme Harmony.

Near the gate you pass through on your way to the Nine Dragon Screen there is a fascinating **Clock Museum ⓭** (Zhongbiao Guan; 钟表官; separate entrance fee payable), filled with a spectacular array of timepieces, mostly originating from Europe, which were collected by Qing emperors. As the temporal guardians of the harvest, emperors were responsible for predicting weather patterns, and were intensely interested in the scientific knowledge brought to China by the Jesuits.

Opposite the Nine Dragon Screen is the **Gate of Peace and Longevity** (Ningshoumen; 宁寿门), which leads to the **Palace of Peace and Longevity ⓮** (Ningshougong; 宁寿宫). The 18th-century emperor Qianlong had this complex built for his old age. The **Imperial Treasury ⓯** (Zhenbao Guan; 珍宝馆; separate entrance fee payable), which gives some idea of the wealth and magnificence of the Qing imperial court, is now housed in the adjoining halls to the north. On display are golden cutlery and table silver, jewellery, robes, porcelain, cloisonné, hunting equipment and golden religious objects (many of the Qing emperors were followers of Tibetan Buddhism), as well as pictures made of precious and semi-

The Real Last Emperor?

Following the forced abdication of child emperor Pu Yi by Yuan Shikai, military strongman and former courtier, the Qing dynasty was effectively over and China declared a republic. Yuan was granted presidency in place of Sun Yat-sen, who strongly opposed Yuan and insisted a new government should be centred in Nanjing. Thanks to a fabricated coup d'état, Yuan consolidated his position and a capital of the Republic of China was established in Beijing. Considering this merely a transitional phase, Yuan declared himself "Emperor of the Chinese Empire" in 1915. Faced with widespread opposition, he abdicated just three months later. Some historians argue Yuan, not Pu Yi, was the last emperor of China.

precious stones, usually depicting animals and landscapes – symbols of longevity, health and good fortune.

The northern exit

On the way to the northern exit at Shenwumen is a small well, the **Well of the Concubine Zhen** ⑯ (Zhenfeijing; 珍妃井). Rumours were reported in the Western press, and passed down by historians who had no other record, that Cixi ordered Zhen Fei to be thrown to her death down this well before the imperial family fled to Xi'an in the wake of the Boxer Rebellion. It was said that Zhen Fei, a favourite of Guangxu, had supported the emperor in his ill-fated reforms of 1898, and that she begged Cixi to let her stay with him in Beijing to continue the fight. Cixi, the story goes, disapproved, ordered Zhen Fei to be executed, and forced Guangxu to accompany her to Xian. There is, however, little evidence to support these claims, and the well in question seems too small for someone to drown in. The legend may have more to do with reports from

foreign armies entering the city, who found frightened concubines hiding in wells for fear of being raped.

Follow the red palace walls to the west. Before leaving the palace it's worth taking time to see the **Imperial Flower Garden** ⑰ (Yuhuayuan; 御花园). Laid out during the Ming period, it exemplifies the traditional Chinese skill at landscape gardening. The artificial rocks, pavilions, pines, cypresses, flowers and bamboo work together to produce a harmonious whole. This garden was the only chance for many of the people who lived in the palace to catch a glimpse of nature. The hill of rocks in the garden's northeast corner is one of the few places from which the world beyond the palace could be viewed. The imperial family climbed it each year on the Double Ninth Festival to pray for family members and friends who lived in far-off places.

Leave the Imperial Palace by way of the **Gate of the Divine Warrior** ⑱ (Shenwumen; 神武门). There is a panoramic view of the entire Forbidden City – and much of the modern city – from Jingshan (Coal Hill), across the street *(see page 150)*. ❏

ABOVE: the Forbidden City is Beijing's number-one tourist attraction.
BELOW: the Imperial Flower Garden.

SOUTHERN BEIJING

Sprawling for miles beyond ancient Qianmen Gate, this part of the city was traditionally poorer than areas further north. In the southeast is the spectacular Temple of Heaven complex, set within one of the city's largest parks

The southern area of Beijing has long been the poorer side of town, ever since the Manchu invasion of 1644 relocated the local Han Chinese here – away from the nobles and military officials who chose to reside in elegant homes further north. The streets deviate from the strict grid pattern of most of Beijing, the pavements are narrower and the drainage inferior. Yet this has been a key area of development in recent years, resulting in large-scale development and the demolition of many historic neighbourhoods. Some interesting old streets remain, as well as important historical sites including the magnificent Temple of Heaven, together with the scant remnants of the Muslim Quarter at Ox Street and Niu Jie Mosque.

The Qianmen area

Just to the south of Tiananmen Square, beyond Qianmen Gate, is the area known as **Qianmen**. This used to be one of the busiest sections of town, situated as it was close to the gates in the wall linking the Inner (Tartar) City with the Outer (Chinese) City. In earlier times, officials would leave their horses outside Qianmen or Tiananmen gates before

passing through the gates into the Forbidden City (see page 105).

To the north of Qianmen Gate was the so-called Tartar City, the spacious estates of the imperial household and tranquil temples set aside for ancestral and godly worship. To the south was the bustling mass of everyday life, where the pursuit of more earthly delights was also allowed. The brothels and opium dens of Qianmen were so renowned that Manchu officials – and even emperors in disguise – would come to sample their

LEFT: teapots on Liulichang. **RIGHT:** outside the old railway station at Qianmen.

ABOVE: name stamps, known as chops, make good souvenirs.

pleasures. The area was also famed for its opera houses – Mei Lanfang made his start in the now shuttered Guanghe Theatre in a little street just off Qianmen. Brothels are a thing of the past, at least in theory, and opera theatres are fast joining them. The area is now dominated by Qianmen Dajie, an ambitious and controversial pedestrianised shopping street done up in traditional style whose authenticity has been questioned by some. Two reproduction 1920s trams run slowly up and down its length, more popular as a photo opportunity than as a means of transport.

Named after the famous novelist, **Laoshe Teahouse** (Laoshe Chaguan; 老舍茶馆; daily 9am–10pm) on Qianmen Xidajie aims to give patrons a taste of Old Beijing with nightly performances of opera and vaudeville, traditional snacks and pricey cups of tea poured by staff bedecked in flowing gowns. It's all for the tourists, of course, but certainly entertaining.

Dazhalan and Liulichang

Dazhalan ❶ (大栅栏) is a long *hutong* heading west off Qianmen Dajie that boasts a 600-year heritage and is famous for its old shops and businesses that draw customers from the suburbs and the provinces, as well as overseas tourists. It was completely renovated before and after the Olympic Games and is now a pedestrianised zone. The name Dazhalan (often referred to as "Dashilar" in Beijing dialect) literally means "big stockades", and is an echo of Ming times when the streets were closed off at the evening curfew.

One of Dazhalan's best-known shops is the **Tongrentang Pharmacy**, which hoards secret recipes of the Qing court and is reputed to be the oldest Chinese medicine shop in the country, founded back in 1669. Tongrentang has not only survived, but flourished – it now has branches throughout China, around Asia, and even in such far-off places as London

Southwestern Beijing

and Sydney. Other famous shops include the Neiliansheng Shoe Store, the Ruifuxiang Silk and Cotton Fabrics Store and various shops specialising in tea leaves and musical instruments.

A few unrenovated side alleys remain in the more chaotic style of old, though their days are certainly numbered. Further to the west through the maze of *hutong* is **Liulichang ❷** (琉璃厂), literally meaning "glazed tile factory", a shopping street restored in the 1980s to its original style, which offers a wide range of Chinese arts and crafts with a generous helping of kitsch. Its name derives from the five kilns that were established nearby during the Ming dynasty to provide glazed tiles for the palaces and halls being built in the new Imperial Palace. During the Qing dynasty, the area was inhabited by Chinese officials serving a Manchu government who were not permitted to live in the Tartar City to the north. A thriving economy grew up around the community, catering to the mostly male officials, young men studying for their civil service exams and the many itinerant merchants who passed through here.

There are many long-established companies on Liulichang. On the eastern stretch are most of the antique (or purported antique) shops. Here you can also find the **Cathay Bookstore** (at No. 115), with its collection of old books, while **Yidege** (No. 67) has been selling artists' and calligraphers' supplies since 1865. **Daiyuexuan** (No. 73) is the place to go for quality paintbrushes, which it has been selling since 1916. The western branch of the street has bookshops and art galleries as well as more calligraphic supplies.

A short distance to the north is the **Zhengyici Beijing Opera Theatre** (Zhengyici Xilou; 正乙祠戏楼), the oldest Beijing Opera theatre constructed entirely of wood. It was built in the 18th century and has hosted many opera masters, including Mei Lanfang, but was later converted into a hotel, which eventually closed in 1949. Through much effort, the theatre finally reopened in 1995. It can seat 150 people.

The **Huguang Guild Hall ❸** (Huguang Huiguan; 湖广会馆) on Hufang Lu near the western

> *Loo-le-chang appeared to be the 'Pasternoster Row' of Peking. The street is nearly a mile in length, and almost every shop in it is a bookseller's.*
>
> Robert Fortune, 1863

BELOW: traditional shops on Liulichang.

Daguanlou Cinema

Opened in 1903, Daguanlou is the oldest operating cinema in the world. Originally a teahouse that put on opera performances, the venue started to show foreign short films between acts on a piece of suspended white cloth. The forward-thinking owner shot China's first movie, *Dingjun Shan*, an adaptation of a well-known Beijing Opera, when these imports started to lose their novelty. The film, starring "King of Beijing Opera" Tan Xinpei, was a huge success. Daguanlou remains on the frontline in the fight between domestic movies and stiff foreign competition, though a remake of *Dingjun Shan*, starring the great grandson of the original actor, can still be viewed here. See page 267.

ABOVE: Beijing Opera at the Liyuan Theatre.

end of Liulichang was, along with Zhengyici, considered one of Beijing's "Four Great Theatres" in its heyday and is one of the best place to see opera in the city. There is also a small museum on site.

Alternatively, a few minutes' walk south, the **Liyuan Theatre** (Liyuan Juchang; 梨园剧场) at the Qianmen Hotel has performances every evening. *For more on opera, see pages 88–9, and for venues see page 267.*

Hidden away in Dazhiqiao Hutong off Xuanwumenwai Dajie is the **Yang Memorial Temple** ❹ (杨椒山祠), built to commemorate Ming-dynasty official and would-be reformer Yang Jiaoshan. In 1895, six scholars met here before presenting Emperor Guangxu with their own blueprints for reform. Like Yang Jiaoshan before them, they were executed for their ambitions *(see panel, page 132)*. Today the small temple is somewhat neglected but serves as an interesting stop within a warren of narrow, unrestored *hutong*.

After the founding of the People's Republic in 1949, prostitution was officially abolished. Some 3,000 troops marched into the area south of Qianmen on 21 November and shut down more than 200 brothels.

South Cathedral ❺

Address: 141 Qianmen Xidajie
Tel: 6602-6538
Opening Hrs: daily 6am – 4pm
Entrance Fee: free
Transport: Xuanwumen subway station (lines 2 & 4)

A few hundred metres west, across Xuanwumen Dongdajie, is Beijing's oldest extant church, **South Cathedral** (Nantang; 南堂; daily). The church was established in the late Ming and early Qing periods, when Christianity began to establish itself with the arrival of Matteo Ricci (1552–1610) and Johann Adam Schall von Bell (1592–1666). Schall von Bell was responsible for the original structure which burned down in 1775. Money from Emperor Qianlong helped to rebuild it, but it was later destroyed by the xenophobic Boxers in 1900.

The spires of the missionary churches that seemed so breathtaking to Westerners were considered to be bad feng shui by the Chinese, and blamed for many current evils. It did not take much to encourage people to destroy the foreign building that was held responsible for the bad harvests of the previous few years. The current structure dates from 1904, but this in turn was heavily damaged during the Cultural Revolution. The building has been open to the faithful again since the early 1980s.

The cathedral also serves as the seat of the Chinese Catholic Patriotic Association, founded by the government in 1957 as a means of co-opting Catholics while at the same time attempting to give the appearance of religious freedom. The Association does not recognise the authority of the Pope, and Catholics who remain true to the papacy have to practise their religion in secret.

Niu Jie Mosque ❻

Address: 18 Niu Jie, Xuanwu District
Tel: 6353-2564
Opening Hrs: daily 8am–4pm
Entrance Fee: charge
Transport: Caishikou subway station (line 4)

The largest concentration of Muslims in Beijing – an estimated 10,000 or more – live along **Niu Jie** and in its many little side streets and *hutong*. The street's name – which translates as "Ox Street" – is often said to indicate an association with the Hui (Chinese Muslim; *see panel, below*) community, but is in fact a corruption of an earlier name, Liu Jie, which derived from the presence of a pomegranate orchard in the vicinity. The Niu Jie area has been rebuilt recently and looks similar to other Beijing neighbourhoods, but a careful eye can still pick out Hui shops and schools, signs of the community's unique Muslim background.

The focal point of the community, the **Niu Jie Mosque** (Niu Jie Qingzhensi; 牛街清真寺), with its curved eaves and colourfully painted support and cross beams, looks more like a Chinese temple than a Muslim place of worship – in common with all mosques in the city, there is no dome and no minaret. Instead, it follows the Chinese palace style, with main and side buildings laid out symmetrically, and roofs of glazed tiles; roof arches and posts are often adorned with texts from the Koran

牛街礼拜寺
Niujie Mosque

ABOVE: the Niu Jie Mosque is the centre of the city's Muslim community. **BELOW:** Beijing's Hui Muslim population is mainly concentrated in the south of the city.

Beijing's Muslims

There are more than 200,000 ethnic Chinese Muslims living in Beijing today. Known as the Hui minority, they number around 6 million across China. Many of them are no longer orthodox Muslims, but, whether believers or not, they share one custom important to all Muslims: they don't eat pork. For this reason, there are in Beijing, as in many other Chinese cities, Huimin Fandian, or Hui restaurants, in which ritual-clean hands prepare snacks and meals, substituting mutton for pork. The Hui can be distinguished from non-Muslim Chinese by their white skullcaps, while many Hui men sport long beards. They speak Mandarin Chinese. There are also several thousand Uighur Muslims in the capital – *see page 67*.

TIP

The Niu Jie Mosque is open to non-Muslims (including women), but it is important to dress respectfully – no shorts or sleeveless tops. The prayer hall is closed to non-Muslims.

or other Islamic motifs. Also unusually for a mosque, there is a shop inside the complex, selling necklaces and teapots as well as copies of the Koran.

The mosque dates all the way back to the 10th century, and was built in the style of a Buddhist temple, after the Islamic faith had spread into China during the Tang dynasty (618–907). Right behind the main entrance is a hexagonal building, the **Tower for Observing the Moon** (Wangyuelou; 望月楼). Every year, at the beginning and at the end of the fasting month of Ramadan, the imam climbs the tower to observe the waxing and waning of the moon and to determine the exact length of the period of fasting.

Beyond the tower is the main prayer hall. This is where the faithful come for religious ceremonies, after ritually cleansing themselves in the washrooms. Like all mosque prayer halls, this one has no adornment or pictures inside. There is a sign requesting people not to enter the hall unless they are Muslim. Since Islamic tradition dictates that Mus-

lims have to pray facing Mecca, the front of the hall faces west. Beyond the prayer hall are a few smaller religious buildings and steles. In the little courtyard garden that runs east is the tombstone – with an Arabic inscription – of the founder of the mosque. During the Cultural Revolution, the faithful managed to save this by burying it next to the wall.

With state support, the mosque was restored in the 1990s, and it is once more a meeting place for Muslims. Many Hui children also come here to study the Koran. Other regulars here include the staff of the embassies of Islamic countries, and the local Uighur community.

Fayuansi ❼

Address: 7 Fayuansi Qianjie
Tel: 6317-2150
Opening Hrs: Mon–Tue, Thur–Sat 8.30am–4pm
Entrance Fee: charge
Transport: Caishikou subway station (line 4)

Just to the east of Niu Jie Mosque, on Fayuansi Qianjie (a *hutong* leading off Niu Jie), is what is thought

BELOW RIGHT:
Buddhist monks at Fayuansi.

Buddhist Academy

The Buddhist Academy at Fayuansi is China's most prestigious and accepts only one out of every four applicants who pass tests in Buddhism, Chinese, politics, English and scripture. Once accepted, a young novice will be educated in Buddhist theory and history and required to take courses in philosophy, Chinese history, politics, writing and foreign languages. Elective courses include tea ceremony, calligraphy, music, art, computers and law. While this curriculum may sound rather worldly for a monk, the fact is that Chinese Buddhist monks do not live in isolation – many have cellphones, email addresses and even websites. Those with high positions in their temples also have cars and drivers. Upon finishing their studies, most monks either stay on for further cultivation, become abbots at local temples or pursue further studies abroad. Unfortunately, those who leave tend not to return, and school leaders complain of a Buddhist brain drain.

Buddhism has become China's most popular religion, with an estimated 100 million practitioners, and some classes are reporting four-fold increases in applications. Its popularity is often seen as a reaction to increasing material wealth.

to be the oldest temple in the Inner City, **Fayuansi** (Temple of the Source of Buddhist Teaching; 法源寺). It was built on the orders of the Tang emperor Li Shimin, in honour of soldiers killed in battle in the unsuccessful Korean campaign, and took over 40 years to construct before finally being completed in 696. Almost the entire structure has been renewed over the centuries, although the front courtyard contains ancient pine trees from the Tang dynasty, and the drum and bell towers are flanked by cypresses from the Song.

The temple houses the **Buddhist Academy** (*see panel, opposite*), formed in 1956 by the Chinese Buddhist Society. The academy is devoted to the teaching and study of Buddhism, and trains young monks for four to five years before they can enter other monasteries in China. There is also an extensive library with over 100,000 volumes.

The large complex has six halls. Enter through **Shanmen** (Mountain Gate; 山门), guarded by two stone lions. In the first temple courtyard, two bronze lions guard the **Hall of the Celestial Kings** (Tianwangdian; 天王殿). The Celestial Kings rule the four points of the compass and can keep away all evil spirits and the enemies of Buddhism. Enthroned in the middle of the hall is a Milefo, a laughing, fat-bellied Buddha, who encourages the faithful to "come in, follow me on the way to release in nirvana".

Such Milefo Buddhas represent Maitreya, the Buddha of the Future. They can be seen at the entrance to almost all Chinese Buddhist temples, and are always flanked by the four Celestial Kings. These five statues are Ming-dynasty bronzes, a rarity in Chinese Buddhist temples.

Behind the Milefo Buddha is the Guardian of Buddhism, with his face turned to the main hall of the temple, the **Hall of Heroes** (Daxiongbaodian; 大雄宝殿). This is reached by leaving the first hall and crossing a garden

ABOVE LEFT: incense burners are a feature of Buddhist and Daoist temples. **ABOVE:** the Hall of the Celestial Kings at Fayuansi. **BELOW:** a dragon guards one of the Fayuansi halls.

ABOVE: Daoist priests sometimes earn extra income as fortune-tellers, as here outside Baiyunguan Temple.
BELOW RIGHT: certain animals are linked with Daoist deities; touching the donkey at Baiyunguan brings good health.

with a bronze cauldron and stone steles. Within the hall is a Buddha flanked by two Bodhisattvas and surrounded by 18 Luohan, or saints, the lowest rank in the Buddhist divine hierarchy.

Leaving the main hall, you will pass a small hall with stone tablets and come to the **Hall of a Thousand Buddhas**. Here, on a stone base, is a 5-metre (15ft) high sculpture dating back to the Ming dynasty, showing the Buddhas of the five points of the compass; towering over all of them is the Dharma Buddha.

In the last hall there is a Reclining Buddha and an exhibition of Buddhist sculpture, with some pieces dating back to the Han dynasty. A splendid Guanyin Bodhisattva with 1,000 arms is also on display.

Baiyunguan ❽

Address: 6 Baiyunguan Jie, Xuanwu District
Tel: 6617-6164
Opening Hrs: daily 8.30am–4.30pm
Entrance Fee: charge
Transport: Muxidi subway station (line 1)

To the northwest of Fayuansi, in an unpromising area dominated by thundering traffic and tower blocks, is one of the few Daoist temples left in Beijing, **Baiyunguan** (Temple of the White Cloud; 白云观). Used as a factory during the Cultural Revolution, the temple was restored to its original purpose and today is a thriving centre for China's only indigenous religion, popular with pilgrims and home to around 35 monks – easily identified by their white stockings and top-knotted hair.

The temple site dates from the Tang dynasty (although the building itself dates from the Ming) and is the centre of the Daoist Dragon Gate sect. Daoist temples on the grand scale were not built until the Yuan dynasty and the reign of Kublai Khan, who appointed a priest named Qiu Chuji as "National Teacher"; Qiu took up residence in the temple, and from that time on Baiyunguan has been the centre of Daoism in northern China (the other principal Daoist centre in Beijing is Dongyue Temple, in the east of the city, *see page 173*).

The complex contains several

Caishikou Execution Ground

The old execution ground at Caishikou (south of the Yang Memorial Temple) has a blood-soaked history of beheadings, gruesome punishment and ghost stories. It was also the stage for one of the most important events in modern Chinese history. In 1895, six Confucian scholars presented Emperor Guangxu an ambitious plan for modernisation that included political and social reform. Guangxu sought to implement the Hundred Days Reforms with edicts covering a move away from Confucian examinations, staid bureaucracy and absolute monarchy. Empress Dowager Cixi – then de facto ruler – promptly ordered Guangxu's imprisonment and the six were executed soon after at Caishikou in September 1898. The failure of the Qing to accept reform is seen as the cause of imperial China's downfall.

The hurried beheadings of the would-be reformers could have been worse, however. Written and photographic records detail a far more unpleasant penalty practised at Caishikou known as the "lingering death" or "death by a thousand cuts". The unfortunate convict would be bound and have portions of flesh from the torso and limbs methodically sliced off before his eventual death and dismemberment.

Baiyunguan is well endowed with English signage which explains each of these.

In the centre of the furthest courtyard is the **Hall of the Four Celestial Emperors**, and on its upper floor is the **Hall of the Three Purities**. Daoist manuscripts are kept here in a compendium similar to those found in Buddhist temples. In a hall off one of the side courtyards of the western section there are old bronze guardian figures, and in a building behind this are 60 relatively new figures of Daoist divinities, each one appointed to a year of the traditional 60-year Chinese calendar. Visitors can find their personal Daoist divinities according to this calendar. The Daoist priests who reside here will be pleased to help.

Daoist temples use obvious symbolic motifs more frequently in their decoration than Buddhist temples. Common designs include the Lingzhi mushroom (which is supposed to prolong life), Daoist immortals, cranes and the eight trigrams from the *Book of Changes* (more commonly known in the West as the *I Ching*).

LEFT: the hexagonal pagoda at Tianning Si.
ABOVE: throwing coins at the central bell brings good luck at Baiyunguan.
BELOW: *pailou* gateway at Baiyunguan Temple.

courtyards, the overall design being similar to Buddhist temples in that it faces south and its structures lie one behind the other along a straight line. Pass through the entrance gate into the first courtyard; the main attraction here is the pair of gong-like copper coins with a bell in the centre suspended on strings. The idea is to throw (normal-sized) coins from the bridge – hitting the bell means good luck. As Chinese currency is almost exclusively in paper form, you must buy a bag of "coins" from the nearby kiosk. Other ways to bring luck involve touching animal motifs and figures – the stone monkey at the entrance gate, or the bronze donkey in a western courtyard – or rubbing the belly on the large bronze statue of Wen Cheng, the scholar-deity in one of the western courtyards.

There are several halls spread around the large complex, each dedicated to a different deity or group of deities, concerned with everything from health to wealth. Unusually,

Tianning Si ⑨
Address: Guang'anmen, Xuanwu District
Tel: 6343-2507
Opening Hrs: daily 9am–4pm
Entrance Fee: free
Transport: Changchunjie subway station (line 2)

A short distance to the south of Baiyunguan is **Tianning Si** (Temple of Heavenly Tranquillity; 天宁寺), thought to be the oldest building in Beijing. All that remains of the original building is the spectacular 58-metre (190ft) hexagonal pagoda. This was one of the few tall buildings in the city at the time it was built in the 12th century, towards the end of the Liao dynasty – of which its style is thought to be typical. It now peers out from behind a threatening overpass, tower blocks and smokestacks.

The pagoda rises in 13 storeys from a richly decorated podium that symbolises the mountain of the gods, Sumeru. The first level has windows and doors but is otherwise unadorned. The temple was comprehensively restored in 2004.

ABOVE: an urn for burning incense at the Temple of Heaven.
RIGHT: guards at the Temple of Heaven wear Qing-dynasty attire on certain occasions.
BELOW: Chengzhen Gate at the Temple of Heaven.

Taoranting Park
South of Fayuansi and close to the Second Ring Road is the pleasant open space of **Taoranting Gong-yuan** ⑩ (Happy Pavilion Park; 陶

然亭), with the **Temple of Mercy**, dating from the Yuan dynasty, close to its southern gate. In 1695 a three-room wing west of the old temple was built, from which the park gets its name. Li Dazhao, co-founder of the Chinese Communist Party, rented one of these rooms while he was in Beijing working to further the revolution, and held many meetings here. Nearby are two *pailou* (gates of honour) which once stood on Chang'an Jie. In the past, Taoranting Park was one of the few open spaces open to common people who did not have access to the imperial parks. The boating lake and swimming pool are very popular in the summer.

The Temple of Heaven ⓫

Address: Yongdingmen Dajie
Tel: 6702-8866
Opening Hrs: park daily 6am–9pm all year; temple complex daily 8am–5.30pm
Entrance Fee: charge. It's best to buy an all-inclusive ticket *(tao piao)*, although if you only wish to visit the park then a separate, much cheaper, ticket is available
Transport: Tiantan Dongmen subway station (line 5)

The spectacular **Temple of Heaven** (Tiantan; 天坛) complex is set in the middle of one of the city's most visited parks, popular with Beijing residents, Chinese tourists and foreigners alike.

It is easy to get here from the city centre by bus or by taxi, and the park can be entered through several gates. The buildings are divided into two main groups: northern and southern. The northern group, built to a semi-circular layout representing Heaven, gathers around one of the most impressive – and famous – buildings in China, the Hall of Prayer for Good Harvests. The southern group, meanwhile, has a square layout that symbolises Earth.

The sizeable park surrounding the ancient buildings is a favourite place for locals to practice t'ai chi and various other forms of exercise. It is also very popular with men wielding traditional Chinese musical instruments, or playing dominoes or Go – it's all very picturesque, and not just a show for the tourists. Come early in the morning before the tour groups arrive.

A place of ritual

Built in 1420, the Temple of Heaven served as a place of ritual for Ming and Qing emperors. Every year at the time of the winter solstice the emperor would come here in a magnificent procession lasting several days, in order to honour his ancestors and to pray for a good harvest in the season to come. In the middle of the first lunar calendar month, the emperor prayed once more in the Temple of Heaven, this time in the Hall of Prayer for Good Harvests. This ceremony was last carried out in 1914 by the self-proclaimed emperor Yuan Shikai.

The observation of such ritual was more than a mere formality. The sacred nature of the emperor's

When lightning destroyed the Hall of Prayer for Good Harvests in 1889, officials were blamed for having allowed a caterpillar to ascend the holy structure and incur the wrath of Heaven. More than 30 were executed.

BELOW: the park is popular with musicians.

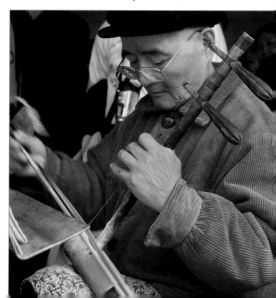

rule had been established in the 3rd century BC: as the Son of Heaven, he administered heavenly authority on earth. According to the Chinese, natural catastrophes, bad farming practices, failing harvests and increasing corruption were all signs that the emperor had lost the favour of Heaven and of his ancestors. In such circumstances, it was considered a legitimate act to overthrow him. The sacrificial rites in the Temple of Heaven were therefore treated with the utmost reverence by the ever-wary emperor.

The Hall of Heaven and the Echo Wall

The procession for the winter solstice began at Qianmen Gate at the southern edge of the Forbidden City. When it arrived at the Temple of Heaven the emperor changed his robes in the **Hall of Heaven A** (Huangqiongyu; 皇穹宇). Built in 1530 and restored in 1730, this hall

has a round, pointed roof with a golden spire. The ancestor tablets of the emperors were stored inside (the spirit of the ancestor was thought to be present in the tablet during the ceremony).

A brick wall surrounding the courtyard of the Hall of Heaven has become famous as the **Echo Wall B** (Huiyin Bi; 回音壁). If you stand facing the wall and speak to someone who is also standing by it, he or she will be able to hear every word at every point anywhere along the wall. Of course, it is necessary to wait until only a few people are present, which, unfortunately, is very rarely the case.

The three stone slabs in front of the stairs to the main temple are the Echo Stones (Sanyinshi), which produce another peculiar effect. If you stand on the first slab and clap your hands, you will hear a single echo. On the second step you will hear a double echo, and on the third, a triple. The secret of this ingenious

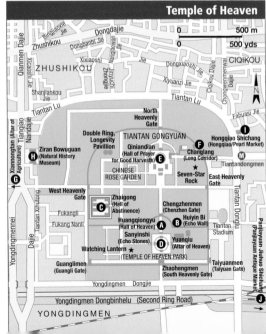

Temple of Heaven

phenomenon has to do with the different distances at which each stone slab is placed from the wall. Again it's practically impossible to witness the acoustics because every other visitor is trying the same thing.

The Hall of Abstinence and Altar of Heaven

Before the winter solstice ritual, the emperor would fast in the **Hall of Abstinence** ❻ (Zhaigong; 斋宫), which stands in the west of the temple complex. Then, by the first rays of the sun on the day of the solstice, he would offer sacrifices and prayers at the **Altar of Heaven** ❼ (Yuanqiu; 圆球). This is the most spectacular of the city's eight imperial altars (Xiannongtan, Ritan and Ditan are others), consisting of a stone terrace of three levels surrounded by two walls – an inner round one and an outer square one. The lowest level symbolises the Earth, the second, the world of human beings, and the last, Heaven. The altar is built from stone slabs,

and its construction is based on the number nine and its multiples.

In earlier times, odd numbers were considered the attribute of Heaven (*yang*). Nine, as the highest odd unit, was the most important number of all, and therefore became associated with the emperor. The innermost circle on the top level consists of nine slabs, the second of 18, the third of 27 and so on until the final ring on the lowest level, which, as the 27th circle, contains 243 slabs.

Here another odd sound effect can be heard. If you stand in the middle of the upper level on the round stone slab and speak in a normal voice, your voice is heard more loudly than those of any other people around you. This effect is caused by the echo retained by the balustrades, and by a hollow space within the stone slab that functions as a resonating cavity. This stone in the centre was considered by the Chinese to be the most holy place in the Chinese empire, indeed the centre of the Earth.

LEFT & ABOVE:
the magnificent Hall of Prayer for Good Harvests.

TIP

Entering the park by the southern entrance you will approach the Hall of Prayer for Good Harvests via the Danbi Bridge, the route the emperor would take to "step up to Heaven". To access the south gate, take bus 958 from Tiantan Dongmen subway station.

SHOPPING

Dazhalan

Beijing's time-honoured brands have weathered the gentrification of this venerable street, and some small shops are testing the water offering gifts and crafts to tourists.

Made in Paradise
天堂制造
41 Dazhalan Jie.
Tel: 6303-7218. p288, A2
Silver rings and pendants, sparkly bangles, dyed bags and tapestries are made by the owner's family to cater for the trend in all things Tibetan.

Qianxiangyi 谦祥益
50 Dazhalan Xijie.
Tel: 6301-6658. p288, A2
Established in 1840, Qianxiangyi is a silk buyer's paradise with a huge selection of bolts sold by the metre, plus shirts, pyjamas and tapestries on the second floor.

Liulichang

Cathay Bookshop
中国书店
57 Liulichang Xijie.
Tel: 6303-2104. p291, E2
A famous bookstore of interest for its books on Chinese art and calligraphy, as well as antiquarian tomes, maps and photographs.

Markets

Beijing Curio City
北京古玩城
21 Dongsanhuan Nanlu.
Tel: 6774-7711. p289, E4
Just south of Panjiayuan, this four-storey complex houses a huge range of antiques, reproductions, kitsch and curios.

Hongqiao Market (Pearl Market) 红桥市场
44 Hongqiao Lu.
Tel: 6713-3354. p288, C3
Clothes, shoes, watches and fake designer goods are sold on the first and second floors; antiques, silk and – emphatically – pearls on the second and third. China supplies 95 percent of the world market of cultured freshwater pearls, and most vendors come from families that produce them. They can talk you through their products and string pearls to order. Careless shoppers still face the risk of walking away with painted beads, however.

Panjiayuan Antique Market 潘家园旧货市场
South of Panjiayuan Bridge.
Tel: 6775-2405. p289, E4
Most of the "antiques" in this huge market are reproductions, but interesting purchases can still be picked up from hundreds of shops and stalls packed with paintings, porcelain, silk items, Cultural Revolution memorabilia, ethnic clothing, books and souvenirs. A flea market is held at weekends, adding to the treasure-hunt appeal of a visit. Bargain hard in the knowledge that other

stalls probably offer the same "unique" items.

Qianmen Pedestrian Street

High rents kept many small businesses away from this central shopping street in its opening months, leaving international brands to fill up the empty outlets.

H&M
72–82 Qianmen Dajie.
Tel: 6706-0508. p288, A2
Simple, stylish and moderately priced clothes from the Swedish retailer. This expansive flagship store offers the full collection, with jeans from Rmb 300 and T-shirts from Rmb 100.

Zara
54–6 Qianmen Dajie.
Tel: 6701-7060. p288, A2
The Spanish fashion success story is taking over Beijing. The Qianmen branch supplies mainly women's clothes and shoes with a smaller section for men and children.

LEFT & ABOVE: Hongqiao Pearl Market.

The Hall of Prayer for Good Harvests

Walk along the central causeway that links the southern and northern buildings to reach the most striking building of the Temple of Heaven complex, the **Hall of Prayer for Good Harvests** ❺ (Qiniandian; 祈年殿). First constructed in 1420, the hall was struck by lightning in 1889 and burned to the ground. It was rebuilt according to the original plans.

The structure is built on a three-level marble terrace, each level surrounded by a balustrade. The pointed roof, with its three levels, its 50,000 blue-glazed tiles – blue symbolises heaven – and its golden point, was constructed without using a single nail and has no spars or beams. It is supported by 28 pillars made of wood from the southwestern province of Yunnan. The central four, the **Dragon Fountain Pillars**, are almost 20 metres (66ft) tall and represent the four seasons. The first ring of pillars surrounding them represents the 12 months; the outer ring, also of 12 pillars, the 12 divisions of the day. In the centre of the floor is a marble plaque with veining showing a dragon and a phoenix (symbolising the emperor and the empress).

To the east are more imperial buildings and the **Long Corridor** ❻ (Changlang; 长廊), a favoured spot for elderly musicians. This can be accessed with a simple "park only" ticket.

West of the park

Leave the Temple of Heaven via the west gate, and follow Tianqiao Nandajie. Before 1949, this was a meeting place of acrobats, fortune-tellers, sellers of miraculous elixirs, and other shady characters. Even today, the markets around here bustle

ABOVE LEFT: a tour group in Tiantan Park. **ABOVE:** Panjiayuan market is one of the best places in Beijing to look for scroll paintings, lacquerware, silk items such as cushion covers, and all kinds of interesting odds and ends. **BELOW LEFT:** dancing at the Long Corridor in the Temple of Heaven park. **BELOW:** animatronic dinosaurs at the Natural History Museum.

with life, and the residents of this district are considered a separate breed.

A sports park on this street marks the site of the **Altar of Agriculture** (Xiannongtan; 先农坛; daily 9am–5pm; entrance fee), which stood symmetrically opposite the Temple of Heaven and was dedicated to the legendary emperor Shennong, the "first farmer" in China. This was one of the eight altars which, in addition to the Temple of Heaven, were central to the ritual life of Ming and Qing emperors. Parts of the site have been demolished or converted in recent times, but some old structures survive intact, notably the Hall of Jupiter, now housing the instructive **Museum of Ancient Architecture** (Gudai Jianzhu Bowuguan; 古代建筑博物馆; daily 9am–4pm; entrance fee). The museum houses a large model of Old Beijing and actual fragments of buildings long since demolished, and is notable for extensive English descriptions of exhibits.

ABOVE & BELOW: all kinds of odd items are on sale at Panjiayuan Antique Market.

Natural History Museum

Address: 126 Tianqiao Nandajie
Tel: 6702-4431

Opening Hrs: daily 8.30am–5pm
Entrance Fee: charge
Transport: Bus 20 from Qianmen subway station (line 2).
200-metre/yd walk from Temple of Heaven's west gate

Beijing's **Natural History Museum** (Ziran Bowuguan; 自然博物馆) is in an ivy-clad building just to the west of the Temple of Heaven. The museum has an exhibition of more than 5,000 species in palaeontology, zoology and botany, but captions are in Chinese only. It has a number of dinosaurs: in the centre of the hall is the skeleton of the one-horned Qingdaosaurus. The skeleton of Mamenchisaurus, twice the size, was dug up in the village of Mamenxi in Sichuan province. In contrast to these giants, there are the remains of a Lufengsaurus – 2 metres (6½ft) high and 6 metres (20ft) long – from Yunnan province, and of a parrot-beaked dinosaur that was no bigger than a cat. There is also an entertaining collection of animatronic dinosaurs in the poorly lit basement, which growl and bellow at passers-by, sometimes in Mandarin, and several gruesomely preserved human cadavers on the third floor.

East and south

Just across the street from the Temple of Heaven's east gate and reached via a footbridge across the busy road is an ugly twin-towered building housing **Hongqiao Market** (Hongqiao Shichang; 红桥市场), also called the Pearl Market, which continues to draw busloads of tourists seeking cheap knick-knacks.

About 4km (2½ miles) further east, past Longtan Park and close to the Third Ring Road, is **Panjiayuan Antique Market** (Panjiayuan Jiuhuo Shichang; 潘家园旧货市场;), a sprawling collection of shops and stalls selling antiques and curios – a sight, and cacophony, without equal in the capital. *For more on both markets, see page 138.* ❑

BEST RESTAURANTS, BARS AND CAFÉS

Restaurants

Beijing/Chinese

Fengzeyuan 丰泽园
83 Zhushikou Xi Dajie.
Tel: 6318-6688. Open:
11am–2pm, 5–9pm. **$$$**
8 p288, A3
With a long and glittering
history - top Communist
brass dined here in the
1950s – Fengzeyuan
serves up sure-fire
Shandong cuisine, nota-
bly sea cucumber and
sautéed fish.

Jinyang 晋阳饭庄
24 Zhushikou Xi Dajie. Tel:
6303-1669. Open: 10am–
10pm. **$$** **9** p288, A3
Besides a full range of
noodles, the staple of
Shanxi cuisine, Jinyang
serves a signature duck
dish which is steamed
and then baked – popular
with those who may find
Peking Duck too greasy.

Old Beijing Noodle
老北京炸酱面大王
29 Chongwenmen Dajie.
Tel: 6705-6705. Open:
11am–2.30pm, 5–9pm. **$**
10 p288, C3
This restaurant has
revived the lively tradition

Prices are for a typical
dinner for one (three
dishes with beer in
Chinese restaurants, or
a three-course meal
with a half-bottle of
house wine in Western-
style restaurants).

$ = under Rmb 50
$$ = Rmb 50–100
$$$ = Rmb 100–200
$$$$ = over Rmb 200

of (old-style) Beijing fast
food with hand-pulled
noodles and other afford-
able dishes in a rowdy
atmosphere. *Zhajiang
mian*, noodles served
with soybean paste and
vegetables, are Beijing's
most famous.

European

Capital M
2 Qianmen Pedestrian
Street. Tel: 6702-2727.
www.capital-m-beijing.com
Open: 11.30am–10.30pm.
$$$$ **11** p288, A2
The sister restaurant to
Shanghai's famous M on
the Bund. The Qianmen
location affords impres-
sive terrace views across
Tiananmen Square to
match the glamorous
interior and fine continental dining. Afternoon tea
served from 2–5pm.

Maxim's de Paris
2 Chongwenmen Xi Dajie.
Tel: 6512-1992. Open:
11am–2pm, 5–10pm. **$$$$**
12 p288, C2
Beijing's first joint-venture
restaurant is now past its
prime, though the sheer
size and opulence still
make it worth a visit for
classic French cuisine.

Huimin (Muslim)

Lao Ciqikou Bean Juice
老磁器口豆汁店
Opposite Temple of Heaven
north gate. Tel: 6703-5725.
Open: 6.30am–7.30pm. **$**
13 p288, B3
Authentic snacks from
Beijing's Hui minority

including halal meat and
the increasingly rare
douzhi, a fermented mung
bean juice beloved by
Beijingers that can be per-
plexing to the uninitiated.

Peking Duck

Liqun Roast Duck
利群烤鸭店
11 Beixiangfeng. Tel: 6705-
5578. Open: 11.30am–
1.30pm, 4.30–10pm. **$$$**
14 p288, B2
Hidden away in the
labyrinth of *hutong* east
of Qianmen, this atmos-
pheric family-run eatery
turns out crispy ducks to
packed tables of diners
for whom an immaculate
environment is not a
concern. Reserving a
table, and a duck ahead
of time, is advised.

Quanjude 全聚德
32 Qianmen Dajie.
Tel: 6701-1379. Open:
11am–2pm, 4.30–9pm.
14 Qianmen Xi Dajie.
Tel: 6302-3062. Open same
hours. **$$$** **15** p288, A2
www.wfjquanjude.com.cn
The first Quanjude
opened its doors in 1852.
It continues to serve
Beijing's most famous,
and some say overrated,
roast duck at several
palatial branches around
the city. Judge for yourself
if this Beijing institution
deserves all the hype.

Vegetarian

Bodhi-Sake
菩提缘素食斋
10–16 Heiyaochang Jie. Tel:

Bars

The Jialana Bar
嘉兰娜酒吧
175 Yongan Lu, Xuanwu
District. Tel: 6318-7748.
1 p288, A3
Simple food and drinks
are served at this quiet
bar.

Eveni Wine Club
品酒会所
Eveni, 16 Zhushikou Dong
Dajie. Tel: 6701-6256. **2**
p288, B3
Offering wine to enjoy
with a spot of foot
massage. Free wine
tastings.

6354-
2889. www.3puti.com
Open: 10am–9.30pm. **$$$**
16 p291, E4
This renovated ancient
nunnery serves unpreten-
tious but delectable
monastic vegetarian food
(thus excluding onion and
garlic) such as Tibetan
grilled mushrooms and
imitation meat to rival the
real thing. The serene
courtyard setting is the
perfect antidote to the
hectic city outside.

Jubao Yuan 聚宝源
1 Niu Jie Xili. Tel: 8354-
5602. Open: 11am–10pm.
$$ **17** p291, D3
Well located for visitors to
the Muslim district, this
hotpot restaurant keeps
things simple with old-
fashioned charcoal-
heated metal pots and a
variety of high-quality
meat dishes.

BEIJING'S PARK LIFE

From first light, Beijingers begin to fill parks, pavements, alleys, grass verges and any space large enough to swing a leg or bat a shuttlecock. It's a fascinating spectacle

Walk along any Beijing street early in the morning, and you will see old men shuffle out of their homes to escape the chaos of their tiny apartments. In their hands are birdcages, which they swing back and forth as they make their way to the nearest park, where they join people of all ages enjoying a wide variety of activities.

Stroll through one of the larger parks, such as Longtan, Tiantan or Ditan, and watch the fascinating mixture of martial arts, breathing exercises, Beijing Opera, calligraphy, ballroom dancing, *Yang Ge* dancing, badminton, jogging, hanging from trees, shouting exercises, meditation, kite-flying and, the newest addition, walking the dog. T'ai chi shadow boxers draw the eye with slow, flowing movements as they practise "monkey's retreat" or "send the tiger over the mountain".

As the exercisers disperse, elderly people spread out chessboards, mah-jong tiles, dominoes or playing cards. Spectators roll jangling steel balls around their hands, a practice said to prevent rheumatism.

By the time of the rush hour, the parks have regained a little of their tranquillity – until the onslaught of lunchbreakers arrives on the scene to break the quiet once more.

BELOW: qigong in Beihai Park. Practitioners use slow, precise breathing to focus their strength.

ABOVE: ballroom dancing is popular with older citizens.
BELOW: the Chinese are world-beaters at table-tennis.

MUSICIANS IN THE PARK

It's not all limb-stretching in the parks of Beijing. In Temple of Heaven Park, aficionados of folk music and traditional Han music gather with their instruments to practise their skills (and earn a few *kuai* from passing tourists).

In keeping with the Confucian ideals of moderation and harmony, musicians keep it simple, playing variations on a single melodic line. The instruments, which have changed little over the centuries, range from the *erhu* (a simple, two-stringed fiddle) and the *zheng* (zither) to the *pipa* (four-stringed lute) and *dizi* (wooden flute).

With the advent of recent Western influences on China, traditional music has taken a back seat to pop and rock music. The latter, which developed as a youthful expression of protest, was outlawed until the late 1980s, when an official ban was reluctantly lifted by the authorities. Pop anthems are today the mainstay of the music scene. Still, it isn't hard to track down the traditional strains of Chinese music – either at formal performances in the Beijing Concert Hall (Beixinhua Jie, just south of Beihai Park) or at casual gatherings in Temple of Heaven Park.

ABOVE: communal exercises, a common early-morning sight in parks across the city.

ABOVE: Yangge folk dancing in Beihai Park.
RIGHT: keep-fit equipment in Ditan Park.

ABOVE: water calligraphy is thought to stimulate mind and body. The characters are usually painted with plain water, with the result that the fine brushwork quickly disappears.

THE LAKE DISTRICT AND THE NORTH

To the north of historic Beihai Park, Beijing's most attractive neighbourhoods are found in the leafy streets and *hutong* around Houhai and its adjoining lakes. Further east is the impressive Lama Temple

Though there are records of a natural body of water and marshy islets in central Beijing dating back to the Tang dynasty, it was during the Liao and Jin periods (10th–13th centuries) that the man-made lakes of Beihai (North Lake), Qianhai (Front Lake), Houhai (Back Lake) and Xihai (West Lake) took shape. As well as serving as termini to the city's canal network, their aesthetic appeal attracted the city's ruling elite – who built fine residences in the area, including an imperial lodge on Jade Island.

Today some of Beijing's most expensive courtyard properties can still be found here, though this attractive area mostly has an egalitarian atmosphere; in the warmer months, locals indulge in simple pleasures such as boating, fishing and passing the time playing mah-jong or cards by the lakeside. Tourists come for the historic sights, though many spend a good deal of their time in the proliferation of bars, cafés and restaurants that seem to fill every corner around the lakes.

To the north and east, a large area of *hutong* extends past the Bell and Drum towers all the way to the Confucius and Lama temples. Beyond the

Second Ring Road lies ancient Ditan Park, after which the sprawling modern suburbs take over.

Beihai Park ❶

Address: 1 Wenjin Jie, Xicheng District
Opening Hrs: summer daily 6am–10pm, winter 6.30am–7pm
Entrance Fee: charge
Transport: the South Gate is a short walk from Forbidden City North Gate (Shenwumen)

The area around the North Lake, **Beihai Park** (Beihai Gongyuan; 北

LEFT: the banks of Xihai (West Lake).
RIGHT: goldfish, a form of carp, have been bred in China for over 1,000 years. They are traditionally associated with art and poetry.

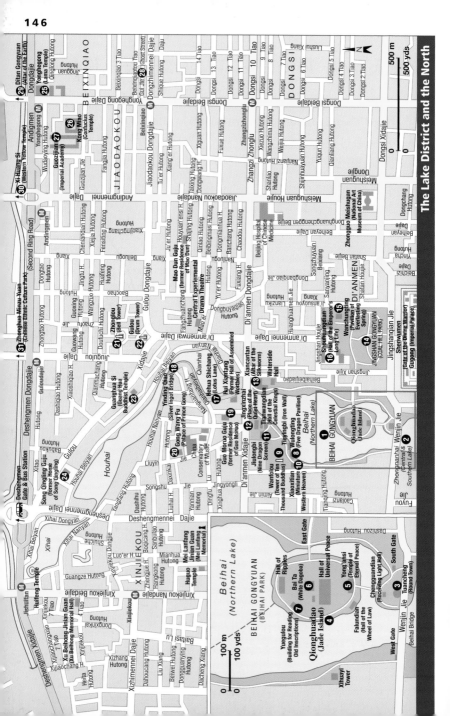

The Lake District and the North

海公园) is one of the most beautiful and popular places to spend a day out in central Beijing, no matter what the season. In winter, the lake is used for skating. The very youngest enjoy themselves on ice sledges – daring contraptions consisting of a wooden chair, or sometimes just a large plank, fastened onto two runners. In days gone by, the ice was smoothed with glowing irons for imperial celebrations. During the rest of the year, the lake is used for boating – some children even swim in it during the summer – and its banks attract those who enjoy strolling and alfresco dining.

The other part of the lake, **Zhongnanhai ❷** (中南海), literally, "Central and Southern Lake", and its surroundings, were a pleasure garden for the court. Right next to the Forbidden City, this is where horse races and hunts, birthday receptions and celebrations of the Lantern Festival took place. After 1949, Mao, Zhou Enlai, Liu Shaoqi and other notables lived in the area, and Mao's private library is still here today. Surrounded by its massive wall, Zhongnanhai has been the seat of the politburo and the state

council since 1949. Foreigners are not admitted into this modern-day Forbidden City unless they are invited to an audience.

Islands in the lake

The location of the park – west of Jingshan (Coal Hill) and northwest of the Imperial Palace – marks the centre of Kublai Khan's Mongol capital, Khanbaliq (known as Dadu in Chinese). In the south of the park, with a separate entrance, is the **Round Town ❸** (Tuancheng; 团城; Tue–Sun 8am–4.30pm; entrance fee), one of three islands in the Northern Lake. The khan had this island landscaped, along with the surrounding area, and from this spot, according to Marco Polo, he ruled in inimitable splendour. However, only the trees remain from that time, all the architecture of the Mongol Yuan dynasty having been destroyed.

An exquisite 1.5-metre (5ft) wide nephrite container, in which Kublai Khan kept his wine, also survives; it stands next to the entrance of a pavilion with white marble pillars and a blue roof. In the 18th century, a poem

TIP

As with the Forbidden City and Temple of Heaven, it's worth buying an all-inclusive ticket (tao piao) when visiting Beihai Park. This entitles you to access all the places of interest within the park.

BELOW LEFT: a pavilion at Round Town in the south of the park.
BELOW: musicians using traditional instruments perform in the Temple of Eternal Peace in Beihai Park.

by the emperor Qianlong praising the beauty of this work of art was engraved on the inside of the vessel. A second jewel in the Round Town is a 1.5-metre (5ft) white jade statue of Buddha with inlaid jewels. It can be seen in the **Receiving Light Hall** (Chengguangdian; 承光殿).

Jade Island ④ (Qionghuadao; 琼华岛) is the most impressive part of the park as far as scenery and history are concerned. The main path leads from the South Gate to a 600-year-old bridge, across which is the **Temple of Eternal Peace ⑤** (Yong'ansi; 永安寺), and beyond that, the **Hall of the Wheel of Law** (Falundian; 法轮殿).

From here, a twisting path leads up uneven steps to the 35-metre (115ft) **White Dagoba ⑥** (Bai Ta; 白塔), an onion-shaped shrine in the Tibetan style, built on the ruins of a Ming palace in honour of the fifth Dalai Lama on the occasion of his visit to Beijing in 1651. It was this onion shape that led foreigners living in Beijing during the republican era to refer to it as "the peppermint bottle". In 1679, and again in 1731, the dagoba was destroyed by earthquakes, but was

ABOVE: Beihai Park is a popular venue for weddings. **BELOW:** the Hall of the Wheel of Law (Falundian). **BELOW RIGHT:** the White Dagoba.

rebuilt on both occasions. It suffered only cracks during the 1976 Tangshan earthquake, and during restoration a golden reliquary containing two small bone fragments, probably of prominent lamas, was found. The view from here of the Forbidden City, Beihai and Zhongnanhai, and the numerous *hutong* of the Inner City, is only surpassed by the view from the peak of Jingshan.

On the northern side of the dagoba, the path leads through a labyrinth of stairs, corridors, pavilions and rock formations carved into grottoes intended to resemble the houses of Daoist saints, and heads steeply down to the lake shore, which is bordered by a long, semicircular covered walkway.

Halfway up the northwestern slope of Jade Island is a statue called the **Plate for Gathering Dew** (露盘), which was placed here by Emperor Qianlong. It is thought to represent one of the Eight Immortals and records a legend from the life of the emperor Wudi, who ruled early in the 1st century. When Wudi heard that drinking dewdrops would make him immortal, he commanded a

line over the water and connected by walkways. The largest pavilion, with its double-stepped, curved roof, forms the head of a curving dragon when seen from above. Emperors used to fish from this point. Beside the quay where the boats tie up is the 700-year-old, 4-metre (13ft) wide **Iron Wall** (Tieying Bi; 铁影壁), although it is not iron at all, but igneous rock. It was originally placed in front of a Buddhist convent which had been a bell foundry in the Ming dynasty: hence the idea that it was made of iron. It was moved to its present location in 1947.

The path leads west from the waterfront to the **Tower of Ten Thousand Buddhas** ❾ (Wanfolou; 万佛楼), built by the emperor Qianlong in the 18th century on the occasion of his mother's 80th birthday. The pure gold statuettes of Buddha that filled the niches inside the tower were stolen – like so many other treasures – by European troops in 1900.

To the south stands what is probably the biggest pavilion in China, the **Miniature Western Heaven** ❿ (Xiaoxitian; 小西天), which was built in 1770

slave to sit outdoors overnight with a bowl to catch the dewdrops falling from Heaven, and bring them to him so that he could refresh himself and become immortal.

Directly below this statue is the **Building for Reading Old Inscriptions** ❼ (Yuegulou; 阅古楼). A collection of 495 stone tablets is kept here, engraved with the work of famous Chinese calligraphers. Most of them date from the 18th century; some, however, go back more than 1,500 years. Rubbings were taken from the tablets – one of the earliest forms of printing.

Next door, in the Hall of Ripples, is the Fangshan Restaurant (see page 162), established by chefs of the imperial household who were suddenly left unemployed when Pu Yi was forced out of the Imperial Palace in 1924.

By the lake shore

From here, a ferry takes visitors to the **Five Dragon Pavilion** ❽ (Wulongting; 五龙亭), on the northwest lake shore. These buildings from the Ming era are built in a zigzagging

LEFT: communal dancing in a park pavilion. **ABOVE:** detail at the Tower of Ten Thousand Buddhas. **BELOW:** one of the Dragon Pavilions at Beihai Park.

as a shrine to Guanyin, the goddess of mercy. In the Mahayana Buddhist tradition that established itself in China, the idea of the "Western Heaven" is similar to Christian concepts of paradise. Inside, Buddhist paintings are exhibited. The **Nine Dragon Screen** ⓫ (Jiulongbi; 九龙壁) originally served to ward off the god of fire from a workshop for translating and printing Lamaist scriptures that Qianlong had built in honour of his mother. When, in an ironic twist of fate, that building succumbed to a conflagration in 1919, a gymnasium was built in its place, and the screen was moved here. A few steps to the east of the Dragon Screen is the **Hall of the Celestial Kings** (Tianwangdian; 天王殿, a Ming-dynasty workshop for the translation and woodblock-printing of Buddhist scriptures.

The **Place of the Quiet Heart** ⓬ (Jingxinzhai; 静心斋), just beyond, invites walkers to rest and pause in contemplation. It is a delightful garden within a garden laid out by Qianlong, interspersed with lotus pools, halls, pavilions and living quarters. Empress Cixi often used to lunch

here. At other times, Manchu princes found the peaceful surroundings conducive to reading the Confucian classics, while Pu Yi wrote his memoirs, *From Emperor to Citizen*, here.

On the other side of the bridge is the **Altar of the Silkworm** ⓭ (Xiancantan; 先蚕坛), one of the eight altars that played a large part in the ritual life of Ming and Qing emperors. Here the empress would come to perform a ceremony honouring the goddess of silkworms – the wife of the mythical Yellow Emperor, who supposedly discovered the secret of the silkworm – and to pray for a good harvest. Turned into a teahouse during the republican era, it presently serves as a nursery school for children of high-level officials.

Jingshan Park (Coal Hill Park) ⓮

Address: 1 Jingshan Qianjie
Tel: 6404-4071
Opening Hrs: Jan–Mar 6.30am–8pm, Apr–May & Sept–Oct 6am–9pm, June–Aug 6am–10pm, Nov–Dec 6am–8pm
Entrance Fee: charge

ABOVE: water calligraphy at Jingshan Park. **BELOW:** there are views across the Forbidden City and much of central Beijing from the five pavilions perched on top of Jingshan. **BELOW RIGHT:** the Nine Dragon Screen at Beihai Park.

Transport: Dongsi (line 5) or Xisi (line 4) subway stations

Directly behind the Forbidden City is **Jingshan Park** (Jingshan Gongyuan; 景山公园), an artificial hill which came into existence at the beginning of the 15th century, when the emperor Yongle had moats dug all around the Forbidden City. Feng shui – Chinese geomancy – probably played a decisive part in the choice of a suitable spot to tip the spoil. Jingshan served to protect the Forbidden City from malignant influences from the north. Pragmatism must also have played a role in the choice, as any approaching enemy could be seen at a distance by a lookout placed at such a height.

Five pavilions, dating from the 16th century, crown the chain of hills and emphasise their zigzagging lines. Each pavilion once housed a bronze figure of Buddha, but four of these were plundered by European troops in 1900. The surrounding park was not opened to the public until 1928. Before that date, it was a private imperial garden where palace ladies and imperial family members spent their leisure time.

It was at Jingshan that Chongzhen, the last Ming emperor, committed suicide in 1644, after the rebellious peasant armies walked into Beijing through gates left open by traitorous eunuchs. Upon hearing the terrible news, the beleaguered emperor jumped on a horse and tried to flee the city, but was forced to turn back. His route took him past the Jesuit residence, and Father Johann Adam Schall von Bell saw him – for the first and last time – as he galloped by. When he got back to the palace, Chongzhen ordered his wife to hang herself and his sons to hide. He attempted to kill his 15-year-old daughter, but she defended herself, losing a hand to his sword in the process. The emperor then went out the back gate of the palace, climbed Jingshan and hanged

ABOVE LEFT: Buddha at Jingshan. **ABOVE:** spring blooms in front of Shouhuangdian, on the northern slope of Jingshan. The park is known for its peonies.

Today Yingding Qiao (Silver Ingot Bridge) marks the boundary between Qianhai and Houhai lakes, but it used to represent the final end of China's Grand Canal, which stretches some 1,800km (1,125 miles) south all the way to Hangzhou. Traders would bring grain, bolts of silk and tributary offerings for the emperor and exchange them there.

himself from a locust tree. The tree was uprooted during the Cultural Revolution, but was replaced in 1981 and is now a favourite photo spot for Chinese tourists.

At 48 metres (157ft), the hill is the highest point of land in central Beijing, and the view from the **Pavilion of Everlasting Spring** ⑮ (Wanchungting; 万春亭), on the middle of the five peaks, is quite superb. Looking straight along the north–south axis of the city, the sea of curved golden roofs that is the Forbidden City lies to the south, with the White Dagoba towering over Beihai Lake to the west. To the north are the massive Drum and Bell towers; and on a clear day you can see, on the horizon to the northwest, the silhouette of the Western Mountains.

In the north is the **Hall of the Emperor's Long Life** ⑯ (Shouhuangdian; 寿皇殿), where the corpses of empresses were laid before being moved to tombs outside the city.

Shichahai and the Back Lakes

Shichahai (The Sea of the Ten Buddhist Temples; 十刹海) is a complex

ABOVE RIGHT & BELOW: Houhai Lake.

of lakes north of Beihai Park. Historically, this area has harboured many beautiful courtyard palaces of Manchu princes and Qing-dynasty officials. Today it remains one of the most attractive parts of Beijing.

In the last few years the attractions of the so-called "back lakes" have been increasingly capitalised on by entrepreneurs, who have opened innumerable restaurants, bars and cafés here. The most bustling thoroughfare is **Lotus Lane** ⑰ (Hehua Shichang; 荷花市场), a pedestrian-only area on the southwestern shore of Qianhai Lake; the lane is lined with bars, restaurants and coffee houses. On sultry summer nights, it is packed with young people eager to enjoy the lake, the stars, the bars and each other. Another nightlife area is concentrated around dinky little **Yinding Bridge** ⑱ (Silver Ingot Bridge; 银锭桥), where Houhai meets Qianhai Lake, and Nanluoguxiang (南锣鼓巷) – a long, renovated *hutong* and heartland of Beijing's nascent coffee-house culture.

Former Residence of Guo Moruo

Nearby on Qianhai Xijie is the **Former Residence of Guo Moruo** ⑲ (Guo Moruo Guju; 郭沫若故居; Tue–Sun, 9am–4.30pm; entrance fee), an influential figure in the rise of Communism in China. Guo was born in Sichuan Province in 1892, the son of a wealthy landlord. Following a spell in Japan, where he studied at Kyushu Imperial University, he returned to China in 1921 and became known as a respected author as well as a proponent of change, having been profoundly influenced by the Russian Revolution of 1917. The buildings are set in leafy grounds; inside, among the polished floors and old furniture, are photographs and quotations from the great man, but most are captioned in Chinese only.

Palace of Prince Gong ⑳

Address: 17 Qianhai Xijie
Tel: 8328-8149
Opening Hrs: daily 7.30am–4.30pm
Entrance Fee: charge
Transport: Pinganli subway station (line 4)

A short distance through the *hutong* to the west of the Yinding Bridge is the **Palace of Prince Gong** (Gong Wang Fu; 恭王府), the world's largest extant courtyard house and a very popular destination for tour groups. Prince Gong, the brother of Emperor Xian Feng, virtually ran the country during the minorities of the emperors Tongzhi and Guangxu, from 1861 to 1884. His home and its 5.7-hectare (14-acre) grounds, including lush gardens, are now occupied by the China Conservatory of Music. The historic structures in the complex include Beijing's only preserved Qing-dynasty theatre. Here, guests are served by women wearing traditional costumes of the period and treated to a sample of Beijing Opera.

Bell and Drum towers

Address: Di'anmen Dajie
Tel: 8402-7869
Opening Hrs: daily 9am–5pm
Entrance Fee: charge
Transport: Gulou Dajie subway station (line 2)

On the eastern side of the back lakes are two towers dating from the rule

ABOVE: the Palace of Prince Gong is thought to have provided inspiration for the classic novel *Dream of the Red Mansions*. **BELOW LEFT:** keeping guard at the Bell Tower. **BELOW:** Lotus Lane.

of the city gates. The drums were struck again every two hours, the last time being at 5am. By that hour, the officials to be present at the imperial morning audience were supposed to have taken up their kneeling positions just in front of the Hall of Supreme Harmony – failure to do so brought heavy penalties.

The day officially began at 7am with the ringing of the huge iron bell of the Bell Tower. When this proved too quiet, an even bigger bronze bell was installed in the tower, which could be heard 20km (12 miles) away. The bronze bell has now disappeared, but the iron bell is on display behind the tower. The building is so sturdy it survived the earthquake of 1976 without significant damage: only one stone ornamental figure on the roof is said to have fallen down.

Inside the recently refurbished Drum Tower is the one remaining original drum, damaged during the Opium Wars of the 19th century, now flanked by two brightly painted replicas. Climb the steep staircase of 69 steps for a fascinating view of the neighbourhood. Looking down upon the grey and often grass-covered tile roofs, separated into a variety of geometric shapes by the walls of the *hutong*, you can get a sense of how

of Kublai Khan. They have endured so many twists and turns of history that surviving the wars and revolutions of the 20th century seems relatively unremarkable. Both of the towers stand at the northern end of Di'anmenwai Dajie, and once formed the northernmost point of the city – although as the Mongol city expanded northwards they eventually stood close to the centre. Under the Ming emperor Yongle, the towers were rebuilt in 1420, somewhat to the east of their original position.

After the original wooden **Bell Tower** ㉑ (Zhonglou; 钟楼) was destroyed in a fire, the present tower, 33 metres (108ft) high, was built in 1747. The structure of the **Drum Tower** ㉒ (Gulou; 鼓楼) remains largely intact from Yongle's time. In earlier years, 24 big drums were kept inside – only one has survived – which were struck 13 times every evening at 7pm to signal the start of the night hours and also the closing

each *siheyuan* courtyard is a community in itself.

Nearby sights

The **Former Residence of Mao Dun** (Mao Dun Guju; 茅盾故居; open Tue–Sun 9am–4pm; entrance fee) can be found in a quiet *hutong* not far from the Drum Tower. Mao Dun *(see page 188)* was a precocious novelist and journalist whose influence lives on in the form of the Mao Dun Literature Prize. His courtyard home has been preserved in the simple style in which he lived.

Beyond the Yinding Bridge, on the east bank of Houhai, is the **Guang Hua Buddhist Temple ㉓** (Guanghua Si; 广化寺; daily 8am–4pm; entrance fee). Constructed during the Yuan dynasty, it is now home to the Beijing Buddhist Society. Relatively modest in size, it is well preserved and stocked with the usual colourful array of Buddhist statues and artefacts.

Former Home of Song Qingling ㉔

Address: 46 Houhai Beiyan
Tel: 6404-4205
Opening Hrs: daily 9am–4pm
Entrance Fee: charge
Transport: Jishuitan subway station (line 2)

The **Former Home of Song Qingling** (Song Qingling Guju; 宋庆龄故居), wife of Sun Yat-sen and honorary president of the People's Republic of China, is nearby at 46 Beiheyan Jie close to the northern end of Houhai. The grounds were formerly part of the palace of Prince Chun, Pu Yi's father. The house where Pu Yi was born is just south of here, and occupied by the Ministry of Health.

Song Qingling moved into the house in 1963 and lived there until her death in 1981. The guest room contains an exhibition of photographs, documents and objects from her life: her pampered Shanghai childhood as a daughter of one of

ABOVE: the former home of Song Qingling, full of period charm.

China's most prominent families; her years as a student, her marriage to Sun Yat-sen, and her political activities and support for the resistance to Japanese occupation. An extract from her most famous speech, the essay "Sun Yat-sen and his cooperation with the Communist Party", is also on display.

The Lama Temple ㉕

Address: 12 Yonghegong Dajie
Tel: 6404-4499
Opening Hrs: daily 9am–4pm
Entrance Fee: charge
Transport: Yonghegong subway station (line 2)

Some 2km (1½ miles) east from the lakes is the **Lama Temple** (Yonghegong; 雍和宫), one of the city's most beautiful and interesting temples. A visit here can easily be combined with a walk in Ditan Park *(see page 160)*, on the far side of the Second Ring Road, or the Confucius Temple and the Imperial Academy, just to the west.

At first glance, you might think it odd that a Tibetan Buddhist

TIP

Houhai has one of the largest concentrations of *hutong* and courtyard houses in the city. Pedicab drivers hawk their "tours" enthusiastically to tourists, though many hostels in this area rent bicycles for a more leisurely exploration of the winding back alleyways.

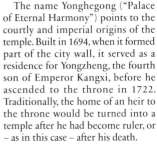

The thick scent of incense being burned inside the Lama Temple is so strong it can often be detected from inside a taxi passing by on the Second Ring Road. Outside the temple are dozens of stalls selling incense sticks of all sizes and other interesting Buddhist items.

ABOVE RIGHT: Tibetan-style prayer wheel at the Lama Temple. Spinning the wheel despatches one of the mantras inscribed on its surface.
BELOW: burning incense.

temple enjoys such prominence in the capital, given Beijing's high-profile squabbles with the Tibetan government-in-exile. But China's relationship with Tibet and its religion goes back further than the contemporary clashes. The presence of a Lamaist temple has been part of a centuries-long policy of pacifying the fractious "Land of the Snows", as well as other Lamaist states, such as Mongolia, and several emperors – notably Qianlong *(see below)* – were followers of Tibetan Buddhism.

The name Yonghegong ("Palace of Eternal Harmony") points to the courtly and imperial origins of the temple. Built in 1694, when it formed part of the city wall, it served as a residence for Yongzheng, the fourth son of Emperor Kangxi, before he ascended to the throne in 1722. Traditionally, the home of an heir to the throne would be turned into a temple after he had become ruler, or – as in this case – after his death.

Yongzheng's son and successor, Qianlong (under whose rule the Chinese empire extended westwards into Tibet), sent for 300 Tibetan monks and 200 Chinese pupils and installed them in his father's old palace. The palace then served as a temple-cum-monastery from 1744 to 1960, and was considered one of the most notable centres of Lamaist Buddhism outside Tibet. During the Qing period, the temple was closed to the public except for the annual performance of the "devil dance", which was staged as a warning against succumbing to human weaknesses – anger, greed, wine, sex and so on. The dance can still be seen today during the Chinese New Year festival.

During the Cultural Revolution, the monastery was closed, with parts of it converted into a shoe factory. Red Guards took over the complex, but they were forbidden to destroy or plunder it by order of Zhou Enlai. In spite of this, many monks were ill-treated and sent away to do manual labour in the countryside. In the early 1980s, the monastery was reopened and completely restored. More than 70 monks now live here in the rear part of the complex.

The Lama Temple belongs to the Yellow Hat or Gelugpa sect of Buddhism, predominant in Tibet, whose spiritual head is the Dalai Lama. While the Dalai Lama lives in exile, the second spiritual head of Tibetan Buddhism, the Panchen Lama, resides in Beijing. In contrast to the Dalai Lamas, the Panchen Lamas have recognised Chinese authority since the beginning of the 20th century. However, they have also defied the Chinese on at least one occasion.

Following the death of the 10th Panchen Lama in 1989, the Chinese government assembled a group of lamas known to be sympathetic to their wishes, and asked them to find a successor – a boy reincarnation of the previous Panchen Lama. But in 1995 it was revealed that the abbot in charge of the search committee had quietly asked for the Dalai Lama's approval of the chosen boy. When they discovered this, the Chinese authorities had the abbot arrested and put the boy and his parents under detention. They then announced that a new boy would be selected by the old method of drawing ivory lots from a golden urn. A new Panchen Lama was thus proclaimed in November 1995. His validity is contested by Tibetans in exile but the Panchen Lama's role in state propaganda on the Tibet issue remains. In 2010, at the age of 19, he was made vice president of China's Buddhist Association – the religion's state-run supervisory body.

The Hooligan Priests of the Lama Temple

Though hard to imagine today, the monks of the Lama Temple once held an appalling reputation for harassing visitors and even turning to robbery. Missionary and translator W.A.P. Martin once described their manners as those of "highwaymen" and claimed they had been known to "lay rough hands on visitors in order to extort a charitable dole". The infamy of these delinquent Mongol priests was such that a guidebook from the turn of the century advised visitors to carry a pistol. Another missionary, Arthur Judson Brown, was equally unimpressed by their immorality, saying that brass statues at the temple were "as filthily obscene as anything that I saw in India".

Visiting the temple

Coming from the south, enter the temple grounds through a gate. After crossing the gardens, you pass into the inner courtyard with its Bell and Drum towers and two pavilions with steles in them. To the north is the **Hall of the Celestial Kings** (Tianwangdian; 天王殿), with statues of the Maitreya Buddha and two guardian divinities.

Beyond the pavilion is a stone representation of the World Mountain, Sumeru. In the **Hall of Eternal Harmony** (Yonghegong; 雍和宫) there are three statues of Buddha surrounded by 18 Luohan. The buildings to the left and right of this inner courtyard house a mandala and valuable *thangka* – figures representing the founder of the Yellow Hat sect, Tsongkhapa. Crossing the next courtyard, you come to the **Hall of Eternal Protection** (Yongyoudian; 永佑殿), with statues of the Buddhas of longevity and medicine.

The halls to the left and right of the following courtyard contain,

ABOVE: the Lama Temple. **BELOW:** incense sticks can be purchased from stalls at Chinese temples.

ABOVE: tea for sale. There is a bewildering range of varieties, some of which command very high prices.

among other items, statues of Yab-Yum, a male and female divinity whose intimate sexual connection symbolises the cosmic unity of all opposites. This courtyard is bounded by the **Hall of the Wheel of Dharma** (Falundian; 法轮殿), in the middle of which is a 6-metre (20ft) high statue of Tsongkhapa. Behind this statue is the monastery's treasure: a miniature mountain of sandalwood, with 500 Luohan figures of gold, silver, copper, iron and tin.

The fifth inner courtyard ends at the **Pavilion of Ten Thousand Happinesses** (Wanfuge; 万福阁).

This contains a 25-metre (80ft) high Maitreya Buddha made from a single piece of sandalwood. The three-storey pavilion is linked by bridges to the two-storey side buildings that flank it.

The Confucius Temple 26

Address: 13 Guozijian Jie
Tel: 6404-2407
Opening Hrs: daily 9am–4.30pm
Entrance Fee: charge
Transport: a short walk from the Lama Temple (Yonghegong subway; line 2)

To the west, Guozijian Jie is graced by two of only a few existing *pailou*

SHOPPING

Dianmen Xidajie

Three Stones Kite Store
29 Dianmen Xidajie, Xicheng District. Tel: 8404-4505. p285, E3
Just north of Beihai Park you'll find most of the traditional styles of Chinese kites including long-tailed fish, butterflies and, of course, dragons.

Drum Tower

Gulou Dongdajie has become a bustling commercial street with shops selling musical instruments and several retro clothes outlets.

Ruoshuitang Umbrella
若水堂典油纸伞
144 Gulou Dongdajie. Tel: 136-9113-0149. p286, B2
These traditional handmade paper parasols are sturdier than you might imagine and decorated with Chinese designs such as classical landscapes or floral patterns.

Ye Rocks
49 Gulou Dongdajie. Tel: 136-0131-2554. p286, B2
Owned by a drummer, this store is where Beijing's would-be rockers come to buy hats, scarves and retro leather jackets.

Guozijian Jie

The pleasant lane on which the Imperial Academy and Confucius Temple lie has a number of traditional craft shops.

Bannerman Tang's Toys and Handicrafts
38 Guozijian Jie. Tel: 8404-7179. p286, B2
The art of making toys and traditional crafts such as Beijing Opera masks has been in this family for generations.

Old-Toxin Tin Toys
46 Fangjia Hutong. Tel: 138-1091-6465. p286, B2
Standing apart from the more traditional craft shops on Guozijian, this shop is stocked

with reproductions of old tin toys

Houhai

A number of street-side stalls selling paper lanterns and neon toys dot Houhai Lake. Other shops try their luck flogging anything with a Chinese feel to the tourist crowds.

Naxi Popo 纳西婆婆
14 Yandai Xiejie. Tel: 8404-1300. p286, A2
Wooden wall-hangings and puppets in the vibrant style of the Naxi minority.

Nanluoguxiang

In the *hutong* east of Qianhai lake, one of the best shopping streets in town for quirky Chinese contemporary and retro gifts and clothes. Many of its shops are barely bigger than a large cupboard.

Plastered T-shirts
61 Nanluoguxiang. Tel: 134-8884-8855. p286, B2.
www.plastered.com.cn
Tapping into the retro

craze, Plastered T-shirts takes simple designs from everyday Beijing life such as subway tickets, beer labels, and the outdated Xiali taxis.

Wudaoying Hutong

Seeking to replicate the success of renovated *hutong* Nanluoguxiang, this alleyway, just north of the Confucius Temple, is attracting some ambitious retail outlets.

Brand Nu
61 Wudaoying Hutong. Tel: 150-1115-3421. p286, B2
Sells products handmade by women's groups across China, and accepts charitable donations of old clothes, books, etc.

Dong Liang Studio
63a Wudaoying Hutong. Tel: 6406-2337. p286, B2
Boutique clothes shop promoting local fashion design talent for both womenswear and menswear. .

(decorative gates) left standing in Beijing. Along this street are two important landmarks.

The **Confucius Temple** (Kong Miao; 孔庙) remains one of the largest in China outside of the city of Qufu, the birthplace of Confucius in Shandong province.

For many years after 1949, Confucianism was seen as the embodiment of the feudal ways that Communism was trying to eradicate. Most Confucian temples throughout China were thus converted to other uses, or simply abandoned. Beginning in the late 1980s, there was an effort to revive some of the basic precepts of Confucianism, such as respect for authority and the elderly, and in recent years the teachings of the ancient sage have become more popular (*see panel, below*).

Before the wide staircase leading up to the main hall, the **Hall of Great Achievements** (Dachengdian; 大成殿), look out for a cypress tree. It is said that a branch came loose from this tree and brushed off the head of a disloyal officer as it fell to the ground. Inside the hall are some of the musi-cal instruments which were so important in Confucian ceremonies.

Confucian thought is the basic underpinning of traditional Chinese society. The philosophy was especially apparent in the system of choosing mandarins for the civil service, which endured for 2,000 years. Candidates – who were locked up in cells for three days as they wrote the exam – were required to demonstrate flawless knowledge of the Confucian classics and mastery of a highly formulaic "three-legged" essay. Practical knowledge was not valued in this system.

One of the most impressive sights in the temple is the 198 stone tablets recording the names and hometowns of 51,624 candidates who successfully passed such tests held during the Yuan, Ming and Qing dynasties. The stone tablets can be seen in the pavilions around the **Gate of the First Teacher** (Xianshimen; 先师门).

The Imperial Academy

Tradition dictated that on the right of a temple there should be an academy. So in the year 1306, during the

Although the Confucian examination system was eventually overturned, China's National College Examination is its legacy: a ferociously competitive, high-pressure exam and prerequisite for entrance into Chinese universities. Some parents of students preparing for the examination visit the Imperial Academy to pray for the all-important pass mark.

BELOW LEFT: a traditional drum at the Confucius Temple.

The Confucius Institutes

Headquartered in Beijing, the Confucius Institute is a non-profit organisation run, ostensibly, to promote the Chinese language and culture around the world. The ancient sage was deemed a suitable "figurehead", combating uncertainties over a rising, authoritarian regime through the peaceful figure of a man of traditional values and erudition. Some academic institutions abroad have elected to run their Chinese language courses without the influence of the Institutes, however, fearing they are a vehicle for Chinese Communist propaganda. By the end of 2009 there were almost 400 institutes in 87 countries and regions.

Domestically, Confucius is enjoying something of a renaissance, with populist author and TV lecturer Yu Dan breaking sales records for her interpretations of the *Analects*. A recent state-sponsored movie starring Chow Yun-fat as the sage was careful to avoid tainting Confucius' reputation with awkward questions about his anti-authoritarianism and sexual exploits. Many in China would like to see a return to the cultural richness and values of the past, though the irony of Communist leaders hijacking the reputation of the sage – Mao vilified Confucius as a symbol of backward conservatism – has not gone unnoticed.

ABOVE: The Altar of the Earth was used for ceremonies relating to agriculture. To mark the start of the farming season the emperor would act out tilling a field with a ceremonial plough and whip. Actors dressed as peasants would then present him with the five sacred grains to symbolise an abundant harvest.

BELOW: performance at the Chinese Ethnic Culture Park.

Yuan dynasty, the **Imperial Academy** ㉗ (Guozijian; 国子监; daily 9am–4.30pm; entrance fee) was founded as a school to teach the Chinese language to Mongol boys and Mongol to Chinese boys, as well as educating all pupils in all of the martial arts. Later, the academy became a university which, in 1462, had 13,000 students. In total, the academy was responsible for producing 48,900 successful *jinshi* scholars.

Gui Jie, food street

A short walk south of the Confucius Temple is **Gui Jie** ㉘ (Ghost Street; 簋街), the city's traditional "food street". Red lanterns and neon illuminate this all-night dining boulevard of spicy hotpots, de luxe private rooms and rowdy street life. The restaurants sit side-by-side for just over a kilometre between Beixinqiao and Dongzhimen subway stations (try the Huajia Yiyuan restaurant – *see listings, opposite*).

North of the Lama Temple

North of the Lama Temple is **Ditan Park** ㉙ (地坛公园; daily 6am–9pm; entrance fee), which spreads around

the **Altar of the Earth** (Ditan; 地坛), one of the original eight altars, along with the Temple of Heaven, that played a great role in the ritual life of the Ming and Qing emperors.

To the northwest, between the Second and Third ring roads and near the junction of Huangsi Dajie and Gulouwai Daijie, is the **Western Yellow Temple** ㉚ (Xi Huang Si; 西黄寺; no fixed opening times or fee), among the best surviving examples of Lamaist architecture in Beijing. Two temples, Eastern and Western, were built here in the mid-17th century, but they were destroyed in 1958 during the Great Leap Forward. The most spectacular surviving structure is the White Pagoda, which Qianlong had built in 1780 to honour the sixth Panchen Lama, who died of smallpox while visiting Beijing. Subsequent Chief Lamas at the Lama Temple were required to have had smallpox and recovered (and be therefore immune) so that they could avoid similar fates.

The **Chinese Ethnic Culture Park** ㉛ (Zhonghua Minzu Yuan; 中华民族园; daily 8.30am–6pm; entrance fee) on Minzu Lu, just west of the main Olympic complex and south of the Fourth Ring Road, is a large "cultural" theme park popular with school groups. It's the place to come for a (government-approved) crash course in minority culture in China. Most visitors, however, are likely to find it rather tacky.

A short walk from the **Bird's Nest Stadium** (*for details on the Olympic sites, see page 59*) and just outside the Olympic Green subway station, **Chocolate Wonderland** (Chaokeli Menggongyuan; 巧克力梦公园; Jan–Apr Mon–Fri 9am–5.30pm, Sat–Sun 9am–7.30pm; entrance fee) is a theme park for the sweet-toothed showcasing numerous improbable items all crafted from chocolate. Previous sculptures have included the Great Wall, the Terracotta Warriors and a full-size BMW. ❏

BEST RESTAURANTS, BARS AND CAFÉS

Restaurants

Beijing/Chinese

Beijing Noodle King
京味面大王
35 Dianmen Xidajie,
Xicheng District. Tel: 6405-
6666. Open: 10.30am–
10.30pm. $ ⑱ p286, A3
A bustling, bright place
with a sedan chair out-
side, and doormen in
old-style clothing and
fake braids who shout out
the arrival of each guest.

Drum and Gong 锣鼓
104 Nanluoguxiang. Tel:
8402-4729. Open: 10am–
midnight. $$ ⑲ p286, B3
Simple, home-cooked
Beijng-style dishes, a
rooftop terrace and
English menu make this
a popular choice.

Huajia Yiyuan 花家怡园
235 Dongzhimennei Dajie
(Gui Jie). Tel: 6405 1908.
Open: 10.30am–4am. $$
⑳ p286, C2
Gui Jie, sometimes called
"Ghost Street", is a neon-
lit all-night dining boulevard of spicy hotpots, de
luxe private rooms and
rowdy street life. The perfect choice for beginners,

Prices are for a typical
dinner for one (three
dishes with beer in
Chinese restaurants, or
a three-course meal
with a half-bottle of
house wine in Western-
style restaurants).

$ = under Rmb 50
$$ = Rmb 50–100
$$$ = Rmb 100–200
$$$$ = over Rmb 200

Huajia Yiyuan is an
impressive traditional
courtyard restaurant
with a comprehensive
picture menu detailing
plentiful home-style
dishes.

Jin Ding Xuan 金鼎轩
77 Heping Xijie, just north
of the Lama Temple.
Tel: 6429 6888. Open: 24
hours. $ ㉑ p286, C1
Popular dim sum joint
famous for a characteris-
tic bustling atmosphere.

Jiumen Xiaochi
九门小吃
1 Xiaoyou Hutong, Houhai.
Tel 6402 5858. Open 10am–
10pm. $ ㉒ p285, E2
A collection of traditional
Beijing snack stalls
recreated in a large
courtyard.

Ken de rouge 红邸
22 Houhai West Bank,
Houhai. Tel: 6402-6665.
Open: 11.30am–2.30pm,
5.30–11.30pm. $$$ ㉓
p285, E2
The contemporary Asian
interior design and
nouvelle Chinese cuisine
is sure to impress. Try
one of the restaurant's
specialities such as
Yunwu Tea Shrimp.

Mei Mansion 梅府家宴
24 Da Xiang Feng Hutong.
Tel: 6612-6845. Open:
11am–2pm, 5–10pm. $$$$
㉔ p286, A2
This pleasant restaurant
features food created for
the great Beijing Opera

RIGHT: the brightly lit
Noodle King restaurant.

star Mei Lanfang. Mei
was a northerner, but his
chef was a southerner
who created a kind of
north-south fusion
cuisine which the family
reportedly still eats to
this day.

Yueming Lou 月明楼
21a Ya'er Hutong, Shicha-
hai, Xicheng District. Tel:
6400-2069. Open: 9am–
midnight. $$ ㉕ p286, A2
A former church that has
been converted into an
Old Beijing-style
restaurant, with beautiful
views of the lakes and
surrounding *hutong* from
its third-floor terrace.

European

Fish Nation
31 Jiaodaokou, Nanluogu-
xiang. Tel: 6401-3249.

Open: 9.30am–1am. $$ ㉖
p286, B2
The intention was to make
Britain's national cuisine
as popular in China as
Chinese food is in
England. A "Big British
Breakfast"and carefully
prepared fish and chips,
pizzas and salads.

Hunanese

**Yuelu Mountain Dining
Place** 岳麓山屋
10 Lotus Lane (He Hua Shi
Chang). Tel: 6617-2696.
Open: 11–2am. $$ ㉗
p286, A3
Splendid Hunanese food
in a sleek setting that
combines traditional and
modern. Chinese readers
will find interesting books
on its wooden shelves,
while those seeking

privacy can reserve rooms upstairs.

Imperial

Fangshan Restaurant 仿膳饭庄

1 Wenjin Jie, inside Beihai Park South Gate. Tel: 6401-1889. Open: 11am–1.30pm, 5–8pm. **$$$$** ㉘ p286, A4

Opened in 1925 by three imperial chefs in a traditional courtyard on the shore of Beihai Lake, Fangshan produces dishes once served to Qing emperors. Calligraphy and antique furniture adorn the stylish dining rooms. An extensive menu features haute cuisine from across China. Set banquets start at Rmb 150 per person for a relatively simple meal to more than Rmb 1,000 for a truly imperial feast.

Li Family Restaurant 厉家菜

11 Yangfang Hutong, Deshengmennei. Tel: 6618-0107. Open: 6–8pm. **$$$$** ㉙ p286, A2

This family-run place in an old courtyard house specialises in imperial cuisine. It's very popular, so book at least four days in advance.

Muslim

Kaorouji 烤肉季

14 Qianhai Dongyan. Tel: 6404-2554. Open: 11am–2pm, 5–11pm. **$$** ㉚ p286, A2

This is an old Muslim restaurant popular with Beijing's Hui residents. The caged mynah birds that greet diners in Chinese as they enter the restaurant are always a hit with children. Staff may also be able to

arrange for a meal to be eaten on a boat on nearby Qianhai Lake.

Shaoxing

Kong Yiji 孔乙己

Shichahai Houhai Nanan. Tel: 6618-4917. Open: 10am–2pm, 4–10.30pm. **$$** ㉛ p285, E2

This popular themed diner recreates the ancient flavours of Shaoxing, the southern home town of famed writer Lu Xun. Reservation advised.

Sichuanese

Beijing Bamboo Garden Hotel 北京竹园宾馆

24 Xiaoshiqiao Hutong Jiugulou Dajie. Tel: 6403-2229. Open: 7–11am, noon–2pm and 6–9pm. **$$** ㉜ p286, A2

Delicious Sichuan food served in the middle of a bamboo garden; eat on

the terrace or in the wide-windowed dining hall.

Sichuan Restaurant 四川饭店

14 Liuyin Jie, Xicheng District. Tel: 6615-6924. Open: 11am–2pm, 5–9pm. **$$** ㉝ p286, A2

This well-known restaurant serves excellent Sichuan food in the midst of the gardens of the Prince Gong Palace, one of the best-preserved – and most elaborate – courtyard homes in the city. A memorable experience.

Southeast Asian

Buffalo Stone 水牛石

6 Lotus Lane (He Hua Shi Chang). Tel: 6617-2242. Open: 9.30–2am. **$$$** ㉞ p286, A3

Artistic decor and traditional-style wooden furniture adorned with

rant offers a set menu only according to what the chefs are prepared to cook on a given day.

No name restaurant
无名云南餐厅
1 Dajinsi Hutong, Houhai. Tel: 8328-3061. Open 11am–1am. **$$** 38 p286, A2
Well-priced and accessible Yunnanese cooking. A table on the roof and bowl of delicious cold noodles is highly recommended in summer.

---

plush silk pillows. An excellent place for a candlelit dinner of Southeast Asian cuisine.

Café Sambal
43 Doufuchi Hutong (east of Jiugulou Dajie). Tel: 6400-4875. Open: noon–midnight. **$$–$$$** 35 p286, A2
Flavoursome Malaysian food in stylish surround-

ings, with an attractive courtyard for the summer.

Vietnamese

Nuage 庆云楼
22 Qianhai Lake East Bank. Tel: 6401-9581. Open: 11–1am. **$$** 36 p286, A2
This Vietnamese restaurant's languid style and lakeside location give it the sultry, airy atmosphere of a tropical escape.

Yunnanese

Dali Courtyard 大理
67 Xiaojingchang Hutong, Gulou Dongdajie. Tel: 8404-1430. Open: 11am–2pm, 6–11pm. **$$** 37 p286, B2
Set in a beautiful courtyard, this popular restau-

Prices are for a typical dinner for one (three dishes with beer in Chinese restaurants, or a three-course meal with a half-bottle of house wine in Western-style restaurants).

$ = under Rmb 50
$$ = Rmb 50–100
$$$ = Rmb 100–200
$$$$ = over Rmb 200

Bars and Cafés

Bed Bar 床
17 Zhangwang Hutong, Jiu Gulou Dajie. Tel: 8400-1554. 3 p286, B2
One of the top spots in town to be seen, were it not for the murky interior. A fashionable clien-tele lounge on *kang*-style beds and sip mojitos and other well-prepared cocktails.

Drum and Bell Café
41 Zhonglouwan Hutong. Tel: 8403-3600. 4 p286, B2
One of the best spots in town to enjoy a coffee or a beer on a roof garden overlooking a public area between the ancient Drum and Bell towers where locals practice t'ai chi, spin diabolos and gossip.

Café Heaven and Earth
天与地茶餐吧
2 Qianhai Beiyan. Tel: 6657 1870. 5 p286, A2
This café stocks a variety of herbal teas and well as coffee, beer and cocktails. Wifi available.

ING
55a Wudaoying Hutong. Tel: 6401-7769. 6 p286, C2
Hutong bar and cafe striving to carve a niche out for itself on trendy

Wudaoying Hutong. It has a loft, comfy couches downstairs, goldfish and even two iguanas.

MAO Live House
111 Gulou Dongdajie. Tel: 6402-5080. www.maolive.com. 7 p286, B2
This no-nonsense rock venue has become a mainstay in Beijing's music scene. Cheap drinks and loud music attract a young crowd.

Passby Bar 过客
108 Nanluoguxiang. Tel: 8403-8004. 8 p286, B3
Opened 10 years ago when, believe it or not, this was the first bar on Nanluoguxiang. Has an outside courtyard and a fair-sized library of travel books.

Vineyard Cafe
葡萄院儿
31 Wudaoying Hutong. Tel: 6402-7961. 9 p286, C1
Classy bistro serving simple but delicious food and a number of well-chosen wines.

Xiao Xin's Cafe
小新的店
103 Nanluoguxiang. Tel: 6403-6956. 10 p286, B3
Filled with Beijing memorabilia and excellent cakes. Wifi available.

LEFT: imperial cuisine and surroundings at Fangshan.
ABOVE: modern chic at Café Sambal.

LIFE IN THE HUTONG

The heart of Beijing lies behind its modern facade, in the tranquil *hutong*, narrow alleys that have been the hub of the city's street life for 700 years

Since the time of Genghis Khan, Beijingers have built single-storey homes with tiled roofs, facing into a central courtyard and protected by high walls. They are set within a labyrinth of crumbling grey alleyways, some dating back many centuries. These are the *hutong* (the word itself is of Mongolian origin), the heart of traditional Beijing and one of its most alluring sights.

There are two main areas of *hutong* in Beijing: a collection of narrow, winding streets surrounding the newly renovated Qianmen Dajie, and the attractive area around the Drum and Bell towers and back lakes to the north of the Forbidden City. Strolling or cycling around these areas is an experience not to be missed, giving a glimpse of the city as it used to be. Tiny workshops dimly lit by a single bare bulb, street vendors selling steamed *baozi*, snot-nosed children, old men carrying their songbirds in bamboo cages, coal smoke and bicycles – all form part of this vaguely Dickensian scene. For those who bemoan the increasingly standardised, international facade of modern Beijing, these alleyways provide instant succour. See them before they disappear.

ABOVE: family members wrap up against the Beijing winter to dine together in an old courtyard. Privacy, security and a close-knit sense of community are some of the upsides of life in a *hutong*. To many residents, these benefits make up for the prevalence of substandard housing and often grimy living conditions.

ABOVE: Chinese chess *(wei ch'i)* contends with backgammon for the right to be called the oldest game still played in its original form. **LEFT:** it is possible to take a cycle-rickshaw tour of the *hutong* around Houhai Lake.

A DISAPPEARING WAY OF LIFE

As Beijing continues to modernise, the *hutong* are under threat. The least salubrious were cleared in the 1950s to make way for apartment blocks, but sizeable areas of courtyard houses remained until the late 1980s. Unfortunately, most of the *hutong* have now gone, and those that have survived as tourist attractions are often renovated in a style that is attractive and accessible but lacks authenticity.

It is easy for outsiders to be sentimental about the destruction of old buildings, but the fact is that many *hutong* dwellings are cramped and squalid. Some are comprised of just one or two small rooms, functioning as combined kitchens, living rooms, bedrooms and washrooms. The families use a public toilet in the alley, not pleasant at the best of times, let alone in the freezing winter months. A 15th-floor apartment with all modern conveniences naturally holds great appeal.

Yet some families prefer to stay put, fearing exile to distant suburbs with poor infrastructure. Others believe *hutong* should be preserved for their historical value. In a country where government control normally restricts public debate to the most trivial issues, the fate of the *hutong* has prompted academics to write articles stressing the importance of the alleys to Beijing's cultural heritage and urging residents to petition officials and courts.

BELOW: behind protective walls, inside the courtyards of the *hutong*, is another world. Assorted jumble collects in doorways, pot plants catch the sun's angled rays, and caged songbirds hang from the eaves. The secret to a sweet voice, so they say, is frequent baths and a diet of cornmeal and ground peanuts.

BELOW: a typical *hutong* street near Houhai Lake. Washing dries in the dry spring air; pedal-powered three-wheelers, used for delivering vegetables, coal and other goods, obstruct the pavements.

LEFT: these buildings near Liulichang are scheduled for demolition.

EASTERN BEIJING

Home to five-star hotels and gleaming high-rise office blocks, this busy commercial area, Beijing's business hub, has long been the most Westernised part of the city. It's a prime shopping and nightlife area, too

Most travellers to Beijing arrive in the city's burgeoning eastern area, be it on a flight into Capital Airport or a train into Beijing Zhan, the main railway station. It is also in this part of the city that many find themselves staying, in a gleaming high-rise hotel where English is the official language and a McDonald's or Starbucks is certain to be just around the corner. For first-time visitors, it is not uncommon to feel shocked – even cheated – by the international modernity of it all, as though China should for ever eschew high-rises, foreign fast-food outlets, ring roads and cars in order to preserve a more authentically "Chinese" environment for tourists.

The reality, of course, is that the West does not hold the patent on modernity. Eastern Beijing – especially Chaoyang District – may look a lot like big metropolitan cities around the world (albeit with more construction work), but it is still Chinese. This is the economic heart of the modern capital, home to scores of embassies and the diplomats who staff them. It is also the area in which, in the past, international journalists were required to live, and in which most still do. Beijing's first modern office building – the Citic

Building – was built here soon after Deng Xiaoping started his economic reforms, and the area is now home to the China headquarters of hundreds of companies from around the world.

The Central Business District occupies an area of roughly 4 sq km (1½ sq miles), set to double by 2017, centred roughly on the iconic CCTV headquarters east of the Third Ring Road and overlooked, since 2009, by the World Trade Centre Tower III: at 330 metres (1,083ft), this is Beijing's tallest building. The uniform, boxlike home/

LEFT: the New Poly Plaza, one of the city's most distinctive modern structures.
RIGHT: Wangfujing.

office complex is a major landmark doubtlessly poised to serve as a backdrop for business deals that will shape the future of Beijing and the world.

Little of the past remains in these parts, offering few sites for visitors beyond marvelling at the new, gleaming buildings and perhaps stumbling upon a back alleyway where pockets of a more traditional and humble lifestyle live on in the shadows of the 21st-century capital. Even in the centre of this modern metropolis, office workers may earn as little as Rmb 2,000 (around 300 US dollars) each month, while the army of construction

ABOVE: upmarket shopping at Oriental Plaza.

labourers, security guards, cleaners and shopkeepers take home even less.

To the north, the embassy district of Sanlitun has exploded into a neon-lit and ever-expanding zone of entertainment and hedonism where Rmb-60 Martinis are glugged down by Chinese professionals whose parents would never have set foot in a bar. Entrepreneurs from around the world dip a toe into the restaurant trade, creating a cornucopia of foreign cuisines; some are successful, while others fall foul of the whims of spoilt diners and city bureaucrats and end up facing huge financial losses.

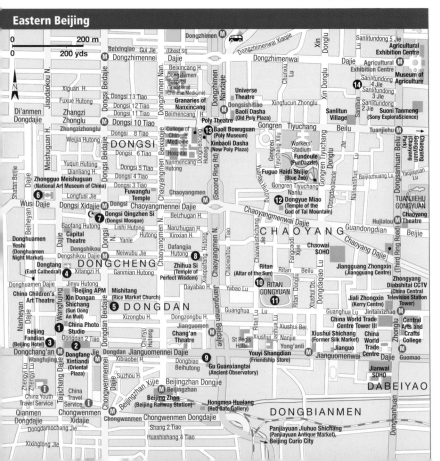

In the northeast, the huge green expanse of Chaoyang Park offers some respite and room to breathe away from the congested city-centre roads, with plenty of facilities to keep children entertained. Further out to the northeast a once loosely knit community of penniless artists has thrived and morphed almost unrecognisably into the 798 Art District, a venue for international galleries, the exhibition spaces of China's new generation of super-rich creative talent and stopping point for busloads of camera-wielding art tourists from home and abroad.

On the downside, and somewhat paradoxically, much of Chaoyang district can be somewhat insular – there are many people, both Chinese and foreign, who rarely ever venture out of its comfortable confines, or even into its side roads and back alleys.

Wangfujing

A short distance to the east of the Imperial Palace is **Wangfujing ❶** (王府井大街). Always a smart address, in recent times this famous thoroughfare has established itself as Beijing's pre-mier shopping street. Pedestrianised as far up as Dong'anmen Dajie, it's a great place to stroll, window-shop and people-watch. Over the past few years, practically every building has been rebuilt, with the assistance of huge amounts of Hong Kong capital. This is the place to come to browse in upmarket Western-style shopping malls and department stores, both above and below street level.

For a time in the 1990s there was a flagship McDonald's on the southeast corner, at the junction with Chang'an Jie; it was knocked down to make way for Li Kai-shing's enormous **Oriental Plaza ❷** (Dongfang Xintiandi; 东方新天地), a gleaming Hong Kong-style shopping mall with a vast array of shops and food courts. The huge **Beijing Hotel ❸** (Beijing Fandian; 北京饭店) once the only place where foreigners could stay in the capital, is on the corner of Wangfujing and Dong Chang'an Jie. It was built in four stages. The earliest part of the building is the centre, dating from 1917, where ornate French-style vaulted ceilings and a sweeping staircase evoke the decadent days of

The crowds of Wangfujing coalesce slightly more thickly at the window of shop number 180, the prestigious China Photo Studio. A portrait of Mao Zedong is proudly displayed, flanked by Zhou Enlai and Liu Shaqi. In fact, this is China's only studio authorised to display the photographs, as they are originals taken at the studio some 50 years ago. Still operational, you can have your own portrait taken here, though it's unlikely it will be placed in the shop window.

BELOW: shops on Wangfujing.

George Ernest Morrison

Few shoppers on today's Wangfujing realise the bustling commercial district was once also known as Morrison Street. In the last instance of a Beijing road taking its name from a foreigner, George Ernest Morrison, traveller and influential journalist, gave his name to the popular curio hunting ground. This dual name lasted from the 1920s until the founding of the PRC in 1949. Morrison's travels across the Middle Kingdom – published in the book *An Australian in China* – were a stepping stone to a post as Beijing correspondent for *The Times* of London. He witnessed and reported the formation of the Republic in 1912, even influencing domestic policy as an adviser to Yuan Shikai's government.

Beijing's New Architecture

With the Olympic impetus showing little sign of waning, Beijing has invested huge sums in bringing its architecture bang up to date

After decades of somnolence, Beijing has been experiencing an architectural revolution that has transformed the city in the past few years. Controversially, many of the new generation of buildings have been designed by foreign architects.

The first of the foreign invaders was French architect Paul Andreu, whose **National Centre for the Performing Arts** (see page 104) is a dramatic glass-and-titanium dome located behind the Great Hall of the People. Its high cost, futuristic design and the significance of allowing a foreigner to tamper with such politically sensitive ground made it a lightening rod for criticism. It remains most commonly known as "The Egg", a term which in Chinese is not entirely flattering. The howls of protest were in vain, however. Whatever their rationale, the central government allowed Beijing to become a design labora-tory for the world's architects. The vast media coverage and column inches full of superlatives and laudatory reporting may have been some small recompense.

The Egg's counterpart is the "**Bird's Nest**", as the Beijing Olympic Stadium has been nicknamed. Designed by the firm of Herzog & De Meuron, in cooperation with the China Architecture Design Institute, the bowl-shaped, steel stadium does indeed resemble a nest – rather more than the cracked veneer of a piece of traditional Chinese pottery that designers claim was its inspiration. The stadium is occasionally used for big-name performances and remains one of the city's top tourist attractions.

Arguably the most avant-garde of all the Olympic-era buildings is the new headquarters for **China Central Television** (**CCTV**), designed by Dutch architect Rem Koolhaas and his firm. The building, which stands just outside the eastern section of the Third Ring Road, consists of two leaning towers that bend to 90-degree angles at the top where they meet and form a tube. Some liken it to a Möbius strip, while those scornful of the state broadcaster prefer to imagine it as a pair of giant underpants. The building features a public observation deck. Another landmark structure is the **New Poly Plaza**, completed in 2007, featuring a 90-metre (300ft) atrium enclosed by the world's larg-est cable-net-supported glass wall.

The capital's new architectural wonders are now an inspiration for young Chinese design talent, such as Pan Shiyi, for whom the future could not be rosier. Each of his SOHO brand projects is unique, although all cater to urban professionals by creating a city-within-a-city lined with apartments, offices, shopping areas and other facilities.

The Central Business District is set to double in size by 2017. Plans are currently at the proposal stage, but all are necessar-ily ambitious and feature rows of skyscrap-ers that will make downtown Beijing look more like Manhattan than the ancient capi-tal still within living memory. The **Beijing City Planning Museum** (see page 111) provides a glimpse of this future. ❑

LEFT: the CCTV building.

the 1920s. The hotel was extended in 1954, and this section reflects the optimism of the early years of the People's Republic. The East Wing, added in 1974 towards the end of the Cultural Revolution, is, not surprisingly, somewhat bleak. The western section was added in 1989 and is a tribute to the financial freedoms of the Deng era. To the north is the Sun Dong An Mall, a pedestrian area renovated for the PRC's 50th anniversary.

Mixed among, and dwarfed by, the commercial high-rises are a few remnants of times past. At 74 Wangfujing Dajie, the **East Cathedral** ❹ (Dongtang; 东堂; Mon–Sat 6.30am– 8pm), also known as St Joseph's, was burned to the ground in 1900, and had to be rebuilt. Prior to that the site was occupied by part of the house of Schall von Bell (see page 184), who died here in 1666. The grey-brick cathedral has an active congregation, and with the redevelopment of Wangfujing, the churchyard has been converted into one of Beijing's most popular, and attractive, squares. Nearby on Dong'anmen Dajie is **Donghuamen Night Market** (Donghuamen Yeshi; 东华门夜市), a good place to try street food. A long line of vendors sell a variety of regional specialities, including outlandish delicacies such as fried locusts, scorpions and silkworms.

The **Rice Market Church** ❺ (Mishitang; 米市堂) at Dongdan Bei Jie (the next main street to the east, previously known as Rice Market Street) is an important Protestant church. The grey-brick building with its Chinese roof and double wooden eaves dates from the 1920s, when it was the seat of the Bible Society. Today it is home to the Chinese Christian Council. There are 21 million Protestants in China.

National Art Museum of China ❻

Address: 1 Wusi Dajie, Dongcheng District
Tel: 6401-7076. www.namoc.org
Opening Hrs: daily 9am–5pm
Entrance Fee: charge
Transport: Dongsi subway station (line 5)

At the northern end of Wangfujing is the **National Art Museum of China** (Zhongguo Meishuguan; 中国美术馆), a large Chinese-style edifice completed in 1962 with a white-tiled exterior and traditional roof typical

ABOVE LEFT: the East Cathedral. **ABOVE:** sea horse on a stick at Donghuamen Night Market. **BELOW:** more conventional street fare.

of the period. The sign overhanging the entrance way is carved in Mao Zedong's distinctive handwriting.

The museum is a good place to discover both new and old trends in Chinese art, though most shows focus on traditional styles such as calligraphy, landscape and folk art. Keen to shake off its stuffy reputation, it has recently injected a more contemporary feel into its shows, with experimental themes and multimedia exhibitions now in evidence. Beijing's more controversial exhibitions are still found in the 798 Art District, however.

Dongsi Mosque

Dongsi Mosque ❼ (Dongsi Qingzhen Si; 东四清真寺) is not open to the general public, so an appointment must be made for a visit. From the street one would hardly notice that there is a mosque at all – like Niu Jie Mosque *(see page 129)* it has no minaret or muezzin. The building dates from 1447, and in 1450 the Ming emperor Jiangtai gave it the title Qingzhen Si (meaning "Temple of Purity and Light"), which is how all mosques are now referred to in Chinese.

ABOVE: Beijing's booming economy means that luxury European cars are now part of the city scene.
BELOW RIGHT: the Ancient Observatory.

Zhihua Si

Located to the east of Wangfujing, not far from the Second Ring Road, is **Zhihua Si ❽** (The Temple of Perfect Wisdom; 智化寺; daily 8.30am–4.30pm; charge). It was built as a family shrine by a eunuch named Wang Zhen in 1443, during the Ming dynasty, but closed six years later when Wang was executed. Woodblocks used for printing the "Grand Collection of Buddhist Scriptures" are kept here.

The Ancient Observatory ❾

Address: 2 Dongbiaobei Hutong
Tel: 6524-2202
Opening Hrs: daily 9am–4pm
Entrance Fee: charge
Transport: Jianguomen subway station (lines 1 and 2)

At the junction of Jianguomennei and the Second Ring Road is the **Ancient Observatory** (Gu Guanxiangtai; 古观象台). Originally constructed in 1279 north of its present-day site, the observatory that you see today was built in the mid-15th century and sits atop a watchtower that was once a part of the city walls. It served both the Ming and Qing dynasties in

Reading the Stars

In the 13th century, astronomers at the Yuan-dynasty imperial observatory fixed the length of the year at 365.2424 days – within one-1,000th of a day according to modern calculations. They achieved such precision with the aid of bronze astronomical instruments such as those on display in the Ancient Observatory. The three armillary spheres, quadrant for finding stars, celestial globe, equatorial theodolite for determining angles of elevation, altazimuth for determining the height of stars in the sky, and sextant were all used by these early Chinese scientists.

Such astonishing accuracy benefited astrology as much as astronomy. The casting of horoscopes earned the scientists the fortune and patronage they needed to develop their instruments and observatories. The *luo pan* (net tablet), a wooden or brass disc covered in hundreds of characters, was the most complicated astrological instrument. Seventeen concentric rings surround a small compass, which represents the *tai qi* (Great Origin or Ultimate Cause). The *luo pan*, backed up by the consultation of charts, was used in complex forms of divination based on calculating changes in the position of the stars and planets.

making predictions based on astrology, as well as helping navigators who were about to go to sea.

Today the observatory is surrounded by ring roads and the roar of traffic, yet it remains an evocative reminder of the era in which Jesuit priests advised Chinese emperors, and reading the stars was of crucial importance to governance.

A short walk south, immediately to the east of Beijing Railway Station, is **Red Gate Gallery** (Hongmen Hualang; 红门画廊), one of China's first private contemporary art galleries located in an ancient and magnificent Ming dynasty watchtower. Regular exhibitions here promote established domestic artists.

Altar of the Sun

Beyond the Second Ring Road to the east of the observatory, along the vast thoroughfare of Jianguomenwai Dajie, are the famous old Friendship Store and nearby Silk Street Market *(see shopping listings, opposite)*. Further to the north, in the Jianguomen diplomatic quarter, is the **Altar of the Sun** ❿ (Ritan; 日坛; daily 6am–9pm; entrance fee), one of the eight altars which, along with the Temple of Heaven, played a prominent role in the ritual life of the Ming and Qing emperors. The rebuilt altar still stands, and is sometimes used for alternative art exhibitions. **Ritan Park** ⓫ (Ritan Gongyuan; 日坛公园) itself is a pleasant place for a stroll if you are in the neighbourhood – with rocks, ponds, meandering paths and a lakeside café that resembles a Qing-dynasty boat.

Dongyue Miao ⓬

Address: 141 Chaoyangmenwai Dajie
Tel: 6551-0151
Opening Hrs: Tue–Sun 8.30am–4.30pm
Entrance Fee: charge
Transport: Chaoyangmen subway station (line 2)

Further north, on the other side of Chaoyangmenwai Dajie, **Dongyue Miao** (Temple of the God of Tai Mountain; 东岳庙) is one of the few Daoist temples in the city. It was built to honour the highest celestial ruler of the Tai mountain, one of the five Daoist holy mountains in China. Dating back to

BELOW: nightclub in Sanlitun.

SHOPPING

Eastern Beijing affords near-limitless shopping opportunities. For each new glistening mall that rises from the dust of countless construction sites, smaller stores cluster round offering similar – though sometimes counterfeit – items at lower prices.

3.3 Shopping centre

An oft-overlooked mall housing hundreds of small shops and boutiques well worth browsing for unique items. A good option for men's clothing with craft and houseware shops on the basement floor.

Vivienne Lee
Stall 2125, 3.3 Shopping Centre, Sanlitun. Tel: 5136-5125. p287, E3
Gorgeous cashmere jumpers in a range of sizes and styles.

Antiques

Although many low-quality household items are much cheaper than they are in the West, antiques and works of art often fetch surprisingly high prices. Objects dating from before 1840 cannot be exported. Most antiques date from the early 20th century, which covered the final period of the late Qing dynasty and the early republic. In recent years, factories have produced many replicas of antiques, and it is harder to find really beautiful pieces, such as woodblock prints of traditional pictures.

Jianguomen

Friendship Store
友谊商店
17 Jianguomen Waidajie. Tel: 6500-3311. p289, D1
Though long past its heyday, when the Friendship Store was the only place in town that sold imported goods, this is still a reliable spot to pick up foreign news-papers and traditional Chinese souvenirs.

Shin Kong Place
新光天地
87 Jianguo Road. Tel: 6530-5888.
www.shinkong-place.com. off p289, E1
This Taiwanese depart-ment store is packed full of international brand names. The bottom floor is filled with small stalls providing nicely pack-aged gift ideas, such as tins of high-quality tea and other consumables.

Silk Street Market
秀水服装市场
8 Xiushui Dongjie, Jianguomen. Tel: 5169-9088. p289, E1
Beijing's legendary shopping destination moved from the old alleyway to an indoor location in 2006, but its character has remained essentially unchanged. It is packed with up to 20,000 shoppers a day bargaining furiously for shirts, silk ties, jackets, shoes and countless other items. It is regularly targeted for intellectual property violation – and has even inspired a movie. Bargain hard, otherwise you will pay well over the odds.

Sanlitun/ Sanlitun Village

A dream for international brand-seeking Chinese shoppers and foreign visitors after a glimpse of Beijing commercial future. Apple, American Apparel, Paul Smith and The North Face have all set up shop here.

Steve Madden
F9-13 Sanlitun Village. Tel: 6416-7215. p287, E3
One of many flagship stores in Sanlitun Village popular with the city's trendy set, Steve Madden stocks an international style
of accessories and famous shoes.

Yashow Market
雅秀服装市场
58 Gongti Beilu. Tel: 6416-8945. p287, E3
Perennially popular with foreign visitors and residents for larger-sized clothing, knock-off brands and the daily circus of boisterous haggling.

Solana

A Mediterranean-style "lifestyle" mall near Chaoyang Park encom-passing some 600 shops, a dining street, ice rink and cinema.

Khawachen 喀瓦坚
BL 2-03, Solana Lifestyle Shopping Park. Tel: 5905-6311. off p287, E3
Exquisite Tibetan hand-woven carpets both off the shelf and made to order.

Wangfujing

Several malls lie on Beijing's most famous shopping street for quality clothes, jewellery and electrical items. Other large stores provide shoppers with a broad range of options.

Beijing Painting & Calligraphy Store
北京画店
289 Wangfujing. Tel: 6513-8413. p288, B1
Four floors of arts, crafts and jewellery. Look out for solid gold Chairman Mao lapel badges.

Foreign Languages Bookstore 外文书店
235 Wangfujing Dajie. Tel: 6512-6903.
www.bpiec.com.cn. p288, B1
Still the best foreign-language bookstore in town, selling potboilers for long train journeys, hefty books on art and photography and Chinese-language learning materials.

the Yuan dynasty, it was once the largest of its kind in northern China.

Dongyue is a thriving Daoist centre, and an interesting place to visit. The complex consists of three courtyards. Off the main courtyard is the **Hall of Tai Mountain** (Daxiong Baodian; 大雄宝殿), in the centre of which is a statue of the god of Tai Mountain, surrounded by his high-ranking servants. Elsewhere are hundreds of other Daoist deities, dedicated to a wide variety of moral and spiritual codes – on controlling bullying and cheating, caring for animals and upholding piety. *(For more on Daoism see pages 63 and 132.)*

Poly Museum

Perched on the corner where the Second Ring Road meets Gongren Tiyuchang Beilu is the distinctive glass-curtain front of the **New Poly Plaza**, a tall office tower that houses the **Poly Museum**  (Baoli Bowuguan; 保利博物馆; Mon–Sat 9.30am–4.30pm; charge). The small museum displays

valuable Chinese artefacts recovered from abroad, including ancient bronzes, Buddha statues and several fountainheads looted from the Old Summer Palace *(see page 199).*

Sanlitun

Further east is **Sanlitun**  (三里屯), Beijing's throbbing heart of nightlife and bacchanalia. In 1996 there was only one bar here, but in true Beijing style it was not long before copycat venues emerged, hoping to cash in on the obvious success. The main strip is lined with a relatively humdrum succession of bars, though the Nali Patio and Tongli Studio area a few minutes' walk north house the favourite spots of many long-term residents. On the corner of Sanlitun Lu and the Workers' Stadium North Road (Gongti Beilu) is the unrepentantly conspicuous all-in-one entertainment district of **Sanlitun Village**, greeting passers-by with the curved metallic facade of the world's largest Adidas

SHOP

Centred on Yabao Lu, immediately west of Ritan Park, the Russian District is a wholesale traders' paradise. Countless fur dealers advertise their wares in Cyrillic and pedicab drivers ply their trade in Russian. The area also has a number of very reasonably priced Russian restaurants.

BELOW: neon-drenched Sanlitun bar street.

Northeastern Suburbs

The iconic curves of the 798 District's Bauhaus-style factory roofs are best viewed from inside 798 Space, a 1,980 sq-metre (22,000-sq-ft) exhibition area rumoured to have cost some US$20 million to renovate. Bold, red Maoist slogans have been left on the ceiling for visitors' appreciation.

RIGHT: Beijing's best art bookstore, Timezone 8 occupies a former factory canteen on Jiuxianqiao Lu in the Art District. There is a café attached. **BELOW:** the 798 Photo Gallery.

store. Cafés, restaurants and shops sit side by side in this ambitious international project.

Chaoyang Park

With an area of some 320 hectares (800 acres), **Chaoyang Park** (Chaoyang Gongyuan; 朝阳公园) is Asia's largest urban public park and surrounded by some of Beijing's most expensive high-rise apartments. It's great for kids, with fairground rides, boating, inflatable castles and room to run around. **Sony ExploraScience** (Suoni Tanmeng; 索尼探蒙; daily 9am–5.30pm; entrance fee) is an interactive museum of technology and the natural world located near the south gate.

798 Art District ⓭

Address: Main entrances are alleys 2 and 4 on Jiuxianqiao Road
Tel: 5978-9798; www.798art.org
Opening Hrs: daily 10am–5pm
Entrance Fee: some galleries charge
Transport: Bus 401 (or taxi) from Sanyuanqiao subway station (airport line)

Taking its name, or rather number, from the German-built arms-factory-turned-gallery that serves as its symbolic heart, the **798 Art District** (Qijiuba Yishuqu; 798艺术区) is a thriving community of contemporary artists, shops, studios and galleries great and small. Though the area was under threat of demolition for years, it finally received government protection as a state-approved cultural zone in 2006. Under such watchful eyes, public performance art was banned and some of its more controversial artists decamped to other corners of the city. A massive rise in rental costs has also closed many smaller exhibition spaces, but for the casual visitor this could merely represent an improvement in quality.

Though still, in parts, an unpolished and loose collective of grass-roots talents and personal spaces, some impressive – and even spectacular – galleries have emerged here, not least of which is The **Ullens Centre for Contemporary Art** (Youlunsi Dangdai Yishuqu; 尤伦斯当代艺术中心; Tue–Sun 10am–6pm; www.ucca.org.cn), a multi-million-dollar not-for-profit exhibition space. The **Xin Dong Cheng Space** (Chengxindong Guoji Dangdai Yishu Kongjian; 程昕东国际当代艺术空间; daily 10am–6.30pm; www.chengxindong.com) is worth a visit, while the **798 Photo Gallery** (Bainian Yinxiang Sheying Hualang; 百年印象摄影画廊; daily 10am–6pm; www.798photo.gallery.com) is a district mainstay, displaying both talented contemporary Chinese photographers and historical pictures. Don't be afraid to explore the district's many winding alleyways, open galleries and the huge, decommissioned factory equipment on the eastern side, though be aware that not every building is open to the public. *For more on the modern art scene, see pages 180–1.* ❑

BEST RESTAURANTS, BARS AND CAFÉS

Beijing/Chinese

The East is Red
红色经典
266 Baijialou, East Third
Ring Road. Tel: 6574-8289.
Open: 9am–2.30pm,
4–9.30pm. **$$** 39 p289, E3
Cultural Revolution-era
nostalgia and plenty of
kitsch. Rousing nightly
performances of Communist song and dance and
period fare.

Green T. House
紫云轩茶事
6 Gongti Xilu, Chaoyang.
Tel: 6552-8310. Open:
11am–midnight. **$$$$** 40
p287, D3
This beautifully decorated
restaurant gets its name
from the tea that is
featured in many of its
dishes. Good and reliable
as the food is, the
atmosphere and decor
are the main draws.

Made in China
长安一号餐厅
Grand Hyatt Hotel, Oriental
Plaza. Tel: 6510-9608.
Open: 11.30am–2.30pm,
5.30–10pm. **$$$$** 41
p288, B1

Prices are for a typical
dinner for one (three
dishes with beer in
Chinese restaurants, or
a three-course meal
with a half-bottle of
house wine in Western-
style restaurants).

$ = under Rmb 50
$$ = Rmb 50–100
$$$ = Rmb 100–200
$$$$ = over Rmb 200

Country-style cooking at
Western prices, an inter-
esting contrast of peasant
food in one of Beijing's
plushest hotels.

Noodle Loft 面酷
20 West Dawang Lu,
Chaoyang. Tel: 6774-9950.
Open: 11am–11pm. **$$** 42
p286, C1
Food from Shanxi
province and noodles of
every kind. Watching the
skilled chefs make
noodles by hand before
your eyes is almost as
much fun as eating them.

French

Bleu Marine 海蓝法餐厅
5 Guanghua Xili. Tel: 6500-
6704. Open: 11.30am–
11.30pm. **$$$$** 43 p289, E1
The chefs buy fresh ingredients daily, and the
French menu changes
regularly. Irresistible to
homesick Europeans.
Reservations are
essential.

Fusion

The Courtyard 四合苑
95 Donghuamen Dajie. Tel:
6526-8883. www.courtyard
beijing.com. Open: 6–10pm.
$$$$ 44 p288, B1
Close to the east gate of
the Forbidden City, this is
one of Beijing's top res-
taurants, serving an interesting range of East-West
fusion dishes. The gallery
features contemporary
Chinese art.

RIGHT: period charm at
the Red Capital Club.

Guizhou

Three Guizhou Men
三个贵州人
West Gate of the
Workers' Stadium (above
Coco Banana). Tel: 6551-
8517. Open: 24 hours. **$$**
45 p287, D3
Hip, spacious restaurant
offering authentic, spicy
Guizhou food of reliable
quality. Full picture menu
and lip-smacking milk tea.

Hotpot

Mengguren 蒙古人
Dong Chang'an Dajie. Tel:
6522-9500. Open: 11am–
2pm, 5.30–10pm. **$$$** 46
p288, B1
Enjoy hotpot, roast lamb
and other Mongolian
dishes while you listen to
live traditional songs in
this centrally located four-
storey restaurant.

Imperial

Red Capital Club
(Xin Hongzi Julebu)
新红资俱乐部
66 Dongsijiu Tiao,
Dongcheng. Tel: 6402-7150.
Open: 6pm–1am. **$$$$** 47
p286, C3
Located in a lovingly
restored courtyard house,
the decor here evokes
1950s China – and
authentically so, as much
of the furniture was once
used by high-level
leaders. The menu
features the favourite
dishes of Mao Zedong
and Deng Xiaoping.

Indian

Asian Star
亚洲之星新马印
26 East Third Ring Road
(Dongsanhuan Beilu).
Tel: 6582-5306.

Open: 11am–2.30pm, 5–10.30pm. **$$$** 48 p287, E3
This large, glitzy restaurant features food from China and Southeast Asia, but its best dishes are Indian.

Italian

Annie's 安妮
A1 Nongzhanguan Nanlu, Chaoyang Park. Tel: 6591-1931. Open: 11am–11pm. **$$** 49 p287, E3
Child- and wallet-friendly Italian. Puts service and affordability ahead of strict authenticity.

Assaggi 尝试
1 Sanlitun Beixiaojie. Tel: 8454-4508. Open: 11.30am–2.30pm, 6–11.30pm. **$$$$** 50 p287, E2
Italian food served in an elegant setting; the glassed-in rooftop patio is particularly pleasant.

Peking Duck

Da Dong Roast Duck Restaurant 大董烤鸭店
Building No. 3, Tuanjiehu Beikou. Tel: 6582-2892. Open: 11am–2pm, 5–9.30pm. Reservations are always required. **$$$–$$$$** 51 p287, E3
One of the classiest of duck restaurants (formerly called the Beijing Roast Duck Restaurant), where the meat is a little crisper than that of most competitors and every part of the duck is served in a range of side dishes.

Wangfujing Quanjude 王府井全聚德
9 Shuaifuyuan, off Wangfujing. Tel: 6525-3310. Open: 11am–2pm and 4.30–9.30pm. **$$$** 52 p288, B1
A branch of the famous Peking Duck restaurant.

Sichuanese

Sichuan Restaurant

四川饭店
37a Donganmen Jie, Wangfujing. Tel: 6513-7591. Open: 11am–11pm. **$$** 53 p288, B1
The Wangfujing branch of this famous restaurant (the original is at 51 Xirongxian Hutong in Xidan District) serves the same combination of Sichuan standards laced with chillies and peppers.

Xiheyaju 羲和雅居
Northeast corner of Ritan Park. Tel: 8561-7643. Open: 11am–2.30pm, 5–10pm. **$$** 54 p287, D4
An ever-popular Sichuan restaurant in attractive Ritan Park, Xiheyaju has indoor and outdoor dining.

Spanish

Mare 古老海
14 Xindong Lu, Sanlitun. Tel: 6417-1459. Open: noon–midnight. **$$$$** 55 p287, E3

Offering a lengthy tapas and wine menu for enjoyable lunches and romantic evenings.

Thai

Phrik Thai 泰辣椒
Gateway Building, 10 Yabao Lu. Tel: 8561-5236. Open: 11.30am–2pm, 5.30–11pm. **$$** 56 p289, D1
A good Thai restaurant in the Russian market area. Access via the small road running due south from Yabao Lu.

Purple Haze 紫苏庭
Opposite the Workers' Stadium North Gate. Tel: 6413-0899. Open: 11am–11.30pm. **$$** 57 p287, E3
Provides reasonably priced, reliable Thai classics such as red chicken curry and tom yum soup.

Tibetan

Makye Ame 玛吉阿米
A11 Xiushui Nanjie, Jianguomenwai. Tel: 6506-

Bars and Cafés

The Boat
8 Liangmaqiao South
Road. Tel: 6460-5512. ⑪
p287, E2
*See Gay & Lesbian
Travellers, page 274.*

The Bookworm 书虫
Bld 4, Nansalitun Lu.
Tel: 6586-9507.
www.beijingbookworm.com.
⑫ p287, E3
Beijing's best English-
language bookstore,
café and venue for
regular literary events.

Café Yo
30 Sanlitun Beilu. Tel:
6413-2168. ⑬ p287, E2
Excellent café for warm,
buttered croissants,
fresh salads and Illy
coffee. Wifi available.

Destination 目的地
Opposite Workers' Stadium
West Gate. Tel: 6551-5138.
⑭ p287, D3
*See Gay & Lesbian
Travellers, page 274.*

Drei Kronen 1308
China View #5, Workers'
Stadium East Road. Tel:
6503-5555. ⑮ p287, E3
A counterintuitively
large microbrewery
serving wallet-lightening
but excellent steins
of pilsner, wheat beer
and dark beer.

Face Bar
Just South of Workers'
Stadium South Gate.
Tel: 6551-6788. ⑯
p287, D4
Tasteful Asian cocktail
lounge with thoughtful
bartenders and red-
baize pool table.

LAN Club 兰会所
4/F LG Twin Towers, B12
Jianguomenwai Dajie.
Tel: 5109-6012. ⑰
p289, D1
Glamorous, Philippe
Starck-designed interior
with impressive wine
cellar and cigar lounge.

Paddy O'Sheas
28 Dongzhimenwai Dajie,
Sanlitun. Tel: 6415-6389.
⑱ p287, E2
Irish pub popular for
draught Guinness,
televised sports
matches and pool/
darts upstairs.

Vics 威克斯
Inside Workers' Stadium
North Gate. Tel: 5293-
0333. ⑲ p287, E3
Hard to ignore, Vics is
the largest nightclub in
the Workers' Stadium
North Gate section.
Expect crowds of fash-
ionable young people
and loud volumes.

9616. Open: 11.30–2am. **$$**
㊳ p289, D1
An intimate restaurant
with Tibetan art and fur-
nishings and Tibetan-
style dishes.

Prices are for a typical
dinner for one (three
dishes with beer in
Chinese restaurants, or
a three-course meal
with a half-bottle of
house wine in Western-
style restaurants).

$ = under Rmb 50
$$ = Rmb 50–100
$$$ = Rmb 100–200
$$$$ = over Rmb 200

Vegetarian

Pure Lotus Vegetarian
净心莲
10 Nongzhan Nanli,
Chaoyang Park. Tel: 6592-
3627. Open: 11am–11pm.
$$$ ㊹ p287, E3
Tofu, grains and special
spices make the fake
meat almost indistin-
guishable from the real
thing.

Xinjiang

Afunti 阿凡提
A2 Houguaibang Hutong,
Chaoyangmennei Dajie.
$$$. Tel: 6527-2288 or

6525-1071. Open: 11am–
11pm. **$$** ㊿ p287, C4
A fun pub atmosphere at
this boisterous Xinjiang
restaurant with belly
dancers and other shows.
The roast mutton, kebabs
and naans are good.
Book ahead if possible.

Xinjiang Red Rose
新疆红玫瑰餐厅

7 Xingfu Yicun, opposite the
Workers' Stadium North
Gate. Tel: 6415-5741.
Open: 11am–11pm. **$$** ㊱
p287, E3
Hookah pipes, nightly
music, Uighur dancing
girls and excellent *dapaiji*
("big plate chicken").
Large groups can get
rather boisterous.

FAR LEFT & LEFT: The Courtyard, one of Beijing's most
exclusive restaurants. **ABOVE:** Beijing duck meat at
Quanjude's Wanfujing branch.

MODERN ART

Having captured the imagination of the West, contemporary Chinese art has experienced a roller-coaster ride in recent years

Though modern China lags behind other nations in creative fields, its contemporary art has long fascinated the world and Beijing was, until recently, the epicentre of the scene. The peak of profitability was 2007 when Yue Minjun's *Execution* fetched US$6 million at auction. The painting was inspired by the 1989 Tiananmen crackdown, giving the work the political overtones that prove irresistible to Western audiences. Similar prices for other pieces caused a frenzy of speculation, imitation – and ultimately decline.

The abandoned industrial workshops that aspiring artists had converted into the studios and galleries of the 798 Art District *(see page 176)* became a new kind of factory, churning out derivative works that cynically pandered to foreign buyers. When the global economic crisis tightened purse strings the market crashed, and hard.

The big players – artists of genuine talent as well as the main galleries – survived, however, and some see the current creative environment as more grounded and realistic. In 2009, a more interactive approach was in evidence. Derelict *hutong* became makeshift galleries, small shops were turned into communal exhibition spaces, and at least one local journalist was "kidnapped" as part of a collaborative project. Some may lament the passing of the heady days of dizzying prices and boundless optimism, but for the casual enthusiast Beijing now offers a contemporary art scene that seems to suit its character better.

ABOVE: *About Circle No. 4* by Hong Hao, 2004 comprises photographs of hundreds of daily objects rearranged to form a complex still life.
LEFT: a converted warehouse in the 798 Art District.

ABOVE: *Chat* by Jin Jiangbo, 2008. An installation that articulates the pressure brought about by information technology.
LEFT: *Miss Mao* statues by the Gao Brothers.

ROLL CALL: BEIJING'S CREATIVE CROWD

Artist, activist, iconoclast, Ai Weiwei's improbable oeuvre includes destroying an ancient Han-dynasty urn in the name of art, and co-designing the National Stadium – which he later compared to a toilet bowl. Conceptual artists the Gao Brothers delight in taunting the establishment – for example, their signature "Miss Mao" statues boast naked female breasts. Cao Fei worked in photography and video before moving into the virtual world of Second Life where fantasy improves on mundane reality. Sheng Qi famously severed a finger on his left hand and fled China following the Tiananmen Square massacre. He has now returned to the capital to create his emotionally charged paintings. Pioneer Huang Rui helped stage the first exhibition of Chinese contemporary art in 1979 and is regarded as one of the fathers of the 798 Art District, while Yue Minjun produces some of China's most recognisable works of contemporary art, invariably depicting identical, maniacally laughing figures. Photographer Hong Hao is popular among collectors, particularly for works depicting his personal possessions: from chess pieces to condoms, magazines to Mao badges.

ABOVE: *Leaving the Garden of Dreams No. 1* by Lu Peng.
BELOW: *Royal Pond* by Du Yi and ChART Contemporary, 2009 – an abandoned building converted into a temporary exhibition space.

ABOVE: *Catching Prostitute B* by the Gao Brothers, 2007. A sculpture inspired by a photograph of the arrest of a sex worker.

ABOVE: *RMB City* by Cao Fei, 2009. An installation of a virtual art piece originally created on internet platform Second Life.

WESTERN BEIJING

The university, haven for revolutionaries, sets the tone for this fascinating section of the city, home to important temples, churches and attractive parkland

Western Beijing has long been the home of intellectuals and students. Most of the city's hundreds of universities and other institutes of higher learning are located in Haidian District, and the area has also been a base for some of the nation's best-known writers, revolutionaries and martyrs. In more recent years, its historic role as a centre of higher learning and research led the Zhongguancun area *(see page 193)* to be selected as the site for what is billed as "China's Silicon Valley". The idea to create a hotbed of future-oriented research and development in Western Beijing seemed like a fantasy when it was announced in 1988, but the Zhongguancun sub-district is now occupied by an increasing number of internationally funded research and development centres, as well as the regional headquarters of IBM, Microsoft and Intel.

South of the university area is the Financial District, the streets lined with banks, ministries and regulatory commissions. Though still lacking a stock exchange, the pivotal Financial Street (Jinrong Jie) – close to the Second Ring Road west of the Xidan shopping mall – has been the recipient of a multi-billion-dollar upgrade, enabling it to rival New York's Wall Street and adding several luxury hotels and respectable bars to Beijing's entertainment scene in the process.

Walking between sights is not always practical in this sprawling part of town, though several good museums are clustered close together on Fuxing Lu – an otherwise dizzying thoroughfare stretching east as far as the eye can see until it morphs into Chang'an Avenue.

LEFT: *jiaozi* are a local favourite. **RIGHT:** the striking facade of the North Cathedral.

North Cathedral ❶

Address: 33 Xishiku Dajie
Tel: 6617-5198
Opening Hrs: daily, services Mon–Sat
6am, 7am, Sun 6am, 7am, 8am, 10am
Entrance Fee: free
Transport: Xisi subway station (line 4)

Situated not far to the northwest of
Beihai Park, in a side *hutong*, is the
imposing Gothic-style **North Cathedral** (Beitang; 北堂; also known as
Xishiku; 西什库), built by Jesuits in
1889. It is best known for its role in
the frenzied Boxer Rebellion of 1900;
when the Boxers' hostility to foreigners reached fever pitch they lay siege
to the cathedral, in which about
3,000 converted Chinese Christians
had taken refuge under the protection of the French bishop Favier.

Although most of the other Boxers
were rounded up, incorporated
into imperial militias and marched
off to face the approaching Allied
troops, the Qing court allowed this
one group to continue attacking the

ABOVE: Johann Adam
Schall von Bell (1592–
1666) is buried at the
Old Jesuit Cemetery. The
site is seen as an
important emblem of
China's long links with
the West, and several
scholars and officials
have proposed that it be
renovated and fully
opened to the public.

cathedral for seven weeks, resulting in
the deaths of numerous Chinese converts. The siege was finally ended by
the intervention of Japanese soldiers.
The church survived, only to be shut
down and looted during the Cultural
Revolution. It was restored, and today
has a sizeable congregation made up
of Catholics of the Patriotic Church.

Earthenware and Brick Market Church

A short distance northwest, the
**Earthenware and Brick Market
Church ❷** (Gangwashitang; 缸瓦市
堂), in Xisi Beidajie, is one of the two
most important Protestant churches
in Beijing (the other is the Rice
Market Church east of the Imperial
Palace, *see page 171*). It was built at
the beginning of the 20th century for
the London Bible Society.

Another Christian monument
is the Old Jesuit Cemetery, in the
courtyard of the Beijing Administrative College on Maweigoulu, in

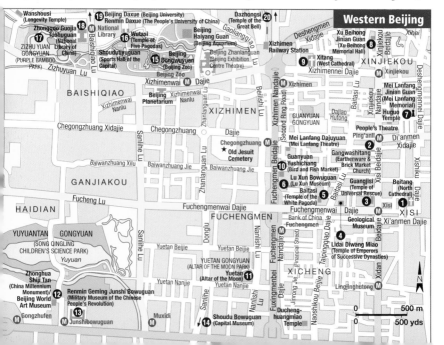

Western Beijing

the Fuchengmen District further west beyond the Second Ring Road. Sixty-three Jesuits, both Western and Chinese, are buried here. Most prominent among the tombs are those of Matteo Ricci, Johann Adam Schall von Bell and Ferdinand Verbeist. Although the cemetery is not technically open to the public, guards at the gate will generally allow visitors to enter.

Guangjisi ❸

Address: Fuchengmennei Dajie
Tel: 6616-0907
Opening Hrs: daily 8am–4pm
Entrance Fee: free
Transport: Xisi subway station (line 4)

At the eastern end of Fuchengmennei, wedged between apartment blocks and warehouses, stands **Guangjisi** (Temple of Universal Rescue; 广济寺), a well-used and atmospheric Buddhist temple. It is often a stop on the popular cycle-rickshaw "Hutong Tour" which starts from the North Gate of Beihai Park *(see page 277)*.

Under the Ming emperor Tianshun, an existing Jin-dynasty temple on the site was renovated. This was in turn restored and extended in 1669, under Emperor Kangxi. The temple was rebuilt in 1935, following a fire, and more restoration work was completed in 1952, although it was kept closed during the Cultural Revolution. The design of the temple follows the classic Buddhist architectural plan. In the third hall, the Hall of Guanyin, is a thousand-armed statue of the goddess of mercy, gilded during the Qing period. A copper Guanyin figure and a Guanyin on a lotus blossom dating from the Ming period are also on view.

Stored in the library of the monastery are valuable handwritten sutras dating back to the Tang dynasty, along with more than 30,000 old rubbings of stone inscriptions.

Lidai Diwang Miao

A five-minute walk west from Guangjisi, towards the zoo, is the **Lidai Diwang Miao ❹** (Temple of Emperors of Successive Dynasties; 历代帝王庙; 9am–4.30pm; entrance fee), built in 1530 during

ABOVE: the *hutong* neighbourhoods extend west beyond Guangjisi temple. **BELOW:** a tour of the *hutong*.

the reign of Jiajing for the ceremonial worship to past rulers. Jiajing was the only Ming emperor to pay homage to his predecessors here, though several Qing emperors later adopted the practice. The entrance is flanked by stone stelae ordering riders to dismount and guarded by an exceptionally long shadow wall. Several huge buildings matching the imperial majesty of the Forbidden City lie within the perimeter. English-speaking guides are available for a fee.

Baitasi **⑤**

Address: Fuchengmennei Dajie
Tel: 6613-3317
Opening Hrs: Tue–Sun 9am–4.30pm
Entrance Fee: charge
Transport: a short walk from Fuchengmen (line 2) or Xisi (line 4) subway stations

Continuing west a few more minutes is another Buddhist shrine, **Baitasi** (Temple of the White Pagoda; 白塔寺), which was built in 1096 during the Liao dynasty. Kublai Khan restored it in Tibetan style in 1271, but it was destroyed by fire soon after-

wards. The monastery was rebuilt in 1457 and at the same time received its official name of Miaoyingsi (Temple of Divine Justice).

The temple is best known for its 51-metre (167ft) white dagoba (a Tibetan-style shrine), which dates from 1279; it is larger and older than the similar structure in Beihai Park. Its top is adorned by an engraved copper canopy, from which little bells hang, moving in the wind in order to drive away evil spirits. In the fourth hall there are sculptures of the three Buddhas and two Buddha pupils, as well as some *thangka* – Tibetan scroll pictures.

Baitasi and its grounds were restored in the late 1970s, when valuable objects were found in the dagoba, including Buddhist manuscripts and calligraphy by Emperor Qianlong, as well as jewellery and coins from various dynasties. A further restoration in 2000 revealed more treasures. Within a series of antechambers and private gardens is the Temple Kitchen (*see restaurant listings*), whose imperial-themed decoration includes a mirror that belonged to Qianlong.

ABOVE: China is nothing if not bureaucratic, and there often seem to be petty laws and restrictions on almost everything. There is an army of officialdom – from policemen to traffic controllers, security guards and park wardens. **BELOW:** the museum inside Lu Xun's former residence.

Lu Xun Museum ⑥

Address: 19 Gongmenkou Ertiao
Tel: 6616-5654
Opening Hrs: daily 9am–4pm
Entrance Fee: charge
Transport: Fuchengmen subway station (line 2)

The **Lu Xun Museum** (Lu Xun Bowuguan; 鲁迅博物馆), comprising the former residence of one of the great Chinese writers of the 20th century as well as an exhibition hall, is situated on a small street between Baitasi and the Second Ring Road. The typical Chinese courtyard house – which he bought with borrowed money – is situated near **Fuchengmen**, an old imperial gate due west of Beihai Park. The eastern room in the northern part of the courtyard belonged to Lu Xun's mother, the western room to his wife. The rooms to the south served as living quarters and a library.

The small room added to the north side was the study and bedroom that Lu Xun called the "Tiger's Tail". Here he wrote the two stories *The Tomb* and *Wild Grasses*. Photographs, unpublished manuscripts, letters and a copy of the entry he made in his diary on the day of his death are all on display.

Mei Lanfang Memorial ⑦

Address: 9 Huguosi Jie
Tel: 8322-3598; www.meilanfang.com
Opening Hrs: daily 9am–4pm
Entrance Fee: charge
Transport: Pinganli subway station (line 4)

The former residence of Beijing Opera's brightest star and relentless innovator Mei Lanfang (1894–1961; *see panel, below*) has been converted into the **Mei Lanfang Memorial** (Mei Lanfang Jinian Guan; 梅兰芳纪念馆), a museum dedicated to his costumes, personal effects and the history of the art.

Approximately 1km (²/₃ mile) to the west and conveniently located by Chegongzhuang subway station (line 2), the **Mei Lanfang Theatre** (Mei Lanfang Dajuyuan; 梅兰芳大剧院) was built in 2007 to accommodate and promote Beijing Opera to the masses: over 1,000 seats line the high-tech auditorium that spans three floors.

TIP

The website of the National Peking Opera Company (www.cnpoc.cn) has English listings of the Mei Lanfang Theatre's upcoming performances as well as opera news, and even audio and video recordings.

BELOW LEFT:
Mei Lanfang, star of the opera.

Hitting the High Notes

The most celebrated Beijing Opera performer, Mei Lanfang (1894–1961) was a master of the *dan* role, a central female character traditionally played by a man. Mei was born into a family of performers. He began studying opera as a child, making his stage debut at 11. By the time he was 20, he was already a household name. In 50 years as a *dan* performer, Mei played more than 100 female roles, including concubines, generals and goddesses. He was also an innovator, designing new dances and other routines to enhance his roles. He added a sword dance to the opera *Conqueror Xiang Yu Parts with His Concubine*, and a ribbon dance, based on drawings in ancient Buddhist frescos, to *The Fairy Scattering Flowers*. Mei was an ambassador abroad for his ancient art form, visiting various European cities as well as Japan, Russia, India, Egypt and the US – which he toured in 1929 – and making many friends, including actor Charlie Chaplin and singer Paul Robeson. As Beijing Opera enjoys something of a renaissance in modern times, the graceful figure of Mei Lanfang once more takes the lead. The 1,035-seater Mei Lanfang Theatre opened in Beijing in 2007 with a Chen Kaige biopic released the following year.

Writers of Beijing

Follow in the footsteps of the city's famous writers, including Lu Xun, Cao Xueqin and Guo Moruo

Many of China's most important literary figures composed their influential and lasting works in the capital. Their footsteps can be retraced on a paper trail of their homes and hangouts.

Lu Xun: undisputed father of modern Chinese literature

Born in Zhejiang and having penned some of his most famous works in Shanghai, the so-called father of modern Chinese literature lived in Beijing from 1912 to 1926 and, in 1919, took part in the May Fourth Movement – a cultural renaissance that sought to overturn China's ancient traditions. The use of vernacular was one literary innovation, notable in Lu Xun's most famous work, *The True Story of Ah-Q*. His former residence is in the west of the city *(see opposite)*.

The founding of the National Library of China drew on the contributions of Lu Xun and still holds handwritten volumes by the author totalling some 5,000 pages.

Mao Dun: novelist and "contradiction"

Born Shen Dehong and writing under the pen name Mao Dun, one of China's most famous novelists dropped out of Peking University in 1916 due to financial troubles. He took up work as an editor in Shanghai, the setting for his most famous novel, *Midnight* (1933), regarded as a classic of social realism. An early supporter of Communism, Shen became Minister for Culture upon the founding of the People's Republic in 1949 and even served as personal secretary to Mao Zedong. His former residence in Yuanensi *hutong (see page 155)* houses original manuscripts and letters as well as the austere furnishings of a lifelong socialist.

Cao Xueqin: dreamer of red mansions

Regarded as pre-eminent among China's four great classical novels, *The Dream of the Red Mansions* – written by Cao Xueqin in the mid-18th century – has spawned an entire field of study known as "redology", and even a type of elaborate cuisine based on recipes described in the book *(see Laijinyuxuan restaurant, page 111)*. Cao worked as a teacher in Shihu *hutong* and, it is believed, lived there until he moved to the western suburbs to pen his great work, an epic account of intrigue and indecency centred on two aristocratic houses. His former residence *(see page 212)* is sparse on exhibits, but offers a chance to see a handwritten manuscript of his greatest work.

Guo Moruo: revolutionary

The influential revolutionary author and philosopher has now fallen out of favour with China's younger generation though, the courtyard house he occupied from 1963 until his death *(see page 153)* is an opportunity to experience the spacious and well-preserved residence of a Communist official – Guo was the first president of the Chinese Academy of Sciences and his work applying Marxist theories to Chinese history was praised by Mao. Here he wrote his theses, poems and other works. Many of his manuscripts and documents are still housed within these walls.   ❑

LEFT: a scene from *The Dream of the Red Mansions*.

Xu Beihong Memorial Hall

Further north is the **Xu Beihong Memorial Hall ❽** (Xu Beihong Jinian Guan; 徐悲鸿纪念馆; Tue–Sun 9am–4.30pm; entrance fee). Xu Beihong (1895–1953) was one of China's most famous modern artists, well known for his numerous paintings of horses.

When she died, his widow, Liao Jingwen, left this house, along with his books, calligraphy and other work, to the People's Republic, and a memorial to Xu was built in the grounds. Later, the Memorial Hall was moved here, to 53 Xinjiekou Beidajie.

Xu's studio was rebuilt in the new hall exactly as it was shortly before his death. Hanging on the walls are a copy of his painting, *Rich Harvest*, works by Ren Bonian and Qi Baishi, and a photograph of Xu taken in 1913 by Rabindranath Tagore, the Indian poet and Nobel Prize winner.

The works of art exhibited in the Memorial Hall were almost all collected by the artist himself during his lifetime. They include more than 1,200 examples from the Tang, Song, Yuan, Ming and Qing dynasties, as well as works from the time of the May Fourth Movement (1919). One of the most valuable items is a cartoon of the Tang painting *The Scroll of the 87 Immortals*, by Wu Daozi.

West Cathedral

Not far from Xizhimen stands another Catholic church, the **West Cathedral ❾** (Xitang; 西堂). Built in the 18th century, it was destroyed during the persecution of Christians in 1811. A second church, built in 1867, was in turn a victim of the Boxer Rebellion. The present building dates from the beginning of the 20th century.

Bird and Fish Market

Next to the Xizhimen overpass nearby is the **Bird and Fish Market ❿** (Guanyuan Yushichang; 官园鱼市场), which is particularly large and active at weekends. Keeping caged birds and crickets is especially popular with older Chinese men, a traditional activity that lends the market a flavour of Old Beijing. The tradition of cricket fighting, and associated gambling on the outcome, goes back at least as far as the Song dynasty. There are regular cricket-fighting events all over China; punters study the insect's form (fighting records are kept) and other attributes to make a qualified bet. Other vendors sell Koi carp, among other highly decorative fish. The best specimens can fetch astronomical sums.

Altar of the Moon

Situated symmetrically opposite the Altar of the Sun (Ritan, *see page 173*) is another of the eight altars that played such a great role in the ritual life of the Ming and Qing emperors. The **Altar of the Moon ⓫** (Yuetan; 月坛; daily 6am–9.30pm; entrance fee) stands in a public park – easy to find because of its large telecommunications tower. The northern section features traditional Chinese architecture, while the

ABOVE: Xu Beihong's innovation was to combine Western and Chinese techniques, to great effect.
BELOW: a flavour of Old Beijing at the Bird and Fish Market.

On the northern side of Fuchengmen overpass several curious iron camels accompanied by handlers can be seen. The site was one of the old city gates through which coal was brought from western Beijing on the backs of such beasts.

southern section is characterised by a series of pools and rockeries.

Just to the east, across the Second Ring Road is **Financial Street** (Jinrong Jie), Beijing's financial nexus since its completion in 2008. an ideal spot for tourists to take a break in one of the many hotel cafés and bars.

Millennium Monument

The **China Millennium Monument** ⑫ (Zhonghua Shiji Tan; 中华世纪坛) is an odd, "futuristic" structure that includes a spire, bronze crossways, "Holy Fire Square" and fountains, all rife with symbolism, most of it so obscure that even the explanations offered in publicity brochures are of little help. In essence, the building seems intended as the government's answer to the Temple of Heaven – minus the religious significance – and as one of Jiang Zemin's legacies to the city. It was here that the government officially rang in the year 2000 in a huge ceremony that included the running of a torch here from the site of Peking Man. It is now carving out a role for itself as the **Beijing World Art Museum**, and has

held several large exhibitions of local and foreign artists. The museum's permanent exhibition is devoted to ancient civilisations.

Behind the monument is **Yuyuantan Park** (Yuyuantan Gongyuan; 玉渊潭公园; daily 6am–10.30pm), a scenic spot popular with Beijing's emperors for its gardens and serene lake. A famous cherry blossom festival is held here every spring.

PLA Museum

To the south, on Fuxing Lu, is the **Military Museum of the Chinese People's Revolution** ⑬ (Renmin Geming Junshi Bowuguan; 人民革命军事博物馆; Tue–Sun 8.30am–4.30pm; entrance fee), with four floors of weapons and a motley band of tanks, planes and other military hardware lined up at the front. Its Ming-dynasty weapons are a highlight, while the modern military history displays completely omit events that officials would prefer to brush over.

Capital Museum

Another notable history lesson awaits a 1km (2/3-mile) walk to the

BELOW: ringing in the 21st century at the Millennium Monument.

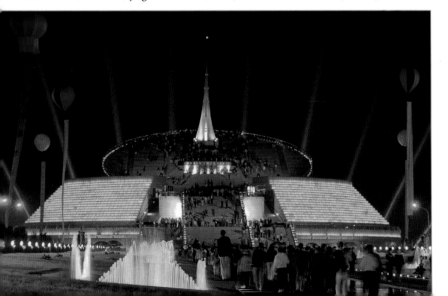

east (or by taking bus 1 and alighting at Gonghua Dalou stop) at the **Capital Museum** ⑭ (Shoudu Bowuguan; 首都博物馆; Tue–Sun 9am–4pm; entrance fee). This state-of-the-art museum was opened in 2006 to house collections once held at the Confucius Temple. It boasts a permanent exhibit on Beijing's 850-year history as capital, its urban development, culture and customs. There are also fine art collections of bronze, jade, calligraphy and porcelain. Generous funding has provided a much higher standard of English captioning than in many Chinese museums, as well as multimedia displays and a dedicated movie hall. The museum is also an architectural curiosity, with its distinctive overhanging roof a nod to ancient Chinese design.

Beijing Zoo ⑮

Address: 137 Xizhimenwai Dajie
Tel: 6831-4411
Opening Hrs: daily 7.30am–6pm

Entrance Fee: charge
Transport: Beijing Zoo subway station (line 4)

Further to the west, past the Second Ring Road, is **Beijing Zoo** (Beijing Dongwuyuan; 北京动物园). Around 1900, a Manchu high official returned from a long journey abroad bringing a special gift for the Empress Dowager Cixi: a great number of animals, which he had mainly bought in Germany. To accommodate them, Cixi had a decaying park transformed into the "Park of Ten Thousand Creatures". In time this became the present-day zoo. Be warned that standards are not up to those of most Western zoos. The main attraction, of course, is the giant pandas, whose quarters are right by the entrance. Also within the zoo complex is the **Beijing Aquarium** (Beijing Haiyang Guan; 北京海洋馆; same hours as zoo; separate entrance fee) which manages to create a more refined demonstration of the natural world.

ABOVE: artillery piece at the PLA Museum.
BELOW: Beijing Zoo was the first in the world to breed giant pandas. Cubs weigh just 100 grams (3½oz) – no other mammal, except marsupials, gives birth to offspring so much smaller than the adult.

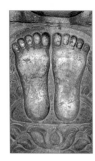

ABOVE: Buddha's footprints are honoured at Wutasi.

Wutasi ⑯

Address: 24 Wutaisi Cun
Tel: 6217-3543
Opening Hrs: daily 9am–4.30pm
Entrance Fee: charge
Transport: National Library subway station (line 4) or by exiting Beijing Zoo North Gate

Just behind the zoo, to the north of the Shoudutiyuguan sports hall, is **Wutasi** (Temple of Five Pagodas; 五塔寺). The temple dates back to the 15th-century reign of the Ming emperor Yongle. It was restored during Qianlong's reign but devastated by European troops in 1860 and again in 1900. The building, with five small pagodas standing on a massive square base, is in what is known in Buddhism as the "Diamond Throne Pagoda" style, and quite different from other temples in Beijing. Worth seeing above all else are the bas-reliefs on the outside, which depict Buddha figures, symbolic animals, lotus flowers, heavenly guardians, the wheel of Buddhist teaching, and other Buddhist symbols.

Go up two flights of stairs to the terrace where the bases of the pagodas are also adorned with reliefs. In the cloisters down below, visitors can study the various styles of pagoda architecture in China through an exhibition of photographs. An impressive collection of steles also awaits in this courtyard. The temple is a peaceful place, and does not get as crowded as most others in the city.

Purple Bamboo Park and the Longevity Temple

Across Baishiqiao to the west is the **Purple Bamboo Park ⑰** (Zizhu Yuan; 紫竹公园; daily 6am–8pm; entrance fee), popular for its amusement park and playground. Around the three lakes are 10 different varieties of bamboo – a rare plant in northern China – including *Phyllostachys nigra*, known as "purple bamboo" in Chinese and "black bamboo" in Eng-

SHOPPING

Haidian

Golden Resources Shopping Mall
金源时代购物中心
Yuanda Lu, Haidian District. Tel: 8887-5888. www.global. newyanshamall.com.
off p284, A1
What used to be the world's largest shopping mall is a sight in itself, with its vast, often empty corridors and incredible quantities of expensive designer clothes. Marvel at high-end imported Japanese toilets and faux-European furniture.
Lao Jian Handmade Leatherwear
老茧手工制品

38 Xinjiekou Beidajie. p285, E2
A tailor-made service at keen prices.
Zoo Market
Opposite Beijing Zoo, Haidian District. Tel: 8837-8056. p284, B2
This wholesale clothing market is well known to Beijing residents for its low prices. Not all stalls offer retail sales.

Wudaokou

The student area has many cool cafés and arty shops.
Wudaokou Clothing Market
五道口服装市场
261 Beisihuan Zhonglu.

Popular and inexpensive clothing market.
Yufeng Bookstore
雨枫书馆
69 Chengfu Lu.
Tel: 6270-1928.
Specialising in female authors and children's books. Holds regular writers' salons.

Xicheng/Xidan

Joy City
131 Xidan Beidajie, Xicheng. Tel: 6651-7777.
www.xidanjoycity.com.
p291, D1
Xidan shopping district's newest big mall is impressive, and is packed with international brands from Japan, Korea, the US and Europe.

Art Box
Joy City Mall, B1, 18a. Tel: 5971-6246. p291, B1
Korean designer gifts, clothes and accessories.
UNIQLO 优衣库
Floor 3, Joy City Mall. Tel: 6528-1788. p291, B1
Trendy Japanese casual clothing brand.

Zhongguancun

Beijing's hi-tech zone is the best place in town to purchase electronics and computers.
Hailong Market
海龙大厦
Zhongguancun Dajie.
off p284, B1
A towering mall packed full of stalls selling all kinds of electronics.

lish. Boats set sail from here to the Summer Palace *(see margin, page 206)*.

A short distance northwest of the park is the Buddhist **Wanshousi** (万寿寺; Longevity Temple; Tue–Sun 9am–4.30pm; entrance fee), built in 1577 and featuring a fine collection of bronze statues, ceramics and various other ancient artefacts. The temple was a favourite of Cixi, who would break the journey to the Summer Palace here.

North to Beijing University

Just north of the park is an enormous complex housing the **National Library of China** ⑱ (Zhongguo Guojia Tushuguan; 中国国家图书馆; daily 9am–5pm). Established in 1909, this is the largest library in Asia and the fifth-largest in the world, with some 21 million items. The library has an unrivalled collection of ancient Chinese texts.

From here you can go north to **People's University** (Renmin Daxue; 人民大学), not far from the Friendship Hotel *(see NW suburbs map, page 200)*, which is home to foreign experts from all over the world.

A short distance further north is **Zhongguancun**, which has been dubbed China's "Silicon Valley". Zhongguancun has nothing of the physical beauty of the other, more famous Silicon Valley in California, but it is an interesting window into the Chinese government's plans for the future. The area claims to be home to more than 400,000 of China's brightest scientists and teachers, and has become one of the nation's most important centres of science and technology research.

Still further north, out beyond the Fourth Ring Road close to the Old Summer Palace, is the prestigious **Beijing University** ⑲ (Beijing Daxue, or "Beida"; 北京大学). The institution was founded in 1898, but its first campus was in the city centre, in the eastern part of the old Imperial City. The present campus, in the western district of Haidian, was previously the site of the American-founded Yanjing University, which merged with the main institution in 1953. The campus has park-like grounds with a quiet lake, and a classical Chinese pagoda with pavilions and stone figures.

WHERE

In 1918, a graduate of Hunan First Normal School arrived at Peking University to take up a poorly paid job as library assistant. Mao Zedong worked here for six months, spending his free time at meetings of the Society for the Study of Marxism. The site of the former library is now a monument to his humble beginnings. Xinwenhua Movement Memorial Hall, 29 Wusi Dajie, Tue–Sun 8.30am–4.30pm.

BELOW: bikes are increasingly outnumbered by cars.

How Beijing Fell out of Love with the Humble Bicycle

Though once known as a city of bicycles, Beijing has been embracing the motor vehicle in recent years with a passion that has seen private car ownership double from 2 million vehicles in 2003 to 4 million by the end of 2009. The ranks of sedate riders that ruled the capital's roads had a romantic quality for Western visitors, but for the people of Beijing the bicycle was never more than a practical necessity. A car is now seen as the ultimate status symbol for the emerging middle class, with convenience barely an issue: the average daily commute time for rush-hour drivers has now exceeded an hour – one of the longest in the world.

Despite the concerns of environmentalists, the government seems reluctant to change its policy of tax discounts and cheap licence fees. In fact, the removal of high-polluting vehicles from Beijing's urban areas in recent years has been cited as opportunity to allow even more cars onto the roads. The powerful auto industry is

considered a major contributor to China's growing economy, and Beijing has always been unwilling to bar its people the same luxuries that are enjoyed in the developed world. In a remarkably flat city renting a bicycle is still a good option for visitors, however. Getting to know the extensive and cost-effective subway system is also an excellent way to beat the rush-hour traffic jams.

Today, more than 30,000 students are studying at Beida, many of them foreigners. The students have been involved in most of the political upheavals of the 20th century; from the May Fourth Movement of 1919 to the Cultural Revolution and the 1970s and 1980s pro-democracy protests – which resulted in the demonstrations and "Democracy Wall" newspapers of 1979 and, tragically, in the Tiananmen massacre of 1989. In recent years, the students have become known for their conservative nationalism, and some argue that the school is now dominated by the so-called "new leftists".

The remains of the old Beijing University – the so-called **Red Building** (Hong Lou; 红楼; daily 8.30am–5.30pm; entrance fee), at the eastern end of Shatan Jie – can still be seen. Here, Li Dazhao, one of the founders of the Chinese Communist Party, used to teach, and Mao Zedong used to work in the library. Chen Duxiu, the first General Secretary of the Chinese Communist Party, also taught at the old Beida.

ABOVE: the 7-metre (23ft) bell at Dazhongsi, the Temple of the Great Bell. **BELOW:** Beijing University students.

The university area is well supplied with bars and cheap restaurants, with the main concentrations on Weigongcun and around Wudaokou.

Dazhongsi ⑳

Address: 31 North Third Ring Road
Tel: 6255-0819
Opening Hrs: Tue–Sun 9am–4.30pm
Entrance Fee: charge
Transport: Dazhongsi subway station
Around 2km (1¼ miles) to the east of the modern Beida on the Third Ring Road, squeezed in among the new buildings and the factories, is **Dazhongsi** (Temple of the Great Bell; 大钟寺), dating from AD 743. This temple, like many others in the city, was badly damaged during the Cultural Revolution, but has been restored. On display are some 160 ancient bells, from tiny 150-gram (6oz) specimens to the bronze giant that gives the temple its name, housed in the further part of the grounds in a 17-metre (56ft) high tower.

The Great Bell was made in 1406 on the orders of Emperor Yongle and measures 7 metres (23ft) in height, has a diameter of 3 metres (10ft) and weighs 46.5 tonnes. Inscribed on the bell is the entire text of the *Huayan Sutra*, consisting of some 200,000 characters. At the top of this, and other every bell, is a *pulao*, a mythical creature.

The Huayan sect has had great influence over traditional Asian attitudes to nature and inspired many artists. It was founded in AD 630 and endured until about 1000. Its teaching states that all creatures and things are imbued with a cosmic principle, that everything exists in harmony with everything else, and that every grain of dust contains all the wealth of Buddha. This teaching does not preach the need to influence the cosmic powers or to use magic, as is the case with Tantric (Tibetan) Buddhism. It relies, instead, on contemplation and observation. ❏

BEST RESTAURANTS, BARS AND CAFÉS

Restaurants

Beijing / Chinese

Amigos Lounge
5 Yude Alley, Jinrong Jie
(Financial Street). Tel: 6651-
0999. Open: 11am–1am.
$$$ 62 p285, D3
A spacious interior and
three gardens for
imperial-inspired cuisine.

Ding Ding Xiang 鼎鼎香
Bld 7, Guoxing Jiayuan. Tel:
8835-7775. Open: 11am–
10pm. **$$$** 63 p284, B3
A popular hotpot joint
with secret-recipe sesa-
me dipping sauce for the
meat and vegetables.

Temple Kitchen
今风古韵食府
171 Fuchengmennei Dajie,
Baitasi. Tel: 6618-1119.
www.jinfengguyun.com.
Open: 9am–11pm. **$$$$**
64 p285, D4
Exquisite private dining
rooms and tranquil
atmosphere.

Tongheju Restaurant
同和居
72 Sanlihe Nanjie, Yuetan,
Xicheng. Tel: 6852-2917.
Open: 10am–9.30pm. **$$**
65 p284, B4
A venerable establish-

Prices are for a typical
dinner for one (three
dishes with beer in
Chinese restaurants, or
a three-course meal
with a half-bottle of
house wine in Western-
style restaurants).

$ = under Rmb 50
$$ = Rmb 50–100
$$$ = Rmb 100–200
$$$$ = over Rmb 200

ment, with food from
Shandong province.

Tongxinju Mao Jia Cai 童
心居毛家菜
16 Minzu Daxue Lu, Haidi-
an. Tel: 6843-9049. Open:
9.30am–11pm. **$$** 66
p284, A1
Specialises in serving up
Mao's favourite dishes.

Xiang E Qing 湘鄂情
3 Jiaoyu Jie, Jinrong Jie
(Financial Street). Tel: 6656-
6468. Open: 11am–9pm. **$$**
67 p290, A3
Home-style Hunan and
Hubei fare. Many diners
opt for the fish head with
minced red pepper.

Yuguotianqing 雨过天晴
35 Tonglingge Lu, Xicheng.
Tel: 6608-9265. Open:
10.30am–10pm. **$** 68
p291, D1
This poetically named
establishment – "the rain
is over and the sky is
clear" – serves good
dumplings and *baozi*.

European

Blu Lobster 蓝韵
Shangri-La Hotel, 29
Zizhuyuan Lu. Tel: 6841-
2211. Open: Tue–Sun 5.30–
11pm. **$$$$** 69 p284, A2
Brian Mckenna's molecu-
lar gastronomy includes a
42-ingredient salad, chilli
ice cream and other
implausible wonders.

Moscow Restaurant
莫斯科餐厅
135 Xizhimenwai Dajie.
Tel: 6835-4454. Open:
11am–2pm, 5–9pm. **$$$**
70 p284, C2
A cavernous restaurant in

the old Soviet-built
exhibition centre.

Hotpot

Hongbinlou 鸿宾楼
11 Zhanlanguan Lu,
Xicheng. Tel: 6899-4561.
Open: 11am–8.30pm. **$$$**
71 p284, B3
Very good hotpot, plus
other specialities includ-
ing Peking Duck.

Minority Cuisine

**Golden Peacock Dai
Ethnic Flavour**
金孔雀傣家酒楼
2 Minzu Daxue Bei Lu,
Haidian. Tel: 6893-2030.
Open: 11am–10pm. **$$** 72
p284, A1
Popular place featuring
the sweet, spicy food of

Yunnan province.

Miao Minority Restaurant
盛祥农家院
54 Fuxingmen Dajie. Financial Street. Tel: 6607-9738.
Open: 11am–1.30pm,
5–9pm. **$$** 73 p285, D4
Miao dance performan-
ces accompany dishes
such as roast bullfrog
and dog-meat hotpot.

**Tutu Mongolian
Restaurant** 图图
2/F, 16 Minzu Daxue Beilu,
Haidian. Tel: 6846-8500.
Open: 11am–2pm,
5–9.30pm. **$$** 74 p284, A1
The area around the
Minorities University has
some excellent restaur-
ants, mostly at reason-
able prices. This is for
devout carnivores only.

Bars and Cafés

Buzz Bar
The Westin Beijing, Jinrong
Jie (Financial Street). Tel:
6606-8866. Open: 7am–
1am 20 p285, D4
A 1970s-style lounge
bar serving up
signature cocktails.

Café d'Or
Tangla Hotel, 19 Fuxing-
menwai Dajie, Jinrong Jie
(Financial Street). Tel:
5857-6688. Open: 8am–
8pm. (off map)
A cosmopolitan place
with fine international
food and drinks.

Cigar Legends Bar
3 Jincheng Fangjie,
Jinrong Jie (Financial
Street). Tel: 6607-9899.

Open: 10.30am–midnight.
21 p285, D4
Focuses on the enjoy-
ment of fine cigars in
an elegant setting.

CupofChino
5/F, InterContinental Hotel,
11 Jinrong Jie (Financial
Street). Tel: 5852-5888.
Open: 6am–11pm. 22
p285, D4
New York-style deli and
coffee bar.

Crystal Bar 水晶吧
The Ritz-Carlton Beijing,
Jinrong Jie (Financial
Street). Tel: 6601-6666.
Open: 8am–1am. 23
p285, D4
Hotel bar with fine port
and cigars.

SPECTACULAR RESTAURANTS

Few cities can match Beijing when it comes to distinctive cuisine – and distinctive restaurants in which to enjoy it. The attention to detail can be astonishing

Though many foreign visitors may baulk at tucking in to some of the more exotic fare served up in Beijing's restaurants, an unprejudiced approach to dining in China – the result of a long-standing scarcity of protein-rich foods that still exists today in poorer provinces – means there are some truly unique culinary experiences on offer for the gastronomically daring. Chicken's feet, offal and the distinctively pungent "stinky" tofu are but an initiation into unusual foods that are not only edible but can be surprisingly tasty. The craze for minority restaurants has put ants, locusts and bamboo worms onto the capital's dining tables. Some restaurants (such as Middle Eight, at 8 Sanlitun Zhongjie) even serve up bee pupae – deep fried and with a spicy dipping sauce. Sometimes resembling more a study in zoology than a row of popular food stalls, Donghuamen Night Market (see page 171) can fix you up with skewered centipedes, fried scorpions and the ever-elegant sea horse. Though such delicacies are mostly for tourists' amusement, the plump silkworms are a reasonably tasty, nutritious and low-fat snack. Perhaps the most extraordinary of all Beijing's dining spots is Guolizhuang (at 34B Dongsishitiao, Dongcheng District), which deals almost exclusively with just one part of the anatomy – the penis. Deer, cow, sheep and snake all face the chop for your dining pleasure, with enhanced virility the supposed nutritional payback.

ABOVE: fish cakes wrapped in beancurd skin.
BELOW: supreme elegance at the Green T-House.
BELOW LEFT: ox and snake penis, an acquired taste.

ABOVE: the East is Red has cornered the Cultural Revolution nostalgia market. Diners are treated to full-scale theatrical performances.
RIGHT: skewered delights at Donghuamen Night Market include sea horses and cockroaches.

ABOVE: spectacular surroundings and spectacular food at the Fangshan restaurant.

DRESSED TO IMPRESS

Eating out is one of China's most popular entertainments, so perhaps it's not surprising that Beijing has many unique and eye-catching restaurants. Though an unlikely period of history to inspire a cabaret, the Cultural Revolution is the setting of the dinner show and decor at The East is Red *(see page 177)*. Waitresses dressed as Mao's Red Guards take your orders rather more sedately than the intellectual purges of the 1960s, though the nightly shows are more rousing. Audience members wave red flags and shout slogans in support of the Great Helmsman as performers dance and sing revolutionary hits.

Imperial cuisine comprises the often elaborate dishes popular with China's royalty, particularly during the Qing dynasty and the reign of the famously demanding Empress Dowager Cixi. At Fangshan Restaurant *(see page 162)* waitresses in exquisite Manchu outfits escort diners to their tables and regale them with stories on the history and significance of each dish. For pure imperial indulgence, the "Manchu-Han Banquet" includes 134 dishes to be eaten over six days.

BELOW: Donghuamen Night Market, the place foreign tourists are most likely to encounter the exotic culinary delicacies of the city.

THE SUMMER PALACES

The great landscaped gardens and lavish palaces built outside Beijing for the pleasure of the emperor and his court are now open to anyone who wants to escape the bustle of the city

There are two "summer palaces" in the northwestern suburbs of Beijing. Between them, they were used by the Qing emperors for more than 150 years. During this time dozens of palaces, pavilions and temples were built in carefully crafted idyllic landscapes of artificial hills, lakes and canals. The older complex, Yuanmingyuan, was largely destroyed by foreign troops in 1860 at the end of the Second Opium War.

The "New" Summer Palace, Yiheyuan, built as a replacement by the empress dowager Cixi at the end of the 19th century, was also plundered by foreign troops, in 1900 during the Boxer Rebellion. This time, however, most of the buildings survived or were restored, and Yiheyuan is today one of Beijing's major sights, attracting large numbers of visitors, particularly on summer weekends. Its popularity so outweighs that of its predecessor that it is generally referred to simply as "the Summer Palace".

The Old Summer Palace ❶

Address: Qinghua Xilu, Haidian District
Tel: 6262-8501
Opening Hrs: Apr–Oct daily 7am–7pm, Nov–Mar daily 7am–5.30pm

Entrance Fee: charge
Transport: Yuanmingyuan subway station (line 4), or by taxi

Little remains of the original Summer Palace, **Yuanmingyuan** (圆明园), although its expansive grounds are now a park providing a quiet retreat from the city, and are a popular place for weekend picnics. The main entrance is at the southern end of the complex. Inside, a web of paths make their way through the park. There is a fair amount of tourist tat for sale, as well as snack

LEFT: the Theatre Museum at the Garden of Virtue and Harmony. **RIGHT:** ruins at Yuanmingyuan.

vendors, children's playgrounds and boating lakes. The rebuilt maze (*see below*) is fun. Past a wide depression in the terrain is a broad field of ruins, where the remains of ornate pillars and frescos are more reminiscent of European Baroque buildings than the architecture of imperial China.

The magnificent complex of park and palace that once stood here was the creation of Emperor Qianlong (1736–95). He called it Yuanmingyuan: the Garden of Perfect Purity. Qianlong was an enthusiastic admirer of southern Chinese landscape gardening, having appreciated the quiet beauty of the West Lake in Hangzhou, and the gardens and canals of Suzhou, sketches of which were used to transform the surroundings of Yuanmingyuan into a gigantic masterpiece of landscape gardening. Here, natural and artificial landscapes were merged into a perfect whole.

Similarly inspired by pictures of princely French and Italian palaces,

ABOVE: Emperor Qianlong created the once magnificent palace and gardens at Yuanmingyuan.

Qianlong gave orders for buildings in the European style to be constructed in the northeastern part of the park. The architect was a Jesuit missionary and artist, Giuseppe Castiglione, from Genoa, later to be the emperor's confidante and teacher. Between 1747 and 1759, Castiglione created a complex of buildings unique in China. There were little Rococo palaces with horseshoe-shaped staircases, marble halls, fountains and even a maze (now reconstructed in stone) – a piece of Versailles in the Middle Kingdom, the counterpoint to the chinoiserie so prized by the European princes of the time.

Qianlong was particularly fond of European fountains, simple or elaborate. The remains of some of these can still be seen just south of the present **Palace Museum** (daily 9am–5pm; no extra charge). The fountains were composed of several levels of waterspouting figures; water sprayed from stone lions' heads, dogs' mouths and

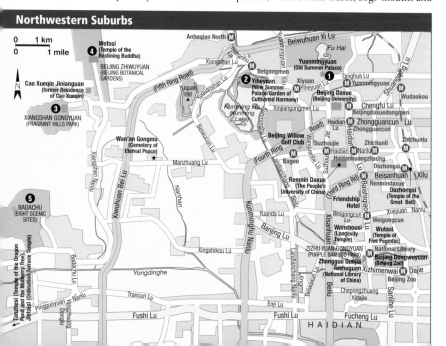

Northwestern Suburbs

stags' antlers. In the museum itself are old photographs, prints and a large map of the site.

An interesting symbiosis of Chinese thought and European architecture was the water clock, designed by the French Jesuit Benoît. Close to the Palace of the Quiet Sea, the ruins can be seen between the museum and the restored maze. Traditionally, the Chinese divided the 24-hour day into 12 segments, with every segment attributed to an animal. Benoît designed a construction with 12 stone animals with bronze heads, each of them spouting water for two hours.

In Qianlong's time, as tentative diplomatic relations developed with the West, the French court contributed to the decoration of the buildings "in the Western style" and sent rare gifts. One hundred years later, it would be French troops, together with the British, who destroyed these very palaces.

Destruction of the palace

During the Second Opium War (1858–60), when China vastly overestimated its strength and tried to expel permanently the unscrupulous foreign merchants, the Europeans took brutal revenge. The imperial house was considered personally responsible for the xenophobic policies, and Lord Elgin, the commander-in-chief of the British forces, ordered the destruction of Yuanmingyuan. It was said that he wanted to spare the common people and only punish the court. Before the troops attacked in October 1860, the emperor Xianfeng, together with his womenfolk (among them the concubine Cixi), managed to escape to the safety of Chengde, some 250km (150 miles) to the north.

The allied soldiers plundered the palace, taking away anything they could carry – some items have ended up in museums and auctions in the West. Then they set fire to the buildings, and for three days the Summer Palace blazed. The traditional wooden buildings were almost completely destroyed, and only a few of the Western-style structures survived. Attempts at restoration failed because of a chronic lack of finance, and the palace's demise was complete when, following the Boxer Rebellion,

Yuanmingyuan's potency as a symbol has led to a lively debate over its future. Some believe it should be restored to its original glory as proof of China's triumph over weakness and imperialism. Others argue that to rebuild the ruins would be tantamount to sacrilege. Both palaces are now protected by a Unesco World Heritage listing, obligating the city to preserve Yuanmingyuan in its current state.

BELOW: the ruins at Yuanmingyuan make a backdrop for patriotic productions.

Looted Bronze Animals

Among the treasures plundered from Yuanmingyuan in 1860 were 12 bronze fountainheads of the water clock, representing the signs of the Chinese zodiac. Five of these – the ox, tiger, horse, monkey and pig – were recovered and are now exhibited at Beijing's Poly Museum *(see page 175)*. There was a public outcry in March 2009 when auctioneers Christie's put two – the rat and rabbit – up for bidding. "China will never consent to illegal possession of stolen cultural relics," China's Deputy Culture Minister said. A Chinese collector, apparently acting alone, bid successfully for them but refused to pay, disrupting the sale on grounds of patriotism. The whereabouts of the five remaining heads are as yet unknown.

ABOVE: soldiers on a
day out at Yiheyuan.
ABOVE RIGHT: the
Pagoda of Buddhist
Virtue (Foxiangge).

peasants from the surrounding countryside took away valuable ceramic
tiles and marble to build houses.

Yuanmingyuan today

For modern Beijingers, what was once
the exclusive haunt of emperors is
now a place for a day out. They come
especially to enjoy **Fu Hai Lake**. In
the summer, hundreds of paddle and
rowing boats bob in the water, and,
in the winter, skaters glide over the
ice. Also popular is the eastern section, the **Eternal Spring Garden**
(长春园), with the European fountain ruins – one of the more intact
structures in the complex.

The ruins of Yuanmingyuan
remain a powerful symbol of China's
humiliation at the hands of the West.
The memory of its destruction is
regularly evoked as a reminder of the
dangers of both Western imperialism and domestic political and military weakness. Indeed, the large sign
just outside the eastern gate of the
ruins greets visitors with the words,

"Do not forget the national shame,
rebuild the Chinese nation."

The New Summer Palace ❷

Address: Yiheyuan Lu, Haidian District
Tel: 6288-1144
Opening Hrs: Apr–Oct daily 6.30am–
8.30pm, Nov–Mar daily 7am–7pm
Entrance Fee: charge
Transport: Xiyuan or Beigongmen
subway stations (line 4), or by taxi.
There is also a boat service *(see
margin, page 206)*

A short distance southwest of Yuanmingyuan is the site of the "New"
Summer Palace, **Yiheyuan** (颐和园;
Garden of Cultivated Harmony).
The area had been used as an imperial pleasure garden for centuries, pre-
dating the gardens of Yuanmingyan,
the "Old" Summer Palace. However,
it wasn't until the 1880s, when the
empress dowager Cixi set about
expanding the original park, and
rebuilding and adding to the existing buildings, that the new Summer
Palace was created to replace the old.
The resulting mosaic of imperial
pleasure gardens and grand buildings, harmoniously arranged on hills
around a beautiful lake, was partially

TIP

For entry to the New
Summer Palace, as with
the Forbidden City and
Temple of Heaven, it's
best to purchase an all-
inclusive ticket (*tao
piao*), unless you only
want to visit the park
and not the buildings.

destroyed in 1900 but quickly rebuilt – and has since survived civil war and the Cultural Revolution to become one of Beijing's top tourist attractions, visited by hundreds of thousands every year.

Cixi loved her new creation. She and her entourage effectively abandoned the Forbidden City and ruled China from here for 20 years until her death in 1908.

As in every Chinese garden, rocks and water feature prominently, while blossoming shrubs and a colourful arrangement of flowering plants in tubs have been preferred to European-style flower beds. There is also a conscious use of walls and buildings to screen sections of the gardens, so that small pieces of the landscape appear like framed pictures through windows in chequered, rhomboid, fan, vase and peach shapes. Sometimes a sudden and dramatic change of scene is possible within only a few yards. A walk through the Summer Palace can be likened to the slow unrolling of a Chinese scroll painting.

Beautiful **Kunming Lake**  (Kunming Hu; 昆明湖) covers about two-thirds of the area of the Yiheyuan complex, adding a sense of serenity and silence. In summer, the lake is covered with a carpet of huge, round, green lotus leaves, while pale pink lotus flowers rise between them. The three islands in the lake recall a 2,000-year-old Daoist myth of three islands in the Eastern Sea supposedly inhabited by immortals.

The great artificial hill, about 60 metres (200ft) in height, which rises behind the palace was named **Longevity Hill** ⑧ (Wanshou Shan; 万寿山) by Qianlong, in honour of his mother on her 60th birthday. Like a giant screen, it divides the grounds of the Summer Palace into two completely different landscapes. The southern section, with the broad lake in the foreground, is reminiscent of the idyll of the West Lake

in Hangzhou; the northern section, with its romantic groves and canals, creates an atmosphere akin to that of Suzhou.

Around the site

The main path into the grounds, some 800 metres/yds' walk from Xiyuan subway station, leads through a mighty wooden *pailou*, a kind of Chinese triumphal arch, past the ghost wall that is supposed to ward off all evil influences, directly to the **Eastern Gate** (Donggongmen; 东宫门). Alternatively, Beigongmen subway station allows convenient access to the **Northern Gate** (Beigongmen; 北宫门) and entrance to the Palace via Suzhou Street, a canal-side walk over quaint bridges and past replica shops in the style of Old Suzhou.

Visible beyond the Eastern Gate is the **Hall of Benevolence and Longevity** ⑥ (Renshoudian; 仁寿殿), with its opulent furnishings and decorative objets d'art. This is where young Emperor Guangxu dealt with state business when the imperial court resided in Yiheyuan; here, grand audiences were held for imperial

ABOVE: pleasure boats of various shapes and sizes cruise the waters of Kunming Lake. Most depart from the jetty next to the Marble Boat.
BELOW: the view across Kunming Lake from the Pagoda of Buddhist Virtue (Foxiangge).

ABOVE: Cixi was an enthusiastic fan of Beijing Opera, and had an open-air stage built at the Summer Palace.
BELOW RIGHT: opinion is divided on the true character and motivations of the Empress Dowager Cixi.

ministers, advisers, mandarins, and later for foreign diplomats as well.

It was in the nearby **Hall of Jade Ripples ⓓ** (Yulantang; 玉澜堂) that Cixi supposedly kept Guangxu under house arrest for his folly at attempting to reform a crumbling dynasty by opening China to foreign ideas in 1898. It has been argued, however, that it was pressure from a powerful faction at court which convinced her that Guangxu was endangering the regime, and told her that if she did not resume her position as regent, the dynasty would collapse.

Not far from the Hall of Jade Ripples, on the southeastern slopes of Longevity Hill, were Cixi's private living and sleeping apartments, the **Hall of Happiness and Longevity ⓔ** (Leshoulang; 乐寿堂). Served by a staff of 48, she did not want for much except privacy.

Cixi was passionate about Beijing Opera. There was an excellent ensemble at court, composed of 384 eunuchs. Cixi herself was supposed to have appeared in some operas as Guanyin, the goddess of mercy. She had an impressive open-air stage

built in the **Garden of Virtue and Harmony ⓕ** (Deheyuan; 德和园). Its three stages, one above the other, were connected by trap doors, so that supernatural beings, saints and immortals could swoop down into the operatic scene and evil spirits could rise from the depths of the underworld. There was even an underground water reservoir for "wet" scenes.

Today, the Deheyuan has been turned into a Theatre Museum. Costumes can be seen in glass cases, and the attendants wear the clothes and hairstyles of the Qing dynasty. Under their Manchu shoes are high platforms, which gave women a swaying walk. Unlike the Han Chinese, the Manchu women – the palace elite – did not have their feet bound.

A highlight in the further eastern part of the palace gardens is the **Garden of Harmonious Interest ⓖ** (Xiequyuan; 谐趣园), a complete, perfect and beautiful replica of a lotus pool from the Wuxi area in central China.

The Long Corridor

Covered walkways and galleries are established features of Chinese land-

Who Was the Real Cixi?

The founder of the New Summer Palace, the apparently omnipotent empress dowager Cixi, began life as a concubine of the third rank. Her rise to prominence began when she became pregnant with Emperor Xianfeng's son, Tongzhi. She was appointed as one of the two regents who ruled during Tongzhi's subsequent minority, following the death of Xianfeng in 1861. The accepted wisdom is that she was ruthlessly ambitious, removing anyone who stood in her way, and that it was she, rather than Guangxu, who effectively ruled China in the late 19th century.

There is, however, an alternative view which maintains that Cixi was merely a puppet, installed on the throne by officials who actually made policy, so that they could hide behind her and act as they pleased. As a woman she had little personal power, and was further handicapped by her inability to read or write. Her defenders point out that Cixi was unable ever to know what was really going on because the only people she had contact with were inside the court – as a woman of imperial rank she was not allowed to venture beyond the confines of the imperial palaces. The only weapon she had was her son, the royal heir, and her ambition for him was merely a form of self-defence.

scape gardening. These light, elegant, wooden structures link scattered individual buildings to make a composite whole. The **Long Corridor** ❶ (Changlang; 长廊) is a magnificent example; 728 metres (796 yds) in length, it runs along the foot of the hill parallel to the shore of Kunming Lake.

The ceilings and rafters of the walkway are decorated with countless bird-and-flower motifs. If humans or human-like creatures appear in the pictures, they are either in scenes from famous legends, episodes of Chinese history, or scenes from classical novels such as *The Dream of the Red Mansions*, *The Bandits of Liangshan Moor* or *The Journey to the West*, with its hero the Monkey King, Sun Wukong.

In the middle of the walkway, where the east–west axis of the palace park meets the north–south axis, the **Gate of Dispelling Clouds** ❶ (Paiyunmen; 排云门) – a great *pailou* triumphal arch – marks the start of the climb up Longevity Hill. Next

to 12 massive, oddly shaped stones symbolising the signs of the Chinese zodiac is an elegant pair of lions cast in bronze – perhaps the most beautiful in all of Beijing – guarding an imposing Buddhist temple complex, which is surrounded by a red wall. Go through two gates and over a bridge to reach the **Hall of Dispelling Clouds** ❶ (Paiyundian; 排云殿).

A temple once stood on this site during the Ming dynasty. Qianlong had it rebuilt and, on his mother's 60th birthday, renamed it the Temple of Gratitude for a Long Life. It was destroyed in 1860, and the present form dates from Cixi's time in 1892. This was where she celebrated her birthdays with extravagant and elaborate ceremonies. Many of the presents given on these occasions are on exhibition in the rooms here, often with yellow paper labels attached, marked with words of adulation such as "Given in honour and respect by your true and loyal subject..."

One day two bandits entered the Summer Palace. The one pillaged, the other burned … We Europeans, we are the civilised, and for us the Chinese are the barbarians, but look what civilisation has done to the barbarians.

Victor Hugo

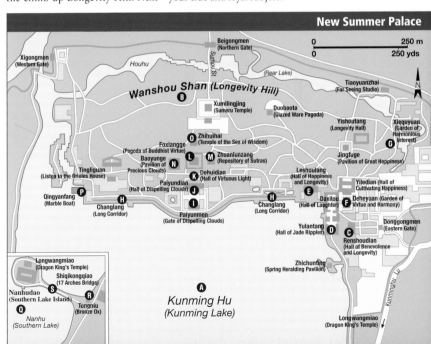

New Summer Palace

0   250 m
0   250 yds

Beigongmen
(Northern Gate)

Xigongmen
(Western Gate)

Houhu

(Rear Lake)

Suzhou St.

Tiaoyuanzhai
(Far Seeing Studio)

Wanshou Shan (Longevity Hill) ❶

Xumilingjing
(Sumeru Temple)

Duobaota
(Glazed Ware Pagoda)

Yishoutang
(Longevity Hall)

Xiequyuan
(Garden of Harmonious Interest) ❶

Foxiangge
(Pagoda of Buddhist Virtue)

Zhihuihai
(Temple of the Sea of Wisdom) ❶

Baoyunge
(Pavilion of Precious Clouds) ❶

Dehuidian
(Hall of Virtuous Light) ❶

Zhuanlunzang
(Repository of Sutras) ❶

Jingfuge
(Pavilion of Great Happiness)

Tingliguan
(Listen to the Orioles House)

Leshoutang
(Hall of Happiness and Longevity) ❶

Yiledian (Hall of Cultivating Happiness)

Paiyundian
(Hall of Dispelling Clouds) ❶

Deheyuan (Garden of Virtue and Harmony) ❶

Qingyanfang
(Marble Boat) ❶

Changlang
(Long Corridor) ❶

Daxilou
(Hall of Laughter) ❶

Paiyunmen
(Gate of Dispelling Clouds) ❶

Changlang
(Long Corridor) ❶

Donggongmen
(Eastern Gate)

Yulantang
(Hall of Jade Ripples) ❶

Renshoudian
(Hall of Benevolence and Longevity)

Longwangmiao
(Dragon King's Temple)

Shiqikongqiao
(17 Arches Bridge)

Nanhudao
(Southern Lake Island) ❶

Tongniu
(Bronze Ox)

Nanhu
(Southern Lake)

Zhichunting
(Spring Heralding Pavilion)

❶

**Kunming Hu
(Kunming Lake)**

Kunminghu Lu

Longwangmiao
(Dragon King's Temple)

If the subway simply isn't good enough for you, travel to the Summer Palace in the style Cixi would have been accustomed to: by boat. Craft leave from Purple Bamboo Park every hour in summer, with the voyage taking about an hour. Call 6852-9428 for more information.

ABOVE: the Bronze Ox pacifies the water spirits. **BELOW:** the Marble Boat, two storeys of spectacular excess.

Go past the Hall of Dispelling Clouds and through the **Hall of Virtuous Light** (Dehuidian; 德慧殿), then up a steep stone staircase to reach the 38-metre (125ft), octagonal **Pagoda of Buddhist Virtue** (Foxiangge; 佛香阁). This is the highest point of the palace and commands a wonderfully panoramic view.

To the east is a group of buildings, the **Repository of Sutras** (Zhuanlunzang; 转轮藏), once used as the archives for copies of Confucian classics and Buddhist scrolls. To the west is a rare and quite extraordinary masterpiece of Chinese architecture – the **Pavilion of Precious Clouds** (Baoyunge; 宝云阁), framed on all four sides by smaller pavilions and walkways. In Cixi's day, Lamaist monks gathered here to pray on the 1st and 15th day of every lunar month. Its stepped roof, and its beams, columns and struts, make it look like a wooden building, yet they were all cast from bronze in 1750 with the help of wax moulds. This is why it is usually called the Bronze Pavilion (Tongting). It is one of the few buildings of the Summer Palace to have survived the destruction of 1860 and 1900 relatively unscathed.

Behind the pagoda on Longevity Hill, a narrow path leads to the **Temple of the Sea of Wisdom** (Zhihuihai; 智慧海). There are countless small statues of Buddha in the niches of its greenish-yellow ceramic facade.

Sights around the lake

A little further to the west, at the end of the Long Corridor lies the famous **Marble Boat** (Qingyanfang; 清宴舫), misleadingly named as it is neither made of marble nor capable of floating. Cixi is generally thought to have squandered a fortune on this spectacular folly, money that should have gone to the Chinese navy – with the direct result a humiliating naval defeat by the Japanese in 1895. Prince Chun, Guangxu's father, was in the habit of flattering Cixi as a way of encouraging her to support his policies, and squeezed funds from wealthy gentry and rich officials in order to pay for it. It should also be pointed out that Qianlong had already built the base of the boat, which, like so much in the palace, was damaged in 1860.

From the Marble Boat, it is possible to cross the lake by ferry, landing either on **Nanhudao**  (Southern Lake Island; 南湖岛), or on the neighbouring mainland. Close to the bridge leading to Nanhudao crouches the **Bronze Ox** ® (Tongniu; 铜牛). Its task, as the characters engraved on its back make clear, is to pacify the water spirit and to protect the surrounding land from floods. The script also relates how Qianlong decided to enlarge the lake; in recording this on the statue, he was identifying with the legendary Emperor Yuan, a mythological hero who is described as having commanded the damming of a flood from the back of an ox.

Seventeen Arches Bridge ® (Shiqikongqiao; 十七孔桥) crosses the water in a supremely graceful curve, linking Nanhudao with the mainland. Stone lions and other exotic creatures keep watch on the balustrades. On the small island itself is the **Dragon King's Temple** (Longwangmiao; 龙王庙).

The demise of the palace

The 1900 Boxer Rebellion grew out of economic hardship combined with a rise in Chinese nationalism, promoted by the government. The desire was to preserve Chinese traditions at all costs and to expel all things foreign. However, it didn't work out that way, and the foreigners ended up plundering the capital city, making off with untold cultural riches.

As the European powers plundered, Cixi fled to Xi'an. She is said to have become apoplectic with rage when she heard that her throne had been flung into Kunming Lake, her robes stolen, and the walls of her bedchamber scrawled with obscene words and drawings. When at last she returned to Beijing, she set about restoring the palace to its former glory with typical energy. Some buildings were not restored – the Lama Temple, for instance, on Longevity Hill, has only been partially rebuilt in the last few years. Following her death in 1908, imperial China itself was to survive only three more years. ❑

ABOVE: yellow roof tiles were reserved for imperial palaces.
BELOW LEFT: *pailou* gateway at the main entrance to the Summer Palace.

RESTAURANTS

Imperial

Bai Family Mansion
白家大院
15 Suzhou Jie, Haidian District. Tel: 6265-4186. Open: 11am–10.30pm. **$$$**
Based on imperial cuisine, Bai dishes would certainly have helped cool Cixi's fiery temper. The Qing dynasty-style ornamentation of the interior and waitresses creates an impressive regal atmosphere. An interesting and unusual experience.

Tingliguan Restaurant
听鹂馆
Inside the New Summer Palace (Yiheyuan). Tel: 6288-1955.
www.tingliguan.com. Open: 11am–2pm, 5–7pm. **$$$** and up
The Tingliguan serves more than 300 dishes that were popular at court in Ming and Qing times. Fresh fish caught from Kunming Lake is a house speciality.

Sichuan

Meizhou Dongpo 眉州东坡4
27 Zhongguancun Dajie. Tel: 8285-6945. Open: 10.30am–10.30pm. **$$**
Popular among Sichuan natives, this chain restaurant provides reasonably priced and dishes such as wontons and *dandan* noodles featuring the signature fiery spice from China's southwest.

• • • • • • • • •

Prices are for a typical dinner for one (three dishes with beer in Chinese restaurants, or a three-course meal with a half-bottle of house wine in Western-style restaurants). **$** = under Rmb 50, **$$** = Rmb 50–100, **$$$** = Rmb 100–200, **$$$$** = over Rmb 200.

WESTERN FRINGES

In the hills and valleys to the immediate west of the city are a number of tranquil temples and other sites of historical – and prehistorical – significance. Further north are the impressive imperial tombs of the Ming emperors

I f you're staying in Beijing for more than a few days, you may want to break up your sightseeing with a trip to the hills and valleys of the pleasant rural areas to the west of the city. Not only will you get to see a China markedly different from that experienced in the urban sprawl, but you will also gain an insight into some important events from the country's past. The hills are popular with hikers, and the more visited trails often have English signage, safety rails and refreshments on sale. Lesser-known spots require more planning and care, but the quiet, crowd-free atmosphere is worth the effort.

The Fragrant Hills ❸

Address: Haidian District
Tel: 6259-1155
Opening Hrs: summer daily 6am–7pm, winter daily 6am–6pm
Entrance Fee: charge
Transport: bus 630 from Bagou subway station (line 10), 112 from Pingguoyuan subway station (line 1), or by taxi

Whether you're escaping the heat of a Beijing summer, or just the madding crowds, a trip to **Fragrant Hills Park** (Xiangshan; 香山公园), around an

hour's drive to the northwest (beyond the Summer Palace), is a convenient way to get away from the metropolis for a day. If you are lucky enough to make the trip on one of the increasingly rare haze-free days, you will be rewarded by an excellent view of the city you have left behind.

In the Liao dynasty (916–1125), noble and wealthy merchant families built elegant villas on the cool slopes of these hills, to which they could flee when temperatures in the city soared. Those that could not afford to buy or

LEFT: figure at the Ming Tombs.
RIGHT: visitors dress up in Qing costume to have their photograph taken.

build their own property rented guest quarters in temples. The journey was undertaken on mule at an easy pace, travelling through the woodlands, enjoying the feeling of communion with nature and staying overnight in Daoist or Buddhist shrines.

Later, the Ming emperors turned the area into an imperial game preserve, and the Qing emperor Kangxi is reputed to have killed a tiger here. Qianlong turned it into a landscaped park, a complex of 28 scenic zones, named the Park of Tranquillity and Pleasure. As with both of the Summer Palaces, however, it was badly damaged by foreign troops in 1860, and again in 1900. Few of the buildings have survived.

The Fragrant Hills were opened to the public in 1957, and quickly became one of the most popular excursions for city dwellers. Bear in mind that on summer and autumn weekends the crowds are so large it can sometimes feel as if you are still in the city. The

ABOVE: Spectacles Lake. **BELOW:** the Glazed Tile Pagoda.

hills are particularly popular from late October to early November because of the blazing reds and yellows of the sycamore leaves.

Turn right inside the main eastern gate to the park and you come to the Tibetan-style **Temple of Clarity** Ⓐ (Zhaomiao; 昭庙), built in 1780 for the Panchen Lama. In its grounds is the octagonal **Glazed Tile Pagoda** Ⓑ (Liulita; 琉璃塔), which has little bells hanging from the corners of its eaves, the lightest breeze making them chime delicately. The **Chamber of Introspection** Ⓒ (Jianxinhai; 见心斋), to the east of the pagoda, has a courtyard in the southern Chinese style with a semicircular pond, as well as the usual walkways and pavilions. Only a few steps ahead lie two lakes separated by a jetty, and known, because of their shape, as the **Spectacles Lake** Ⓓ (Yanjinghu; 眼镜湖).

Beyond this is the northern gate, from which a chairlift will take you to the 550-metre (1,830ft) summit of

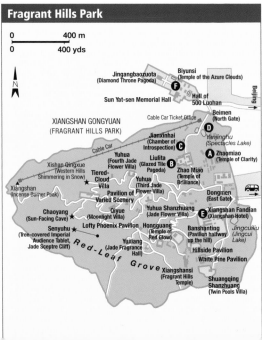

Fragrant Hills Park

0   400 m
0   400 yds

N

XIANGSHAN GONGYUAN
(FRAGRANT HILLS PARK)

Jingangbaozuota
(Diamond Throne Pagoda)

Biyunsi
(Temple of the Azure Clouds) Ⓕ

Sun Yat-sen Memorial Hall

Hall of 500 Luohan

Cable Car Ticket Office

Beimen
(North Gate)

Beijing

Cable Car

Jianxinhai
(Chamber of Introspection) Ⓒ

Yanjinghu
(Spectacles Lake) Ⓓ

Zhaomiao
(Temple of Clarity) Ⓐ

Yuhua
(Fourth Jade Flower Villa)

Liulita
(Glazed Tile Pagoda) Ⓑ

Zhao Miao
(Temple of Brilliance)

Xishan Qingxue
(Western Hills Shimmering in Snow)

Tiered-Cloud Villa

Yuhua
(Third Jade Flower Villa)

Pavilion of Varied Scenery

Dongmen
(East Gate)

Xiangshan
(Incense Burner Peak)

Chaoyang
(Sun-Facing Cave)

Qiyue
(Moonlight Villa)

Yuhua Shanzhuang
(Jade Flower Villa)

Xiangshan Fandian
(Xiangshan Hotel) Ⓔ

Lofty Phoenix Pavilion

Hongguang
(Temple of Red Glow)

Banshanting
(Pavilion halfway up the hill)

Jingcuilu
(Jingcui Lake)

Senyuhu
(Tree-covered Imperial Audience Tablet, Jade Sceptre Cliff)

Yuxiang
(Jade Fragrance Hall)

Hillside Pavilion

White Pine Pavilion

Xiangshansi
(Fragrant Hills Temple)

Red-Leaf Grove

Shuangqing Shanzhuang
(Twin Pools Villa)

the "Fragrant Hill". From here you can gaze over steep, thickly wooded slopes and deep ravines to Biyun Temple (in a side valley on the northeast side of the park). Further away is the Jade Spring Hill, with its ancient pagoda, with the Summer Palace and Kunming Lake beyond. In the far distance are the skyscrapers of Haidian District – on a clear day, you can get a good impression of the immensity of Beijing. If you're feeling fit you can climb the hill on foot instead of taking the chair lift, but you will need good shoes and at least a couple of hours to spare. The steepest part of the hill bears the name Guijianchou, which means "Even the devil is afraid of it!"

Near the East Gate stands the I.M. Pei-designed **Xiangshan Hotel** **E** (Xiangshan Fandian; 香山饭店), probably the most beautifully situated hotel in the region. The southern part of the park beyond the hotel is excellent for picnics. Yet only a few visitors ever seem to find their way here. Past the remains of the once massive Xiangshan Temple (destroyed in 1860) that rose over six levels, you will reach the remote **Twin Pools Villa**

(Shuangqing Bieshu; 双清别墅) and the **Pavilion Halfway up the Hill** (Banshanting; 半山亭). Here, a small tower has been restored, and from it you get a good view of the park.

Biyunsi (Temple of the Azure Clouds) **F**

Address: northern end of Fragrant Hills Park
Tel: 6259-1155
Opening Hrs: daily 8am–5pm
Entrance Fee: charge
Transport: can be reached directly by bus 630 from Wofosi (Temple of the Reclining Buddha; see page 212), or by taxi

Just to the north of Xiangshan Park is the spectacular, 600-year-old **Biyunsi** (Temple of the Azure Clouds; 碧云寺). The structure is made up of four great halls, the innermost being the memorial hall for Sun Yat-sen. Here lies an empty coffin, a gift from the Soviet Union, which could not be used because it did not arrive until two weeks after the funeral.

To the left of the main entrance of the hall, letters and manuscripts left by Sun Yat-sen are on display. On the

ABOVE: replica of an ancient Chinese coin at Biyunsi. This decorative motif is seen in temples and pagodas. **BELOW:** Biyunsi high in the hills.

TIP

The Botanical Gardens
are one of the few
places in Beijing where
sitting on the grass is
not only permitted but
encouraged, making it a
great place for a picnic.

ABOVE: dragon detail
on a Biyunsi roof.
BELOW: the Temple of
the Reclining Buddha.

wall is an inscription in marble: a letter from Sun Yat-sen addressed to the Soviet Union. There are exhibition rooms on both sides of the memorial hall showing photographs from Sun's life.

Beyond the memorial hall is the pagoda courtyard. The marble **Diamond Throne Pagoda** (Jingangbaozuota; 金刚宝座) was built in 1748 under the rule of Emperor Qianlong, and is modelled on Wutasi (the Temple of the Five Pagodas) in northwest Beijing *(see page 192)*. In March 1925, Sun Yat-sen's coffin lay in state in the pagoda, before being moved in 1929 to Zhongshanling, the Sun Yat-sen mausoleum in Nanjing. His clothing and personal belongings, however, remained here. The pagoda itself is 35 metres (114ft) high, and its base is adorned with numerous statues of Buddha.

The Botanical Gardens and Wofosi

There are other places nearby worth seeking out. The **Beijing Botanical Gardens** (Beijing Zhiwuyuan; 北京植物园; daily summer 6am–7pm, winter 7am–5pm; entrance fee), to the east of the main park, contains a large conservatory and pleasant grounds.

Located within the gardens is the **Former Residence of Cao Xueqin** (Cao Xueqin Jinianguan; 曹雪芹纪念馆; Tue–Sun 8am–4pm), where it is thought Cao wrote one of China's four great classical novels, *The Dream of the Red Mansions*, sometimes translated as *The Dream of the Red Chamber*. The central building is now a memorial hall housing a few exhibits, including a handwritten manuscript of Cao's great work.

To the north is **Wofosi** ❹ (Temple of the Reclining Buddha; 卧佛寺; daily 8.30am–4.30pm; entrance fee), dating from the Tang dynasty. The 54-tonne, 5-metre (18ft) Buddha is made of lacquered and painted bronze, and is of indeterminate age, although experts have expressed doubts that it is the original statue. Surrounding the Buddha are transcendental Bodhisattvas. Beyond the temple is the **Cherry Ravine** (Yingtao Gou; 樱桃沟), a romantic spot.

Eight Scenic Sights ❺

Address: Badachu Lu, Shijingshan District
Tel: 8896-4661
Opening Hrs: summer daily 5am–7.30pm, winter daily 6am–6pm
Entrance Fee: charge
Transport: bus 972 from Pingguoyuan subway station (line 1), bus 992 from Bagou subway station (line 10), change to 489 at Tongjiafen bus station, or by taxi

On a hillside 8km (5 miles) to the south of Xiangshan is a group of former temples and monasteries that can be visited together, and are collectively known as the **Eight Scenic Sites** (Badachu; 八大处). The first, the **Temple of Eternal Peace** (Chang'an Si; 长安寺), dating from the Ming dynasty, is located just outside the park. Somewhat ironically, it houses a bronze statue of Guan Yu, a hero of the Three Kingdoms period who was later worshipped as the god of war. The second, the **Temple of the Sacred Light** (Lingguang Si; 灵光寺),

is still home to a number of Buddhist monks and holds a holy relic reputed to be a tooth of the Buddha. Built in 1956 as a replacement for an earlier structure, the Buddha Tooth Pagoda is used for worshippers who seek health and longevity. The **Temple of Great Compassion** (Dabei Si; 大悲寺) is renowned for its 18 Luohan statues. The largest structure, the **Temple of the Fragrant World** (Xiangjie Si; 香界寺), served as an imperial retreat during the Qing dynasty. An inscription by Emperor Qianlong remains inside. The temple below the peak, the **Cave of Precious Pearls** (Baozhu Dong; 宝珠洞), is built around a cave in which a hermit is supposed to have lived for 40 years. The highest of the eight sights, it affords splendid views of Beijing on a clear day.

Tanzhesi ❻

Address: Tanzhe Shan, Mengtougou District
Tel: 6086-1699

ABOVE: there are over 2,000 species of trees and plants at the impressive Botanical Gardens, some in hothouses, others in formal gardens outside.

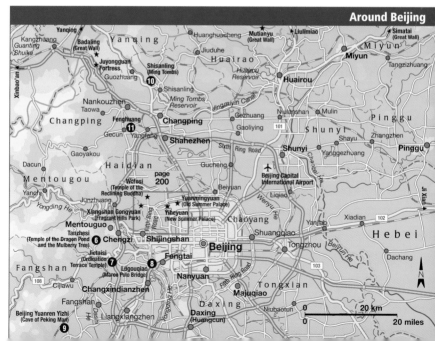

Around Beijing

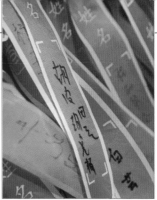

ABOVE: an offering at Tanzhesi. **ABOVE RIGHT:** bright red ribbons marked with prayers are attached to trees at Tanzhesi.

> ❝
>
> *[Jietaisi temple] is a great religious foundation in Beijing, in full and serene activity. Here the monastic life of a thousand years ago... is unrolled before the Western eyes of the weekend visitor from Peking, breathing, actual, undecaying.*
>
> Ann Bridge, from *Peking Picnic*
>
> ❞

Opening Hrs: daily 8am–5pm
Entrance Fee: charge

Beijing's oldest Buddhist temple is not to be found the city centre but in the Mentougou District on Tanzheshan Hill, southwest of the Eight Scenic Sights and about an hour by taxi from downtown. It is easy to combine a visit to **Tanzhesi** (Temple of the Dragon Pond and the Mulberry Tree; 潭柘寺) with a side trip to Jietaisi (Ordination Terrace Temple, *see opposite*). Both are delightful because of their rural setting and the sense of peaceful isolation which you can experience, particularly on weekdays.

Tanzhesi was built between AD 265 and 316 on terraces carved in dense woods – both Buddhists and Daoists traditionally withdrew to such beautiful places where they can meditate undisturbed. The temple is made up of three parts set along a north–south line across the hill slope. Enter following the central axis from the south, through the

Gate of Honour, and the adjoining **Mountain Gate**. The path is lined by picturesquely gnarled old pine trees. Beyond the Mountain Gate, one behind the other, are the **Hall of the Celestial Kings** (Tianwang Dian; 天王殿), the **Daxiongbaodian Hall** (the main hall), the **Zhaitang Hall** and the **Piluge Pavilion**, dedicated to the Buddha Vairocana. Above the main hall are legendary beasts, sons of the Dragon King, who are supposed to have captured a monk and chained him to the roof.

There is a great view of Tanzhesi and its surroundings from here, the highest point in the grounds. Beyond Daxiongbaodian Hall are two gingko trees, called the Emperor's Tree and the Emperor's Companion's Tree, thought to date from the Liao dynasty (916–1125).

Take the western path from here and look into the **Temple of Guanyin**, where you can see the Paving Stone of Beizhuan, on which the nun Miaoyan, a daughter of the Mongol emperor Kublai Khan (1260–94), is supposed to have prayed to Buddha daily in penance for her father's misdeeds. The path continues to the Temple of the Dragon King and the Temple of the Founding Father.

In the eastern part of the grounds are a white dagoba dating from 1427, two groups of 12th-century pagodas, a bamboo grove and the **Pavilion of the Moving Cup**, where Qianlong stayed during his visits to the temple.

Jietaisi

Eight km (5 miles) to the southeast, at the foot of Ma'anshan Hill, is **Jietaisi** ❼ (Ordination Terrace Temple; 戒台寺; daily 8am–5pm; entrance fee). This imposing temple dates from 622 and owes its name to the three-level stone terraces which were surrounded by statues and upon which the dedication ceremony of monks took place. The main hall is the **Daxiongbaodian**, and beyond it is the **Thousand Buddhas Pavilion**. Steles with Buddhist inscriptions dating from the Liao and Yuan dynasties can be seen in front of the Mingwang Hall. There is no longer much to be seen inside the halls, but it is worthwhile taking a walk to enjoy the temple grounds with their old pine trees.

Dajuesi and Fahaisi

Out past the New Summer Palace (take a taxi, or bus 346 from the main gate) is **Dajuesi** (Temple of Enlightenment; 大觉寺; daily 8am–5pm; entrance fee), at the foot of Yangtai Hill. It was founded in 1068, but the present buildings date from 1428, when the temple was rebuilt. It is known for its "six wonders", which include a 1,000-year-old stele, a millennial gingko tree and the beautifully clear Dragon Pool fed by a nearby spring.

To the south, in the district of Shijingshan, is **Fahaisi** (Law of the Sea Temple; 法海寺; 9am–4.30pm; entrance fee), built by the eunuch Li Tong in 1439 and today visited chiefly for its murals dating from the Ming dynasty.

Marco Polo Bridge ❽

Address: Wanpingcheng, Fengtai District
Tel: 8389-3919
Opening Hrs: daily 7am–7pm
Entrance Fee: charge
Transport: bus 624 from Gongzhufen subway station (lines 1 & 10), or by taxi

The **Marco Polo Bridge** (Lugouqiao; 卢沟桥) is 15km (9 miles) southwest of central Beijing. The Italian merchant Marco Polo, who stayed at the court of the Mongol emperor Kublai Khan in the 13th century, admired this bridge: "Ten miles past Cumbaluc [Khanbaliq]… a magnificent stone bridge crosses the river, and it has no equal anywhere in the

ABOVE: the Marco Polo Bridge. **BELOW LEFT:** Chinese soldiers in 1937.

The Troubled Waters of 1937

Though the Marco Polo Bridge incident of 7 July 1937 is considered the trigger for the Sino-Japanese War that would last eight years and claim more than 35 million lives, detailed information on the fateful day remains sparse. The event was not covered by local reporters at the time because of Beijing's desire to maintain the fragile relations between Chinese and Japanese troops. Professor Hata of Nihon University blames the clash on a badly timed toilet stop by a Japanese soldier. He says the Japanese believed the man had been kidnapped and taken to the town of Wanping. They demanded entry to search for him and were refused. The Japanese artillery bombarded the town, were met with resistance and Wanping became arguably the first battlefield of World War II. Beijing's official line is that Japan had long harboured plans to control all of northern China and the claim of a missing soldier was merely an excuse. The incident remains of historical importance to Chinese historians wary that Japan could lay the blame for the war on their doorstep. Though the details of that day remain contested, the Japanese troops continued to advance into Chinese territory, taking Beijing (then Beiping) on 29 July.

Nobody knows for sure who first called Lugouqiao the "Marco Polo Bridge", though it seems likely the term originated in Beijing's foreign community after the publication of Sir Henry Yule's The Book of Ser Marco Polo *in the 1870s.*

world… The 24 arches and the 24 pillars are of grey, finely dressed and well-placed marble blocks. Marble slabs and pillars form a balustrade on both sides… It is wonderful to see how the row of pillars and the slabs are so cleverly joined together."

Lugou means "Black Ditch", and is an earlier name for the **Yongding River**, which flows under the bridge. The first crossing was built here in 1189, improved in 1444 and rebuilt following a flood in 1698. On the balustrade on either side are 140 stone posts crowned with lions, some only a few centimetres tall, others comparative giants; no two are exactly alike. At each end is a 5-metre (15ft) stele; one records the rebuilding of the bridge in the 17th century, while the other is inscribed: "The moon at daybreak over the Lugou Bridge", one of the eight wonders of Old Beijing.

As the river is prone to flooding, the 11 arches of the bridge have been fastened with iron clamps to strengthen it, and it has been closed to road traffic. Upriver, a dam has created an artificial lake, so that the river bed is usually dry in summer, which

Political Science

The scientific importance of the Peking Man bones has diminished over the years as older hominid bones have been found elsewhere, but its symbolic importance in China has correspondingly increased. Every few years there are patriotic calls to find the missing bones, including a 1998 plea from leading palaeo-anthropologists and a 2000 manifesto that opened with the words, "We call on everybody to come together and search for the lost 'Peking Man'!"… A 2003 discovery at the site of human cultural artefacts that pre-date Peking Man caused renewed interest, and led the government to channel much-needed funding into preservation of the site, though the bones remain missing.

has taken away some of its appeal. The river was navigable here until the early 20th century, and there was a landing place from which travellers embarked on journeys to the south.

The bridge gained notoriety in the 1930s because of the incident which is seen as the start of the Japanese invasion of Asia during World War II. On 7 July 1937, Japanese troops of the Tianjin garrison attacked the bridge, provoking the Chinese guards to fire at them. This retaliation provided a pretext for further aggression by the Japanese. By August, China and Japan were at war. A **Memorial Museum** (same hours as bridge, separate entrance fee) at the bridge explains the full background to these events.

Peking Man Cave ❾

Address: Zhoukoudian, Fangshan District
Tel: 6930-1278
Opening Hrs: daily 8.30am–4.30pm
Entrance Fee: charge
Transport: bus 917 from Tianqiao long-distance bus station (just west of Temple of Heaven), or by taxi

BELOW: archaeologists at work in the Zhoukoudian Caves.

The site of the discovery of Peking Man, *Sinanthropus pekinensis*, lies close to the small town of Zhoukoudian, about 50km (30 miles) southwest of Beijing. The **Cave of Peking Man** (Beijing Yuanren Yizhi; 北京猿人遗址) is on the northern slopes of Longushan (Dragon Bone Mountain).

About 450 million years ago, the site was underneath an ocean. As the waters receded, limestone caves gradually developed. Much later, around half a million years ago, early hominids settled in these caves; they were to inhabit them for the next 300,000 years. When this species of hominid disappeared, the caves naturally filled in, and the tools, food scraps and bones in them remained covered by deposits until modern times.

As early as the Ming dynasty, workers digging for lime found many animal fossils, which were believed to be the bones of dragons. By the beginning of the 20th century, peasants were finding human teeth at this site. In 1921, the Swede John Gunnar Andersson found a rich source of fossils that attracted many other scientists.

More discoveries were made in the following years, until, in 1927, systematic excavations began. Two years later the complete upper skull of Peking Man was found. Java Man and Heidelberg Man were known at

that time, yet the discovery of Peking Man surprised scientists and caused a great sensation.

Up until the beginning of the Japanese invasion in 1937, fossil remains of more than 40 individuals of both sexes had been found. The men were some 1.5 metres (5ft) tall, the women slightly smaller. They had skulls about a third smaller than people of today, but could walk upright, use stone tools, and understood the use of fire. In the Upper Cave, the remains of *Homo sapiens*, who settled here some 18,000 years ago, were also discovered.

Work at the site was interrupted by the Japanese occupation of China in 1937, and by 1941 it had practically come to a halt. The decision was made to get the bones out of China. Packed in specially built wooden crates, they were delivered to the office of Trevor Bowen, the American administrator of Peking Union. Mr Bowen brought the crates to the US embassy and from there they were transferred to the United States Marine Corps.

The plan was to put them aboard the SS *President Harrison*, for shipment

ABOVE: an artist's impression of Peking Man. **BELOW LEFT:** the museum at the Peking Man Cave. **BELOW:** the entrance to the cave.

to the US. However, whether the skulls actually made it onto the ship is unclear – all that is known for sure is that they have never been seen since.

The actual work that led to the discovery of Peking Man seems to have been a model of international cooperation, with Chinese and Western researchers working amicably and productively side by side. In subsequent years, however, there has been a great deal of undignified squabbling over who should get the credit for finding the bones and who should take the blame for losing them. In Europe, it is common to credit the find to the Jesuit Teilhard de Chardin, who is said to have discovered the first skull. It is more likely, however, that it was discovered by the Chinese site worker Pei Wenzhong, as the Chinese have long attested.

There is a small **museum** (same hours as main site; entrance fee included) on the site, close to the Peking Man Cave and the Upper Cave. The exhibits are divided into three sections and provide information on evolution in general, of Peking Man in particular, and on the development of Chinese palaeontology. There are also displays of other fossils found in the area – ancient bears, tigers, elephants and rhinoceros. A sort of eternal flame at the museum symbolises the importance of Peking Man's early use of fire.

ABOVE: lion pillars guard the main entrance to the Ming Tombs complex.
BELOW: visiting the rural hinterland of Beijing offers a different perspective.

The Ming Tombs ⑩

Address: Changping District
Tel: 6076-1334; www.mingtombs.com
Opening Hrs: 8am–5pm
Entrance Fee: charge
Transport: Nanshao subway station (Changping line). Tourist buses from Qianmen bus station; bus 845 from Xizhimen to Changping, then change to bus 345, or by taxi

Although Beijing was the capital of the Middle Kingdom for five dynasties, the tombs of the Ming emperors are the only ones in relatively close proximity to the city. The tombs of the Qing emperors, both the western and eastern sites, are further out, although still within reach (*see pages 243 and 244*). The burial site of the Liao (916–1125) are in distant northeast China;

those of the Jin (1125–1234) were destroyed at the end of the Ming era. The rulers of the Yuan dynasty (1279–1368) had no special burial rites and left no mausoleums behind them.

A visit to the **Ming Tombs** (Shisanling; 十三陵) is often combined with a trip to the Wall at Badaling (see page 229). Thirteen of the 16 Ming emperors are buried here, in a valley to the south of the Tianshou Mountains, 50km (30 miles) northwest of Beijing. The foothills of the Yanshan Mountains form a natural entrance to the 40-sq-km (15-sq-mile) basin, "defended" on both sides by the Dragon and Tiger Mountains, which are said to keep harmful winds away from the holy ground.

The completion of the eight-lane Badaling Expressway has made the site more readily accessible. A visit here is usually part of an organised tour to the Great Wall, although tourist buses 1, 2, 3 and 4 all call in regularly en route to Badaling.

Behind the **Great Palace Gate**  (Dagongmen; 大宫门) at the entrance to the Ming necropolis is a square stele pavilion, on which can be seen a great tortoise bearing another stele on its back. The gate marks the beginning of the **Avenue of Stone Figures** (Shixiang Sheng; 石像生), also known as the Avenue of Ghosts. This 7km (4-mile) road leading to the tomb of Emperor Yongle is flanked by pairs of stone lions, elephants, camels, horses and mythological creatures, followed by 12 military and civil dignitaries representing the imperial court.

Beyond these figures is the **Dragon and Phoenix Gate** (Longfengmen; 龙凤门) with its three entrances which in earlier years were sealed off behind heavy doors.

The **Tomb of Emperor Yongle** (Changling; 长龄; same hours as site; entrance fee) is the biggest and best preserved of the 13 surviving tombs. Built on a south-facing slope, its three

ABOVE: Ming-dynasty relics on display at the Ming Tombs Museum.
BELOW: Emperor Wanli's crown.

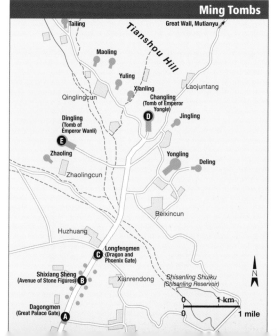

The opulence of the Ming Tombs is a clear example of the importance of ancestor worship to the ancient Chinese but also of the self-aggrandisement of their emperors, many of whom began constructing their final resting places as soon as they ascended the throne.

courtyards are surrounded by a wall. The first courtyard stretches from the massive three-arched entrance gate to the **Gate of Eminent Favours** (Ling'enmen; 祾恩门). In the east of this courtyard is a pavilion with a stone tablet, a stone camel and a stone dragon. The **Hall of Eminent Favours** (Ling'endian; 陵恩殿) is in the second courtyard. The central section of the stone steps leading up to the hall is adorned with sea monsters and dragons. In the east and the west parts of the hall there are "fire basins", in which balls of silk and inscriptions were burned as offerings to the imperial ancestors. Four mighty wooden pillars, each made out of a single trunk of a *nanmu* tree, along with 28 smaller posts, support the construction.

In the third and last courtyard, a stele tower can be found, with an incense basin and other ritual objects in front of it – the so-called "nine stone utensils". On the stele is the inscription "Tomb of the emperor Chengzu of the great Ming dynasty" (Chengzu was the temple name of Emperor Yongle). A wall with

a circumference of about 1km (²/₃ mile) was built to enclose the burial mound which is 31 metres (102ft) long and 38 metres (125ft) broad. To the east and west are the tombs of the 16 imperial concubines, who were buried alive to serve their emperor in the underworld.

The **Tomb of Emperor Wanli** Ⓔ (Dingling; 定陵) lies to the southwest of Changling. Wanli (1573–1619) was buried here in 1620, together with his two wives, Xiaoduan and Xiaojing. About 30,000 workers took a total of six years (1584–90) to complete the tomb, which cost 8 million taels of silver (equivalent to the total land tax for two years). It is said that during excavation of the tomb, several workers were struck by lightning, almost perishing. The team sacrificed two live chickens to placate the spirits.

A tunnel leads down to a depth of 7 metres (23ft), to the first massive gate of a subterranean palace, with five rooms, mighty marble vaulting and a floor of 50,000 highly polished stones. The marble thrones of the emperor and his wives stand in the central hall. An "eternal lamp" (an

BELOW: the magnificent 7km (4-mile) Avenue of Stone Figures.

oil lamp with a floating wick that was believed to burn for ever) and five sacrificial offerings (an incense bowl, two candelabra and two vases of yellow-glazed earthenware) can be seen in the room. Next door are two side chambers that contain pedestals for coffins. These platforms, which are covered with the "golden stones" and filled with yellow earth, are known as the Golden Fountains. No coffins were found in this chamber.

The rear hall is the largest and the most imposing in the subterranean palace. It is 9.5 metres (30ft) high, 30 metres (100ft) long and 9 metres (30ft) wide. On pedestals in the middle of the hall are the coffins of Wanli and his empresses, surrounded by 26 lacquered chests filled with crowns, gold and jade pitchers, cups, bowls, earrings and wine containers. There are also sacred objects of jade and items of blue-and-white Ming porcelain. An extraordinarily fine filigree crown of gold adorned with two dragons playing with a pearl (pictured on page 219) can be viewed in the two exhibition halls within the complex, together with a valuable embroidery showing 100 playing children, and other exhibits.

Other Ming emperors' tombs are not open to the public at present – they have government protection against excavation – but you can wander around the grounds for several miles, discovering the ruins of other tomb structures and escaping from the crowds.

ABOVE: imperial suit of armour excavated at the Ming Tombs.

Fenghuang Mountain ⑪

Address: Haidian District
Opening Hrs: 6am–6pm
Entrance Fee: charge
Transport: bus 346 from the New Summer Palace (Yiheyuan), or by taxi

Some 25km (16 miles) northwest of the New Summer Palace, **Fenghuang Mountain** (凤凰岭) is well worth the trip for a less crowded hiking experience than that offered by the Fragrant Hills. The charming **Dragon Spring Temple** (Longquan Si; 龙泉寺), dating from the Liao dynasty (AD 907–1125), is at its foot, guarded by two Maidenhair trees said to be as old as the temple. Three un-signposted dirt paths zigzag up the mountain, each requiring several hours. ❏

RESTAURANTS

THE GREAT WALL

The greatest fortification in human history was built to prevent invasion by nomadic tribes from the steppes to the north. Today it is one of the most famous sights on earth

The Great Wall is the single greatest tourist attraction in China, and one of the greatest in all the world. It has excited fascination and wonder among Westerners ever since tales of its immensity and scale began trickling back to Europe in the 17th and 18th centuries. Its popularity as a tourist attraction among Chinese is a more recent phenomenon, one given a considerable boost by Mao's comment to the effect, "If you haven't been to the Great Wall, you're not a real Chinese." An unattributed, but similar, aphorism directed at Westerners says, "If you haven't been to the Great Wall, you haven't been to China".

Thanks in part to the widespread expression of such sentiments, the Great Wall receives an estimated 10 million visitors each year, the vast majority of them heading to the parts most easily reached as a day trip from Beijing.

It is possible to visit the Wall in all seasons. It looks as spectacular flanked by summer greenery as by winter snow, or by autumn yellows, oranges and browns. Spring and autumn are best for hiking, however, as summer heat and dense vegetation make an excursion more of an ordeal, and in midwinter it is often uncomfortably cold, while snow and ice make the steep slopes dangerous. In any season, solid and comfortable footwear is advised.

The rise and fall of the Wall

The "Ten Thousand Li Great Wall" (Wan Li Chang Cheng; 万里长城) represents the pinnacle of 2,000 years of wall-building in northern China. The construction visible today dates mostly from the 15th century and

PRECEDING PAGES: Juyongguan Fortress. **LEFT:** an empty stretch of Wall at Juyongguan Pass. **RIGHT:** patriotic tourists at Mutianyu.

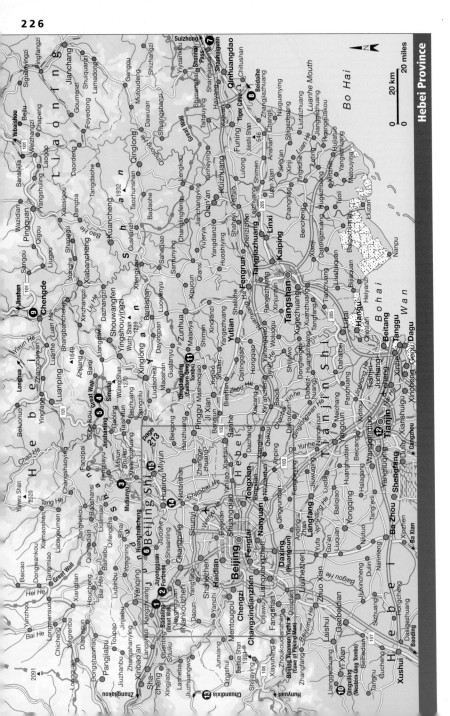

Hebei Province

N

0   20 km
0   20 miles

stretches for some 4,000km (2,500 miles). It is a structure of overwhelming physical presence, a vast wall of earth, brick and stone topped by an endless procession of stout towers, rolling over craggy peaks and across deep ravines and barren deserts. But the Great Wall is more than a remnant of history. It is massively symbolic of the tyranny of imperial rule, the application of mass labour, the ingenuity of engineers commissioned to work on the grandest scale, and the human desire to build for immortality.

It is, however, misleading to speak of one wall. Archaeologists have identified many walls, some of which date back to the 5th century BC. These fortifications came into being because the flourishing agricultural settlements on the fertile plains along the Yellow River and its tributaries had to protect themselves against constant plundering by nomadic tribes. Each settlement built its own "great wall" of rammed earth, the earliest probably being in the state of Qi, in modern Shandong province. The length of all such walls so far discovered totals some 50,000km (30,000 miles).

It was Qin Shi Huangdi, considered to be the first Chinese emperor (221–210 BC), who conceived the idea of a single, protective Great Wall. He forced all the states of China to submit to his rule. After removing internal threats in this way, he linked the northern walls into a single defensive bulwark against the nomads. Under the leadership of General Meng Tian, an army of 300,000 forced labourers is said to have constructed the Great Wall. In those days, the Wall began in the west of Lintao (to the south of Lanzhou) and ran east through Inner Mongolia, Shaanxi and Hebei provinces. It ended in the east of what is now Liaoning province.

The Great Wall did not always fulfil its purpose of keeping enemies out. It was breached regularly even before the Tang dynasty (618–907) extended the borders of its empire well beyond it. Sometimes it simply had no purpose at all. The Mongol conquerors who ruled northern China from 916 to 1368 had no need of the Wall, since it lay in the middle of their territory, and served as neither a boundary nor a defence.

ABOVE: cable cars ensure swift access to the higher sections of the Wall at Badaling and Mutianyu. **BELOW:** security guard on the Wall at Badaling.

The Great Wall: Fact vs Fiction

A number of myths surround the Great Wall, perhaps unsurprisingly for such a remarkable, improbable structure. Contrary to popular belief, the Wall is not visible to the human eye from the moon. It is also not filled with the bodies of dead labourers, as such material would prove unstable. For some, the Wall represents a monumental folly, but historian David Spindler says it is wrong to say that it was ultimately ineffective – as, after all, it helped the Ming army to maintain its sprawling territory for hundreds of years. Spindler cites two major instances of the Mongol hordes being kept at bay: in 1554 at the Jinshanling section and in 1561 at Badaling.

ABOVE: the Wall at Badaling is illuminated during the summer, and on special occasions at other times of the year.
ABOVE RIGHT: dressing up as a Mongol warrior.
BELOW: hiring a taxi for the day makes a trip out to the Great Wall a more relaxed experience.

However, the overthrow of the Mongols by the first Ming emperor, Zhu Yuanzhang (1368–98), changed the situation. The maintenance of the Great Wall became a matter of life or death for the new Ming dynasty, which had to defend itself against attacks from the Mongols and other hostile northern neighbours. For more than 200 years, work went on to strengthen the Wall. New sections were built, fortified towers were extended, and the logistics of defending and administering it were overhauled and improved.

The Wall was mostly left to decay from the 18th century. The Manchu rulers of the Qing dynasty were invaders from beyond the Wall, and were intent on expanding rather than consolidating their empire. Wind and weather gradually eroded away some sections of the once-more redundant fortifications. Peasants recycled bricks and stones to build farmhouses and stables. This process of deconstruction continued into modern times.

During the Cultural Revolution, army units built whole barracks out of bricks taken from the Great Wall.

Preserving the Wall

Since Deng Xiaoping launched a campaign in 1984 to "Love China, Restore the Great Wall", many sections have been rebuilt and opened to tourists. The intentions of the campaign were good and have generally led to much greater respect for and interest in the Wall. However, over the years this increased interest has produced certain inevitable side effects.

The chief source of the problems is tourism itself. As more people visit the Great Wall, the popular restored areas become increasingly crowded, causing those interested in a more genuine – or at least private – Wall experience to seek out less crowded parts of the 675km (420 miles) of Wall in the Beijing area. However, it is hard to keep anything secret in China, and as more hikers show up on a particular unrestored section of the Wall – commonly referred to as "Wild Wall" – local people begin appearing to sell drinks and other items. Such small-scale entrepreneurial activity gradually grows until, in the blink of an eye, an entire village erects a bridge or a barricade on the Wall so they can charge tourists to cross it. Local officials get involved and build guesthouses or cable cars. Sometimes they even undertake hastily to repair the Wall with limestone and paint. More tourists come, bringing with them their litter, noise and graffiti, and causing the more adventurous to seek undiscovered sections of Wild Wall – and thus the entire cycle begins again.

Even at the central government level, the lack of will and the failure to commit sufficient funding led the World Monument Fund to place the Great Wall Cultural Landscape in the area of Beijing on its list of the world's most endangered monuments in 2002. This helped bring more attention to the problem, and in 2003 the Beijing government promulgated stricter regulations banning the construction of buildings on or near the Wall, and forbade hikers from walking on the most fragile sections. Beijing has pledged to commit part of its Rmb 3 billion cultural heritage conservation project (2010–14) to opening and restoring several more sections of the Wall to attract yet more visitors, all the while protecting restricted areas.

Badaling ❶

Address: Yanqing County
Tel: 6912-1737
Opening Hrs: daily 7am–7pm
Entrance Fee: charge
Transport: tourist bus 1 from Qianmen, 2 from Beijing Railway Station, 919 from Deshengmen, or by taxi

The most accessible section of the Wall – and consequently the most crowded – is at **Badaling** (八达岭), 60km (38 miles) northwest of Beijing. It is easily reached by the fast road from Beijing, and despite the hordes of sightseers – avoidable in the early mornings and in the colder months – Badaling has great scenery, restored forts and exhibitions to see.

The Wall here was strategically important and heavily fortified by the Ming emperors. The way up on both sides of the valley leads to high beacon towers, from which you can see the northern plain and the Wall snaking across faraway hills. The western side is a steeper climb. The watchtowers on this stretch are solidly built, with high arrow slits.

The only drawback of Badaling is that it can seem unbearably crowded

> *This is a great wall and it had to be built by a great people,*
>
> US President
> Richard Nixon, 1972

BELOW: a replica of one of the famous Terracotta Warriors stands guard at Juyongguan Fortress.

and commercialised. Vendors of tacky souvenirs and T-shirts compete for sales, not only as you approach but also on the Wall itself. In the evening, karaoke sessions and laser shows are sometimes held. Only by a brisk walk of an hour or so can you escape from the tour groups.

The majority of tourists visit Badaling as part of a tour, often taking in the Ming Tombs *(see page 218)* en route and sometimes also stopping at **Juyongguan Fortress ❷** (Juyongguan; 居庸关), built to guard the narrow, 20km (13-mile) long valley, and Beijing, against invading armies from the north. In the middle of the valley is a stone platform of white marble, the **Cloud Terrace** (Yuntai; 云台). Built in 1345, it once served as the foundation for a great gate with three stone pagodas. An arched gateway still survives. In the vaulted passage of the gate there are splendid reliefs, mostly Buddhist motifs, among them the four Tianwang (Celestial Kings), and inscriptions of Buddhist Sutras in six different languages: Sanskrit, Tibetan, Tangut, Uighur, Mongol and Chinese.

ABOVE: a steep climb to the strategically important Juyong Pass.
BELOW RIGHT: an unrestored section of the Wall.

The Wall climbs steeply on both sides from the fortress; this was an important section, and is one of the oldest. It has been renovated in recent years but is usually quite empty, and the scenery is dramatic.

Mutianyu ❸

Address: Mutianyu Town, Huairou District
Tel: 6162-6505
Opening Hrs: daily 6.30am–6.30pm
Entrance Fee: charge
Transport: tourist bus 6 from Xuanwumen, or by taxi

The Wall at **Mutianyu** (慕田峪) is equally spectacular but less crowded than Badaling. A long section of restored Wall follows a high ridge, giving views over wooded ravines 90km (55 miles) northeast of Beijing. The nearest point on the Wall is a steep one-hour climb from the car park, though the cable car provides a breathtaking alternative and a luge-like slide offers a quick way down. Mutianyu was not part of the main Wall but a barrier wall shielding passes to the north towards Zhangjiakou. High parapets, crenel-

Rambling on the Ramparts

To experience the true splendour of the Wall, you need to hike on it. Of old, parts of the wall were used as routes for porters and itinerant traders. In this age of leisure-walking many enthusiasts hope it will become the world's ultimate long-distance footpath.

Since so much of the Wall is unrestored, seeing wilder sections need not be an endurance test. Walking is mostly on the Wall itself, so it's difficult to get lost, but the going is often slow. Take great care on steep, crumbling sections. In some places, you may have no alternative but to leave and rejoin the Wall; in others, rickety piles of fallen bricks may be your only climbing aid.

Jinshanling, Huanghuacheng and Simatai are three of the more popular stretches, the last being the most popular place – and the most challenging, if you traverse the whole ridge. You can combine a trip to Simatai and Jinshanling, to the immediate west, perhaps camping overnight in one of the many towers along the Wall. Camping is not officially allowed but, while numbers remain small, it seems to be tolerated. The views from your beacon tower at dusk and dawn are rewarding. Do not light fires, and, of course, take all your litter with you.

lated on both sides, are part of the major Ming-dynasty renovations completed in 1569. As at Badaling, large blocks of granite were used in the foundations because of the strategic importance of the area, which became known as the North Gate of the Capital.

Simatai ❹

Address: Gubeikou Town, Miyun County
Tel: 6903-1051
Opening Hrs: daily 8am–5pm
Entrance Fee: charge
Transport: bus 980 from Dongzhimen long-distance bus station to Miyun station, then transfer to Simatai (or take a taxi from Miyun)

Well established as a favoured section of Wall for hikers, **Simatai** (司马台) shows the unrestored Great Wall at its most majestic, crowning a narrow ridge and sharp pinnacles. The site is quite remote, 115km (70 miles) northeast of Beijing, and many visitors find it best to take a tour.

You can either take the cable car to a point 20 to 30 minutes' walk below the Wall, or make a longer excursion on foot. If you opt for the latter, from the car park you will see a small reservoir between two steep sections of Wall. Go through the entrance gate and take the path to the right (east) leading to the higher section of Wall. This is the most spectacular stretch. Alternatively, turn left (west) for a quieter, easier walk towards Jinshanling.

The scramble to **Viewing the Capital Tower** (Wangjing Lou; 望京楼) via the ridge demands a good head for heights, but rewards you with some of the best views and most exciting walking anywhere on the Wall. In places, you walk on sections just two bricks (40cm/16 inches) wide, which locals call the *tianti*, or "stairway to heaven". Yet even on the most inaccessible parts you may find someone waiting to sell you a soft drink. On the lower reaches, inscriptions on bricks give details such as "made by the infantry camp of suppressing enemy troops in the sixth year of the Wanli reign".

Jinshanling ❺

Address: Gubeikou Town, Miyun County
Tel: 0314-883-0222
Opening Hrs: 24 hours
Entrance Fee: charge
Transport: take the Chengde bus from Dongzhimen long-distance bus station alighting at Jinshanling, from where the Wall is a short taxi ride away

First built by the Northern Qi dynasty in AD 555, **Jinshanling** (金山岭), like neighbouring Simatai 10km (6 miles) to the east, was part of a 3,000-

A 1931 issue of Popular Mechanics reported that the Nationalist government planned to turn the Wall into an elevated highway extending 2,400km (1,500 miles) westwards from Beijing, an unlikely scenario, as any visitor to the steeper sections would contest.

ABOVE LEFT: souvenir T-shirts. **BELOW:** the Wall at Mutianyu.

ABOVE: the Wall meets the sea at Shanhaiguan. The town can be accessed by several daily trains from Beijing. Journey time on the faster trains is three or four hours. Book tickets two days in advance of travel. There are also buses from Xizhimen and Majuan bus stations in Beijing. Frequent buses and trains operate between Shanhaiguan and Beidaihe. **BELOW:** Great Wall scenery at Huanghuacheng.

li wall from Shanhaiguan to northern Shaanxi Province. Some 7km (4 miles) distant, **Gubeikou** (古北口) was considered a weak point in the defence of the capital. It occupies a broad valley among low mountains cut by streams and rivers, allowing many possible routes to Beijing. Tribes of Mongol and other nomads repeatedly forced their way through here. In 1554, the same group raided Beijing three times via Gubeikou. Heavy fortification followed in the late 16th century, including "arrow walls", small walls built across steep sections of the main Wall, giving protection to archers.

In the late 17th century, when Emperor Kangxi built his summer resort in Chengde, the pass which lies on the route there was heavily guarded. The 158 fortified towers are particularly remarkable for their variety of shapes: rectangular, round, oval and polygonal. Most of the towers on the section east of Gubeikou have been restored, but this is usually the quietest of all the tourist stretches. It makes a good choice for an easier walk with views east towards the more dramatic Simatai.

Huanghuacheng ❻

Address: Chengguan town, Huairou District
Tel: 8353-1111
Opening Hrs: daily 8am–5.30pm
Entrance Fee: charge
Transport: bus 916 from outside Dongzhimen subway station (line 2) to Huairou Nan Dajie, then change to bus 936 to Huanghuacheng station

Once one of the main garrison areas guarding the capital, **Huanghuacheng** (黄花城), or Yellow Flower Wall, lies 60km (38 miles) north of Beijing, the closest the Wall gets to the city. Climb up on either side from a small reservoir to the east of the road.

The more spectacular section begins across the reservoir – and across the narrow dam. If you are scared of heights, you will have to take a detour to cross the stream below the dam, leaving a steeper climb up to the Wall. Several large towers along the ridge offer great views on both sides. A stone tablet lies on the floor of the largest tower. Further on, the Wall resembles a saw blade as it drops steeply into the valley to your right (south).

To complete a circular route, descend to the valley on a path leading down from the large tower, which is the lowest point on the ridge. Once at the bottom, head west through orchards of apples, walnuts and apricots, until you reach the road back to the reservoir.

The Hebei coast

Ancient walls still enclose about half of the small market town and former garrison of **Shanhaiguan** (山海关) ❼, in Hebei province, the place where the Wall meets the sea. The East Gate, rebuilt in 1639, is known as the First Pass Under Heaven. Manchu troops rode through here to Beijing to replace the deposed Ming emperors in 1644. There is a small museum here offering some historical details on the Great Wall and a scale model of the area.

As the Great Wall (daily 8am–5.30pm; entrance fee) rises steeply inland, two sheer drops have to be climbed by ladder. From the top, you get a fantastic view of the Wall dropping below you and then bounding over the plain towards the sea. In the

opposite direction is the Old Dragon's Head, where reconstructed barracks of the Great Wall cross golden sands to meet the Bohai Sea. The **beach** itself is not unpleasant, and it's worth walking to the end of the jetty for views of the Old Dragon's Head and to take in the bracing sea air.

Shanhaiguan is a favourite photo spot for the hordes of day-trippers who arrive from nearby **Beidaihe** (北戴河) ❽, a beach resort long favoured for company conferences and official junkets – although it was the small foreign community in Beijing and Tianjin who made the place popular in the early 20th century. China's top leaders still meet here annually to enjoy a welcome respite from Beijing's polluted air, hidden away at a private beach to the south of town.

An abundance of cheap seafood restaurants line a small boardwalk area on the sandy 10km (6-mile) main beach. On the rolling, rather Mediterranean-looking hills behind the town, old brick villas overlook the sea. Party officials and organisations have access to many of the 700 villas built around Beidaihe before 1949. ❏

ABOVE: a sandy stretch of beach, good transport links and warm shallow waters have made Beidaihe one of the main seaside resorts in China.

RESTAURANTS

Badaling Great Wall

Badaling Restaurant
八达岭饭店
Badaling Great Wall.
Tel: 6912-1486. Open:
11am–8pm. **$$$**
This is the main, state-owned restaurant at Badaling, the only one tourism officials will promote to groups. It is enormous – the space can accommodate up to 1,000 people. Reasonable Sichuan and Jiangsu food, served in clean surroundings.

Simatai Great Wall

Great Wall Villa 长城山庄
Simatai Great Wall, Jingqu Lu. Tel: 6903-5159. Open: 7am–9pm. **$**
A small restaurant in this inexpensive hotel serves basic home-style food to hungry hikers.

Simatai Restaurant
司马台饭馆
Simatai Great Wall, 98 Jingqu Lu. Tel: 6903-5311. Open: 8am–9pm. **$**
Home-style food prepared by an experienced Sichuanese chef.

Beidaihe

Hai Tian Xiang 海天香
Dongjing Lu. Tel: 0335-404-7159. Open: 8.30am–midnight. **$$**
Home-style cooking – and a menu in English – with seafood as a speciality; the restaurant is a quick five-minute walk from the CITS office.

Kiessling's 起示林
96 Dongjing Lu. Tel: 0335-404-4284. Open: 7.30am–10.30pm. **$$$**
The Beidaihe branch of the famous Austrian restaurant serves both Western and Chinese food. In the distant past, diners could expect to be served Viennese chocolate and caviar on sparkling crystal while White Russian musicians serenaded them at table. Things aren't quite like that these days, but you can still get a good, and substantial, nostalgia-laced meal.

• • • • • • • • • •

Prices are for a typical dinner for one (three dishes with beer in Chinese restaurants, or a three-course meal with a half-bottle of house wine in Western-style restaurants). $ = under Rmb 50, $$ = Rmb 50–100, $$$ = Rmb 100–200, $$$$ = over Rmb 200.

How They Built the Greatest Wall in History

The astonishing project, conceived as the ultimate defence, took nearly 20 centuries to complete and involved millions of conscripted labourers

The Ming-dynasty Ten Thousand Li Great Wall averages 8 metres (26ft) high and 7 metres (21ft) wide. Some sections are broad enough to allow five or six soldiers to ride side by side. Surveyors planned the route so that, where possible, the outer (generally north-facing) wall was higher. Countless parallel walls, fortified towers, beacon towers, moats, fortifications and garrisons completed a complex system. Local military units supervised construction. In a simple contract, officers and engineers detailed the time, materials and work required.

Hidden Sentries

Many sections of the wall around Beijing were built on granite blocks, with some foundation stones weighing more than 1 tonne.

Elaborate wooden scaffolding, hoists and pulleys, and occasionally iron girders, aided the builders. To speed up the construction process, prefabricated stone parts were used for beacon towers, including lintels, gate blocks and gullies.

ABOVE: construction of the Great Wall varied according to the terrain and the perceived level of threat. With the aim of maximising its defensive capabilities, surveyors often chose unlikely routes across near-vertical hillsides. Engineers coped with the topography by using stretches of "single" wall, bridges, viaducts, and incorporating natural features.

BELOW: the 7-metre (23ft) thick wall was constructed of an outer layer of brick and stone enclosing an inner core of earth and rubble.

ABOVE: stone tablets, like this one set into the wall at Huanghuacheng, serve as invaluable artefacts by which to measure the progress of construction down the centuries. The tablets record what was built when and by whom, as well as listing command structures.

BELOW: Ming-dynasty bricks were extremely heavy; pulleys, shoulder poles, handcarts, mules and goats were used to move them into place.

LEFT: towers in remote areas were built close enough together to enable the beacon system devised in the Tang dynasty to function. When trouble was spotted, guards used smoke, fire or gunpowder blasts, which could be interpreted by neighbouring guard posts.

LIFE ON THE EDGE: A GUARD'S STORY

From their small rooftop sentry boxes, Great Wall guards, though they kept their weapons and torches primed, saw no enemies for months on end. If an assault came, the guards' main function was not to defend the wall but to alert the nearest garrison using a complex system of torch signals.

Most guards lived in remote watchtowers shared with 5–10 others. During the day, those not on lookout tilled small patches of farmland on the hillside, collected firewood and dried cattle or wolf dung, and sometimes hunted. They ground wheat flour in stone mortars and carried out minor repairs to the wall and tower. To supplement food supplies brought by road, migration of farmers was encouraged or enforced, and guards helped them construct irrigation canals and farmhouses.

The guards' crowded living quarters also served as storage for grain and weapons. Doors and windows had heavy wooden shutters to keep out the winter cold, and often guards shared a *kang*, a heated brick bed.

ABOVE: a Ming-dynasty watchtower window.

BELOW: to minimise transportation costs, brick kilns were constructed as close to the wall as possible. Brick makers often recorded their names and the date of production on the bricks as a guarantee of quality. So far, some 50 brick kilns have been excavated. Archaeologists believe dozens – if not hundreds – more remain buried along the length of the wall.

FURTHER AFIELD

Beyond the Great Wall, the Imperial Resort at Chengde offers blessed relief from the noise and summer heat of the city. Closer in are the port city of Tianjin, ancient tombs and some scenic countryside

Main Attractions

CHENGDE:
 IMPERIAL RESORT
 LITTLE POTALA TEMPLE
EASTERN QING TOMBS
TIANJIN:
 ZHONGXIN PARK
 ANTIQUES MARKET
CHUANDIXIA
NINE VALLEYS (JIUGUKOU)

Maps and Listings

The region extending from the immediate surroundings of Beijing, largely encompassed by Hebei province, has a great deal to offer anyone who wishes to see a different side of China, away from the frenetic energy of the capital city. Within reach are resorts of both imperial and seaside variety – mountains, lakes and grasslands, imperial tombs, and the enjoyable city of Tianjin. In the countryside, enter another world, where the air is clean, trees and grass are abundant, and life is lived at a slower pace. This rural tranquillity is being eroded, however, as increasingly well-heeled tourists head out of Beijing on weekends and holidays to scenic spots for outdoor activities such as rock climbing, hiking, horse-riding and even bungee-jumping.

CHENGDE

Chengde **9** (承德), 250km (150 miles) to the northeast of Beijing, is a city of more than 200,000 people that feels a lot smaller than it actually is. It is several degrees cooler than the capital, and even though there are tall buildings and busy roads, it has

somehow managed to retain the feel of the summer resort it once was.

Around the end of the 17th century, the Qing emperors began to look around for somewhere cool and green to retreat to when the summer heat of Beijing became oppressive. They found what they were looking for beyond the Great Wall, in the hilly countryside around the Wulie River. Here they established a summer residence, creating carefully structured landscapes set against the natural backdrop of mountains and woods,

LEFT: overview of the Chengde palaces, with the Little Potala Temple in the background.
RIGHT: fur hats help to protect against the freezing winter cold.

TIP

There are several trains daily from Beijing Zhan to Chengde, generally taking around 4½ hours – although some take considerably longer. Buses and minibuses go from Deshengmen, Xizhimen and Dongzhimen bus stations.

and populated them with innumerable pavilions, palaces and temples.

The resort was first established when Emperor Kangxi (1661–1722) ordered the building of a summer palace here in 1703, and construction continued through most of the reign of Qianlong (1736–95). The result is the largest imperial residence in China that has survived in its original condition – the buildings and gardens cover an area of 560 hectares (1,400 acres), and are surrounded by a wall 10km (6 miles) long. Outside the palace walls, to the north and west, a total of 11 temples – mostly in the Tibetan style – were built. Seven of these can still be visited.

For over 100 years, the emperors and their retinues passed the summer months here, spending their time on hunting excursions, equestrian games and other diversions, as well as on state business. Yet it all came to an abrupt end in 1820, when a bolt of lightning killed Emperor Jiaqing, who was in residence at Chengde at the time. Fearing that fate might deal them a second blow, the court stayed away, and the buildings and gardens fell into ruin.

Xianfeng was the only emperor ever to stay here again, and he only did so when forced to flee Beijing during the Second Opium War in 1860. It was at the Imperial Resort that he was obliged to sign the Treaty of Peking, which granted far-reaching concessions to foreigners. He died the following year.

The Imperial Resort

Address: Central Chengde
Tel: 031-4216-3761
Opening Hrs: daily 5.30am–6.30pm
Entrance Fee: charge
Transport: taxi, or bus 5, from Chengde railway station

Bordering the northern edge of the town are the beautiful landscapes of the Imperial Resort. The closest section to Chengde itself is **Bishu**

BELOW: Emperor Kangxi.

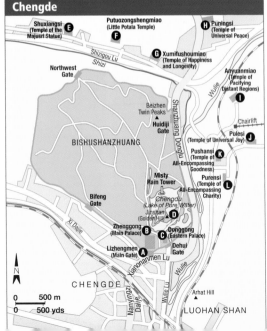

Chengde

Shuxiangsi **E**
(Temple of the Majusri Statue)

Putuozongshengmiao **F**
(Little Potala Temple)

Puningsi **H**
(Temple of Universal Peace)

Shizigou Lu
Shizi

Northwest Gate

Xumifushoumiao **G**
(Temple of Happiness and Longevity)

Anyuanmiao **I**
(Temple of Pacifying Distant Regions)

Wulie

Beizhen Twin Peaks ▲

Huidiji Gate

Shanzhuang Dongliu

Chairlift

BISHUSHANZHUANG

Pulesi **J**
(Temple of Universal Joy)

Pushansi **K**
(Temple of All-Encompassing Goodness)

Misty Rain Tower

Purensi **L**
(Temple of All-Encompassing Charity)

Bifeng Gate

Chengdu
(Lake of Pure Water)
Jinshan **D**
(Golden Hill)

Xi Dalie

Zhenggong **B**
(Main Palace)

Donggong **C**
(Eastern Palace)

Dehui Gate

Lizhengmen **A**
(Main Gate)

Xiaonanmen Lu

Wulie

N

Nanyingzi Dalie

CHENGDE

0   500 m
0   500 yds

Arhat Hill ▲

Wulie Lu

LUOHAN SHAN

Shanzhuang (The Mountain Resort for Escaping the Heat; 避暑山庄), consisting of three great complexes reached by passing through the **Main Gate Ⓐ** (Lizhengmen; 丽正门), which has a tablet bearing inscriptions in Chinese, Mongol, Manchu, Tibetan and Uighur. The **Inner Gate** (Neiwumen; 内午门) bears an inscription in Emperor Kangxi's calligraphy, naming the resort.

As in the Forbidden City in Beijing, the first halls entered are those in which state business was conducted and ceremonies were held, with the private imperial apartments occupying the rear of the palace. The main hall of the **Main Palace Ⓑ** (Zhenggong; 正宫) is built of precious *nanmu* hardwood from southwest China. This was the hall in which, in 1860, Xianfeng reluctantly signed the treaty dictated by the British and the French.

The **Hall of Pines and Cranes** (Songhezhai; 松鹤斋), to the east of the Main Palace, was the private residence of the emperor's mother. Beyond this is the **Hall of Ten Thousand Pine Valleys in the Wind** (Wanhesongfeng; 万壑松风), from which you get a view of the northern grounds. Here, the 12-year-old Qianlong was instructed by his grandfather, Kangxi, in the proper form of answering petitions, and in classical literature. In memory of Kangxi, he later named the hall the **Hall for Remembering Kindness** (Ji'entang; 纪恩堂).

In the southeast corner of the resort are the remains of the **Eastern Palace Ⓒ** (Donggong; 东宫). In 1948 the last part standing, a three-storey theatre, completely burned down.

The **park** adjoining the palaces to the north can be divided into three areas. Directly bordering the palaces is the lake area; to the northwest is a plain; and to the west is a forested, hilly landscape with ravines and valleys.

The **Lake of Pure Water** (Chengdu Lake) is divided by a number of dams into eight smaller lakes. Everywhere are little pavilions, teahouses and resting places, reminiscent of the southern Chinese lakes, such as the area around the West Lake near Hangzhou. The lake is fed from the

ABOVE: a handful of steam locomotives are still in use in northeastern China, and can sometimes be seen on the line at Chengde.
BELOW LEFT: pavillion at the Lake of Pure Water.

A Royal Rebuff

When Lord George Macartney visited China in 1793 in an attempt to open up normal trade relations between Britain and China, Emperor Qianlong received him at Chengde. Their meeting took place in the royal audience tent where Macartney and his delegation were treated to a banquet so splendid that he compared it to the "celebration of a religious mystery". However, although the audience seemed to have gone well, it was followed by Qianlong's famous letter to King George in which he praised the British king for inclining himself "towards civilisation", but informed him that "we have never valued ingenious articles, nor do we have the slightest need of your country's manufactures. Therefore, O King, as regards your request to send someone to remain at the capital, while it is not in harmony with the regulations of the Celestial Empire we also feel very much that it is of no advantage to your country. Hence we have issued these detailed instructions and have commanded your tribute envoys to return safely home. You, O King, should simply act in conformity with our wishes by strengthening your loyalty and swearing perpetual obedience so as to ensure that your country may share the blessings of peace."

Warm Spring (Requan; 热泉) so it does not freeze, even in the frigid north Chinese winter. Smaller lakes and pools have clever features. One, for instance, offers a daytime reflection of the crescent moon – an effect created by rocks carefully placed above the water.

The artificial **Golden Hill** (Jinshan; 金山) is topped by the Jinshan Pavilion where the emperors made offerings to Daoist gods. Further north lies a broad plain, which Qianlong named the **Park of Ten Thousand Trees** (Wanshuyuan; 万树园). Pines, acacias, willows and old cypresses grow in abundance here, and Qianlong delighted in the many birds and deer. The court met in Mongol yurts, feasting and watching wrestling bouts, or enjoying displays of horse-riding or folk arts. To the west of the gardens was a great riding arena where the emperors chose their horses and had them broken in and trained for equestrian performances.

The Eight Outer Temples

Address: 1km (⅔ mile) northeast of the Imperial Resort

Opening Hrs: daily 8am–5.30pm
Entrance Fee: charge
Transport: taxi or bus 6 from the Imperial Resort's southern gate.
All temples are walkable

Many of the temples at Chengde were built in Tibetan style, a sign of the favour shown to the Lamaist religion by the Qing emperors, notably Qianlong. Eleven such temples were built on the hills northwest of the Imperial Resort during the reigns of Kangxi and Qianlong.

Divided into eight groups, they became known as the **Eight Outer Temples** (Waiba Miao; 外八庙). The main gates of these buildings pointed towards the palace, symbolising the unity of China's various ethnic groups under central imperial rule.

Seven temples remain, with halls modelled on famous Tibetan Buddhist buildings. In a kind of giant ancient Buddhist theme park, the 18th-century replicas of the Potala Palace in Lhasa, the Tashilhunpo and Samye monasteries elsewhere in Tibet and other religious buildings from all over China, make an impressive sight. Several of the temples have

ABOVE: the Little Potala Temple (Putuozongshengmiao) is modelled on the Potala Palace in Lhasa. **BELOW:** Puningsi Temple.

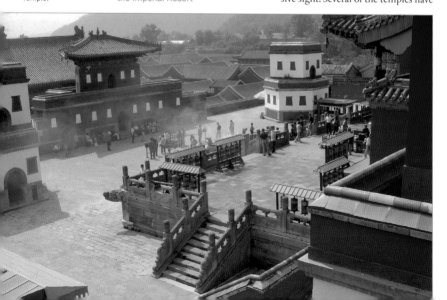

small communities of monks living in them, allowed back in the 1980s after the religious repression of the Cultural Revolution had ceased. All are open daily from 8am to 5.30pm.

In the extreme northwest is the **Temple of the Majusri Statue** (Shuxiangsi; 殊像寺), dating from 1774. A replica of the Shuxiang Temple in the Wutaishan Mountains of Shanxi province, it holds a Manchu translation of the Buddhist scriptures, the *Kanjur*. Further east, due north of the Imperial Resort, is the large and spectacular **Little Potala Temple** (Putuozongshengmiao; 普陀宗乘之庙), which bears the name of Putuoshan, a sacred Buddhist mountain on an island in the East China Sea. It is modelled, however, on the Potala Palace, the residence of the Dalai Lama in Tibet until 1959. Building began in 1767, and the temple was completed four years later. It served as a residence for high Tibetan dignitaries when they stayed at the Chinese imperial court.

From the outside this palace appears to have seven floors, but actually it only has three. Above the Red Palace is a hall, **Wanfaguiyidian.**

This contains many Bodhisattva figures. It is possible to access the roof for panoramic views across the entire complex.

The **Temple of Happiness and Longevity** (Xumifushoumiao; 须弥福寿之庙) was built in 1780 for Qianlong's 70th birthday. The sixth Panchen Lama had announced his intention to travel from Tibet to attend the festivities, and, as a special honour, Qianlong recreated the Panchen Lama's residence (Tashilhunpo Monastery in Xigaze) here. The roof of the main hall is covered with scale-like, gilded copper plates, with eight gilded dragons adorning the roof beams. The bodies of the mythical animals are bent and their tails raised, so that they look as if they are about to launch themselves into the air. The main part of this temple is another Red Palace. A building to the east of it houses a throne in which Emperor Qianlong listened to sermons preached by the Panchen Lama.

A little out of the way to the northeast stands the **Temple of Universal Peace** (Puningsi; 普宁寺), built in 1755. The impressive 37-metre (120ft)

ABOVE LEFT: martial arts outside Puningsi.
BELOW: gateway at the Little Potala Temple.

high **Mahayana Hall** is China's tallest wooden pavilion, and symbolises Meru Mountain (Kang Rinpoche, or Mount Kailash, in Tibet), the cosmic centre of the Buddhist world. It is flanked by a Moon Hall and a Sun Hall, and surrounded by Tibetan stupas. Inside is a carved wooden statue of the Bodhisattva Avalokiteshvara, 22 metres (73ft) tall, measuring 15 metres (49ft) across, and weighing more than 120 tonnes. It is said to be the tallest wooden statue in the world. Known as the Thousand Arm, Thousand Eye Guanyin Buddha, it is an incarnation of the goddess of mercy. Her 42 arms, each with an eye on the palm, symbolise her inexhaustible power of salvation.

A statue of the Buddha Amitabha sits on the head of the goddess. The World Monument Fund has placed this and its two side statues on its endangered list; two-and-a-half centuries of visitors, dust, exposure and neglect have left the statues in "desperate need of conservation".

To the south of the Temple of Universal Peace is the **Temple of Pacifying Distant Regions ❶** (Any-uanmiao; 安远庙), built in 1764 as a replica of the Gu'erzha temple at Ili, in Xinjiang. Only the Pududian (Hall of Universal Conversion) survives, with its statue of the Bodhisattva Ksitigarbha, the king of hell, whom the Chinese know as Ludumu.

Further south lies the **Temple of Universal Joy ❶** (Pulesi; 普乐寺), built in 1766 in honour of Kazhak, Kirghiz and other nobles from northwest China. The building is similar in style to the main hall of Beijing's Temple of Heaven. Beyond the entrance gate, bell and drum towers stand on either side. The main building, the **Pavilion of Morning Light** (Xuguangge; 旭光阁), rests on a square terrace, the combination symbolising heaven and earth according to ancient Chinese cosmology. The Temple of Universal Joy also contains bronze images of Tibetan deities conquering their enemies and in erotic embrace – fine examples of the simultaneously gorgeous and terrifying imagery of Tibetan Buddhism. Behind the temple you can hike or take a cable car to the eroded rock of **Club Peak**.

Adjoining the grounds of the Temple of Universal Joy to the south is the **Temple of All-Encompassing Goodness ⓚ** (Pushansi; 普善寺), which has fallen into ruin. Next to this is the **Temple of All-Encompassing Charity ⓛ** (Purensi; 普仁寺). The southernmost of the Eight Outer Temples, it was built in 1713 to celebrate Emperor Kangxi's 60th birthday.

THE WESTERN QING TOMBS ⓾

Address: Yixian County, Hebei province
Tel: 031-2471-0012
Opening Hrs: summer daily 8am–6pm; winter 8.30am–5pm
Entrance Fee: charge
Transport: tourist bus from Lize Qiao long-distance bus station to Yixian, then change for Western Qing Tombs. Taxis take up to three hours from Beijing

The **Western Qing Tombs** (Qingxiling; 清西陵) lie in a hilly district on the southern slopes of the Yongning Mountains, some 125km (80 miles) southwest of Beijing close to the town of Yixian. The Qing emperors Yongzheng, Jiaqing, Daoguang and Guangxu, along with three empresses, seven princes and many imperial concubines, are buried here. The site is very spread out.

The largest tomb, roughly at the centre of the site, is the **Tomb of Emperor Yongzheng** (Tailing; 泰陵). Yongzheng (1723–35) was extremely suspicious, and developed a network of spies who were supposed to observe the activities of his ministers. He rarely left his palace for any length of time, and only six years after ascending the throne, began to seek a suitable site for his tomb. Because he had gained the throne in an illegal manner, it is said that Yongzheng was afraid of being buried close to his father, Kangxi, in the Eastern Qing Tombs.

The **Gate of Eminent Favours** (Longenmen; 裰恩门) is the entrance to the main part of the Tailing complex. Within the gate there are furnaces for burning offerings, and the former storehouses which now serve as exhibition halls. Offerings were made in the **Hall of Eminent Favours** (Longendian; 裰恩殿), which contains the thrones of the emperor and the empress, together

BELOW LEFT: the Tomb of Emperor Jiaqing at the Western Qing Tombs. **BELOW:** portrait of Guangxu.

with an altar for offerings and gifts. Beyond the hall are two gates, stone receptacles for offerings, and a stele tower, below which lies the underground palace of the emperor.

Not far away to the west of Yongzheng's tomb is the **Tomb of Emperor Jiaqing** (Changling; 昌陵), completed in 1803 but not occupied until 1821. The number of buildings and their style are almost identical.

Five km (3 miles) further west is the **Mausoleum of Emperor Daoguang** (Muling; 慕陵), built between 1832 and 1836. After he had ascended the throne, Daoguang immediately began to have a mausoleum built in the Eastern Qing Tombs. One year after its completion, it was discovered that the subterranean palace was full of water. A new site was found at the Western tombs.

Meanwhile, new homes had to be found for dragons that had been displaced from their homes when the abortive Eastern Tomb had flooded. Hence the unique work of art of the **Hall of Eminent Favours**. On its coffered ceiling of *nanmu* wood, every panel bears a writhing dragon, while the unpainted beams are carved in dragon forms.

The **Tomb of Emperor Guangxu** (Chongling; 崇陵) lies 5km (3 miles) to the east of the Tailing. It was built in 1909, and is the last of the imperial tombs, although Guangxu was not to be the last emperor of the Qing dynasty. That dubious honour is held by Pu Yi, who died in 1967 as an ordinary mortal who could not therefore be buried beside his imperial ancestors. To the east of Guangxu's tomb is a mausoleum for his concubines, including Zhen Fei and her sister, Jinfei.

THE EASTERN QING TOMBS ⓫

Address: Zunhua County, Hebei province
Tel: 031-5694-5471
Opening Hrs: daily summer 8am–5pm, winter 9am–4pm
Entrance Fee: charge
Transport: tourist bus from Xuanwumen subway station (lines 2 & 4), or bus from Dawanglu subway station (line 1) to Zunhua followed by a short taxi ride

Among the largest and most beautiful burial sites anywhere in China

are the **Eastern Qing Tombs** (Qing-dongling; 清东陵), near the town of Zunhua, 125km (80 miles) east of Beijing – a three- or four-hour drive. There is agreeable countryside to look at on the way and, once you arrive, the cobbled courtyards, stone bridges, streams and pathways make the stroll around the wooded tomb complex much more pleasant than the trudge around many tourist sites. The Jingxing mountain range, which resembles an upturned bell, borders the area to the south.

Five Qing emperors are buried in the area: the first dynastic emperor, Shunzi (1644–61), chose this broad valley for the site of his tomb while on a hunting expedition. He was followed by Kangxi (1661–1722), Qian-long (1736–96), Xiangfeng (1851–61) and Tongzhi (1862–75), as well as the empress dowager Cixi (who died in 1908), and a total of 14 other empresses, 136 imperial concubines and princesses.

The main entrance to the tombs is a great white **marble gate**, its rectangular surfaces covered with inscriptions and geometric designs. Pairs of lions and dragons form the base of the pillars. Beyond this is the **Great Palace Gate** (Dagongmen; 大宫门), which served as the official entrance to the mausoleum complex. It has a tower in which a carved *bixi* (a tortoise-like animal) bears a tall stone tablet on its shell. Engraved on the tablet are the "sacred virtues and worthiness" of the emperor Shunzi.

Passing a small hill to the north, you come to a *shenlu* (spirit way) with 18 pairs of stone figures, similar to the one at the Ming Tombs, but a little smaller. This road leads through the **Dragon and Phoenix Gate** (Longfengmen; 龙凤门) and crosses a marble bridge with seven arches. This is the longest and most beautiful of nearly 100 bridges in the complex, and is known as the **Five Notes Bridge**. If you step on one of the 110 stone slabs, you will, it is said, hear the five notes of the pentatonic scale.

At the other end of the bridge is the **Gate of Eminent Favours** (Longenmen; 棱恩门), the entrance to the **Tomb of Emperor Shunzi** (Xiaoling; 孝陵). Beyond is the **Hall of Eminent Favours** (Longendian; 棱恩殿), where the ancestor tablets and the offerings to the ancestors were kept. A stele tower rises behind the hall. The stele within is covered with red lacquer and bears the following inscription in Chinese, Manchu and Mongol: "Tomb of the emperor Shunzi". The underground tomb has yet to be excavated.

The **Tomb of Emperor Qianlong** (Yuling; 裕陵) dates from 1743. Qian-long reigned for 60 years, longer than any of the other nine Qing emperors. The three vaulted chambers of his subterranean palace covers an area of 327 sq metres (126 sq ft). A relief of the goddess of mercy, Guanyin, adorns the eight wings of the four double doors. Behind the doors are fine sculptures of the Tianwang, the Four Celestial Kings. Other reliefs cover the vaulting and the walls of

ABOVE: dragon detail on a wall at the Eastern Qing Tombs. **BELOW:** the Eastern Qing Tombs are set amid attractive scenery.

the tomb, including the Buddhas of the five points of the compass, and Buddhist inscriptions in Sanskrit and Tibetan.

The **Tomb of the Empress Dowager Cixi** (Dingongling; 定陵) can also be visited. The tomb lies about 1km (²/₃ mile) to the west of Yuling. Here, the two wives of Xianfeng lie buried: the eastern empress dowager Ci'an, and the infamous western empress dowager Cixi. The two tombs were originally symmetrical and built in the same style. But Cixi was not satisfied, and had Longendian, the Hall of Eminent Favours, pulled down in 1895. The tomb that she then had built for 4,590 taels of gold is the most splendid and extravagant of all.

As Cixi died before the work on her tomb was completed, the underground part is relatively plain, and is outshone by the fine craftsmanship of the stonework between the steps in front of the tomb and the balustrades in front of the hall. These show some exquisite carvings of dragons in the waves and phoenixes in the clouds – traditional symbols of the emperor and empress. The Hall of Eminent

Favours has an exhibition of Cixi's clothes, articles for daily use and a number of other tomb offerings. Also on display is the Dharani, a robe of sacred verses, woven in pure silk and embroidered with more than 25,000 Chinese characters in gold thread.

The concubines of Emperor Qianlong occupy tombs under 38 burial mounds. Other small tombs worth seeing in the complex are the **Tomb of the Wife of Emperor Shunzi** (Xiaodongling; 孝东陵), the **Changxiling** and the **Mudongling**. These tombs, recently excavated, had already been plundered.

The **Zhaoxiling** stands alone outside the Great Palace Gate. Although Zhaoxi, who was buried here in 1687, was a simple concubine, she was given the title of empress dowager because she had given birth to the future emperor Shunzi.

TIANJIN

A short 30 minutes by high-speed train from Beijing (regular departures from Beijing Zhan, the main station), **Tianjin** ⑫ has long lived in the shadow cast by its big neighbour to the north; the Tianjin Museum even includes several exhibits specific to the nearby capital. But the city is on the up, and there is a fair amount to see here. Most Beijingers have, or plan to, visit Tianjin even if it's just to pay prices for daily goods they last witnessed years ago.

Trading post to treaty port

Tianjin grew up as a trading post. It is the closest port to Beijing, and in imperial times it also thrived on the vast amounts of tribute rice that wended their way north along the Grand Canal. The city became a pawn in the 19th-century trading disputes and wars between the imperial authorities and those European states – particularly the British – who wanted to "open up" China. Attempting to keep the foreigners at bay, while permitting limited and regulated trade, the Chinese allowed Tianjin to become part of the "Canton System" – a scattering of cities in which foreigners could live and trade. Later, it became an outright "concession", similar to the International Settlement and French Concession in Shanghai. A number of Western buildings still dot the cityscape.

During its time as a "treaty port", as the coastal cities of the Canton System were known, Tianjin grew to be far more cosmopolitan than Beijing. Some wealthy Chinese built themselves Western-style villas in and around the city. Pu Yi, the last emperor, lived in the Japanese Concession from 1925 to 1931, fleeing the republican government who had thrown him out of the Forbidden City. **Zhang Garden**, the villa he lived in with his empress, Wan Rong, and his concubine, Wen Xiu, still stands. The house was named after the first owner, Zhang Biao, who built it in 1916.

City sights

Pu Yi was known to frequent another Tianjin landmark, the late 19th-

ABOVE: in common with other coastal cities, Tianjin has visibly prospered in China's economic boom. Prices, however, remain noticeably lower than in Beijing.

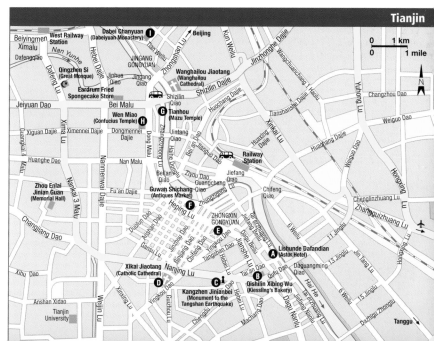

Tianjin

Beiyingmen · Ximalu · West Railway Station · Dabei Chanyuan (Dabeiyuan Monastery) ① · Beijing · Tian Weilu · Kun Weilu · Jinzhonghe Dajie · Wanchuanchang Lu · Hailu

Dafengqiao · Nan Yunhe · Hebei Dajie · Dateng Lu · JINGANG GONGYUAN · Zhongshan Lu · Jinhua Qiao · Jingang Qiao · Qingzhen Si (Great Mosque) · Wanghailou Jiaotang (Wanghailou Cathedral) · Shizilin Dajie · Yuhong Lu · Changzhou Dao

Eardrum Fried Spongecake Store · Shizilin Qiao · Huocheng Dajie · Tianshanshe Dajie

Jieyuan Dao · Bei Malu · ⑥ Tianhou (Mazu Temple) · Tianshanshe Dajie · Xinkai Lu · Weiguo Dao

Wen Miao (Confucius Temple) ⑪ · Dongmennei Dajie · Zhangzizhong Lu · Jintang Qiao · Bei Jianguo Dao · Huping Dajie · Huachang Dajie · Weiguo Dao

Xiguan Dajie · Ximennei Dajie · Xima Lu · Haihe Qiao · Jianguo Dao · Railway Station · Hongxing Lu

Guangli 4 Malu · Nanmennei Dajie · Nan Malu · ⑧ ⑯ · Chifeng Qiao · Huachang Dajie

Huanghe Dao · Nankai 3 Malu · Bei'an Dongqiao · Ziyou Dao · Jiefang Qiao · Chenglinzhuang Lu · Zhangguizhuang Lu

Zhou Enlai Jinian Guan (Memorial Hall) · Fu'an Dajie · Guwan Shichang (Antiques Market) ⑥ · Guangchang Qiao · Chifeng Qiao

Changliang Dao · Diulou Dao · ZHONGXIN GONGYUAN · Zhangzizhong Lu · 6 Weilu · 11 Jinglu

Anshan Dao · Jinchai Dao · Chifeng Dao · Jiefang Beilu · Jiefang Zhonglu · Taierzhuang Lu · 6 Weilu · 13 Jinglu

Xihu Dao · Gansu Lu · Binjiang Dao · ⑥ · Tangchang Dao · Jianshe Beilu · Lishunde Dafandian (Astor Hotel) ④ · Jin Tang Lu

Xikai Jiaotang (Catholic Cathedral) ⑨ · Nanjing Lu · Tai'an Dao · Tai'an Dao · Qufu Dao · Daguangming Qiao · Jingang Nanlu · 6 Weilu · 15 Jinglu

Anshan Xidao · Yingkou Dao · Kangzhen Jinianbei (Monument to the Tangshan Earthquake) · ⑥⑫ · Qishilin Xibing Wu (Kiessling's Bakery) · Machang Dao · Taierzhuang Nanlu · Jingang Nanlu · 6 Weilu · Dazhigu Zhonglu

Tianjin University · Weijin Lu · Xinxing Lu · Guizhou Lu · Chengdu Dao · Machang Dao · Dagu Nanlu · Tanggu

0 — 1 km
0 — 1 mile
N

century **Astor Hotel** (Lishunde Dafandian; 利顺德大饭店), where he enjoyed many pleasant evenings in the ballroom. Due to unfortunate renovations in 1984, the hotel does not retain much of its old-world charm, but it has an interesting array of historical photographs, including one of the future president of the US, Herbert Hoover, and his wife. The couple were married here in 1899, when Hoover was working as an engineer in the city.

Down Tai'an Dao, and then to the south on Zhejiang Lu, is another Tianjin institution, **Kiessling's Bakery**

ABOVE: handcrafted chops for sale in Tianjin's large antiques market. **BELOW:** Tianjin is one of China's largest ports.

(Qishilin Xibing Wu; 起士林西饼屋), set up by an Austrian resident in 1911 to supply bread to foreigners living in the concession. This is in the same building as the Qishilin Hotel. There is another Kiessling's in Beidaihe (*see page 233*).

Following Qufu Dao into Nanjing Lu toward the Friendship Hotel, you will come across the **Monument to the Tangshan Earthquake** (Kangzhen Jinianbei; 抗震纪念碑), which struck on 28 July 1976, just a few weeks before Mao's death. The epicentre was at Tangshan, 80km (50 miles) to the east, but surrounding areas, including Tianjin and Beijing, felt the effects and suffered many collapsed buildings. One of the worst natural disasters of recent times, an estimated 242,000 people died – although this figure went unreported by the government.

Further west along on Nanjing Lu, close to the junction with the large shopping street of Binjiang Dao, is another relic of Concession days, the **Catholic Cathedral** (Xikai Jiaotang; 西开教堂), which was built by French Catholics in 1916.

The "Flying Scotsman" of Tianjin

The 1981 Oscar-winning film *Chariots of Fire* tells the story of Eric Liddell's victory at the 1924 Paris Olympics. Known as the "Flying Scotsman", Liddell is also claimed by China as an Olympic and wartime hero because his birthplace was in fact Tianjin. His former residence at 38 Chongqing Dao even has state protection. In 1925 Liddell returned to work as a missionary and trained Chinese boys in various sports. He also helped build the Minyuan stadium, a replica of Chelsea's football ground and his favourite running track. During the Sino-Japanese War, Liddell elected to stay in China, helping refugees in a rural mission in Hebei province.

Another area evocative of the Concession period is **Zhongxin Park** (Zhongxin Gongyuan; 中心公园) **E**, near the intersection of Heping Lu and Chifeng Dao. Within this attractive circular park, surrounded as it is by old colonial-style buildings, it is easy to feel as if you are in Europe rather than China.

Antiques Market

From the park it is just a short walk to the northwest to Shenyang Dao. On the section of this street closest to the river there is a well-known **Antiques Market F** (Guwan Shichang; 古玩市场). If local lore is to be believed, the true antiques for sale here were confiscated from wealthy families during the Cultural Revolution, and stored in Tianjin. The government is now selling off these treasures to local merchants, who in turn sell them to tourists. Stickers occasionally appear on the merchandise, supposedly indicating from whom the piece was taken, as well as the time and place of the appropriation. The market is also a good place to buy old books and stamps as well as Cultural Revolution memorabilia. Opening hours are approximately 8am to 5pm.

Further north, where Zhangzizhong Lu meets Dongmennei Dajie, is the **Ancient Culture Street** (Guwenhua Jie; 古文化街). Built to look like an old Chinese city, it is now filled with merchants hawking familiar Chinese souvenirs. On some public holidays, Chinese opera performances take place here. In the middle of the street is the **Mazu Temple G** (Tianhou; 天后; daily 8am–4pm; entrance fee), dedicated to the goddess of the sea. It dates back to the Yuan dynasty, and is supposedly the oldest extant building complex in Tianjin.

Worshipped by seafaring people throughout China, the goddess is known as Matsu in Taiwan and Tin Hau in Hong Kong. Mazu's main temple is located on the Taiwanese island of Meizhou, where temple fairs are held every year. Tianjin,

ABOVE: admiring the wares in the antiques market.

EAT

Tianjin is famous for three local snacks. *Goubuli* steamed buns, which can be roughly translated as the snack "dogs don't like" though explanations for this curious name vary; *mahua*, a crispy dough twist with various fillings; and *erduoyan*, fried rice cakes thought to bring both good fortune and taste.

TIP

Chuandixia is directly accessible on bus 929 from Pingguoyuan, the western terminus of Beijing subway line 1. Journey time is approximately 3 hours.

as the largest port city in northern China, has the largest Mazu temple in the area, and still holds an annual temple fair in her honour. Emperor Qianlong once visited this fair, celebrated on Mazu's birthday, the 23rd day of the third lunar month.

Other sights in Tianjin

At the corner of Dongmennei and Dong Malu is the **Confucius Temple** (Wen Miao; 文庙; daily 8.30am–5pm; entrance fee), dating from 1463. Located in what is known as the Old Chinese Quarter, the temple is now surrounded by high-rise shopping malls and apartment buildings. Yet despite this and the strains of pop music that can filter in from the nearby shops, it is mostly quiet and peaceful. Stop in the *cha guan* (tearoom) and sip tea while listening to Beijing Opera on Sunday afternoons.

Further north, across the river on Shizilin Dajie is **Wanghailou Cathedral** (Wanghailou Jiaotang; 望海樓教堂), a Gothic-style Catholic church and monastery built in 1869. Still further north is the **Dabeiyuan Monastery** (Dabei Chanyuan; 大悲禅院; daily 9am–4pm; entrance fee), originally built in 1669 during the reign of Emperor Shunzhi. It managed to survive the Cultural Revolution intact, and was renovated in 1980.

For views of the city's vast urban area, the **Tianjin Eye** (Tianjin Zhi Yan; 天津之眼; Yongle Qiao; open daily; entrance fee) is a 110-metre (360ft) diameter observation wheel on Yongle Bridge which, on a clear day, can provide views of up to 40km (25 miles).

ABOVE RIGHT & BELOW: Chuandixia.

RURAL SIGHTS AROUND BEIJING

A beautifully preserved village in the hills of rural Mentougou District, some 90km (55 miles) west of Beijing, **Chuandixia** (爨地下) **⑬** is a growing tourist destination. Much of the tiny town's architecture dates to the late Ming and early Qing dynasties.

Once a prosperous farming enclave, Chuandixia had been all but abandoned by the mid-1990s. Its young people had all gone to the city to find work, and the only residents were a handful of elderly folk who depended on remittances from their children and on the sales of the honey from the bees they raised in the courtyards of abandoned homes.

However, its beauty was "discovered", and it has quickly become a booming tourist site, with dozens of rooms in which visitors can lodge and eat with local residents. Young people have moved back to manage the inns and restaurants. To avoid the crowds, try to visit on a weekday; bring your walking shoes, as the village is encircled by a trail with great views. There is an entrance fee payable when you first arrive.

Shidu Scenic Spot

Address: Fangshan District
Opening Hrs: daily 8am–6pm for certain sites
Entrance Fee: charge
Transport: trains from Beijing West Station (Beijing Xi Zhan) to Shidu, tourist bus 7 from Beijing South Station (Beijing Nan Zhan)

Some 100km (62 miles) southwest of urban Beijing (but still part of the Beijing municipality), **Shidu Scenic Spot** (Shidu Lüyou Fengjing Qu; 十渡旅游风景区) has a number of natural and man-made assets that draw large numbers of visitors from the capital. Most obvious are the karst mountains that confer Shidu the title of "Guilin of the north" and make it a popular spot with rock climbers. Thrill-seekers can hurl themselves towards the scenic stretch of the Juma River from two bungee-jumping spots. Alternatively, head away from the tourist facilities for hiking in the curiously shaped mountains. If one of the local rustic villages takes your fancy there are usually beds and home-cooked meals on offer for a very reasonable rate.

ABOVE: wall detail at Chuandixia.

SHOPPING

ABOVE: Miyun
reservoir, a weekend
retreat for Beijingers.
BELOW: street scene
in Chuandixia.

TIP

Bus 936 from Beijing's
long-distance Dongzhi-
men bus station goes to
Nine Valleys (60km/
37 miles from the city),
Yunmengshan (80km/
50 miles) and Purple
Cloud Mountain
(75km/47 miles).

Huairou and Miyun

Huairou (怀柔) ⑭ is perhaps best known as the location of the Mutianyu Great Wall *(see page 230).* This was the site to which the International Women's Conference was moved in 1995 after the Chinese government became anxious at the prospect of having Beijing overrun with outspoken feminists from around the world. A generous supply of scenic lakes and mountains has made the area something of a weekend getaway for Beijingers seeking some fresh air, and the locals are increasingly turning from farming to tourism. According to one source, some 2,500 local families now operate family inns and restaurants that host 2½ million tourists a year.

As such numbers indicate, this is not exactly a bucolic retreat, but it is an interesting place to see Chinese tourism in action. It is also still possible to get away from it all if you hike far enough into the Yunmeng Mountains, which are criss-crossed by trails. The **Nine Valleys** (Jiugu-kou; 九谷口) scenic area has rudimentary camping facilities and a gloriously unrestored section of the Great Wall at its entrance. Each valley has its own charm, and there are

entertainment options from the simple, such as fishing and swimming, to the more adventurous hot-air balloon rides. Further north is **Purple Cloud Mountain** (Ziyunshan; 紫云山), pleasantly cool in summer and dotted with dozens of jade-green pools. Hikers can ascend the peaks keeping an eye out for the rainbows that are said to colour the mountain a purple hue.

Miyun (密云) ⑮ is another rural area that has become popular in recent years. It is home to the Jinshanling and Simatai sections of the Great Wall *(see page 231),* as well as a large reservoir. Miyun contains several "folklore villages" that are supposed to show traditional rural life, and also the Nanshan Ski Village, open in winter. The beautiful hills and good hiking, particularly in areas closer to Beijing, attract droves of city dwellers at weekends.

Some 10km (6 miles) west of Miyun reservoir, **Yunmengshan** (云蒙山) has a free campsite which makes a good base for a range of mountain hikes. The highest peak can be reached in around five hours, passing several waterfalls and offering occasional sightings of wild deer in the forests.   ❑

BEST RESTAURANTS

Chengde

Shangke Tang 上客堂
West side of Puning Temple.
Tel: 0314-205-8888.
Open: 11am–8pm. **$$**
A hall built for Buddhist
monks visiting Chengde,
this impressive hotel and
restaurant serves a
variety of food including
a range of vegetarian
cuisine.

Xin Qianlong
新乾隆酒楼
Dijingyuan Building, Xinhua
Lu. Tel: 0314-207-2222.
Open: 11am–10pm. **$$$$**
Just 1km (⅔ mile) from
the Imperial Resort, this
luxury restaurant serves
many cuisines, including
local dishes such as wild
game.

Chuandixia

Chuandixia Farm Cooking
爨底下村农家饭
Zhaitang Village, Mentougou
District. Tel: 6981-6574.
Flexible opening hours. **$**
Located by farmhouses
that provide visitors
accommodation, this
restaurant serves basic
but satisfying country
fare.

Prices are for a typical
dinner for one (three
dishes with beer in
Chinese restaurants, or
a three-course meal
with a half-bottle of
house wine in Western-
style restaurants).

$ = under Rmb 50
$$ = Rmb 50–100
$$$ = Rmb 100–200
$$$$ = over Rmb 200

Huairou

Master Fish Restaurant
鱼师傅餐厅
Huaihuang Road, 3km
(2 miles) to Mutianyu Great
Wall. Tel: 6162-1024.
Open 11am–2.30 and by
appointment. **$$**
A family restaurant
specialising in local trout
– steamed, stewed and
even raw.

Xiaolumian 小庐面
130 Yingbeigou Cun.
Tel: 6162-6506.
www.xiaolumian.com.
Open: 11am–3pm. **$$**
A stone farmhouse
within a stone's throw
of the Mutianyu section
of the Great Wall. The
main dish is hand-
made noodles. Larger
parties can be
accommodated with
advanced booking.

Shidu

Many small restaurants
and guesthouses
operate in this area.
Try the delicious grilled
local trout.

**Shidu Heartfelt Country
Cuisine** 十渡真心农家院
Fangshan District.
Tel: 6134-9802.
Open 9am–7pm. **$**
Provides most of the
region's typical, and
hearty, farmhouse
dishes.

Tianjin

Goubuli 狗不理

RIGHT: steamed *jiaozi*
dumplings.

77 Shandong Lu.
Tel: 022-2730-2540.
Open: 9am–10pm. **$**
Tianjin's most famous
restaurant serves juicy
steamed dumplings
made to a centuries-old
recipe.

Huayun Bowuguan
华蕴博物馆
283 Hebei Lu. Tel: 022-
2339-8888. Open:
11.30am–10pm. **$$$**
An unusual "museum"
restaurant filled with
hundreds of antiques and
historical oddities. Local
cuisine at a range of
prices.

**Richmond International
Restaurant**
里士满西餐酒吧
231 Hebei Lu.
Tel: 022-2311-3397.
Open: 11am–5am. **$$**

A reliable option for
European food such
steak and chips. Serves
imported beers.

South Market Food Hall
南市食品街
Qinghe Dajie, Heping
District. Open: 8am–10pm.
$
Scores of stalls and
restaurants line this
indoor food market. Feast
on local specialities such
as steamed dumplings
and *mahua* (fried dough
twists).

Tianjinwei 1928
天津卫**1928**
1/F, Nuren Jie. Tel: 022-
2728-1928. Open: 11am–
2.30pm, 5–9pm. **$$**
Oozing local character,
traditional food and per-
formances including local
comedy "cross-talk".

INSIGHT GUIDES **TRAVEL TIPS**
BEIJING

LEFT: *weiqi* (go), an ancient board
game still popular across China.

TRANSPORT

ACCOMMODATION

ACTIVITIES

A – Z

LANGUAGE

T RANSPORT

GETTING THERE AND GETTING AROUND

By Air

All visitors need a Chinese visa before embarking on a flight. From London Heathrow flight time is around 10 hours (direct). Economy return fares are typically around £500. Cheaper fares are possible if you are prepared to change planes (Austrian Airlines via Vienna, Finnair via Helsinki and KLM via Amsterdam are often competitively priced). Direct China Air flights can also be well priced.

From North America, flights from the West Coast take around 13 hours, from the East Coast 18 to 20 hours. China Air is often the cheapest option.

Beijing Airport: Fully modernised and expanded for the Olympics, Beijing Capital Airport (Terminal 1: 6454-0100, Terminal 2: 6459-8333, Terminal 3: 6453-0030; en.bcia.com.cn) is about 30km (18 miles) northeast of the city centre.

Opened in 2008, the mammoth Terminal 3 now handles most international and domestic flights. Terminal 2 handles a smaller amount of traffic, while Terminal 1 is used for domestic flights. A free bus links terminals 1 and 2; the journey takes about 10 minutes. Hotels usually have flight-booking services, and most major airlines have offices in Bei-

jing. You must check in at least 30 minutes before departure for domestic flights, although delays are common on many domestic routes, and at least an hour before departure for an international flight.

Transport to/from the Airport

The journey between the airport and the city centre takes about 30 to 40 minutes by **taxi**, but allow an hour or more at busy times. Depending on the destination and category of taxi, the fare will be between Rmb 80 and 120. Beware of drivers who approach you before you reach the taxi rank; ensure the driver uses a meter, or make sure you agree on

AIRLINE OFFICES

Air China, 15 Chang'an Xidajie, Xicheng. Tel: 400-810-0999. www.airchina.com.cn.
Air France, Rm 1609, Kuntai International Mansion, 12A Chaoyangmenwai Dajie, Chaoyang. Tel: 400-880-8808. www.airfrance.com.cn.
British Airways, Rm 2112, Kuntai International Mansion, Chaoyangmenwai Dajie, Chaoyang. Tel: 6459-0071. www.britishairways.com.
China Southern Airlines,

Building A, AVIC Building, 2 Dongsanhuan Nanlu, Chaoyang. Tel: 95539. www.cs-air.com.
Dragonair, 28/F, East Tower, LG Twins Tower, 12B Jianguomenwai Dajie, Chaoyang. Tel: 400-888-6628. www.dragonair.com.
Lufthansa, Rm S101, Lufthansa Centre, 50 Liangmaqiao Lu. Tel: 6468-8838. www.lufthansa.com.cn.
Northwest Airlines, Rm 501, China World Trade Centre, 1 Jianguomenwai Dajie. Tel: 400-814-0081. www.nwa.com/cn.

Qantas, B7-8, 10/F, West Tower, LG Twins Tower, 12B Jianguomenwai Dajie, Chaoyang. Tel: 400-888-0089. www.qantas.com. au/travel/airlines/home/cn/en.
Singapore Airlines, 8/F, China World Tower 2, 1 Jianguomenwai Dajie. Tel: 6505-2233. www.singaporeair.com.
United Airlines, Unit C/D1, 15/F, Tower A, Gateway Building, 18 Xiaguanli, Dongsanhuan Beilu, Chaoyang. Tel: 800-810-8282; 8468-6666. www.cn.united.com.

a price before setting off. The Airport Expressway has an additional Rmb 10 toll fare, for which a receipt is provided. If your hotel is near the airport, drivers may be unwilling to take you unless you pay extra – this is illegal, but agreeing to pay will save you much arguing and changing of taxis. Most of the city's major hotels offer **limousine** pick-ups and free bus transfers.

Air China offers **coach services** from the airport to several stops in the city centre. Destinations include the main Air China booking office on Chang'an Xidajie, close to Xidan; the Lufthansa Centre; and the Beijing International Hotel, north of Beijing Railway station. Public **buses** are regular but can be rather crowded. Taxis are available at all stops.

The **airport express light rail** links the airport to Dongzhimen subway station, which gives access to Line 2 and Line 13. The journey takes about 20 minutes, making it quicker than a taxi at rush hours. The service currently runs from Terminal 3 from 6.21am to 10.51pm and from Terminal 2 from 6.35am to 11.10pm.

By Rail

An exciting way to travel between Beijing and Europe, at least for those with plenty of time, is to take the Trans-Siberian railway. Trains leave from Beijing Railway Station (Beijing Zhan) for a five-day (via Mongolia) or six-day (via northeast China) journey to Moscow. The Beijing International Hotel, a short distance north of the station, has an international ticket-booking office. Allow at least a week to obtain Russian and, if necessary, Mongolian visas in Beijing. Bring plenty of passport photos; otherwise there is a photo booth inside the main entrance to the Friendship Store on Jianguomenwai, or at virtually any photo developing shop. Monkey Business (tel: 6591-6519; www.monkeyshrine.com) has been

arranging Trans-Siberian train trips for many years.

There are also rail routes from Beijing to Moscow via Xinjiang and Central Asia (be aware that visas can take a great deal of time to arrange for the Central Asian republics), and two trains weekly from Vietnam (Hanoi) to Beijing (again, get your visa in Beijing – or in Nanning, southern China).

For travelling by rail to other major cities, an English-language Chinese rail timetable is available at www.chinatt.org, with a comprehensive national timetable available for a small fee.

By Sea

Several ferry services connect China with Japan and South Korea. Boats from South Korea leave the port of Incheon near Seoul for Shanghai, Weihai, Tianjin, Qingdao, Dalian, Dandong and Yantai. The schedules for these trips can be found on www.seoulsearching.com/transportation/boat. Ferries also ply the waters between Japan and China, connecting Osaka, Kobe and Shimonoseki with such cities as Shanghai, Qingdao and Tianjin. The schedules for these can be found at www.seejapan.co.uk/plan/transportation/inter_ferrie.html.

GETTING AROUND

Orientation

Beijing has five main ring roads (the Second, Third, Fourth, Fifth and Sixth; there has never been an authoritative explanation for the lack of a First Ring Road). Most of the other main roads run north–south or east–west, making it relatively easy to navigate through the city. Main streets are commonly divided in terms of *bei* (north), *nan* (south), *xi* (west) and *dong* (east); and in terms of *nei* (inside) and *wai* (outside the Second Ring Road). On the other hand, many housing estates are

full of indistinguishable (unless you can read Chinese) high-rise buildings, making it easy to get lost, especially at night. The words (or suffixes) *jie*, *dajie*, *lu* and *men*, which you'll find on all maps, mean street, avenue, road and gate respectively.

City Maps: see page 283.

Public Transport

Subway

Beijing's subway system, which first opened in 1971, is currently undergoing a rapid expansion. It is fast and very cheap, but can be extremely crowded during rush hours and particularly at interchange stations. Currently, all journeys cost Rmb 2 and there are trains every few minutes from 5am until 11pm. It is easy to find your way around, as signs and announcements are bilingual.

Buy your ticket from the ticket office window or automatic ticket machines. The machines require you to use a touch screen to select your point of departure, which can be confusing, but the flat rate of Rmb 2 means that selecting any station produces the same result. For convenience, carry coins or Rmb 10 notes for the ticket machines. Guards are often on hand to provide change.

An IC transport smartcard, *yikatong*, can be bought for Rmb 20 and charged with a value of up to Rmb 1,000 for journeys on the subway, light rail and many bus lines. More convenient for short-stay visitors, three-, seven- and 15-day passes require a charge of Rmb 10, 20 and 40 respectively. IC cards can be bought and charged at subway counters and ticket machines and some banks.

Line 1 runs east–west underneath Chang'an Avenue through the heart of the city and out to the eastern and western suburbs. Line 2 is a circuit running parallel to the Second Ring Road, more or less following the demolished city wall around the north of the city. Line 4 is convenient for the northwest attractions – the Summer Palaces, Beijing University and Zhongguancun, Beijing Zoo and, in the south, Beijing South Railway station. Line 5 is a new north-south route, line 8 links the Olympic sites to the city, and line 13 forms a large loop extending north from line 2. *There is a map of the subway system at the back of the book.*

By 2015, authorities promise 20 lines with 420 stations and a total distance of 560km (350 miles), which will make it one of the largest networks in the world, and putting every sight within the Fourth Ring Road no more than 1km (⅔ mile) from a station.

Buses

The network of red, yellow and blue buses is comprehensive and operates from 5am to 11pm. Most rides cost around Rmb 1. Journeys are generally slow and crowded and the gaps between stops are sometimes long. Buses are extremely crowded during the rush hours, and you will need to use your elbows, pushing and shoving like the locals do, just to get on board. Remember to secure money and other valuables before you board.

Conductors usually sit at tall metal desks close to the doors. Give the conductor a few *jiao* bills and rely on her help or on that of your fellow passengers, to whom you can perhaps show your destination on a map or name card. You will find people who just struggled violently to get on the bus in front of you will now be only too happy to help if you need assistance. The English-language website www.bjbus.com can help make things easier.

Minibuses

Minibuses ply some of the same routes as the buses but offer a faster, more comfortable service at several times the bus fare, though they are still cheap by Western standards (Rmb 1 to 10, depending on distance). They generally seat 16 people. Tourists

use the services that run between the Summer Palace and the zoo, between the zoo and Qianmen gate, from the zoo to the main railway station, from Qianmen to the station, and from the Summer Palace to Xiangshan Park (and of course return the same way). Minibuses have official stops but, if they have space, will usually stop wherever they are flagged down.

Boats

A boat service operates from two points in Western Beijing to the New Summer Palace, along the Long River. Departures are hourly through the summer months, and journey time is one hour.

Private Transport

Taxis

Beijing's taxi drivers are gruff, overworked and underpaid, but pride themselves on taking every passenger to exactly where they want to go. The sheer number of cabs on the roads and the comparatively low cost of fares make taxi journeys an affordable luxury. The flagfall is Rmb 10 for the first 3km (2 miles) with an additional Rmb 2 for each additional kilometre. All taxis are metered, and drivers are generally reliable at using them. Sometimes a driver may try to quote a flat rate to your destination. Do not accept this if you are just taking a simple one-way journey, as it will never be cheaper than the meter charge.

Drivers occasionally refuse to take passengers, foreign and local, to destinations they consider inconvenient. However, they can be fined for such refusals and simply showing them the number of the Taxi Complaint Hotline – 6835-1150 – is usually enough to convince them that they had better take you where you want to go.

Most taxi drivers speak little or no English, and carrying Chinese name cards for hotels, restaurants, shops or other destinations can be useful for showing where you want

to go. It's always advisable to take along a telephone number of a contact at your destination. If there is a problem the driver can give them a call for directions. Always carry enough change, since taxi drivers are often unable, or unwilling, to change a Rmb 100 note.

Taxis can also be hired for longer trips, such as whole-day tours or visits to the Great Wall or Ming Tombs. You will need to agree the total fare and itinerary in advance. Plan to spend Rmb 400–500 for a full day, depending on distance. Do not pay the full amount in advance.

Beijing Dispatch Service, 1 Binhe Lu. Tel: 6837-3399.
Dial-a-Cab, hotline tel: 96103.
For daily hire:
Beijing Taxi Corporation, 26 Fuchengmenwai Dajie.
Tel: 6852-4088 (24 hours).

Tourist Buses

If travelling in a group, you will rarely need taxis, public transport or bicycles. Most tour groups travel in comfortable, air-conditioned buses. There are bus companies in several places, for instance outside Beijing Railway Station and opposite the Chongwenmen Hotel, which organise regular excursions to the most important sights.

CAR RENTAL

Foreigners are allowed to drive in China, but a local licence is required, which makes this a difficult option for short-term visitors. More practical is to hire a car with a driver. This can be done through most travel agencies and hotels, or from taxi companies. Alternatively, try negotiating a whole-day or half-day price direct with a driver. If you ask at the front desk of your hotel, most will arrange a car for the day for you, giving the driver clear instructions where you want to go and what time you want to return. Do not pay in advance.

From mid-April to mid-October, there are several special tourist bus routes suitable for independent travellers. These are more comfortable and faster than public buses, and cheaper than hiring a taxi. On most routes, several buses leave each morning, starting from about 7am, and return the same afternoon; the ticket allows passengers to get off and on at any designated stop, giving you some flexibility. Routes include Qianmen to Badaling, the Ming Tombs, the Eastern Qing Tombs, and Xuanwumen to Simatai. For a list of schedules and prices see www.bjbus.com and click on "touring Beijing".

Bicycles

The bicycle is still the vehicle most used by Beijingers, although the number of cyclists has declined, with private cars very much in the ascendant. Cycling was once the most enjoyable way to see Beijing (which is mostly pancake-flat), but as cars have spilled over into bicycle lanes and air pollution has worsened, the joys of cycling have diminished and its dangers increased. Nonetheless, if you have steady nerves, strong legs and a high tolerance for pushy, aggressive car drivers, cycling is a great way to get around and will give you a completely different view of life in the city. Perhaps the best option is to rent a bike in a neighbourhood that is relatively quiet – Sanlitun, around Ritan Park and the Houhai area are good bets – until you are more familiar with the rules of the road.

Bicycles must be parked in the special guarded lots (for which you normally have to pay 2 jiao to the attendant). You can have repairs done almost anywhere in the city, as there are repair people on every street corner and in every alleyway.

If you do hire a bicycle, check the brakes first, and make sure the lock is working. Many hotels and hostels have bicycles for hire, usually for around Rmb 20 per day, although prices are much

higher (up to Rmb 100) if you hire from an upmarket hotel.

If you want to experience Beijing at a cyclist's pace but don't feel up to cycling yourself, **pedicabs** (or trishaws) can be hired near many tourist sites.

On Foot

Beijing is too large and too spread out to be seen primarily on foot. This said, most of its major sites demand a lot of walking and some areas of the city do lend themselves to idle strolling. The best parts of the city for wandering about on foot are the back lakes area with its willow-lined paths and meandering *hutong*; the Qianmen shopping district, which is so crowded that it can truly be experienced only on foot; the Wangfujing shopping district, which is largely a pedestrian mall; the old Foreign Legation Quarter, and the Ritan Park embassy district.

Note when crossing the street: a green pedestrian light does not necessarily mean cars and bikes will stop – they are permitted to turn right on a red light signal. Take care at all times.

Domestic Travel in China

By Air

Beijing has flights to all other parts of China. Tourist offices and travel agencies, including many hotel travel desks, can give you the current flight schedule of the various state airlines. Accompanying growth in the aviation business have been improvements in service. But tight budgets, especially for the smaller airlines, and the rapid growth of the industry, have led to overused airports and frequent flight delays.

You can buy tickets from travel agencies or airline booking offices. Travel agencies may be better; although they charge more, they are more likely to have English-speaking staff. Try Beijing Baoshan Air Service, 901, Block B, Jia Hui International Centre, Chaoyang District. Tel: 400-888-

0589. Alternatively, try CITS near the Gloria Plaza Hotel, or China Youth Travel Service (CYTS), around the corner from the CITIC building to the east of the Friendship Store. Since some flights are fully booked, it is advisable to buy your tickets as far as possible in advance.

By Rail

Beijing has three main railway stations: Beijing Zhan (Beijing Station), Beijing Xi Zhan (Beijing West Station) and Beijing Nan Zhan (South Station). Beijing Station is centrally located and connected to the subway system. The west station is out in the southwestern suburbs and less easily accessible. The south station is connected to subway line 4 and is the departure point for the superfast bullet trains that reach Tianjin in just 30 minutes. A few trains to other parts of China run from the city's three smaller stations.

It is possible to buy rail tickets through a travel agency, but it's cheaper to use the foreigners' booking office inside the railway station itself. The many ticket agencies around town – look out for small shops marked with trains and planes on their signage – are a convenient option. If you want a sleeper berth, especially in summer, it is essential to buy your ticket as soon as they go on sale, usually 10 days in advance. Return tickets can be purchased for most routes, provided the return date is within 12 days of the purchase date.

Trains are generally comfortable. Services to Shanghai take 11–14 hours, with most people preferring the overnight services which depart around 7pm: choose between soft sleeper (*ruanwo*; four beds in one compartment) and hard sleeper (*yingwo*; six beds in an open compartment). Trains to Xi'an take 12–13 hours, and to Hong Kong around 26 hours. The **Beijing Railroad Bureau Ticketing Information Office** can be reached at tel: 9510-5105.

A CCOMMODATION

SOME THINGS TO CONSIDER BEFORE YOU BOOK THE ROOM

Choosing a Hotel

Beijing has experienced a boom in hotel construction over the past few years, with some spectacular new or refurbished five-star establishments as well as an increase in the number of lower-end hotels and youth hostels. All should accept foreigners, though some may lack the computer facilities to register foreign guests.

Many of the most palatial hotels, some with rotating rooftop restaurants or classical Chinese adornments, are now prominent landmarks on the city's skyline. Most are either joint ventures or wholly owned by a foreign hotel chain. They are like enclaves, with their own restaurants, shops and other facilities that cater for homesick expats and long-stay business travellers. Some foreign firms also have offices in these hotels. Facilities are, as you would expect, comprehensive, with swimming pools, fitness centres, bars and nightclubs. Most rooms feature plasma-screen televisions hooked up to satellite/cable channels, and broadband internet access. Transport to and from the airport is also often part of the package.

There are also a large number of very comfortable mid-range hotels, which can offer good value and good facilities, including business centres with internet facilities, currency exchange, shops and restaurants.

Even in the budget category, almost all hotels will have air-conditioning and televisions in every room. Most will also have en suite bathrooms, though in some of the cheapest you may have to use a communal shower.

A recent development has been the growth in smaller "boutique" hotels and old-style courtyard hotels. These are full of period features and offer a very different experience to standard hotels.

Hotel Areas

Many of Beijing's luxury hotels are in the business district of Chaoyang, with several along Jianguomenwnwai Dajie between the Second and Third ring roads. To the northeast, the area around the Lufthansa Centre at the city end of the Airport Expressway also has a cluster of top hotels. Another hotel zone, catering to tourists as well as business travellers, is in Dongcheng District, around Wangfujing and Chang'an – this is a lot closer in and within walking distance of the Forbidden City and Tiananmen Square. Other top hotels are scattered around the city, with several close to the Second and Third Ring Roads. Even the former can seem quite a long way out of town, but bear in mind

that subway Line 2 follows this Ring Road in its entirety, so access to the city centre is good.

Less expensive hotels are found all over the city, with a concentration in central tourist areas, particularly south of the Forbidden City (the Qianmen area). There is a growing number of budget options in and around Sanlitun, eastern Beijing's nightlife district. Traditional courtyard hotels such as the Lusongyuan can be found in the *hutong* in the Drum and Bell towers area and elsewhere.

Prices and Booking

There is quite a big difference in price between the handful of top five-star places and the many, perfectly comfortable, mid-to-upper-range hotels. Price categories are included in our listings *(see also Budgeting for Your Trip, page 272)*.

It's always advisable to book in advance during the peak tourist season (June–Oct). At other times, hotels may offer discounts or special packages. Be sure to ask for a discount no matter when you are booking. Most accept reservations from abroad via internet or fax. Websites such as www.beijing-hotels. net, www.sinohotelguide.com and www. tripadvisor.com offer rooms for less than official rates. If you are already in town, asking for a discount at the front desk often saves money.

WANGFUJING AND CHANG'AN AREAS

Luxury

Grand Hotel Beijing
贵宾楼饭店
35 Chang'an Dongdajie
Tel: 6513-7788
www.grandhotelbeijing.com
❶ p288, B1
This Hong Kong joint venture, attached to the Beijing Hotel, offers the height of luxury a stone's throw from Tiananmen Square. Its facilities include a rooftop terrace with views over the square. 217 rooms.

Grand Hyatt Beijing
北京东方君悦大酒店
1 Chang'an Dong Lu, Oriental Plaza
Tel: 8518-1234
www.beijing.grand.hyatt.com
❷ p288, B1
One of Beijing's top hotels, a favourite of businessmen and short-term tourists, that includes top-notch restaurants, excellent service, and houses a museum of ancient Chinese bronzes on its basement ground floor. Great location at the southern end of Wangfujing, within the Oriental Plaza complex. 695 rooms.

The Peninsula Beijing
王府半岛酒店
8 Jinyu Hutong
Tel: 8516-2888
www.beijing.peninsula.com
❸ p288, C1
Now run by the Peninsula Group of Hong Kong fame, the modern, functional construction (with Chinese imperial flourishes) conceals a truly luxurious interior, with a complete range of facilities. The lobby is full of Chinese antiques, while designer labels compete in the shopping arcade. Located in a lively street ideal for shopping and Tiananmen. Service is impeccable. 530 rooms.

Red Capital Residence
新红资客栈
9 Dongsi Liutiao
Tel: 8403-5308
www.redcapitalclub.com.cn
❹ p287, C3
This exclusive boutique-hotel is within a Qing-dynasty courtyard house northeast of Wangfujing (past the Dongsi Mosque). Its rooms are furnished with period antiques and each has a different theme – the Chairman's Suite is dedicated to Mao Zedong and the Concubine's Private Courtyard purports to be for anyone who has ever dreamed of being – or having – a concubine. 5 rooms.

Expensive

Beijing Hotel 北京饭店
33 Chang'an Dongdajie
Tel: 6513-7766
www.chinabeijinghotel.com.cn
❺ p288, B1
Opened in 1917, with a long list of famous guests, this is still considered one of the most prestigious hotels in the city. Period features give it a traditional air, unlike many newer competitors. Centrally located, on the southwest corner of Wangfujing shopping street, near Tiananmen

Square. 1,432 rooms.

Beijing International Hotel 北京国际饭店
9 Jianguomenwai Dajie
Tel: 6512-6688
www.bih.com.cn
❻ p289, C1
With a convenient location near Beijing Railway Station and the Henderson and Cofco Plaza shopping centres, this huge hotel is a well-known landmark. Good facilities, including booking offices for international flights and trains. 1,002 rooms.

Lee Garden Service Apartments
北京丽苑公寓
18 Jinyu Hutong, Wangfujing
Tel: 6525-8855
www.lgapartment.com
❼ p288, C1
Good option for long-term stays or for those who like to have their own kitchen and other comforts of home. Suites range in size from studio to three-room, all with kitchen and full bath. Offers usual luxury hotel facilities, plus childcare and a children's play area. Some rooms have balconies with a view of the Forbidden City. 199 rooms.

Novotel Peace Hotel
3 Jinyu Hutong, Wangfujing Dajie
Tel: 6512-8833
❽ p288, C1
In the same lively street as the Peninsula Palace Hotel, close to Tiananmen and the Forbidden City, this joint venture provides spacious rooms. 344 rooms.

Moderate

Holiday Inn Crowne Plaza
北京国际芝苑皇冠饭店
48 Wangfujing Dajie
Tel: 6513-3388
www.holiday-inn.com
❾ p286, B4
Located on central Beijing's busiest shopping street, close to the Forbidden City, the Crowne Plaza has its own gallery of modern Chinese art, and a salon for performances of traditional Chinese music. 720 rooms.

Novotel Xinqiao Hotel
北京新侨饭店
2 Dongjiaomin Xiang, Chongwenmen
Tel: 6513-3366
❿ p288, C2
A comfortable hotel in the southeast corner of the old Legation Quarter, close to Tiananmen Square and the main

PRICE CATEGORIES

Prices are per night for two people sharing a standard double room in high season, including taxes:

Luxury = over US$200
Expensive = $120–200
Moderate = $40–120
Budget = under $40

TRANSPORT

ACCOMMODATION

ACTIVITIES

A – Z

LANGUAGE

railway station. Good value. 700 rooms.

Budget

Hademen Hotel
北京哈德门饭店
A2 Chongwenmenwai Dajie
Tel: 6711-2244
⑪ p288, C2
Good location diagonally opposite the Novotel

Xinqiao Hotel, and convenient for the railway station and the Temple of Heaven. 196 rooms.

Haoyuan Hotel
好园宾馆
53 Shijia Hutong, Dongsinan Dajie, Dongcheng
Tel: 6512-5557
www.haoyuanhotel.com
⑫ p286, C4
Hidden away in a narrow

alley close to the Peninsula Palace Hotel, the Haoyuan's rooms surround two quiet courtyards. The buildings are a traditional combination of brick and red-lacquered wood. A small restaurant serves hearty traditional fare. Book well in advance. 18 rooms.

Saga Youth Hostel
北京实佳青年旅社
9 Shijia Hutong, Dongcheng
Tel: 6527-2773
⑬ p287, C4
Popular with budget travellers, this hostel offers double rooms and dorms, tour booking and bike rental. Discounts for Hostelling International members.

EAST OF THE SECOND RING ROAD (CHAOYANG)

Luxury

China World Hotel
中国大饭店
1 Jianguomenwai Dajie
Tel: 6505-2266
www.shangri-la.com
⑭ p289, E1
Top-class service and accommodation, with health club, swimming pool and several Western and Asian restaurants. Well located for business. 716 rooms.

Kerry Centre 嘉里中心
1 Guanghua Lu (opposite North Gate of China World)
Tel: 6561-8833
www.shangri-la.com
⑮ p289, E1
Aimed at business travellers and linked to a major commercial and shopping complex, this hotel offers a full range of facilities, from jacuzzis to live jazz performances, and from

movie channels to broadband internet access. 487 rooms.

St Regis Hotel
圣瑞吉饭店
21 Jianguomenwai Dajie
Tel: 6460-6688
www.stregis.com
⑯ p289, D1
Matching Chinese tradition with modern furniture, this luxurious hotel is considered by many to be the best in the city and has a prime Chaoyang location. The hotel's Press Club Bar is a favourite of the foreign business community. 273 rooms.

Expensive

Gloria Plaza Hotel
北京凯莱大酒店
2 Jianguomen Nandajie
Tel: 6515-8855
www.gphbeijing.com
⑰ p289, D1
Opposite the Ancient Observatory. The Sampan restaurant has great dim sum. 423 rooms.

Hotel G
A7 Gongti Xilu, Chaoyang
Tel: 6552-3600
www.hotel-g.com.cn
⑱ p287, D3
Following the trend for boutique hotels in the capital, Hotel G is an ultra-stylish Workers'

Stadium option that is making waves with its attention to detail and service. Includes a Japanese restaurant and popular bar/restaurant serving Beijing's most expensive burgers.

Jianguo Hotel 建国饭店
5 Jianguomenwai Dajie
Tel: 6500-2233
www.hoteljianguo.com
⑲ p289, E1
Convenient for the Friendship Store, Silk Market and most embassies, this is a favourite with long-term visitors. 460 rooms.

Jinglun Hotel
北京京伦饭店
3 Jianguomenwai Dajie
Tel: 6500-2266 ext 8143
www.jinglunhotel.com
⑳ p289, E1
Next to the Jianguo and known for its cuisine, the Jinglun is another businessperson's favourite. 640 rooms.

Opposite House 瑜舍
11 Sanlitun Lu, Chaoyang
Tel: 6417-6688
www.theoppositehouse.com
㉑ p287, E3
This impossibly fashionable Japanese-designed hotel is one of the most stylish spots in town. The lobby seems more like a work of art and the rooms are a minimalist's

dream. Two bars and three restaurants are on site.

Swissotel Beijing
北京港澳中心瑞士酒店
Hong Kong-Macau Centre, 2 Chaoyangmen Beidajie
Tel: 6553-2288
www.beijing.swissotel.com
㉒ p287, D3
Its semicircular, mirrored facade dominates one of Beijing's busy intersections. Popular with business travellers. The fourth floor is barrier-free for travellers with disabilities. 430 rooms.

Traders' Hotel
北京国贸饭店
1 Jianguomenwai Dajie
Tel: 6505-2277
www.shangri-la.com
㉓ p289, E1
Well located at the northern end of the China World Trade Centre business complex, with good service, food and accommodation, this is a cheaper option than the neigh-

PRICE CATEGORIES

Prices are per night for two people sharing a standard double room in high season, including taxes:
Luxury = over US$200
Expensive = $120–200
Moderate = $40–120
Budget = under $40

bouring China World Hotel. 570 rooms.

Moderate

Beijing New World Hotel 北京新世界酒店
Hujia Lou, Dongsanhuan Lu
Tel: 6597-8888
㉔ p287, E4
A 53-storey building on the Third Ring Road, the New World is almost a self-contained town, with a bakery, a medical

centre and a supermarket. Great views from the top floors. 446 rooms.

Budget

Beijing Gongti International Youth Hostel 北京工体青年旅社
Gate 9 Gongren Tiyuchang
Tel: 6551-5362
㉕ p287, E3
Tucked inside the Workers' Stadium, this hostel is conven-

iently located near Sanlitun. Standard hotel services as ticketing and laundry, as well as access to the gardens and lake of the Workers' Stadium.
Beijing Zhaolong Youth Hostel 北京兆龙青年旅社
2 Gongtibei Lu, Chaoyang
Tel: 6597-2299 ext 6111
㉖ p287, E3
Conveniently located with clean, air-conditioned rooms sleeping

2–6 people. Guests can use the health club and other facilities at the adjacent Zhaolong Hotel. 35 rooms.
Jianguomen Hotel 北京欣燕都旅馆连锁建国门店
12 Jianhua Road (south of Jianguomenwai Dajie)
Tel: 6568-5577
㉗ p289, D2
Cheap hotel close to the Friendship Store. 50 rooms.

THE NORTHEAST (AROUND THE THIRD RING ROAD)

Luxury

Kempinski Hotel 凯宾斯基饭店
Beijing Lufthansa Centre, 50 Liangmaqiao Lu
Tel: 6465-3388
www.kempinski-beijing.com
㉘ p287, E2
Attached to Youyi (Friendship) Shopping City, with full facilities, including the authentic Paulaner Brauhaus. 526 rooms.
Kunlun Hotel 昆仑饭店
2 Xinyuan Nanlu (opposite Lufthansa Centre)
Tel: 6590-3388
www.hotelkunlun.com
㉙ p287, E2
Well-established hotel

which hosts art auctions and houses a popular nightclub. 767 rooms.
Radisson SAS Royal Hotel 北京皇家大饭店
6a Beisanhuan Donglu
Tel: 6466-3388
www.radisson.com
㉚ p287, D1
Next to the China International Exhibition Centre, catering mainly to busines travellers. 362 rooms.

Expensive

Great Wall Sheraton 喜来登长城饭店
10 Dongsanhuan Beilu
Tel: 6590-5566

www.sheraton.com/beijing
㉛ p287, E2
This luxury US joint venture is handy for the airport and downtown areas. 850 rooms.
Hilton Hotel 希尔顿酒店
1 Dongfang Lu, Dongsanhuan Beilu
Tel: 6466-2288
www.beijing.hilton.com
㉜ p287, E1
Next to the airport expressway, the Hilton is a supremely comfortable place to stay. 340 rooms.

Moderate

Holiday Inn Lido 丽都假日饭店

Jiangtai Lu
Tel: 6437-6688
http://beijing-lido.holiday-inn.com
㉝ p287, E1
A haven for foreigners, the Lido has a deli and a bakery, supermarket and a Western pharmacy. Just 20 minutes from the airport. 430 rooms.

AROUND THE BELL AND DRUM TOWERS

Moderate

Lusongyuan Hotel 侣松园宾馆
22 Banchang Hutong, Dongcheng District
Tel: 6401-1116
㉞ p286, B3
This delightful courtyard hotel occupies a former Qing-dynasty residence. Rooms are very attractive with period furnishings, although mattresses are

hard. Good location south of the Bell and Drum towers. Dorms available. 50 rooms.

Budget

Beijing Bamboo Garden Hotel 北京竹园宾馆
24 Xiaoshiqiao Hutong, Jiugulou Dajie
Tel: 6403-2229
www.bbgh.com.cn
㉝ p286, A2

Simple, clean rooms open onto a classical Chinese garden, with a great location close to the Drum Tower. What it lacks in facilities is more than made up for in atmosphere. 40 rooms.
Youhao Guesthouse 友好宾馆
7 Houyuanensi, Jiaodaokou, Dongcheng District
Tel: 6403-1114
㉟ p286, B2

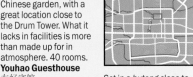

Set in a *hutong* close to the Drum Tower, part of a large compound where Chiang Kai-shek once stayed. 10 rooms.

Southern and Western Beijing

Expensive

Beijing New Century Hotel
北京新世纪即日航酒店
6 Shoudu Tiyuguan Nanlu
Tel: 6849-2001
www.c-b-w.com/hotel/newcentury/
37 p284, B2
This five-star hotel is located near Beijing Zoo. Some rooms have views of the Western Hills.

Moderate

Kelly's Courtyard
凯丽家
25 Xiaoyuan Hutong, Xidan Beidajie
Tel: 6611-8515
www.kellyscourtyard.com
38 p285, D4
Small courtyard hotel

with pleasantly decorated rooms and communal area.
Minzu Hotel
北京民族饭店
51 Fuxingmennei Dajie
Tel: 6601-4466
39 p291, E1
About 3km (2 miles) west of Tiananmen and popular with long-stay businesspeople. Features a Turkish restaurant.
Qianmen Chang Gong
前门长工饭店
11 Yingtao Xiejie, Qianmen
Tel: 6301-5088
40 p288, A2
A 200-year-old hostel centred around a large courtyard offering double rooms and dormitories.
Qianmen Jianguo Hotel 前门建国饭店

175 Yongan Lu
Tel: 6301-6688
41 p288, A3
Comfortable accommodation in the south of the city between the Temple of Heaven and Niu Jie Mosque. Stages nightly Beijing Opera performances.

Budget

Jinghua Hotel 京华饭店
Xiluoyuan Nanlu (past Yongdingmen), Fengtai
Tel: 6721-1671
www.jinghuahotel.com
42 p291, E4
Next to the Third Ring Road, the rooms at this backpacker favourite have en suite showers and air-conditioning.

Dorm beds available. 140 rooms.
Leo Hostel
52 Dazhilan Xijie
Tel: 6303-1595
www.leohostel.com
43 p288, A2
Friendly, bustling hostel on Dazhalan Street offering various tour bookings for travellers, including a popular trip to a "secret" section of the Great Wall.

Northwest Suburbs, Western Hills

Expensive

Fragrant Hills Mountain Yoga Retreat
山地瑜伽
6 Gonfuzhen, Fragrant Hills, Haidian
Tel: 8259-5335
www.mountainyoga.cn
An idyllic retreat for yoga enthusiasts or others who want a unique experience. All rooms are beautifully appointed. Meals are vegetarian, and Hatha yoga classes are offered each morning, including one session on the Great Wall.
Shangri-La Hotel
北京香格里拉饭店
29 Zizhuyuan Lu, Haidian
Tel: 6841-2211
www.shangri-la.com
44 p284, A2
This tasteful high-rise

hotel has meeting rooms, a ballroom, French and Asian cuisine, and a full range of other facilities. On the western edge of the city, the location is rather remote, but there is a shuttle-bus service to downtown areas. 650 rooms.

Moderate

Fragrant Hills Hotel
香山饭店
Inside Xiangshan Park
Tel: 6259-1166
A modern sanctuary from urban noise in the Western Hills. Facilities include a swimming pool. 275 rooms.
Friendship Hotel
友谊宾馆
81 Zhongguancun Dajie, Haidian
Tel: 6849-8888

www.bjfriendshiphotel.com
Part of a huge state-run hotel in pleasant grounds, home to many foreigners working for Chinese state employers. 300+ rooms.

Budget

Xijiao Hotel
西郊宾馆
18 Wangzhuang Lu
Tel: 6232-2288
www.xijiao.com.cn
In the heart of the university district, convenient for the Summer Palaces, Wudaokou's nightlife and the Zhongguancun high-tech area.
Dragon Spring Hotel
龙泉宾馆
21 Shuizha Beilu, Mentougou
Tel: 6984-3366, 6984-3862
For atmosphere and

facilities, the Dragon Spring beats most similarly priced hotels in Beijing. But it is a little remote – out towards the Western Hills, an hour from the city centre. 300+ rooms.
Peking University International Hostel
北京大学青年旅社
150 Chengfu Lu, Haidian
Tel: 6254-9667
An opportunity to mix with Beijing's bright young things and assorted travellers.

Airport

Sino-Swiss Hotel
北京国都大饭店
Xiaotianzhu, Shunyi
Tel: 6456-5588
Convenient access to the airport, plus free shuttle buses into the city are the hotel's biggest assets. A large swimming pool and several restaurants also add to the attraction. **$$$**

Chengde

Mongolian Yurt Holiday Village 蒙古包度假村
Tel: 0314-216-3094
www.cdmgb.com
In summer, the cheapest option is a yurt (circular felt tent) inside the Imperial Resort. You don't have to rough it too much, as the yurts have washrooms and televisions. 40 yurts. **$$**

Puning Hotel 普宁宾馆
Puning Lu, West Yard of Puning Temple
Tel: 0314-205-8888
This traditional-style hotel belongs to the Puning Temple (The Temple of Universal Peace – *see page 241*). It has multiple courtyards, long corridors with painted beam ceilings, and an excellent restaurant specialising in vegetarian food. The plumbing is not perfect and the pool not particularly clean, but the serenity of the location – replete with the early-morning chanting of lamas – more than makes up for such deficits. 100 rooms. **$**

Qianwanglou Hotel
绮望楼宾馆
Bifengmen Lu
Tel: 0314-202-4385

For atmosphere alone this is probably the best option in Chengde. The small, exquisitely refurbished hotel occupies a Qing-dynasty mansion set just inside the grounds of the Imperial Resort. 61 rooms. **$$**

Shanzhuang Hotel
承德山庄宾馆
127 Lizhengmen Lu
Tel: 0314-202-5588
Good location and comfortable rooms, particularly in the older main building. **$$**

Yunshan Hotel 云山饭店
2 Banbi Shanlu
Tel: 0314-215-6171
This is the main tourist hotel in Chengde, close to the station, with good facilities. 190 rooms. **$$**

Great Wall

Commune by the Great Wall
长城脚下的公社
Tel: 5869-6668
www.commune.com.cn
Spectacular villas – with equally spectacular prices – designed by Asia's top architects. Each is furnished by renowned designers and comes with a personal butler. There is a restaurant in the club house. 12 villas, each with multiple bedrooms. **$$$$**

Red Capital Ranch
新红资避暑山庄
28 Xiaguandi Village, Yanxi Township, Huairou
Tel: 8401-8886
www.redcapitalclub.com.cn
This is a Manchurian hunting lodge nestled in the shadow of the Great Wall. Each room is a luxuriously restored private villa filled with antiques.

Guests can hike on the Wall or avail themselves of the Ranch's facilities, which include a fine restaurant and a spa. 10 rooms, closed during winter. **$$$$**

Shanhaiguan and Beidaihe

Beidaihe Friendship Hotel 北戴河友谊宾馆
1 Yongjiao Road
Tel: 0335-404-8558
This beachfront, garden-style hotel was reportedly built at the behest of premier Zhou Enlai. It was renovated in 2002 and the beach is reserved for hotel guests. 250+ rooms. **$**

Beidaihe Guesthouse for Diplomatic Missions
外交人员北戴河宾馆
1 Baosan Lu, Beidaihe
Tel: 0335-404-1807
Just five minutes from the main beach, this hotel has friendly staff and a good seafood restaurant. All rooms have balconies with sea views. 160 rooms. **$$**

Jinshan Hotel
金山宾馆
4 Dongsan Lu, Beidaihe
Tel: 0335-404-1338
On a quiet beach, 4km (2½ miles) north of the town centre. Full facilities include a bowling alley. 600+ rooms. **$$**

Tianjin

Geneva Hotel
天津津利华大酒店
32 Youyi Lu, Hexi
Tel: 022-2835-2222
This relatively cheap hotel has four restaurants, a nightclub, bowling and a health club. 240 rooms. **$**

Tianjin Astor Hotel
天津利顺德大酒店
33 Tai'er Zhuang Lu
Tel: 022-2331-1112
Refurbished in 1997, the Astor opened in 1863. It retains much of its 19th-century elegance and atmosphere, facing the river, while providing full facilities. 220 rooms. **$$$**

Tianjin First Hotel
天津第一饭店
158 Jiefang Bei Lu
Tel: 022-2330-9988
Dating from 1922, this hotel has been tastefully refurbished and offers good value. Opposite the Hyatt. 102 rooms. **$$**

Tianjin Golden Crown Hotel 天津利顺德大酒店
18 Nanjing Lu
Tel: 022-2303-8866
www.gcthotel.com
Great views of downtown Tianjin from luxurious guest rooms and suites in this towering Tianjin landmark. **$$$**

Price Categories

Prices are per night for two people sharing a standard double room in high season, including taxes:
Luxury ($$$$)
= over US$200
Expensive ($$$)
= $120–200
Moderate ($$)
= $40–120
Budget ($) = under $40

ACTIVITIES

THE ARTS, NIGHTLIFE, FESTIVALS, SPORT AND CHILDREN

THE ARTS

Acrobatics

Acrobatics are a traditional form of street theatre in China, with special performances at Chinese New Year (Spring Festival) fairs. It is also an important element in Beijing Opera and in many Chinese martial arts. Most regular acrobatics shows in Beijing are performed by young students, usually including children. Venues include:

Chaoyang Theatre, 36 Dongsanhuan Beilu, Hujialou. Tel: 6507-2421. www.bjcyjc.com
Universe Theatre, 10 Dongzhimennei Dajie. Tel: 6416-9893.
Tianqiao Acrobatics Theatre, 95 Tianqiao Shichang Lu. Tel: 8693-6445.

Art Galleries

Small commercial galleries have flourished in Beijing since the early 1990s. These sell the work of many innovative artists, as well as masters of traditional watercolour, ceramics and sculpture techniques. Exhibitions change frequently. Several art districts have also risen organically in China's capital of culture. During their heyday during the run-up to

the Olympics, most were incredibly successful, although the economic crisis finally took its toll. Some say government control and commercialisation have also weakened the scene at spots such as the 798 Art District.

Several websites showcase fine art in Beijing and other Chinese cities: www.artscenechina.com, www.newchineseart.com and www.sinopop.org

Gallery Districts
798 Art District
(see pages 176, 180–1)
Beijing's best-known art district is a collection of abandoned factory spaces now housing galleries both large and small.
www.798art.org
Caochangdi
The largest refuge of artists escaping from high rents. Situated some 5km (3 miles) south of the 798 Art District.
www.caochangdi.com
Songzhuang Artists Village
A community of artists and gallery owners some distance outside central Beijing. Try the **Artist Village Gallery**. Tel: 6959-8343. www.artistvillagegallery.com

Galleries
Beijing World Art Museum,
9a Fuxing Lu. Tel: 6853-0257. www.worldartmuseum.cn
Open 8.30am–5.30pm.

National Art Museum of China, 1 Wusi Dajie, Dongcheng District. Tel: 6401-7076. www.namoc.org Open 9am–5pm.
Red Gate Gallery, inside Dongbianmen Watchtower. Tel: 6525-1005. www.redgategallery.com. Open 10am–5pm.
Xu Beihong Memorial Hall, 53 Xinjiekou Beidajie. Tel: 6225-2265. Open 9am–4.30pm, closed Monday.

Cinema

Despite the number of pirated DVDs on the streets, Beijing still has many cinemas. Most have morning, matinée and two

WHAT'S ON LISTINGS

Regular Beijing listing magazines *Time Out*, *The Beijinger* and *City Weekend* are available free at bookshops and cafés, mostly at the beginning of the month as copies tend to go quickly. All have useful guides to entertainment, the arts and events. www.timeout.com/cn/en/beijing, www.thebeijinger.com, www.cityweekend.com.cn

For information on the latest exhibitions at Beijing museums, see www.chineseartnet.com

evening showings. The latter usually start around 6.30pm and 8.30pm. Cinemas showing foreign films are especially popular, but more expensive. Hollywood is as well known in China as anywhere, and Hong Kong comedies and action films remain popular. Foreign films are often dubbed into Chinese. You can buy tickets at each venue, but it is often not possible to book in advance by telephone. If you are travelling with a group or on a package tour, you can ask your tour guide.

Cinemas showing both Chinese and foreign films include: **Beijing APM**, 138 Wangfujing, tel: 8511-4393. **Daguanlou** (see page 127), 36 Dashilan, Qianmen, tel: 6308-3312. **Star City**, Oriental Plaza, 1 Dongchang'an Jie, tel: 8518-6778. **Wanda Cinema**, Wanda Plaza, 93 Jianguo Lu, Chaoyang District, tel: 5960-3399.

Classical Music

Beijing has close to a dozen orchestras, several of which maintain regular concert seasons. The China Philharmonic Orchestra generally performs at the **Poly Theatre** (14 Dongzhimen Beidajie, tel: 6500-1188, www.polytheatre.com). The China National Orchestra's regular

venue is the **Beijing Concert Hall** (1 Beixinhua Jie, tel: 6605-5812). The **Forbidden City Concert Hall** in Zhongshan Park (tel: 6559-8285) is also a regular venue for classical music. **The National Centre for the Performing Arts** (see page 104) is now Beijing's premier music performance venue. **The Beijing International Music Festival** (www.bimf.org), held each October, is a major music festival that showcases orchestras and performers from around the world.

Dance

You can see dance and ballet at **the Beijing Exhibition Centre Theatre**, 135 Xizhimenwai Dajie. Tel: 6835-4455; and **Capital Theatre**, 22 Wangfujing Dajie. Tel: 6524-9847.

Beijing's best-known modern dance group is the Beijing Modern Dance Company. www.bmdc.com.cn

Theatre

Theatres generally attract larger audiences than Beijing Opera venues. Both local and foreign plays are performed. The main city theatres are:
Beijing Exhibition Centre Theatre, 135 Xizhimenwai Dajie.

BELOW: acrobatics performance.

WHERE TO SEE BEIJING OPERA

Young people in Beijing seldom appreciate the often complex plays and style of Beijing Opera, and to counter this, some of the traditional Beijing Opera theatres have adapted to modern trends and stage pop concerts, performances of *Xiangsheng* (crosstalk, or comic dialogues) or similar pieces. But most visitors will surely want to see a typical Chinese production, and some of the best-known opera venues are:
Chang'an Theatre, Jianguomennei Dajie (next to the International Hotel). Tel: 6510-1308.

Huguang Guildhall, 3 Hufang Qiao, Xuanwu. Tel: 6351-8284. **Laoshe Teahouse**, 3 Qianmen Xidajie. Tel: 6303-6830. **Liyuan Theatre**, Qianmen Hotel, 175 Yongan Lu. Tel: 8315-7297.
Mei Lanfang Theatre, 32 Ping'anli Xidajie. Xuanwu. Tel: 5833-1211.
Zhengyici Beijing Opera Theatre, 220 Xiheyan Dajie, Xuanwu. Tel: 8315-1649.

Short performances are also held at the **Palace of Prince Gong** (Gong Wang Fu), generally available for tour groups only.

Tel: 6835-4455. **Capital Theatre**, 22 Wangfujing Dajie. Tel: 6524-9847. **Central Experimental Drama Theatre**, 45 Mao'er Hutong, Di'anmenwai Dajie. Tel: 6403-1009. **China Children's Art Theatre**, 64 Dong'anmen Dajie, Dongcheng. Tel: 6251-1425. **Tianqiao Theatre**, 30 Beiwei Lu, Xuanwu District. Tel: 5166-1145. **21st-Century Theatre**, Sino-Japanese Youth Centre, 40 Liangmaqiao Lu. Tel: 6466-0032.

NIGHTLIFE

Where to Go

Many people will tell you that Beijing is not China. The quality and quantity of entertainment available supports that claim. Karaoke no longer dominates the capital's nightlife, especially for more affluent people. Youngsters dance the night away under the laser lights of huge discos. Businessmen frequent garish clubs where hostesses offer *san pei* – three accompaniments: drinking, dancing and sex.

Once you could only find bands, dancing, foreign beer and mixed drinks in the large hotels,

TRANSPORT · ACCOMMODATION · ACTIVITIES · A – Z · LANGUAGE

ABOVE: Workers' Stadium bars.

but for some years now, several areas popular with affluent locals or expats have whole streets full of bars.

Some bars close around 2am, though many stay open until 4 or 5am at weekends. In some, you can find live rock music or jazz; in others, DJs spin dance tunes. Discos break up the dancing and laser shows with performances by singers and cage dancers.

The main bar areas are Sanlitun/Chaoyang Park and the nearby Jianguomenwai/Workers' Stadium area; the back lakes/Nanluoguxiang area; and Weigongcun/Wudaokou in the Haidian university district. Though many bars in Sanlitun and Chaoyang Park are blandly uniform attempts to recreate European or North American style, some local entrepreneurs have opened bars specialising in punk rock, jazz, film, sports and other entertainment. All of the music venues listed stage regular live performances on Friday and Saturday; phone or check publications for other days.

For gay bars, see page 274.

Live Music

The English-language site www.chinamusicradar.com contains a wealth of music-related information and listings.

2 Kolegas, 21 Liangmaqiao Lu, Chaoyang District. Tel: 6436-8998. A popular bar with regular eclectic musical performances. Open 9pm–late.

Cloud Nine Bar, Shangri-La Hotel, 29 Zizhuyuan Lu, Haidian. Tel: 6841-2211, ext. 2723. Luxurious bar with extensive drink list and a regular schedule of nightclub-style live music. Open 8pm–2am.

Lush, 2/F, Huaqing Jiayuan, Chengfulu. Tel: 8286-3566. One of the epicentres of Wudaokou's nightlife. Student-friendly café by day and party house by night. Open 24 hours.

New Get Lucky, A1 Xingba Lu, Nuren Jie. Tel: 8448-3335. This institution of live local rock has local performances every night. Open 11am–2pm.

Yugong Yishan, 3 Zhangxizhong Lu, Dongcheng District. Tel: 6404-2711. One of the hottest spots for local live music in Beijing and one of the few venues successful in regularly attracting foreign talent.

Clubs and Discos

Alfa, 5 Xingfu Yicun, Chaoyang. Tel: 6413-0086. Popular club with a large outdoor patio and a reputation for wild partying, with evenings dedicated to drinks such as absinthe and Martini. Open 10am–late.

Babyface, 6 Gongti Xilu. Tel: 6551-9081. This club chain from Guangzhou feels like an expensive import. Hosts big-name DJ and musical acts from overseas.

The Den, Gongti Lu, next to City Hotel. Tel: 6592-6290. A fluid clientele, and an international cattle market around the crowded, sweaty dance floor. Open 24 hours.

The Loft, 4 Gongti Bei Lu, Chaoyang District. Tel: 6586-7877. A fashionable club and restaurant opened by a prominent Beijing artist couple, The Loft

TEAHOUSES

In addition to the ordinary teahouses, a few establishments entertain their guests, staging short performances of Beijing Opera, acrobatics, magic shows and other entertainment. A good example is the **Laoshe Teahouse**, 3/F, 3 Qianmen Xidajie. Tel: 6303-6830 www.laosheteahouse.com *(see page 126).*

serves good Sichuan food in sleek surroundings that feel more like New York or LA than Beijing. Open 10am–2pm.

Salsa Caribe, 4 Gongti Beilu. Tel: 6507-7821. This over-the-top dance hall is famed for Latin dancing (show up early for lessons). Open 7.30pm–late.

Tango, South Gate of Ditan Park. Tel: 6428-2288. This massive bar/club houses a stage for live performances, as well as numerous private rooms and smaller bars. Open 24 hours.

FESTIVALS

Apart from Spring Festival – New Year according to the Chinese lunar calendar – the other public holidays in modern China are observed according to the Western (Gregorian) calendar. National Day and International Workers' Day, the two most important public holidays, reflect the political changes since 1949 in China. Other important political celebrations that are not public holidays are 1 July, the day of the foundation of the Chinese Communist Party, and 1 August, the founding day of the People's Liberation Army. Several other traditional festivals have revived since the Cultural Revolution, though these are more evident in rural areas.

The origins of these traditional festivals go back a long way, some to the Shang dynasty (16th to 11th century BC). As in the

West, some of these ancient festivals lost their original meaning over time, changed in content or gained a religious meaning; others marked historical events or were reserved for the worship of ancestors or gods. The Spring Festival, the Qingming Festival (Day for Remembering the Dead) and the Moon Festival survive more or less intact. These form one half of the ancient six festivals: three "festivals of the living" (Spring Festival, Dragon Boat Festival and Moon Festival) and the three "festivals of the dead" (Qingming Festival, All Souls' Day and the Songhanyi Festival – for sending winter clothes to ancestors).

Traditional Western festivals such as Christmas and Valentine's Day are increasingly celebrated by young urbanites – but the celebrations have decidedly local characteristics. Christmas Eve, for instance, is a night for dining out with friends, sleeping over in a fancy hotel or going to a classical music concert. Such celebrations have become so widespread – and so profitable – that officials and culture critics have begun to call for a stronger and more commercial celebration of traditional Chinese holidays, which many fear are being outcelebrated and out-spent.

Spring Festival (Chinese New Year)

The most important traditional festival is the **Spring Festival** (Chunjie, or Chinese New Year), which falls between mid-January and mid-February. If you travel in China at this time, expect restricted and crowded public transport services, because many people return to their hometowns for this festival. Trains are often fully booked.

Celebrations are traditionally a family gathering, similar to Christmas in the West. On New Year's Eve, the entire family gathers for a special meal. In Beijing and the north, families make and eat

jiaozi (pasta parcels filled with minced meat and vegetables). At midnight, they welcome the New Year with a volley of firecrackers – more so since a 10-year ban on fireworks was lifted in 2006.

The first day is taken up with meals and visits to relatives. The second and third days are for friends and acquaintances. People visit each other, always taking food, drink or other gifts, and offering good wishes for the New Year. Red envelopes containing money *(hong bao)* are given to the younger generation by the older.

During the Spring Festival, many Beijing parks and temples hold fairs where you can still see stilt walkers, dragon dancers, wrestlers, jugglers, snake charmers, Yang Ge dancers and opera singers. Some of the best fairs are held in Ditan Park, the Summer Palace and Baiyunguan Temple. Longtan Park hosts a spectacular national folk arts competition.

Lantern Festival

The **Lantern Festival** signifies the official end of the New Year celebrations, and takes place on the 15th day of the first lunar month (a full moon). It is a regular

working day, and only the meal of *yuanxiao* (sticky rice balls, usually filled with sweet red bean or sesame paste) follows the old customs. In recent years, Beijing has again promoted Qing-style processions, including musicians, lion dancers, Yang Ge groups and banners with pictures of deities.

Festival of Light

The **Qingming Festival** (Festival of Light, usually 4 or 5 April) was originally a day to celebrate the renewal of life in springtime. Later it became a day to remember the dead. In the past, those who could afford it would make a pilgrimage to the graves of their ancestors, taking cooked chicken, pork, vegetables, fruit, incense and candles. They would burn paper money, often printed with the words "Bank of Hell", and sometimes paper clothes, furniture and houses to ensure their ancestors fared well in the spirit world. After the sacrifice, the cleaning of the graves would begin. Many people, especially in rural areas, have resumed the customs of sweeping graves and burning paper money. In Beijing, schoolchildren lay wreaths and

BELOW: explaining the complexities of Chinese tea.

TRANSPORT

ACCOMMODATION

ACTIVITIES

A – Z

LANGUAGE

SHOPPING

For time-honoured brands such as crafts, silk and writing equipment, head to Dazhalan and Liuliuchang to the south of Tiananmen Square, although the best all-in-one market for Chinese-style gifts is still Panjiayuan, in the southeast of the city. For larger clothes sizes try out Yashow, the Silk Market and Sanlitun Village. Xidan mall, in western Beijing, is good for gifts and clothes for teenagers, as is the area around Joy City Shopping Mall. For quirkier items wander the areas around Nanluoguxiang Hutong near Houhai lake.

See individual places chapters for more detailed shopping listings.

flowers in Tiananmen Square in memory of those who gave their lives for the revolution.

Moon Festival

The **Moon Festival** or Mid-Autumn Festival (Zhong qiu jie), celebrated according to the lunar calendar on the 15th day of the eighth month (a full moon, usually in September) also remains popular in Beijing.

On this day, people eat "moon cakes", filled with various combinations of meat, fruit, sugar, spices, seeds and nuts. The cakes are to remind people of the revolt against Mongol rule in the 14th century, when similar cakes were used to transport secret messages between Chinese leaders. According to ancient Chinese myth, the hare and toad live on the moon. Stories about the moon hare and Chang'e, the "woman in the moon", are still told. If the weather is good, people sit together outside on the day of the Moon Festival, chat, look at the full moon and eat delicious (and very filling) cakes.

SPORT

Chinese people are generally very keen on sport. Many sports halls and stadiums, some of them built to bolster Beijing's Olympic Games bids, host regular competitions and tournaments. Early each morning, the parks fill with people practising t'ai chi, qi gong, martial arts, badminton and table tennis. Chinese television broadcasts local and international sporting events; English Premier League football is hugely popular.

Facilities for Visitors

All large hotels have sports facilities including gymnasia, tennis courts and swimming pools, which are available to guests at no charge; many also allow non-guests to use these facilities for a fee. There are also a number of private gyms in Beijing, including the international chains **Clark Hatch** (tel: 6466-288) and **Bally Fitness** (Basement Level, Chang An Theatre, tel: 6518-1666), some of which offer daily or weekly rates for non-members. Many local gyms are located on the basement level of shopping malls.

A number of Olympic venues are open, or in the process of being opened to the public for sports activities. **The National Aquatics Centre** (www.water-cube.com) has several swimming pools and a water park. **The National Olympic Sports Centre** (www.bjnosc.com) has a wide range of facilities for sports, including tennis and basketball.

Yoga has become extremely popular, and Beijing now has a number of yoga centres, including the **Yoga Yard** (www.yogayard.com), which offers Hatha yoga classes in a courtyard.

The **China World Hotel** (tel: 6505-2266) has good indoor tennis courts open from 6am to 10pm. The **China World Shopping Centre** also has an ice-skating rink. In winter, the frozen **Kunming Lake** at the Summer Palace is Beijing's premier ice-skating venue.

Wealthy locals and expats dabble in horse-riding or golf at a growing number of centres in suburban Beijing. Try the **Equuleus Riding Club** (off Jingshun Lu, tel: 6438-4947) or the **Sheerwood Beijing International Equestrian Club** (off the old Airport Road, tel: 8433-2217). The **High Club** (tel: 6553-2228; www.highclub.cn) organises horse-riding day trips for a range of abilities in the Kangxi Grasslands 80km (50 miles) northwest of Beijing.

Among the golf course options are **Beijing International Golf Club** (50km/30 miles north of Beijing near Changping, tel: 6076-2288) and **Beijing Country Golf Club** (35km/22 miles northeast of Beijing in Shunyi County, tel: 6940-1111). Closer in is the **Beijing Willow Golf Club**, with views of the Summer Palace (Fourth Ring Road, Haidian District, tel: 8262-8899).

Spectator Sports

Football (soccer) has overtaken basketball as the most popular spectator sport in China. Naturally, the capital has one of the top professional football teams, Beijing Guo'an. Like many Chinese teams, Guo'an regularly attract crowds of more than 50,000. They have also bought several foreign players, though the overall level of skill remains far behind that of leading European and South American teams. It is nonetheless worth watching a game to sample the unique atmosphere. Unfortunately – or perhaps fortunately – most visitors will not understand the crude chants. Professional basketball has also taken off, aided by many ex-NBA players.

Tickets for Guo'an football matches, and for basketball games featuring the Beijing Ducks in the CBA league, can be bought from the ticket office on the north side of the Workers' Stadium (tel: 6592-1173).

Hiking and Cycling

The Beijing area offers plenty of opportunities for **hiking** and **cycling**. The Ming Tombs, Eastern Qing Tombs and Chengde are all set in picturesque hiking country, as are the Huairou and Miyun districts north of the city. Beijing has several active hiking clubs which arrange weekend hikes. Try **Beijing Hikers** (tel: 139-1002-5516; www.beijinghikers.com) or the **High Club** (tel: 6553-2228; www.highclub.cn).

Although Beijing does not yet have Western-style campsites, camping is possible so long as you stay far enough away from villages and fields. Equipment can be rented from the **Sanfo Outdoor Club** (tel: 6201-5550; www.sanfo.com.cn, in Chinese only).

Cycling is a good way to see parts of Beijing; rentals and tours can be arranged through **Cycle China** (tel: 6559-3462; www.cyclechina.com). It is also possible to cycle to sights around Beijing, though some of the distances make a day trip too demanding. A small fixed-gear bicycle scene exists along with a shop, Natooke (www.natooke.com). For cycling tours and other information about cycling in China, see www.BikeChina.com.

Walking the Wall

An unusual place to hike – and hopefully get away from the crowds – is on one of the less visited stretches of the Great Wall, such as Jinshanling or Huanghuacheng.

You can arrange your own hike along the Wall, but be warned that accommodation is rudimentary. Simatai has a modern, off-wall guesthouse and a tourist village, and there are several new boutique ranches near less visited areas of the Wall. **CNadventure** specialises in Great Wall hiking, with trips running almost daily in season (tel: 6567-4939;

www.cnadventure.com). Also try www.china-hiking.com/greatwall for more information.

CHILDREN

Beijing can be tough for kids – lots of long meals, long taxi rides and long walks through ancient sites full of staring crowds. And, as friendly as Beijingers are to children, the city itself is by no means child-friendly – grassy areas in parks are sometimes off limits, and playgrounds are uncommon.

Many expats have set up family in Beijing, however, and there is now even a magazine for them called *Beijing Kids* (www.beijing-kids.com), offering parents an impressive amount of information.

Outdoor Activities

Chaoyang Park, **Ritan Park** and, further south, **Taoranting Park** all have playgrounds (fee charged) and rides for children that are open in summer. Other good outdoor destinations are the **Beijing Zoo** (open daily 7.30am – 5pm) and **boating** (or skating) on one of Beijing's lakes (particularly pleasant in **Beihai Park** and **Longtan Park**). Year-round ice-skating can be found at **Le Cool**, in the basement of the China World Centre.

Indoor Activities

Younger children in need of a break can let off steam year-round at **Fundazzle**, a former Olympic-size indoor swimming pool that has been converted into a large play-land in which kids can climb through tunnels, slide down slides, or plunge into the former diving pool now full of plastic balls (just inside the south gate of the Workers' Stadium, tel: 6593-6208, open Mon – Fri 9am – 5.30pm, weekends 9am – 7pm; entrance fee). The **Blue Zoo Aquarium** is located just a few metres away; it has a moving platform that takes viewers through tunnels that bisect the fish tanks

(Workers' Stadium South Gate, tel: 6591-3397, open daily 8am – 8pm, entrance fee).

Those with a scientific bent may enjoy the **Science and Technology Museum** (5 Beichen Dong Lu, tel: 5904-1188, Tue – Sun 9am – 4.30pm) within the Olympic Green, or the **Sony Explora Science Centre** (tel: 6501-8800, open Mon – Fri 9.30am – 6pm, Sat – Sun 9am – 7.30pm) in Chaoyang Park.

Puppet shows can be seen at weekends at the **China Puppet Theatre** (1 Anhuaxili, tel: 6424-3698). For plays and musicals in Chinese, the China Children's Art Theatre (64 Dong'anmen Dajie, tel: 6513-4115) is a good option and even offers acting and dance classes.

The **China Culture Center** offers many classes and outings that are suitable for older children, including painting, calligraphy and martial arts; check their website at www.chinaculturecenter.org or call 6432-9341 to find out what's on.

Children who like crafts can buy items at **Shengtangxuan**, a shop that specialises in traditional handcrafted toys (inside Guozijian Hutong, tel: 8404-7179).

If all else fails, modern toys of all sorts can be found at the **Children's Department Store** (168 Wangfujing) or on the top floor of the Lufthansa Centre.

BELOW: the Blue Zoo Aquarium.

AN ALPHABETICAL SUMMARY OF PRACTICAL INFORMATION

A dmission Charges

Admission is charged at virtually every sight in Beijing – even public parks have a nominal entrance fee (usually Rmb 2 or 3). Most museums, temples and historic sites charge around Rmb 10, but some major sights charge more – Rmb 35 for the Temple of Heaven and Rmb 60 for the Forbidden City, for instance. Some places have different prices, depending upon how many areas or exhibitions are to be visited. Students and those over 55 are often entitled to discounts, but are usually required to have identification proving their status or age. Children under certain ages are allowed in free to some sites, but this is generally determined by height – which can be verified on the spot – rather than age.

B udgeting for Your Trip

Beijing is a city that can be seen on a range of budgets. Hotel prices vary considerably, even for places of a similar standard, so it is always wise to shop around. Price variations will depend on the season (autumn is likely to be the most expensive), the current occupancy and any ongoing promotional events. Hotels frequented by foreign businesspeople or major tour-group operators are likely to be much more expensive for individual tourists than similar hotels in less popular – but still convenient – locations. A perfectly acceptable hotel room can cost under US$50 or $60 (Rmb 340–410) in an area of the city less frequented by Westerners. As the hotel becomes more central, the price will rise, but there is a considerable range between US$60 and US$120 (Rmb 820). For true five-star service with top-notch fitness centres, plasma-screen TVs and the like, expect to pay in the range of US$200 (Rmb 1,360) or more per night, depending on the season.

Food costs vary even more widely: it is possible to eat a delicious and filling meal of noodles or steamed *baozi* for less than US$2 (Rmb 13.6). A typical dinner of three or four dishes with beer and rice for two can be had in the US$10–15 (Rmb 70–100) range at many local restaurants. On the other hand, meals in truly upmarket restaurants will cost almost

CLIMATE AND WHEN TO VISIT

The ideal time for travelling to Beijing is late spring (May to mid-June) and autumn (late August to mid-October). The week following the national holiday on 1 October, however, is not so good, as many Chinese are travelling at this time. The same applies to Chinese New Year, in January or February (date changes each year), probably the worst time to come to China.

Beijing has a continental climate, with four clearly defined seasons. Winter is cold and dry with little snow, and it is usually sunny. Sharp winds blow frequently from the northern steppes and desert regions to the west. Spring, which begins in April, is the shortest season: warm, dry and often windy. In early spring, sandstorms blow in from Central Asia. These cease by mid-May at the latest. The average temperature then climbs quickly.

Summer begins around mid-June and reaches its peak in July and August. Both temperature and rainfall are highest in these two months. It is often muggy; temperatures climb to over 30°C (86°F) and occasionally 35°C (95°F) or more. About 75 per-

cent of the annual rainfall occurs in June, July and August, when afternoon thunderstorms are common.

In autumn the sky is blue most of the time, and the air can be a bit cleaner (Beijing is one of the most polluted cities in the world in terms of air quality). It is usually warm during the day and pleasantly cool in the evening. Early September to late October is ideal, although Beijing can be crowded at this time.

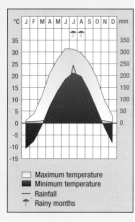

Maximum temperature
Minimum temperature
Rainfall
Rainy months

Tourist Sights

Many tourist sights stop selling tickets one hour before closing for the day. Closing time is generally one hour earlier from October to April. Where historic buildings are located within a public park, such as the Temple of Heaven and Beihai Park, different opening times operate for the park and the buildings.

Crime and Safety

Visitors don't need to take any special precautions in Beijing, though you should never leave money and valuables unguarded. Petty crime in China is low, but rising. Beware of pickpockets on buses, and always keep luggage locked. The most common way for visitors to lose money is through being overcharged by taxi and pedicab drivers. Be sure taxi drivers use the meter and always negotiate the cost of a pedicab journey before you get on board. A common scam in Beijing is to be approached by friendly locals and taken to a teahouse that leaves the visitor with an extortionate bill for drinks and snacks. Chinese police can be identified by their blue uniforms.

Business Hours

Business hours in Beijing seem to lengthen every year. State-owned restaurants and shops still close on the early side, around 8.30 or 9pm, but private establishments stay open much later. Chain grocery stores keep long hours, from early morning until around 11pm. Major shopping malls stay open until 10pm, with stores closing at different times – internet cafés, bars, ice-cream parlours and the like remain open while clothing shops shut down. All stores are open every day, including weekends, and many do not even close on national holidays such as Chinese New Year.

the same as they would at similar establishments in the West, with the bill for two people easily surpassing US$60 (Rmb 400). Bar prices are variable; a beer is usually between Rmb 10 and 25.

Public transport is the most economical way to get around, with subway rides costing about 30 cents (Rmb 2) and buses even less. However, since a taxi ride to most places in town is likely to be only US$3 or $4 (Rmb 20–27), the money saved may not always be worth the time and effort. The exception is during rush hours – around 8am and 6pm on weekdays but extending up to an hour either side – when traffic jams in central Beijing can bring the roads almost to a standstill.

Customs Regulations

Be aware of customs regulations when entering or leaving China, as some unexpected items may be on the restricted list.

A duplicate of the customs declaration which you received on arrival should be shown on departure. Expensive jewellery, equipment and the amount of foreign exchange should all be declared, and all imported items must be taken out again. Items that are imported and not taken out of the country again are subject to customs payments.

Many books, newspaper reports, magazines and videos that are legal in the West may be deemed illegal in China, especially political or pornographic works. Foreign visitors are

advised not to bring more than
one copy of the Bible into China.

Export restrictions apply to
antiques. Antiques that can be
exported carry a special customs
sticker, which normally has a Temple of Heaven symbol. It is advisable to keep receipts for items
bought, in case of spot checks.

D isabled Travellers

Most major hotels have some
form of ramp access, and good
lifts, but it is difficult to avoid
steps when visiting tourist sights.
Ordinary shops and restaurants
seldom provide ramp access.
Some streets have raised tracking
to aid people with impaired vision.

E lectricity

The standard for electricity in
Beijing is 220 volts AC. Hotels
usually have a 110-volt or 120-
volt outlet for shavers.

Embassies & Consulates

Foreign Embassies in Beijing

Australia, 21 Dongzhimenwai
Dajie, Chaoyang District. Tel:

5170-4111, fax: 5140 4204;
www.china.embassy.gov.au
Canada, 19 Dongzhimenwai
Dajie, Chaoyang District. Tel:
5139-4000, fax: 5139-4448;
www.beijing.gc.ca
Ireland, 3 Ritan Donglu,
Chaoyang District. Tel: 6532-
2691, fax: 6532-6857;
www.embassyofireland.cn
New Zealand, Dong'er Jie, Ritan
Lu. Tel: 6532-7000, fax: 6532-
4317; www.nzembassy.com/china
Singapore, 1 Xiushui Beijie,
Jianguomenwai. Tel: 6532-
1115, fax: 6532-9405;
www.mfa.gov.sg/beijing
UK, 11 Guanghua Lu. Tel: 5192-
4000, fax: 6532-1937; www.uk.cn
USA, 55 Anjialou Lu, Chaoyang
District. Tel: 8531-3000;
http://beijing.usembassy-china.org.cn/

Chinese Embassies in the UK and US

UK, Consular Section, 31
Portland Place, London, W1B
1QD. Tel: (020) 7631-1430 (visa
enquiries, Mon–Fri 2–4pm),
(020) 7636-5637, recorded information (premium rate) 0891-880
808; www.chinese-embassy.org.uk
US, Visa Office, 2201 Wisconsin
Avenue, Room 110, Washington
DC 20007. Tel: (202) 338-6688,
fax: (202) 588-9760;
www.china-embassy.org

Entry Requirements

A tourist visa is necessary for
entering China and must be
applied for in person or through
an agent; postal applications are

no longer accepted in the UK or
US. If you need to extend your visa
in China, contact the Public Security Bureau, Visa Section, Andingmen Dongdajie (near the Lama
Temple), tel: 8402-0101. The fine
for overstaying a visa is a punitive
Rmb 500 ($73) per day.

On entry, a health declaration,
entry card and customs declaration have to be completed. These
forms are given out on the plane
or at the airport.

G ay & Lesbian Travellers

Same-sex couples can share hotel
room, and there are generally no
problems for gay travellers in
China. Beijing has a gay scene,
growing in size and confidence,
though many services and gatherings are not widely advertised.
Time Out Beijing magazine has a
gay and lesbian page each month
covering issues and events, while
www.utopia-asia.com is one of the few
websites in English catering to
Beijing's gay and lesbian nightlife.

Destination (opposite the
Workers' Stadium West Gate, tel:
6551-5138) is currently the city's
only dedicated gay bar, with a clientele that is 90 percent male. It's a
popular spot for dancing and cruis-
ing and occasionally holds events
for gay awareness. **The Boat**
(8 Liangmaqiao South Road, tel:
6460-5512) is a converted passenger ferry sitting on the Liangma
River (the northern boundary of the
Sanlitun area) that acts as bar and
party spot for Beijing's gay and lesbian community. Several other
bars and clubs hold gay-friendly
nights and special events.

H ealth & Medical Care

No vaccinations are required for
China. It may be advisable to
strengthen the body's resistance
to hepatitis A infection by having a
gammaglobulin injection before
travelling. Malaria prevention,
recommended by the World
Health Organisation for some
areas of southern China, is not
necessary for Beijing.

FACT FILE

Area: Beijing covers an area of
16,807 sq km (10,443 sq miles).
The city is divided into 16 districts.
Geography: Beijing lies on the
northern edge of the North
Chinese plain at a similar lati-
tude to Madrid and New York:
39° 56' north; longitude 116°
20' east. The city centre is 44
metres (143ft) above sea level.

Population: More than 17 million,
including a migrant population
of about 5 million. The world's
ninth- and China's second-
largest city.
Weights and measures:
China uses a mixture of metric
and more traditional weights
and measures. Distances are
usually in kilometres.

Anyone planning to spend more than one year in China needs a health examination, which includes an Aids test. Travellers suffering from Aids, tuberculosis and other serious illnesses are not normally allowed to enter China.

Getting used to a different climate and foreign food can affect your health. It is worth taking medicines for colds, diarrhoea and constipation in your medical kit, as well as a stock of any regular medication you need. While traditional Chinese remedies are often effective, language difficulties may make it hard to buy the right ones.

Medical Services

Chinese hospitals are divided into those using Western medicine and those using traditional medicine, though some use both (see page 68). You will generally be given Western medicine in the foreigner sections of hospitals, and antibiotics are readily available. If you want traditional Chinese medical treatment, whether herbs or acupuncture, you must request it.

Most tourist hotels offer medical assistance. The Swissotel has its own pharmacy. In case of serious illness, foreigners can get treatment in special sections for foreigners at major local hospitals, but partly because of language problems, the service is not Western-style.

The best hospitals with foreigner sections are the **Sino-Japanese Friendship Hospital**, Heping Donglu, Chaoyang District. Tel: 6422-2952; and Peking Union Medical College Hospital, 1 Shuaifuyuan, Wangfujing, Dongcheng District. Tel: 6529-5274, 6529-5269. More expensive, but the best place for treatment of serious illness, is the private **Beijing United Family Health Centre**, B1/F, St Regis Hotel, 21 Jianguomenwai Dajie, Chaoyang District. Tel: 8532-1221, 6433-2345. All staff speak excellent English.

International SOS Clinic (24hr hospital emergency facilities with English spoken), tel: 6462-9112, 6462-9100.

Pharmacies

Pharmacies in China are of two kinds, those that sell predominantly Chinese medicine and those that sell predominantly Western medicine. All pharmacists will offer advice and suggest medicine, although they may not speak English. Basic cold medicines and antibiotics are inexpensive and available without prescription. Pharmacies keep varying hours, with many open until late at night. Branches of Watson's, such as in the Holiday Inn Lido or the World Trade Shopping Centre, stock a large range of Western medicines and toiletries, or try the Wangfujing Drug Store at 267 Wangfujing.

■ nternet

While hotel business centres generally charge Rmb 2 or 3 per **minute** for internet use, the ubiquitous internet cafés elsewhere charge between Rmb 3 and 5 per **hour**. Many are open from 7am until 2am; the best time to visit is during the day, when the teenagers are in school. All are plastered with no smoking signs, but these are routinely ignored – you can complain, but be prepared for a smoky environment. Some internet cafés may require your passport number, but generally will accept any nine-digit number you provide them without asking further questions.

Travellers with wireless-enabled laptops can connect for free at numerous cafés and restaurants around town, including the Bookworm, Lush and Pass by Bar. Official websites on Beijing include www.bjta.gov.cn, www.cbw.com and www.cits.net.

■ ost Property

Lost property that is presumed stolen should be reported to the Foreigners Section of the Beijing Public Security Bureau, tel: 6525-5486. Beijing does not have a central lost-property office, but the Beijing Tourist Hotline (tel: 6513-0828) may be able to provide some advice on where to seek help. Taxis are a common place to lose things, which is why it's always advisable to ask for a receipt – this will have the telephone number of the taxi company and your driver's identification number on it. For the airport lost and found, tel: 6459-8333.

Maps

Reasonably accurate maps in English are available from most hotels. Bookshops and kiosks mainly sell Chinese maps, which usually include bus and subway routes. Some maps have street and building names in both Chinese characters and English. The Insight Fleximap to Beijing is durable, detailed and easy to use, with a full street index, and its laminated finish means that getting it wet in a Beijing summer rainstorm is not a problem.

■ edia

Newspapers and Magazines

For foreign visitors, China Daily, which is published every day except Sunday, is a nationally distributed English-language newspaper. It includes listings of cultural events in the city, international news and good sports coverage. Global Times is similar, but in a tabloid format. Beijing Today is a weekly English-language paper from the publishers of Beijing Youth Daily, that also carries listings.

Several foreign daily papers can be bought in Beijing (a day late) from the big hotels and the Friendship Store and a small number of bookshops. For local listings, pick up the monthly what's-on magazines Time Out or The Beijinger (see page 266).

(see page 266)

Television and Radio

There are many foreign films shown on Chinese TV, usually dubbed into Chinese but sometimes left in the original language and subtitled. CCTV-9 is an English-language news and information channel. Many large hotels carry CNN and satellite broadcasts from Hong Kong-based Star TV. China Radio International offers an English-language service on 91.5 FM.

Money

The Chinese currency is called renminbi (Rmb; literally, "people's money"). The basic unit is the *yuan*, often called *kuai*. Rmb 1 is worth 10 *jiao*, also called *mao*. Banknotes come in Rmb 100, 50, 20, 10, 5 and 1 denominations; plus 5, 2 and 1 *jiao*. There are also Rmb 1, 5 *jiao* and 1 *jiao* coins.

The currency is pegged to the US dollar at a rate of Rmb 6.82 to $1. At the time of going to press in 2010, there were Rmb 11.1 to £1 sterling, and Rmb 0.88 to HK$1.

Changing Money

Foreign currency and Travellers' Cheques can be changed in most hotels, and at branches of the Bank of China. ATM machines that accept Western cards are located in most major shopping centres and some hotels. For credit card cash advances, there are auto-

matic cash machines scattered throughout the city. Banks will also issue cash advances, but charge a 4 percent commission.

When you change money, you get a receipt that allows you to change Rmb back to foreign currency within six months. Otherwise you are restricted to exchanging US$500 worth of foreign currency into Rmb per day at the Bank of China. Chinese locals are permitted to exchange more.

If you have problems changing money or getting a cash advance, try the main branch of the Bank of China at 1 Fuxingmennei Dajie at the Second Ring Road (tel: 6659-6688), branches inside the China World Trade Centre, or at 8 Yabao Lu (Asia-Pacific Building).

Credit Cards

Major credit cards can be used in most large hotels, shops and restaurants.

Tipping

Tips are not usually expected and are often refused, but waiters in large hotels and restaurants, as well as a few taxi drivers, do court tips. Before you tip, remember that the average wage is low – about Rmb 1,400 (US$200) a month.

P ostal Services

You will find postal facilities in most hotels. Letters and postcards to and from China take around six days. Parcels must be packed and sealed at the post office, to allow customs inspection. The main **International Post Office** (tel: 6512-8120) is on the Second Ring Road, just north of the Jianguomen intersection.

International express courier services, normally with free pick-up, are offered by: **DHL-Sinotrans**, 45 Xinyuan Jie, tel: 800-810-8000, www.cn.dhl.com; **Federal Express**, 101, Tower C, Lonsdale Centre, Wanhong Lu, Chaoyang District, tel: 400-889-1888, www.fedex.com/cn_english; **UPS**, Room 1818, China World Tower 1, tel: 800-820-8388, www.ups.com.

R eligious Services

Beijing has more than 30 Christian churches with regular services on weekdays and Sundays. Catholic mass (including Sunday mass in English) is said in **Nantang Cathedral**, 141 Qianmen Dajie (right outside Xuanwumen underground station), tel: 6602-6538, and **Beitang Cathedral**, 33 Xishiku Dajie, near Beihai Park, tel: 6617-5198. Protestant services are held at Chongwenmen Church, 2 Hougou Hutong, Chongwenmennei, tel: 6513-3549. Muslims can attend several mosques, including **Niu Jie Mosque** on Niu Jie in the south of the city, tel: 6353-2564. Buddhists have plenty of choice among the city's restored temples.

S tudent Travellers

Students from outside China do not get significant travel discounts as they do in some countries, but they can usually get discounted admission to major tourist sights if they have official identification.

T elephones

Calls (land-line) within Beijing are generally free. In most hotels you can telephone direct abroad, though this is expensive and in some you still need to ask the operator to call for you. In top hotels, you can use credit cards and international telephone cards. At around Rmb 8–10 per minute, China's IDD rates are higher than in most Western countries; remember that costs are halved after 6pm and at weekends.

Payphones which accept phone cards can be found along most city streets and in many hotels and shopping centres. These **"IC" cards** (Rmb 30, 50 or 100) can be bought at streetside newspaper kiosks or small shops, as well as from hotels.

Small shops also sell prepaid **internet phone cards** called **"IP"**

TELEPHONE CODES

The international code for China is **86**. The area code for Beijing is **10**, which does not need to be dialled for calls within the city, and is not included in the listed phone numbers in this guidebook.

The prefixes "400" and "800" denote free numbers; "800" numbers cannot be dialled from a mobile phone.

cards, which offer rates considerably lower than standard costs and can in theory be used from any phone – before dialling the number you wish to reach, you need to dial a local number printed on the card followed by a PIN number. US credit phone card codes from China can be accessed by dialling 1087901. Oddly, the cost of an IP card is always lower than its face value. Currently, a Rmb 100 card can be bought for about Rmb 40.

An "unlocked" **mobile phone** brought from outside China can be fitted with a Chinese SIM card in one of the many mobile phone shops dotted around Beijing. SIM cards go from about Rmb 50 upwards – the most expensive cards merely have a more convenient or "lucky" number. Top-up cards, *chongzhika*, can be bought at face value for Rmb 50 or 100.

Dial 115 for operator assistance with long-distance calls, and

BELOW: renminbi (Rmb) notes.

114 for directory enquiries.

Fax: Almost all hotels have fax services, although rates vary widely. Expect to pay about Rmb 10 per page to send or receive.

Time Zone

Beijing time, which applies across China, is GMT +8 hours (EST +13 hours). There is no daylight saving time, so from the end of March/ early April to late October, Beijing is 7 hours ahead of London and 12 hours ahead of New York.

Toilets

All public toilets *(cèsuŏ)* are now free, and their standards are much higher than in the past, particularly in public parks and tourist areas. The public toilets away from major sites and in the *hutong* are best avoided except in cases of dire need (for which it is wise to carry a packet of tissues, as they do not yet have paper). When nature calls, the best option is to go to a hotel or restaurant.

Tourist Information

Beijing's tourist information offices are not especially helpful, and mainly exist to sell tours.

The state-run **China International Travel Service** (CITS), 1 Dongdan, tel: 6522-2991, www.cits.com.cn, has offices in several hotels and at some tourist venues. Most hotels offer guided tours to sights inside and outside Beijing. Larger hotels organise their own tours; others arrange trips through CITS or smaller travel companies.

Beijing Hutong Tourist Agency, Dianmenxi Dajie near the North Gate of Beihai Park, tel: 6615-9097 (or ask your hotel), runs guided pedicab tours through the old *hutong* of what used to be one of Beijing's wealthiest areas, with stops at the Drum and Bell towers. From the same area, starting at the southwest corner of Qianhai Lake, you can take boat tours as

far as the Summer Palace.

Complaints or specific enquiries are handled by the Beijing Tourism Administration hotline on 6513-0828. If you want to book direct with a travel agency, several are listed below, divided into national travel agencies, which deal mainly with tours booked outside China or travel to other provinces, and agencies which deal specifically with the Beijing area.

Travel Agents

Beijing CITIC Guo'an International Travel Service, Guo'an Hotel, 1 Guangdongdian Beijie. Tel: 6501-0841.
Beijing Hutong Tourist Agency North Gate of Beihai Park, Houhai. Tel: 6615-9097.
China International Travel Service (CITS), Beijing Tourism Building, 28 Jianguomenwai Dajie. Tel: 6515-8562. www.cits.net
Panda Tours, Holiday Inn Crowne Plaza, 48 Wangfujing Dajie. Tel: 6513-3388, ext. 1212/13.
IATA, Jia 23 Fuxin Lu. Tel: 5826-3541; email: info@traveling.china.com; www.traveling.china.com

Besides the main travel agencies, Beijing has many small-scale, sometimes unlicensed tour operators. On some of the organised tours, as in many countries, the operators take tourists to shops and restaurants that pay the guides a commission. Others charge double for entrance tickets that you can buy yourself. But most tour companies are reasonably trustworthy, and usually cheap.

W omen Travellers

Women travelling alone generally experience few problems in China. Travelling by public transport or bicycle is usually safe, but there have been occasional reports of Beijing taxi drivers harassing foreign women. When taking taxis, especially at night, or visiting smaller bars and clubs, it may be better to join other tourists.

L ANGUAGE

UNDERSTANDING MANDARIN CHINESE

Mandarin and Dialects

People in Beijing speak *putong-hua*, or "common language", known in the West as Mandarin Chinese. Based on the northern dialect, one of the eight dialects of China, *putonghua* is taught throughout the country. It is promoted as standard Chinese across the country, though most people also, or only, speak a local dialect. In most Beijing hotels you will find someone who can speak at least some English, and in the top hotels good English is spoken. You can generally get by without Chinese in tourist areas; however, taxi drivers speak little English.

Putonghua or other Chinese dialects such as Cantonese is the first language of 93 percent of the population of China. There is considerable difference in the pronunciation of different dialects, though written forms are the same everywhere. Many ethnic minorities, such as Tibetans and Mongolians, have their own written and spoken language. In Beijing, a slightly different dialect is spoken.

Although the pronunciation in Beijing is very close to standard Chinese, it also has some distinctive characteristics, particularly the "er" sound added to the end of many syllables.

The Pinyin System

Since 1958, the pinyin system has been used to represent Chinese characters phonetically in the Latin alphabet. Pinyin has become internationally accepted, so that Peking is today written Beijing (pronounced Bay-jing), Canton is Guangzhou, and Mao Tse-tung is Mao Zedong.

At first this may seem confusing to Westerners, but it is a useful, practical, if imperfect system that is increasingly popular in China. You will find many shop names written in pinyin above the entrance, and the names at railway stations are written in pinyin, so it is helpful to learn the basic rules of the system.

Most modern dictionaries use pinyin. (Taiwan, however, usually uses the older Wade-Giles system.) This transcription may at first appear confusing if one doesn't see the words as they are pronounced. The city of Qingdao, for example, is pronounced *chingdow*.

It would definitely be useful, particularly for individual travellers, to familiarise yourself a little with the pronunciation of pinyin. Even when asking for a place or street name, you need to know how it is pronounced, otherwise you won't be understood. This guide uses the pinyin system throughout for Chinese names and expressions on occasion.

Written Chinese

Written Chinese uses thousands of characters, many of which are based on ancient pictograms, or picture-like symbols. Some characters used today go back more than 3,000 years. There are strict rules in the method of writing, as the stroke order affects the overall appearance of the characters. Because of the slowness of formal calligraphy, ordinary people develop their own simplified handwriting for everyday use. In the past the script was written from right to left and top to bottom, but today it is usually written from left to right.

Some 6,000 characters are in regular use; 3,000 characters are sufficient for reading a newspaper. Mainland China has reformed written Chinese several times since 1949, and simplified characters are now used. In Hong Kong and Taiwan the old characters remain standard.

Tones

It is sometimes said that Chinese is a monosyllabic language. At first sight, this seems to be true, since each character represents a single syllable that generally indicates a specific concept. However, in modern Chinese, most words are made up of two or three syllables, sometimes more. In the Western sense, spoken Chinese has only 420 single-syllable root words, but tones are used to differentiate these basic sounds. Tones make it difficult for foreigners to learn Chinese, since different tones give the same syllable a completely different meaning. For instance, *mai* with a falling fourth tone *(mài)* means to sell; if it is pronounced with a falling-rising third tone *(mǎi)*, it means to buy. If you pay attention to these tones, you can soon tell the difference, though correct pronunciation requires much practice. Taking another example, the four tones of the syllable ma: first tone, *mā* means mother; second tone, *má* means hemp; third tone, *mǎ* means horse; and fourth tone *mà* means to scold.

The first tone is pitched high and even, the second rising, the third falling and then rising, and the fourth falling. There is also a fifth, "neutral" tone. The individual tones are marked above the main vowel in the syllable.

Grammar

Chinese sentence structure is simple: subject, predicate, object. Many Chinese words serve as nouns, adjectives and verbs without altering their written or spoken forms. Verbs have single forms and do not change with the subject. There are no plural forms for verbs or nouns. All of these

have to be inferred from the context. The easiest way to form a question is to add the interrogative particle *ma* (neutral tone) to the end of a statement.

Names and Forms of Address

Chinese names usually consist of three, or sometimes two, syllables, each with its own meaning. Traditionally, the first syllable is the family name, the second or two others are personal names. For instance, in Deng Xiaoping, Deng is the family name, Xiaoping the personal name. The same is true for Fu Hao, where Fu is the family name, Hao the personal name.

Until the 1980s, the address *tongzhi* (comrade) was common, but today *xiansheng* and *furen*, the Chinese equivalents of Mr and Mrs, are more usual. A young woman, as well as female staff in hotels and restaurants, can be addressed as *xiaojie* (Miss). Address older men, especially those in important positions, as *xiansheng* or *shifu* (Master).

Language Guide

There are a standard set of diacritical marks to indicate which of the four tones is used:
mā = high and even tone
má = rising tone
mǎ = falling then rising tone
mà = falling tone

Pronunciation

The pronunciation of the consonants is similar to those in

English: b, p, d, t, g, k are all voiceless; p, t, k are aspirated, b, d, g are not aspirated. The i after the consonants ch, c, r, sh, s, z, zh is not pronounced: it indicates that the preceding sound is lengthened.

Pinyin/Phonetic/Sound
a/a/f**a**r
an /un/r**un**
ang/ung /l**ung**
ao/ou/l**ou**d
b/b/**b**ath
c/ts/ra**ts**
ch/ch/**ch**ange
d/d/**d**ay
e/er/d**irt**
e (after i, u, y)/a/tr**a**m
ei/ay/m**ay**
en/en/wh**en**
eng/eong/**ng** has a nasal sound
er/or/hon**our**
f/f/**f**ast
g/g/**g**o
h/ch/lo**ch**
i/ee/k**ee**n
j/j/**j**eep
k/k/ca**k**e
l/l/**l**ittle
m/m/**m**onth
n/n/**n**ame
o/o/b**o**nd
p/p/tra**pp**ed
q/ch/**ch**eer
r/r/**r**ight
s/s/me**ss**
sh/sh/**sh**ade
t/t/**t**on
u/oo/sh**oo**t
ü (after j, q, x, y)/as German ü (midway between "ee" and "oo"
w/w/**w**ater
x/sh/as in **sh**eep
y/y/**y**ogi
z/ds/re**ds**
zh/dj/**j**ungle

GREETINGS AND BASIC EXPRESSIONS

Hello	Nǐhǎo	你好
How are you?	Nǐhǎo ma?	你好吗？
Thank you.	Xièxie.	谢谢
Goodbye.	Zài jiàn	再见
My name is.	Wǒ jiào	我叫...
My last name is	Wǒ xìng	我姓...
What is your name?	Nín jiào shénme míngzi?	您叫什么名字？
What is your last name?	Nín guìxìng?	您贵姓？
I am very happy	Wǒ hěn gāoxìng	我很高兴...
All right	Hǎo	好

Not all right.	Bù hǎo.	不好
Can you speak English?	Nín huì shuō Yīngyǔ ma?	您会说英语吗?
Can you speak Chinese?	Nín huì shuō Hànyǔ ma?	您会说汉语吗?
I cannot speak Chinese	Wǒ bù huì Hànyǔ	我不会汉语
I do not understand.	Wǒ bù dǒng	我不懂
Do you understand?	Nín dǒng ma?	您懂吗?
Please speak a little slower	Qǐng nín shuō màn yìdiǎnr	请您说慢一点儿
What is this called?	Zhège jiào shénme?	这个叫什么?
How do you say...	...zěnme shuō?	...怎么说?
Please.	Qǐng.	请/谢谢
Never mind	Méi guānxì	没关系
Sorry	Duìbùqǐ	对不起

PRONOUNS

Who/who is it?	Shéi?	谁?
My/mine	Wǒ/wǒde	我/我的
You/yours (singular)	Nǐ/nǐde	你/你的
He/his	Tā/tāde	他/他的
She/hers	Tā/tāde	她/她的
We/ours	Wǒmen/wǒmende	我们/我们的
You/yours (plural)	Nǐmen/nǐmende	你们/你们的
They/theirs	Tāmen/tāmende	他们/他们的
You/yours (respectful)	Nín/nínde	您/您的

TRAVEL

Where is it?	zài nǎr?	...在哪儿?
Do you have it here?	Zhèr... yǒu ma?	这儿有... 吗?
No/it's not here/there aren't any	Méi yǒu	没有
Hotel	Fàndiàn/bīnguǎn	饭店/宾馆
Restaurant.	Fànguǎnr	饭馆
Bank	Yínháng.	银行
Post Office	Yóujú	邮局
Toilet	Cèsuǒ	厕所
Railway station	Huǒchēzhàn.	火车站
Bus station	Qìchē zhàn	汽车站
Embassy.	Dàshǐguǎn	大使馆
Consulate.	Lǐngshìguǎn	领事馆
Passport.	Hùzhào.	护照
Visa	Qiānzhèng	签证
Pharmacy	Yàodiàn.	药店
Hospital	Yīyuàn.	医院
Doctor.	Dàifu/yīshēng	大夫/医生
Translate.	Fānyì	翻译
Bar	Jiǔbā	酒吧
Do you have...?	Nín yǒu... ma?	您有... 吗?
I want/I would like.	Wǒ yào/wǒ xiǎng yào	我要/我想要
I want to buy.	Wǒ xiǎng mǎi...	我想买...
Where can I buy it?	Nǎr néng mǎi... ma?	哪儿能买吗?
This/that	Zhège/nèige	这个/那个
Green tea/black tea	lüchá/hóngchá	绿茶/红茶
Coffee.	Kāfēi	咖啡
Cigarette.	Xiāngyān.	香烟
Film (for camera)	Jiāojuǎnr.	胶卷儿
Ticket	Piào.	票
Postcard	Míngxìnpiàn	明信片
Letter	Yì fēng xìn	一封信
Air mail	Hángkōng xìn.	航空信
Postage stamp	Yóupiào.	邮票

SHOPPING

How much?	Duōshǎo?	多少
How much does it cost?	Zhège duōshǎo qián?	这个多少钱?
Too expensive, thank you	Tài guì le, xièxie	太贵了，谢谢
Very expensive	Hěn guì	很贵
A little (bit)	Yìdiǎnr	一点儿
Too much/too many	Tài duō le.	太多了
A lot	Duō	多
Few	Shǎo	少

MONEY MATTERS AND HOTELS

Money	Qián	钱
Chinese currency	Rénmínbì	人民币
One yuan/one kuai (10 jiao)	Yì yuán/yì kuài	一元/一块
One jiao/one mao (10 fen)	Yì jiǎo/yì mǎo	一角/一毛
One fen	Yì fēn	一分
Travellers' cheque	Lǚxíng zhīpiào	旅行支票
Credit card	Xìnyòngkǎ	信用卡
Foreign currency	Wàihuìquàn	外汇券
Where can I change money?	Zài nǎr kěyǐ huàn qián?	在哪儿可以换钱?
I want to change money	Wǒ xiǎng huàn qián.	我想换钱
What is the exchange rate?	Bǐjià shì duōshǎo?	比价是多少?
We want to stay for one (two/three) nights	Wǒmen xiǎng zhù yì (liǎng/sān) tiān.	我们想住一(两，三)天
How much is the room per day?	Fángjiān duōshǎo qián yì tiān?	房间多少钱一天?

TIME

When?	Shénme shíhou?	什么时候?
What time is it now?	Xiànzài jídiǎn zhōng?	现在几点钟?
How long?	Duōcháng shíjiān?	多长时间?
One/two/three o'clock	Yì diǎn/liǎng diǎn/sān diǎn zhōng	一点/两点/三点种
Early morning/morning	Zǎoshang/shàngwǔ	早上/上午
Midday/afternoon/evening	Zhōngwǔ/xiàwǔ/wǎnshang	中午/下午/晚上
Monday	Xīngqīyī	星期一
Tuesday	Xīngqīèr	星期二
Wednesday	Xīngqīsān	星期三
Thursday	Xīngqīsì	星期四
Friday	Xīngqīwǔ	星期五
Saturday	Xīngqīliù	星期六
Sunday	Xīngqītiān/xīngqīrì	星期天/星期日
Weekend	Zhōumò	周末
Yesterday/today/tomorrow	Zuótiān/jīntiān/míngtiān	昨天/今天/明天
This week/last week/	Zhègexīngqī/shàngxīngqī/	这个星期/上星期/
next week	xiàxīngqī	下星期

EATING OUT

Restaurant	Cāntīng/fànguǎn'r	餐厅/饭馆儿
Attendant/waiter	Fúwùyuán	服务员
Waitress	Xiǎojiě	小姐
Eat	Chī fàn	吃饭
Breakfast	Zǎofàn	早饭
Lunch	Wǔfàn	午饭
Dinner	Wǎnfàn	晚饭
Menu	Càidān	菜单
Chopsticks	Kuàizi	筷子
I want	Wǒ yào	我要
I do not want	Wǒ bú yào	我不要
I did not order this	Zhège wǒ méi diǎn	这个我没点
I am a vegetarian	Wǒ shì chī sù de rén	我是吃素的人
I do not eat any meat	Wǒ suǒyǒude ròu dōu bù chī	我所有的肉都不

FURTHER READING

Beijing

I Love Dollars by Zhu Wen. Columbia University Press, 2006. A satirical journey through Beijing's city streets and darkest corners. Cynical and humorous, this book tells the often soulless yet ultimately human story of economic expansion.
Old Peking: City of the Ruler of the World by Chris Elder (Editor). Oxford University Press, 1997. A collection of passages written by foreigners who visited Beijing at various times during its long history as China's imperial capital.
The City of Heavenly Tranquillity: Beijing in the History of China by Jasper Becker. Oxford University Press, 2008. One of the most respected foreign correspondents in China records a disappearing capital with passion and insight.

General

China Shakes the World: The Rise of a Hungry Nation by James Kynge. Phoenix, 2007. A highly readable account of the economy and its social effects by the *Financial Times*' former Beijing chief.

History

China Remembers by Zhang Lijia and Calum MacLeod. Oxford University Press, 1999. A fascinating and accessible look at New China through the eyes of 33 people; vivid memories of five decades.
Dragon Lady: The Life and Legend of the Last Empress of China by Sterling and Peggy Seagrave. Vintage Books, 1993. Blaming the fabrications of the "Hermit of Peking", Edmund

Backhouse, for the myth of the "evil" empress dowager Cixi, this book shows how Cixi was herself manipulated.
Hungry Ghosts by Jasper Becker. John Murray, 1996. Tells the grim truth about the death of some 30 million in the famines of the Great Leap Forward.
Red Star over China by Edgar R. Snow. Grove Press, 1973. A classic first-hand account of the years of guerrilla war leading up to the 1949 revolution, when Snow followed Mao and other Communist leaders.
The Last Eunuch of China: The Life of Sun Yaoting by Jia Yinghua. China Intercontinental Press, 2009. Biography of China's last living eunuch and his life within Beijing's imperial court.
The Penguin History of Modern China: The Fall and Rise of a Great Power by Jonathan Fenby. Allen Lane, 2008. Comprehensive, up-to-date and essential guide to all of China's major events over the last 150 years.
Wild Swans: Three Daughters of China by Jung Chang. Anchor Books, 1991. Adding plenty of historical detail, Wild Swans records 20th-century China through the lives of three generations of women, starting with the author's concubine grandmother.

Politics

China: Fragile Superpower by Susan L. Shirk. Oxford University Press, 2008. A counterpoint to all those who see China's global domination as inevitable. Examines China's ongoing economic, social and political problems.
Mandate of Heaven: The Legacy of Tiananmen Square and the Next Generation of China's Leaders by Orville Schell. Touchstone

Books, 1995. Schell explores the issues facing China's political leaders from the perspective of writers, artists, musicians, dissidents, underground publishers and venture capitalists. It's out of date – but still fascinating.
Mao, A Life by Philip Short. John Murray, 2004. A masterful, authoritative biography of China's iconic leader.

Culture

Rhapsody in Red: How Western Classical Music Became Chinese. Algora Publishing, 2004. In this engaging book, classical music is a lens for viewing four centuries of China's cultural exchange with the West.
Postcards from Tomorrow's Square by James Fallows. Vintage Books, 2008. A detailed look into a nation reinventing itself.

Other Insight Guides

Over 200 titles in the acclaimed *Insight Guides* series cover every continent. Those highlighting destinations in the region include guides to *China, Southern China, Hong Kong* and *Taiwan*.

The *Insight Step by Step Guides* series has an itinerary-based approach designed to assist the traveller with a limited amount of time to spend in a destination. Titles include *Beijing, Shanghai* and *Hong Kong*.

Insight Fleximaps combine clear, detailed cartography with essential travel information. The laminated finish makes the maps durable, weatherproof and easy to fold. Titles include *Beijing, Shanghai* and *Hong Kong*.

BEIJING STREET ATLAS

The key map shows the area of Beijing covered by the atlas
section. An index of street names and places of interest
shown on the maps can be found on the following pages.
For each entry there is a page number and grid reference

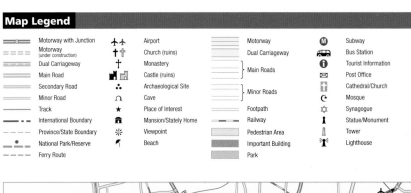

Map Legend

Motorway with Junction	✈ ✈ Airport	Motorway	Ⓜ Subway
Motorway (under construction)	✝ ✝ Church (ruins)	Dual Carriageway	🚌 Bus Station
Dual Carriageway	✝ Monastery		❶ Tourist Information
Main Road	🏰 🏯 Castle (ruins)	Main Roads	✉ Post Office
Secondary Road	⁂ Archaeological Site		✝ Cathedral/Church
Minor Road	∩ Cave	Minor Roads	☾ Mosque
Track	★ Place of Interest	Footpath	✡ Synagogue
International Boundary	🏠 Mansion/Stately Home	Railway	⌿ Statue/Monument
Province/State Boundary	※ Viewpoint	Pedestrian Area	∏ Tower
National Park/Reserve	⚐ Beach	Important Building	🗼 Lighthouse
Ferry Route		Park	

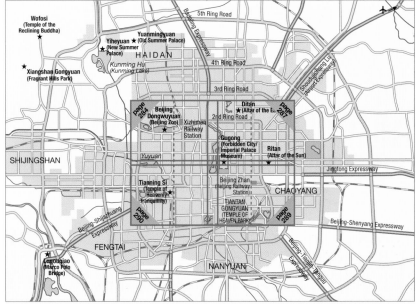

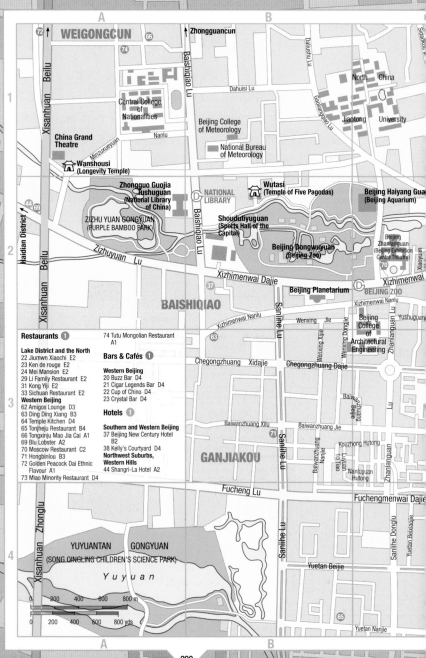

Xisanhuan Beilu

Baishiqiao Lu

Dahuisi Lu

Central College of Nationalities

Beijing College of Meteorology

Nanlu

North China

Jiaotong University

National Bureau of Meteorology

Gaoliangqiao Lu

China Grand Theatre

Minzukueyuan

Wanshousi (Longevity Temple)

Zhongguo Guojia Tushuguan (National Library of China)

NATIONAL LIBRARY

Wutasi (Temple of Five Pagodas)

Beijing Haiyang Gua (Beijing Aquarium)

44 69

Haidian District

Xisanhuan Beilu

ZIZHU YUAN GONGYUAN (PURPLE BAMBOO PARK)

Zizhuyuan Lu

Baishiqiao Lu

Shoudutiyuguan (Sports Hall of the Capital)

Beijing Dongwuyuan (Beijing Zoo)

Beijing Zhanlanguan (Beijing Exhibition Centre Theatre)

Xiaoyuan

Xizhimenwai Dajie

Xizhimenwai

37

Beijing Planetarium

BEIJING ZOO

BAISHIQIAO

Xizhimenwai Nanlu

Saniihe Lu

Xizhimenwai Nanlu

Wenxing Jie

Beijing College of Architectural Engineering

Zhanlanguan

Yushuguan

63

Wenxing Dongjie

Wenxing Xijie

Chegongzhuang Xidajie

Chegongzhuang Dajie

Baiwanzhuang Beijie

Baiwanzhuang Xilu

Baiwanzhuang Jie

71

GANJIAKOU

Kouzhong Hutong

Baiwanzhuang Nanjie

Liyuan 10 Tiao

Nanliuyuan Hutong

Zhanlanguan

Fucheng Lu

Fuchengmenwai Dajie

Saniihe Lu

Saniihe Donglu

Restaurants 1

Lake District and the North
22 Jiumwn Xiaochi E2
23 Ken de rouge E2
24 Mei Mansion E2
29 Li Family Restaurant E2
31 Kong Yiji E2
33 Sichuan Restaurant E2

Western Beijing
62 Amigos Lounge D3
63 Ding Ding Xiang B3
64 Temple Kitchen D4
65 Tonjheju Restaurant B4
66 Tongxinju Mao Jia Cai A1
69 Blu Lobster A2
70 Moscow Restaurant C2
71 Hongbinlou B3
72 Golden Peacock Dai Ethnic Flavour A1
73 Miao Minority Restaurant D4

74 Tutu Mongolian Restaurant A1

Bars & Cafés 1

Western Beijing
20 Buzz Bar D4
21 Cigar Legends Bar D4
22 Cup of Chino D4
23 Crystal Bar D4

Hotels 1

Southern and Western Beijing
37 Beijing New Century Hotel B2
38 Kelly's Courtyard D4
Northwest Suburbs, Western Hills
44 Shangri-La Hotel A2

Xisanhuan Zhonglu

YUYUANTAN GONGYUAN (SONG QINGLING CHILDREN'S SCIENCE PARK)

Yuyuan

Yuetan Beijie

65

Yuetan Beixiaojie

0 200 400 600 800 m
0 200 400 600 800 yds

Yuetan Nanjie

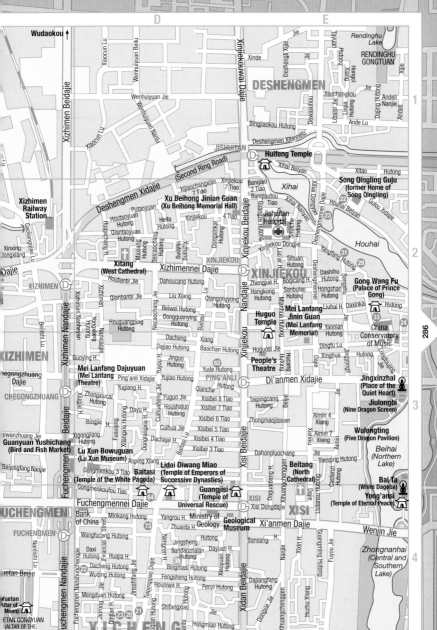

Wudaokou ↑

Xiaocun Lu

Wenhuiyuan Beilu

Xinde

Taiyuan

Deshengli Xijie

Rendinghu Lake

RENDINGHU GONGTUAN

Xizhimen Beidajie

Wenhuiyuan Jie

Xizhimen Railway Station

Xinjiekouwai Dajie

DESHENGMEN

Hongpi Xiang

Dajing Hutong

Andeli Nanjie

Andeli

Jiaochangkou

Ande Lu

Xinxing Yongxiang Lu

Caolangiao Lu

Houtaoyuan Hutong

Putaoyuan

Qiantaoyuan Hutong

Huapichang Lu

Heita Hutong

Beicaochang Hutong

Maxiang Hutong

Deshengmen Xidajie

(Second Ring Road)

Bingjiaokou Hutong

Deshengmen Xibinhelu

Deshengmen Xibinhelu

JISHUITAN

Huifeng Temple

Xihai Beiyan

Xihai

Bangiao 2 Tiao

Banqiaotou Tiao

Xihai Nanyan

Houhai Beiyan

Xitao

Hutong

Song Qingling Guju (former Home of Song Qingling)

Gulou Xidajie

Xijiaochangxiao 7 Tiao

Xinjiekou 7 Tiao

Xinjiekou 4 Tiao

Xu Beihong Jinian Guan (Xu Beihong Memorial Hall)

Jishuitan Hospital

Houhai

Yangfang Hutong

Dazhi Beidajie

Xizhimennei Dajie

XINJIEKOU

Dongmikai Hutong

Baitasi

Xinjiekou Beidajie

Sihuan Hutong

Deshengmennei

Songshu

Xitang (West Cathedral)

Houbanbi Jie

Qianbanbi Jie

Dahoucang Hutong

Liu Xiang

XINJIEKOU

Xinjiekou Nandajie

Zhengjue H.

Hankong Jie

Boqicang H.

Santiao

Dashihu Hutong

Hongshan H.

Gong Wang Fu (Palace of Prince Gong)

Hutong

Xizhimen Nanheyan

Yongkang Hutong

Houguangping Hutong

Beiwei Hutong

Dongguanying Hutong

Qiangonggyong Hutong

Baitasi

Santuao

Jinbao

Liuhai H.

Daxinkai

Mei Lanfang Jinin Guan (Mei Lanfang Memorial)

China Conservatory of Music

XIZHIMEN

Guoying H.

Dacheng

Xiang

Dajiao Hutong

Baochan Hutong

Huguo Temple

Huguosi Jie

Yannian Hutong

Dingfu Lu

Xinghua

Hutong

Mei Lanfang Dajuyuan (Mei Lanfang Theatre)

Ping'anli Xidajie

Jinguo Hutong

Yude Hutong

People's Theatre

Di'anmen Xidajie

CHEGONGZHUANG

Zhongxiucai Hutong

Yugiang H.

Dayu H.

Fuguo Jie

Qianche

Xisibei 8 Tiao

Taipingcang Hutong

Beijie

Jingxinzhai (Place of the Quiet Heart)

Jiulongbi (Nine Dragon Screen)

Bingjie

Fusuijing

Xianqia Hutong

Houshaluo Hutong

Xisibei 7 Tiao

Xisibei 6 Tiao

Zhongmaojiawan

Almin 4 Xiang

Almin 7 Xiang

Wulongting (Five Dragon Pavilion)

Xigongjiang Hutong

Cuihua Jie

Xisibei 5 Tiao

Xishiku

Guanyuan Yushichang (Bird and Fish Market)

Dachaye H.

Xisibei 4 Tiao

Beihai (Northern Lake)

Beiyingfang Nanjie

Lu Xun Bowuguan (Lu Xun Museum)

Anping Xiang

Baitasi

Xisibei 3 Tiao

Dahongluochang

Tianqing Hutong

Caolanzi Hutong

Bai Ta (White Dagoba)

Gongmenkou 3 Tiao

Lidai Diwang Miao (Temple of Emperors of Successive Dynasties)

Beitang (North Cathedral)

Yong'ansi (Temple of Eternal Peace)

Baitasi (Temple of the White Pagoda)

Guangjisi (Temple of Universal Rescue)

XISI

Daguanlou H.

Dajie

Xinhuangchengen

Gongmenkoutou Tiao

Fuchengmennei Dajie

XISI

Xisi Dongdajie

Bank of China

Minkang Hutong

Yangrou H.

Ministry of Geology

Geological Museum

Xi'anmen Dajie

Wenjin Jie

FUCHENGMEN

Wangfucang Hutong

Zhuanta H.

Hutong

Bansang

Guangning Hutong

Fuyou Lu

Zhongnanhai (Central and Southern Lake)

Nanlishi Lu

Daxi Hutong

Jingsheng Hutong

Dayuan H.

Xiaoyuan

Fuchengmen Nandajie

Dacheng Hutong

Huajia H.

Sandaozhalan Hutong

Xihuangchengen

Fuchengmen Nanshunchengjie

Wuding Hutong

Bingmasi Hutong

Jinshihfang Jie

Fengsheng Hutong

Houniwa H.

Fenzi Hutong

Dajiangfang Hutong

Mengduan Hutong

Taipingqiao Dajie

Shifangxiao

Xidan Beidajie

Jetan Beijie

Yuetan Altar of Moon)

ETAN GONGYUAN (ALTAR OF THE MOON PARK)

XICHENG

Jinrong Jie

Qimin H.

Yudan Hutong

Banbi Hutong

Hongmiao Hutong

Dongjie Jie

Huzhi Xiang

Xinhuangchengen

286

Restaurants ❶

Lake District and the North
18 Beijing Noodle King A3
19 Drum and Gong B3
20 Huajia Yiyuan C2
21 Jin Ding Xuan C1
22 Jiumen Xiaochi A2
24 Mei Mansion A3
25 Yueming Lou A2
26 Fish Nation B2
27 Yuelu Mountain Dining Place A3
28 Fangshan Restaurant A4
29 Li Family Restaurant A2
30 Kaorouji A2

31 Kong Yiji A2
32 Beijing Bamboo Garden Hotel A2
33 Sichuan Restaurant A2
34 Buffalo Stone A3
35 Café Sambal A2
36 Nuage A2
37 Dali Courtyard B2
38 No name restaurant A2

Eastern Beijing
40 Green T. House D3
42 Noodle Loft C1
45 Three Guizhou Men D3
47 Red Capital Club (Xin Hongzi Julebu) C3
48 Asian Star E3

49 Annie's E3
50 Assaggi E2
51 Da Dong Roast Duck Restaurant E3
54 Xiheyaju D4
55 Mare E3
57 Purple Haze E3
59 Pure Lotus Vegetarian E3
60 Afunti C4
61 Xinjiang Red Rose E3

5 Café Heaven and Earth A2
6 ING C2
7 MAO Live House B2
8 Passby Bar B3
9 Vineyard Cafe C1
10 Xiao Xin's Cafe B3

Eastern Beijing
11 The Boat E2
12 The Bokworm E3
13 Café Yo E2
14 Destination D3
15 Café Heaven E2
16 Face Bar D4
18 Paddy O'Sheas E2
19 Vics E3

Bars & Cafés ❶

Lake District and the North
3 Bed Bar A2
4 Drum and Bell Café B2

Hotels ❶

Wangfujing and Chang'an Areas
4 Red Capital Residence C3
9 Holiday Inn Crowne Plaza B4
12 Haoyuan Hotel C4
13 Saga Youth Hostel C4

East of the Second Ring Road (Chaoyang)
18 Hotel G D3
21 Opposite House E3
22 Swissotel Beijing D3
24 Beijing New World Hotel E4
25 Beijing Gongti International Youth Hostel E3

26 Beijing Zhaolong Youth Hostel E3

The Northeast (Around the Third Ring Road)
28 Kempinski Hotel E2
29 Kunlun Hotel E2
30 Radisson SAS Royal Hotel D1
31 Great Wall Sheraton E2
32 Hilton Hotel E1
33 Holiday Inn Lido E1

Around the Bell and Drum Towers
34 Lusongyuan Hotel B3
35 Beijing Bamboo Garden Hotel A2
36 Youhao Guesthouse B2

287

Restaurants 🍴

Tianamen Square and Surroundings
1 ZEN 1903 B2
2 Maison Boulud B2
3 Laijinyuxuan A1
4 Tiananmen Fangshan B2
5 Ristorante Sadler B2
6 Tiananmen Donglaishun B2
7 Tiananmen Quanjude B2
Southern Beijing
8 Fengzeyuan A3
9 Jinyang A3
10 Old Beijing Noodle C3
11 Capital M A2
12 Maxim's de Paris C2
13 Lao Ciqikou Bean Juice B3
14 Liqun Roast Duck B2
15 Quanjude A2
Eastern Beijing
39 The East is Red E3
41 Made in China B1

43 Bleu Marine E1
44 The Courtyard B1
46 Mengguren B1
52 Wangfujing Quanjude B1
53 Sichuan Restaurant B1
54 Xiheyaju D1
56 Phrik Thai D1
58 Makye Ame D1

Bars & Cafés 🍸

Southern Beijing
1 The Jialana Bar A3
2 Eveni Wine Club B3
Eastern Beijing
17 LAN Club D1

Hotels 🏨

Wangfujing and Chang'an Areas
1 Grand Hotel Beijing B1
2 Grand Hyatt Beijing B1

3 The Peninsula Beijing C1
5 Beijing Hotel B1
6 Beijing International Hotel C1
7 Lee Garden Service Apartments C1
8 Novotel Peace Hotel C1
10 Novotel Xinqiao Hotel C2
11 Hademen Hotel C2
East of the Second Ring Road (Chaoyang)
14 China World Hotel E1
15 Kerry Centre E1
16 St Regis Hotel D1
17 Gloria Plaza Hotel D1
19 Jianguo Hotel E1
20 Jinglun Hotel E1
23 Traders' Hotel E1
27 Jianguomen Hotel D2
Southern and Western Beijing
40 Qianmen Chang Gong A2
41 Qianmen Jianguo Hotel A3
43 Leo Hostel A2

Map labels:
Xiaoyabao Hutong
Yabaolu Market
Ritan (Altar of the Sun)
RITAN GONGYUAN
Zhongyang Dianshitai CCTV (China Central Television Station Tower)
Dayabao Hutong
Yabao Lu
Asia Pacific Building
Guandongdian Nanjie
Jiali Zhongxin (Kerry Centre)
JINTAIXIZHAO
Guanghua Lu
Zhaotangzi Hutong
Jianguomen Beidajie
Beijie
Guanghua Lu
China World Trade Centre Tower III
International Post and Telecom Office
Embassy District (South)
Xiushui Beijie
Nanjie
Xiushui Shichang (Former Silk Market)
China World Trade Centre
Dongsanhuan Zhonglu
Chang'an Theatre
St Regis Hotel
Youyi Shangdian (Friendship Store)
JIANGUOMEN
GUOMAO
Jianguomennei Dajie
Donghiao Beihutong
Gu Guanxiangtai (Old Observatory)
Jianguomenwai Dajie
YONGANLI
Chaoyang Stadium
Jianwai SOHO
BEIJINGZHAN
CVIK SHOPPING CENTRE
Beijingzhan Dongjie
Jianguoli 1 Xiang
Yong'an Zhonglu
Beijing Zhan (Beijing Railway Station)
Kuijiachang Hutong
Zhuanchang Hutong
Tonghui
DABEIYAO
Hongmian Hualang (Red Gate Gallery)
Dongsanhuan Zhonglu
Zhongwenmen Dongdajie
Donghoupeyan
DONGBIANMEN
Huashizhong 2 Tiao
Huashixia 2 Tiao
Huashizhong 4 Tiao
Huashixia 4 Tiao
Donghuashi
Zhongshili 4 Xiang
Zhongshili Nanjie
Zhongshili 1 Xiang
SHUAGJING
Shangtangzi Hutong
Xiatangzi Hutong
Long'an Temple
Dongsanhuan Nanlu (Third Ring Road)
ZHONGWENMEN
Dajie
Guangqumennei Dajie
Guangqumenwai Dajie
Majuan Bus Terminal
Xizhaosi Jie
Guangqumen Nanxiaojie
Guangqumenwai Nanjie
Guanghedongli Zhongjie
GUANGQUMEN
Xizhaosi
Zhongjie
Guanghe Lu
Chuiyangliu Zhongjie
Chuiyangliu Nanjie
Chuiyangliu Hospital
Beijing Curio City, Panjiayuan Antique Market ↓
DONGCHENG
Tiyuguan Lu
Guangming Lu
Xizhaosi Jie
Yuandushi Temple
LONGTAN GONGYUAN
Longtan
Longtan Lu
BEIJING AMUSEMENT PARK

284

A

YUYUANTAN GONGYUAN
(SONG QINGLING CHILDREN'S SCIENCE PARK)

WEIGONGCUN

Zhonghua Shiji Tan
(China Millennium Monument)/
Beijing World Art Museum

Renmin Geming Junshi Bowguan
(Military Museum of the
Chinese People's Revolution)

GONGZHUFEN

Ministry
of Defense

Fuxing Lu

Fuxing Lu

JUNSHIBOWUGUAN

B

Yuetan Nanjie

Yuetan

Ministry
of Finance

Santihenanheng Jie

China
Academy
of Sciences

Santiheran 2 Xiang

Santiheran Xi Xiang

Santihe Donglu

Nanlishilu

Fuxingmenwai Dajie

MUXIDI

Fuxing
Hospital

Shoudu Bowguan
(Capital Museum)

Zhenwum
2 Tiao

Zhenwum

MUXIDI

Baiyun

Baiyunguan
(Temple of the
White Cloud)

Zhonglu

Xisanhuan

Yangfangdian Lu

Beifengwo Lu

Lianhuachi Donglu

Lianhuachi Donglu

Tianning Si
(Temple of
Heavenly
Tranquillity)

Nanfengwo Lu

Beijing Xi Zhan
(West Railway Station)

Shoupakou

Tianningsiqian Jie

Yongtai
Hutong

Anmenwai
Bejie

Guang'anmen Nanbinhelu

Lianhua
(Lotus Pond)

Maliandao Beilu

Lianhuahe
Hutong

Xiaomaochang Nanli

Maqiang Lu

Shoupakou Xijie

Bejie

Guang'anmenwai Nanjie

SHIJING-
SHAN

Lianhua

Guang'an Lu

Guang'anmenwai Dajie

Hongju Jie

Shoupakou Nanjie

Hongju
Dongjie

67

Xisanhuan
Nanlu

Maliandao Beilu

Maliandao

Maliandao 3 Xiang

Maliandao Zhongxiang

Maliandao
Zhongjie

Hongju 2 Xiang

Nanxinli 2 Xiang

Jie

Guang'anmen
Railway Station

Maliandao Nanjie

Maliandao
Nanjie

Hongjian

Hongju Nanjie

Second Ring Road

Guang'anmen Nanbinhelu

Maliandao
Dongjie

Xuanwu

Maliandao
Hutong

Honglian Nanlu

Lianhua

Guang'anmenchezhan Xijie

Xuanwu

liu oeibuX

Guang'anmen Nanbinhelu

Sanluju Lu

Sanluju Lu

0   200   400   600   800 m

0   200   400   600   800 yds

A

B

285

D **E**

288

1

Children's Hospital

Exhibition Hall of Chinese Arts and Crafts

Ledao Xiang

Guangningbo Jie

Picai

Xueyuan Hutong

Anyuan Hutong

Longtu Xijie

Damucang Hutong

LINGJINGHUTONG

Lingjing Hutong

Shibanfang 3 Tiao

Xinhua

Beiyin Hutong

Taipusi Jie

XIDAN

Piku Hutong

Zhongjingjidao

Minfeng H.

Nanhai

Duchenghuangmiao Temple

China International Travel Service

XIDAN

Xinhuamen (Xinhua Gate)

Fuxingmennei Dajie

Chayuan H.

Wenhua

Xinwenhua

Xidanshoupa Jie

Dongtiejiang Hutong

Jie

Xichang'an Jie

Capital Cinema

Xi'anfu Hutong

Beixinping Hutong

Beijing Concert Hall

Central Music Conservatory

FUXINGMEN

Yongning H.

Toufa

Xirongxian Hutong

Xijulianzi

Xixinlianzi Hutong

Hutong

Dongrongxian Hutong

Dongjiufianzi Hutong

Yuetai Hutong

Wenjia

Xinbi Jie

Dongzhong Hutong

Nantang (South Cathedral)

HEPINGMEN

Xuanwumen Xidajie

Xuanwumen Dongdajie

Qianmen Xidajie

CHANGCHUNJIE

XUANWUMEN

Zhengyici Xilou (Zhengyici Beijing Opera Theatre)

2

Xuanwumen Xiheyanjie

Xuanwumen Dongheyanjie

Shangxie Jie

Hutong

Haibai Hutong

Sanmiao Jie

Chukuying

Yang Memorial Temple

Diangianchang H.

Chunshu-shangtou Tiao

Liulichang Xijie

Liuli Xiang

Liulichang Dongjie

XIBIANMEN

Laoqianggen Jie

Jiaochangxiao 8 Tiao

Jiaochangkou Hutong

Yongguang Xijie

Xicaochang Jie

Qiansongongyuan Hutong

Baishun H.

Xuanwu Hospital

Baiguo Si (Baoguo Temple)

Dingju Hutong

Mianhuaxia 7 Tiao

Luomashi Dajie

3

Guang'anmennei Dajie

CAISHIKOU

Dequan Hutong

Madao H.

Cuzhang Hutong

Beidaji Xiang

Huguang Huiguan (Huguang Guild Hall)

Liyuan Juchang (Liyuan Theatre)

Niu Jie Qingzhensi (Ox Street Mosque)

Fayuansi (Temple of the Source of Buddhist Teaching)

Bao'ansi Jie

HUFANGQIAO

Fayuansiqian H.

Nanheng Xijie

Nanheng Dongjie

Beiwei Lu

CAISHIKOU

4

Chongxiao Hutong

Yingtao 3 Tiao

WANSHOU GONGYUAN

Baizhifang Dongjie

TAORANTING

Taoranting

YOU'ANMEN

Central Academy of Traditional Opera

North Gate

TAORANTING GONGYUAN (HAPPY PAVILION PARK)

East Gate

West Gate

Central Isle

Waterside Pavilion

Xiannongtan Stadium

Taoranting

Temple of Mercy

DAGUANYUAN (GRAND VIEW GARDEN)

XUANWU

Cloud-Depicting Tower

Yongdingmen Xijie

D **E**

STREET INDEX

Art and Photo Credits

Alamy 212B, 249
AP/PA Images 48L, 50
Art Archive 36R
AWL Images 7T, 90/91, 92/93
Gonzalo M. Azumendi 228R
Bodo Bondzio 237
Corbis 28, 38R, 39, 40, 44L, 46L&BR, 54, 81R, 107L, 215B, 218B
David Drakeford 7CBR
The East is Red 8T
Mary Evans Picture Library 41TL&BL, 119T
Laurel Fan 139TL
faungg on Flickr 56T
Fotolia 6CL, 7CTL
Getty Images 34L, 115, 228TL
Alex Havret/APA 42L, 57L
David Henley/APA 4BL, 41R, 43TL, CL&C
Lee Hin Mun/APA 6B, 8B, 9B, 10BR, 11T, 17L, 24L, 52/53, 73BL, 74TR, 76R, 78, 80TR, 81L, 82R, 83BL, 87(all), 95L&R, 103B, 106BL, 123B, 134TR, 136B, 137R, 167, 169, 193L&R, 222/223, 228B, 229, 266, 267, 269
Jack Hollingsworth 80L
Andrew Holt 139BR
ImagineChina 9TL, 20TR, 31, 51, 56BL, 57R, 59L&R, 77R, 86TR&BR, 99, 103T, 111, 133B, 170, 172T, 173, 186B, 189T&B, 190, 191T&B, 201, 216, 217L, 232T, 236, 239T&B, 240T&B, 241T&B, 242B, 243L, 245B, 248B
iStockphoto.com 6TR, 7BR, 9TR, 199, 244T&B, 245T, 253
Anthony Lambert 45
Herry Lawford 161
Tom Le Bas 105B, 106T, 132T&B, 133TR, 153T, 160T
Liu Liqun 172B, 215T
Manfred Morgenstern 30, 32, 33, 35R, 36L, 37R, 61, 63R, 82L, 120, 122T, 183, 184, 200, 204B, 217T, 238, 242T, 243R
Richard Nowitz/APA 1, 4T, 9C,

11B, 18, 25L, 43R, 46TR, 67L, 72T&B, 73R, 75R, 79, 83TL&R, 84L&TR, 85, 98, 100, 101, 104, 108T&B, 113, 114T&B, 117TR&B, 119B, 123T, 125, 135, 139TR, 147R, 148T, 150T&BL, 151L&R, 158, 160B, 168, 186T, 203T, 204T, 206B, 207T&B, 208, 218T, 219T&B, 220, 221, 227T&B, 230T&B, 277
onasia.com 48R, 49, 62, 63L, 84BR, 86L, 194B
Panos 22, 214L, 233
Erhard Pansegrau 26L, 60, 182
Photolibrary 107R, 211B, 247, 252T
Ryan Pyle/APA 55BL, 56BR, 64TR&BR
Ralph Repo 27B, 38L
David Shenkai/APA 55TL&R, 128
Sipa Press/Rex Features 14/15
Hilary Smith 246T&B, 248T
Ming Tang-Evans/APA 4BR, 5T&B, 6CTR&CBR, 7CTR, CBL&BL, 10TL, TR, CR&BL, 11CR, 12/13, 16, 17R, 19, 20L&BR, 21(all), 23(all), 24R, 25R, 42T, 58, 64L, 65(all), 66, 67R, 70, 71, 73TL, 74L&BR, 75TL&BL, 76R, 77L, 94, 102, 105T, 106R, 109, 110, 112, 117L, 121T&B, 122B, 124, 126, 127, 129, 130, 131(all), 134TL&B, 137L, 138L&R, 139BL, 140T&B, 144, 145, 147L, 148BL&R, 149(all), 150R, 152L&R, 153L&BR, 154(all), 155, 156T&B, 157T&B, 159, 162, 163, 166, 171(all), 175, 176T&B, 177, 178L&R, 179, 185T&B, 198, 202L&R, 203B, 206T, 209, 210T&B, 211T, 212T, 213, 214R, 224, 225, 231T&B, 232B, 250T&B, 251, 252B, 254, 256, 260, 268, 271, 272, 278
TopFoto 29, 37R, 44R, 47L&R
Ivan Walsh 188
Marcus Wilson-Smith/APA 80BR, 118, 133L, 136T, 194T, 217BR
Gene Zhang 11CL

GENERAL INDEX